THE
AMERICAN
PROBLEMS, LIFESTYLE

Edith Blicksilver

Georgia Institute of Technology

Atlanta, Georgia

KENDALL/HUNT PUBLISHING COMPANY
2460 Kerper Boulevard, Dubuque, Iowa 52001

To my mother, Fanny Stettner, who graced my girlhood
with optimistic happiness and sang operatic lyrics from
her Austro-Hungarian cultural heritage

and

To my father, Simon Stettner, who told me Polish and
Russian folk tales, exciting heroic episodes from his first
World War experiences, constantly reminded me, as a
patriotic immigrant, that "in America all dreams can be
fulfilled" and he never added "even for a woman."

Cover: Ethnic Women design by Maria de Noronha (Gallman).

Copyright © 1978 by Kendall/Hunt Publishing Company

Library of Congress Catalog Card Number: 78-70677

ISBN 0—8403—1951—7

Printed in the United States of America

B   401951   01

Contents

Note: Contents are also categorized by Literary Form and Ethnic Group in the Appendices of this book. See Appendix A: CONTENTS BY LITERARY FORM, p. 355, and Appendix B: CONTENTS BY ETHNIC GROUPS REPRESENTED BY AUTHOR'S NAME, p. 358.

UNIT THREE: THE CLASSROOM AND BEYOND   117

UNIT FOUR: THAT ELUSIVE IDENTITY   169

UNIT FIVE: EXPLOITATION IN HUMAN RELATIONSHIPS   211

UNIT ELEVEN: SEEKING A BETTER TOMORROW 331

UNIT TWELVE: LITERARY CRITIQUES 343

For the Reader

"Ethnicity" taken from the Greek word "ethnikos," meaning national, designates "any of the basic groups or divisions of mankind or, as defined in this book, *a heterogeneous population, as distinguished by customs, characteristics, language, common history and so forth.*"[1]

The writers selected are by women with different experiences, representing a wide range of ages. They displayed literary merit and, in some cases, selections were chosen for language more precisely mirroring "old world speech patterns" rather than for artistic excellence. Although the search was diligent, some ethnic groups are not represented.

Since "ethnicity" can be categorized by religion (Jews), by nationality (Basques), by religion and nationality (Irish Catholics), and by race (blacks), in addition to language factors and even by region, three tables of contents have been included. The works should be read and enjoyed without the restraints imposed upon them by categorization.

The basic emphasis of the anthology is thematic, stressing the cycle of life, but two alternate tables of contents have been provided for those who prefer either a genre approach or an ethnic listing. Whatever method chosen, each selection speaks to the contemporary concerns of men as well as women, although the focus reflects the ethnic women's point of view.

The editor's goal is to include the wide range of female life experiences to demonstrate the joy and the anguish of being an ethnic woman. It is hoped that the reader, female or male, ethnic or not, will be enriched and edified.

[1] I am grateful to my friend Celestine Sibley, author and staff writer for The Atlanta *Constitution,* who suggested this definition for ethnicity in her column about this anthology written on December 27, 1977, 3B.

Acknowledgments

The following people deserve thanks for their contributions, advice and encouragement:

Weston Nishimura, Marek Web, Esther Brumberg, Bernice Seldon, Lucy R. Darby, Richard Burroughs, Eniko Molnar Basa, Evelyn Shakir, Harry Honda, Kathy Wong, Laura Larry, James Wu, Leonore Hoffmann, Ines Hernandez Tovar, Ruth Dickstein, Jane Gabin, Mrs. James Wu, Sylvania Rodrigues, Joan M. Hartman, Dorothy W. Lunn, Kenny J. Williams, Carlota Cardenas de Dwyer, Marta Cotera, Wolfgang Leppmann, Bob Pennington, Robett Manis, Hannah Lerski, Gerald Thorson, Estela Portillo Trambley, Carol Schoen, Cynthia Secor, Professor Arnold Schrier, Flora Bricker, Jean Fagan Yellin, Daniel Walden, Robert Di Pietro, Mildred Prause, Dorothy Ritsuko McDonald, Priscilla Oaks, Brom Weber, Evelyn Avery, Tomas Rivera, A. LaVonne Ruoff, Carl R. Shirley, Ines Hernandez Tovar, Ernestina N. Eger, Edith and Stan Marlin, Leonore Hoffmann, Lawrence Stettner, Priscilla Stettner, Sonia Lee, Helena Z. Lopata, Sidney Heitman, Klaus Hoffmann, Pranas and Alge Zunde, Sandra Gilbert, M. Perlinda Shelton, Ticki Lloyd, Esther Ann Schapiro, Nadine St. Louis, Antonio V. Romualdez, Marie-Reine Mikesell, Sally Ware, Rufus Greene, Jose Luis Gomez-Martine Father Paul Langsfeld, Ernest Lewald, Professor Pat Scott, Bernice Zamora, Vangie Vigil, Lorna Dee Cervantes, Doris Buchanan Smith, John C. Miller, Carlton C. Qualey, Allene Ross, Natala Belinkov, Yasmin Zaman, Matina S. Horner, Danuta Mostwin, Gloria E. Lemos, Lezley Havard, Pat Pinka, Eileen Sullivan, Margaret Guenther, Linda Ty-Casper, Gilda Cordero Fernando, Edith Tiempo, Nilda Rimonte, George E. Carter, Joan Buckley, Garth Dunleavy, Edward Ifkovic, Ingrun LaFleur, Theodore C. Blegen, Asad Husain, Felix Grosse, Hanna Lerski, Stepas Zobarskas, Reverend Leonardas Andriekus, Gerald D. Nash, Eniko Molnar Basa, Sue Armitage, Carol Fairbanks, Marcus Kulyan, Sona Hoisington, Frank Mocha, Henrietta M. Larson, Francis Puslowski, Don Chang Lee, Ana Castillo, Richard Stites, Ruth Alexander, Wakako Yamauchi, E. Stein, Alla Ktorova, Natasza Belinkov, Sinkewich Valentina, Tatiana Fesenko, Lois Rose, Ellen Gruber, Nancy C. Martin, Caroline M. Whitehead, Sally M. Miller, Sonia R. Rojales, Barbara Kadel, Mollie King, Dolores Brashear, Violet Moore, Matina Souretis Horner, Eclecte Alexander, Mary Nikas, Harold R. Random, Doris P. Random, Doris Buchanan Smith, Wendy Purcell and John Raymond who, as Book Review Editor of the *Atlanta Journal-Constitution,* gave me many books that helped me with this anthology.

I would like to thank the American Association of University Women for the grant which enabled me to complete this project.

I am grateful to the following people from Georgia Tech: President Joseph and Florence Pettit, Vice President Vernon and Helen Crawford, English Department Chairman Karl Murphy and Professor Marguerite Murphy from Georgia State University were always interested in my ethnic studies research. Richard Fuller, Assistant to President Pettit who helped me obtain a grant from the Georgia Tech Foundation to continue my research and Joe Guthridge, Vice President/Development for giving me encouragement with this project.

The following were enthusiastic too: Dean Henry Valk, Jack Walker (Former English Department Head), Professor Merle Walker, David B. Comer III (Former English Department Head), and Tom Almon (Former Associate Head).

The following people gave me excellent advice: Rufus Green, Mel and Doe Kranzberg, James D. Young, Ethel Githii, Robert E. Wood, Larry Rubin, Bob Meredith and Ronald H. Bayor.

I am grateful to Karl Murphy, Chairman of the English Department, and James P. Smith, Assistant Head of the English Department, for giving me a reduced teaching schedule so I can complete this work. They also gave me good advice about thematic topics.

The following secretaries worked diligently on this project: Jean Eberhardt, Elaine Fletcher, Vicki Butt, and Cecilia Anderson.

This monumental job could not have been completed without the conscientious efforts of the following members of the Reference Department at Georgia Tech: Jean Kirkland (Department Head), Susan Clark, Mary Evelyn Gilbert, Mary McMartin, Pamela Mingle, Kathryn Sharp and Celeste Sproul.

In addition the staff members of the Information Exchange Center helped me obtain books with enthusiastic devotion: Ruth Hale, Judith Dyer, Carolyn Eisele, Julia Hornbeck, and Jackie Marvin.

Finally, without the patience and understanding of my children, Paul, Diane and Bob who helped me edit and type this manuscript, I could never have undertaken such a time-consuming project. In conclusion, my husband advised me about all important decisions when I sought his advice. He is both a fine scholar and a devoted friend.

Introduction

Newspaper headlines such as "Indians End Occupation, Claim Victory"—"Chicanos Strike, Seek Better Migrant Working Conditions" indicate that many minority Americans have long suffered grievances which are now finally being aired.

Women, in particular are now seeking a new understanding of their present goals and lifestyles. In assembling impressions in the lives of individual ethnic women, one can explore untapped literary sources of honest expression with which modern women can identify and can recognize aspects of themselves as they too explore life as a re-creative process with facets of love, work, power, fear and failure.

Of course, great literature deals with universal problems that meet the needs of every generation. Antigone is as modern a woman's liberation champion as one can find and the Wife of Bath's anguish as she fears damnation for past sins can reach sympathetic ears.

But the special problems of many ethnic Americans, especially the literary contributions of ethnic American women need more study. Works representing the concerns of Jewish American males and Black American males have already achieved permanent status and recognition, but the problems and social protests of their women and the women of other minority groups such as the Eastern European, the Hispanic American, the Native American and the Asian American deserve attention too.

The following four categories may be explored as the writings of these female ethnic groups are studied.

First, in what way do these women deal with the universal problems of God, life, love, fate, frustration and death? The role of daughter, sister, sweetheart, wife, mother, has not changed throughout the ages, so that similarities, in diffcrent cultures, as well as differences must be recognized. Onc can identify with problems because of the generation gap whether one studies *Hamlet* and *King Lear* or a more modern situation. Consider, for example the unhappiness voiced by this unnamed Russian mother who was rejected by her daughter when she wrote to the editor of the *Jewish Daily Forward* in 1906.

> My own daughter, who was born in Russia, married a Hungarian-Jewish young man. She adopted all the Hungarian customs and not a trace of a Russian-Jewish woman remained with her. This would not have been so bad. The trouble is, now that she is first-class Hungarian, she laughs at the way I talk, at my manners and even the way we cook. She does not avoid me. On the contrary, since her marriage, she has been calling on me more than before. Not an evening passes without quarrels, without mockery and ridicule.
>
> I therefore want to express my opinion that Russian Jews and Hungarian Jews should not intermarry; a Russian Jew and an Hungarian Jew are in my opinion two different worlds and ones does not and cannot understand the other.[1]

Excerpted from Edith Blicksilver: LITERATURE AS SOCIAL CRITICISM: THE ETHNIC WOMAN WRITER, in *Modern Language Studies.* (Vol. 5, No. 2, Fall 1975) pp. 46-54. Reprinted with permission of the editor of *Modern Language Studies,* Northeast Modern Language Association.

The immigrant woman's loneliness in the new world when she had to give up her friends who had not journeyed to America is another universal tragedy facing anyone who leaves family and homeland. Kiev—born, Marya Zaturenska who received the Pulitzer Prize in 1938 for her volume of poetry *Cold Morning Sky* remembered a Russian Easter in 1920 and conveyed her sense of nostalgia, aware of her unique religious heritage that America could not duplicate.

> In the great cathedral with blue windows,
> In great cathedral of Moscow,
> They will kneel before the holy ikons.
>
> . . .
>
> Natasha will be there in a scarlet cloak,
> And Irena's gown will be embroidered in crimson.
> Sergei will be there, and Igor
> Will gaze with mystic Slav-eyes at the gold alter.
>
> . . .
>
> Irena's lover will kiss her on the lips,
> Wild with the love of God.
> Natasha's lover will kiss her forehead
> Reverently as the hands of the high priest.
>
> . . .
>
> But I shall be alone weeping:
> I shall weep remembering the blue cathedral;
> I shall be sad in a strange country,
> Thinking of Igor, Natasha and Sergei,
> Irena, and the singing multitude.

But some ethnic women's problems are not universal and they deal with the tragic consequences of prejudice, discrimination and the unfulfillment of the American dream. So this second category of female social protest should be explored too. Margaret Walker, English Professor and Director of The Institute for the Study of The History, Life and Cultures of Black People Jackson State University, whose collection of poetry, *For My People,*[2] was selected for the library of the Yale Series of Younger Poets expressed her anger, bitterness and contempt for discrimination toward Black women in a poem entitled "Now":

Time to wipe away the slime
from inner rooms of thinking,
and covert skin of suffering;
indignities and dirt
5   and helpless degradation;
from furtive relegation
to the back doors and dark alleys
and the balconies of waiting
in the cleaning rooms and closets
10   with the washrooms and the filthy
privies marked "For Colored Only"
and the drinking-soda-fountains
tasting dismal and disgusting
with a dry and dusty flavor
15   of the deep humiliation;
hearing vulgars shout to mothers
"Hey you, nigger girl, and girlie!
Auntie, Aunt, and Granny;
My old mammy was a wonder
20   and I love those dear old darkies
who were good and servile nigras
with their kerchiefed heads and faces
in their sweet and menial places."
Feeling hate and blood commingled
25   in a savage supplication
full of rites and ceremonies
for the separate unequal—
re-enforced by mobs who mass
with a priest of cult and klan
30   robed and masked in purest White
marking Kleagle with a Klux
and fiery burning cross.
Time to wipe away the slime.
Time to end this bloody crime.

Margaret Walker, "Now" from FOR MY PEOPLE, © 1974. Reprinted by permission of the author.

Discrimination was part of gospel singer Mahalia Jackson's girlhood experiences too and she tells of her hopes and her fears when she moved from her home in New Orleans to Chicago in 1928.

> My aunt Hannah, who was going back to Chicago, took me along with her on Big Number Four—the express train that ran straight through up North. Before we left we cooked up some food and took it along in a big basket. We sat up in our seats for two nights and a day and ate it. It was many years before I ever saw the inside of a railroad dining car without being put behind a screen so the white folks wouldn't have to see me.[3]

A third category of exploration into the problems and protests of ethnic American women should focus upon conflicts between new immigrants and more Americanized members of that ethnic group and/or between one ethnic group and another (e.g., Black and Hisparic Americans). The sense of two-ness, of belonging to a minority group and to the larger American society has been explored by many sensitive young women. The first or second immigrant generation goes through an identity crisis questioning conflicting values, life-styles, loyalties. The school sometimes becomes a place of shames and anguish during a sensitive adolescent stage when conformity is more desirable than uniqueness.

Here is an excerpt from an interview by well known folk singer Joan Baez Harris:

> I have been asked if I think of myself as a Mexican or a Chicano or as being dark-skinned.
>
> This is a difficult question for me to answer, since for the past ten years of my life I have made a point of not categorizing myself. I have refused to accept the title of singer, for instance. I have not particularly identified myself with any special group, but more with humanity as a whole.
>
> I've always thought brown is beautiful, and every chance I've had to get into the sun I've done so, because I like being brown.
>
> When I entered junior high school there was prejudice against brown people. It took me a couple of years to realize that my being brown was why I did not make friends easily.
>
> I have never really regarded myself as Mexican or English. My father was Mexican and was born in Pueblo, Mexico. On my mother's side there was English and a dash of Irish. I never thought of myself as an English girl, and not too much as a Mexican. I feel distant from the cause of any particular minority group in the sense that when I throw myself into "the cause," it is that of mankind. I have never felt I should work just with browns or just with blacks or just with whites.
>
> I know that color made a difference in junior high school. I think I find difficulty talking about this because I never felt I personally was badly discriminated against. When I was in junior high my father was a professor at a university, and although I looked very Mexican I did not speak Spanish. I felt that Mexican kids were getting a dirty deal, but I did not feel that I was. When my father first came to Stanford University, one of the top professors there would hardly speak to him. My father really had to struggle to break through that barrier.
>
> I remember a story my parents told me. In a little town in New York State somebody called me "nigger" because they had never seen anyone as dark as I was. I said, "You ought to see me in the summertime." I loved dark-colored skin.

Once somebody called me a dirty Mexican, and a student asked my teacher, "Is she a Mexican?"

My teacher, attempting to defend me, said, "Joan is the very highest breed of Spanish."

I said, "What do you mean, the very highest breed of Spanish? I'm a Mexican." I made a big point of saying I was a Mexican.

Probably the worst place in my childhood, so far as prejudice is concerned, was southern California. For about a year my younger sister did not want to play with me or be seen with me. She tagged after my older sister, who was fair.

But I've put that thought out of my mind—perhaps because it's unpleasant, but also because I have now done all right for myself. Maybe I feel quilty about my success and don't like to harp on the times I have sensed prejudice in people."

Consider too the problems of the Native American faced with two-fold exploitation from the white man and from the red man who has accepted the artificial standards imposed upon him by the Anglos Society. He has limited choice in order to survive. The land is unproductive and opportunities for a skilled worker are limited. Sometimes younger Indians rebel against tribal customs which they consider impractical, old fashioned, or shameful. Some customs are worth preserving, however, and again, the decision of which to preserve and which to abandon creates difficulties, resulting in family friction.

Majority ignorance sometimes results in sorrows and misunderstandings. For example, the Indian's spiritual affection for the land is not understood by most Americans or by members of other ethnic groups.

Of the not quite two billion acres that Indians once inhabited, the U. S. government permits tribes to reside on only 56 million acres. This land is "critically eroded" (14 million acres), or "severely eroded" (17 million acres), or "slightly eroded" (25 million acres). Nonetheless, this is the most religiously sacred and blasphemed against land in the country, as made clear by a young Apache girl ("What Is an Indian Reservation?" by Marilyn Cosen, *Akwesasne Notes,* Vol. I, No. 7, July, 1969), and an old Cupeno woman ("We Do Not Want Any Other Home," by Celsa Apapas, *Aboriginal American Oratory,* p. 115).

A reservation is a source of security to the Indian. I say this because there he can feel free—freedom in practicing his own customs. Another thing is his land. I think one's environment has a great effect on the person—to the Indian, his land is his own. His ancestors inhabited that land; he was brought up on that land; he knows it; he claims it. What if the reservations were abolished? Then the land would be open for different causes and the Indian would be "lost." I'm not saying that reservations should not be abolished, so that the Indian can practice his part in the reservation communities and learn how to deal with Indian problems and, most important of all, preserve his culture. You asked us to think what place we like next best to this place, where we always lived. You see that graveyard out there? There are our fathers and our grandfathers. You see that Eagle-nest Mountain and that Rabbit-hole Mountain? When God made them, He gave us this place. We have always been here. We do not care for any other place. . . . If you give us the best place in the world it is not so good for us as this. . . . This is our home. . . . We cannot live anywhere else. We were born here and our fathers are buried here. . . . We want this place and not any other. . . .

There is no other place for us. We do not want you to buy any other place. If you will not buy this place, we will go into the mountains like quail, and die there, the old people and the women and children. Let the Government be glad and proud. It can kill us. We do not fight. We do what it says. If we cannot live here, we want to go into the mountains and die. We do not want any other home.[4]

A fourth category of study not only reveals the dilemma of intergroup relations which has resulted in the tragedies of Indian reservations, but also the unfortunate creation of relocation camps for Japanese. For example, what was it like to be a Japanese during the hostilities generated by the attack upon Pearl Harbor? A poem entitled "Nisei, Nisei!" by a sensitive young girl named Ferris Takahashi,[5] an American girl born of Japanese parents, relates an incident of inner anguish more poignantly than the same account could be described by a reporter or a sociologist who is himself emotionally uninvolved.

Indeed, the artistic member of a minority group can have multiple problems. Not only may she feel herself alienated from the majority culture by virtue of her ethnic background, but she may also feel herself alienated from her own ethnic group by virtue of her artistic sensibilities. Being a woman can add to her dilemma, especially if she is of Asian origins.

Diana Chang,[6] a gifted poet, born in New York but taken back to China by her parents during her girlhood years, explores attitudes toward the inner world in a poem called "Second Nature."

Another young Chinese-American artist named Jade Snow Wong points up the problem of the artist disdained by her own compatriots.

> How could I utilize my dual educations? I longed to be in some field which would someday bring me to see China. What work could I do in which I would find no prejudice as a woman? I went alone to the country, where I could think in quiet beauty, close to nature. Troubled, seeking, I had an idea. I liked making pottery and I liked writing. Could I not make a modest living for myself in this combination, which could utilize all I had learned? If I failed, I could return either to the conventional work world or to graduate studies. I was starting from nothing, so I had nothing to lose.
>
> I was already working at my potter's wheel at home. A corner of the sewing factory was allocated for my equipment and cans of clays. At the age of twenty-four, I began a tiny business. I found a Grant Avenue shopkeeper in the heart of Chinatown who permitted me to install my wheel in one of his display windows and to sell my pottery in his store in return for a commission to him. Whenever I was throwing pottery in the window, day or night, great crowds gathered and automobiles caused traffic jams. I sold pottery, too, but not to the curious Chinese. When Chinatown's residents looked at my stoneware bowls made of California clays, they did not see the art in them. "Why, this is a rice bowl!" they would exclaim. "And not even a porcelain one. Only rough clay, suitable for coolies. How can she ask several dollars for something which would cost a few dimes in China? She will soon go out of business." I learned a peculiar human characteristic. People would talk about me as if my presence were not there, and they never thought to ask me for the explanation—that there were no porcelain clays in California and I made one-of-a-kind pieces, not sets of rice bowls. And when I went around Chinatown, I was jeered, "Here comes the girl who plays with mud." They must also have thought, "Here is a college graduate foolish enough to get her hands dirty."
>
> Today, twenty-three years later, they do not jeer or patronize me. A Chinese artist friend tells me that when the popular crowd finds his calligraphy beautiful, he shudders. But when they cannot understand, then he knows that he has risen above the commonplace. By my occupation and my interests, I have become a minority in my own community.
>
> I soon outgrew the store window and moved into a wooden frame building my father had purchased on the western edge of Chinatown, after carefully agreeing to pay my father the full normal rent. Daddy became a frequent visitor, not only to check on his property, but because

he was genuinely concerned with my career. He had told me that his father had always stressed the importance of owning one's business, no matter how small, without partners. Grandfather Wong also thought that anyone who knew how to use his hands would never starve. But the kindest remark Daddy made was that I had vindicated his promise to relatives that he "would bleach the disgrace of out ancestors" in respect to their treatment of women.

In sum, the literature of ethnic minority women is an important new approach to understanding the causes and the consequences of social protest. Meaningful research dealing with such contemporary concerns will help Americans understand why intolerance exists, and why minority groups, especially those representing women, demand a more effective role in determining their own important part in the future of the United States. The impact of dislocation and discrimination, the nature of inter-group and inter-generations relations and the process of adjustment of ethnic women to the dominant male culture will also be better understood. We are all the children of immigrants and our ethnic cultural backgrounds have influenced us as students, as leaders and especially as women. More ethnic women will be elected to high office adding their powerful voices to formulating the decisions of our nation. Social protest cannot be silenced; the literature of social criticism by ethnic women writers should be studied and carefully pondered as a prelude to social programs and political actions.

NOTES

1. Allon Schoener, editor, *Portal to America: The Lower East Side.* (New York: Holt, Rinehart, and Winston, 1967), p. 247.
2. See Ms. Walker's poem "For My People" in Unit Eight, *Memories, Dreams, Hopes.* Notice the similar themes, but the second poem has a more optimistic approach.
3. Gerald Leinwand, editor, *Minorities All.* (New York: Washington Square Press, 1971), p. 143.
4. Shirley Hill Witt and Stan Steiner, editors, *The Way, An Anthology of American Indian Literature.* (Vintage Books, 1972), pp. 59-60.
5. Ms. Takahashi's poem is discussed in detail in Unit Four, *That Elusive Identity.*
6. Ms. Chang's poem is included in Unit Four, *That Elusive Identity.*

GROWING UP ETHNIC

"Girl in Peasant Costume." This girl's Polish grandmother sewed this costume by hand for the granddaughter whom she had never seen, living in America. By permission of Fanny Stettner from a family album.

". . . every generation must create its own traditions. . . ."

Irina Kirk's narrator
in *Born with the Dead*.

from BORN WITH THE DEAD

by Irina Kirk

I first came upon the name Bazaroff at the age of seventeen. A Russian woman, who was our maid in San Francisco, had given me for a Christmas gift an English translation of a novel called *Fathers and Sons,* by Turgenev. I was at once taken by the principal character, who believed in nothing and who, nevertheless, wanted to destroy all traditional beliefs and customs and build a new world of which he himself was not sure. It was not only Bazaroff's rebellious nature that impressed me, but also the intensity of all the other characters in the book, and my own lack of passion began to seem to me like a sin. I decided then that every generation must create its own traditions, and wished that I, too, could think of some new and exciting idea. But my life followed a comfortable pattern and invited no rebellion.

I do not recall much about the woman who had given me *Fathers and Sons,* except that she was a refugee from the 1917 Revolution. I often heard my mother whisper to her guests at tea that our maid was an aristocrat, but I never knew this definitely since the woman seldom spoke of her past. At the time it did not interest me and I did not question her. In the evenings I sometimes went into her room for tea. Though I asked her several times to call me Richard, she continued to address me as Mr. Saunders, and after a while her formality was no longer strange to me, for she managed to combine it with a quiet warmth.

From Irina Kirk, BORN WITH THE DEAD, Chapter One, p. 1. Houghton Mifflin Company, © 1963. Reprinted by permission of the author.

SPECIAL PLACES

Virginia Driving Hawk Sneve

When I was eight years old I made my first trip away from the Rosebud Reservation. My parents, brother, and I drove to the Black Hills which were known to us as *Paha Sapa,* the sacred mountains of the Sioux.

Travel during war time was a hazardous adventure on old patched tires and gas rationing. It was hot and our old Chevy had a canvas water bag tied to the front of the radiator in case the car overheated and for drinking on the 200 mile journey. I had a stomach ache of anticipation for the adventures ahead.

Now as I look back in my memory it is not the Black Hills I see, but a gas station by the side of the road on the outskirts of a western South Dakota town. We had been holding our breaths for miles, praying that the few drops of gasoline left in the tank would get us to the station. I had to go to the toilet again. My father complained at the frequency of my need which

Reprinted by permission of the author.

called for many stops and a run for the ditch. So I was doubly glad to see the gas station and hoped for the privacy of a privy and maybe even running water.

While the car was at the pump I ran to the back of the station and saw three doors. MEN, WOMEN, INDIANS. WOMEN was locked so I rushed into INDIANS trying not to breathe the foul air or sit on the soiled stool.

As we resumed our journey I thought about the three doors. "That gas station had three restrooms," I said to my parents. "One for men. One for women. And one for Indians."

I remember Mom and Dad looking at each other as I went on, "Isn't it nice that there was a special place for Indians?"

No one said anything for a while, then Dad patted my knee. "My girl, I hope there will always be special places for you."

In the years since I have made many journeys which have destroyed the naiveté of that little girl. But there have been many special places for me.

I was a pampered and spoiled child protected against the realities of being an Indian on a reservation. My father was a priest of the Episcopal Church and the only non-Indians I knew were caring Christian missionaries. They made special places in my life by giving me piano lessons and a set of THE BOOK OF KNOWLEDGE.

My family was poor as was every one else on the reservation. My father kept a diary where he confided his fears of not having the money for food and shoes for my brother and myself. He recorded the odd jobs he took and of working for the WPA to supplement his meager mission salary. He wrote daily from fall to spring of chopping wood to keep us warm.

But the recollections of my childhood are of being warm and secure within the family; parents, two sets of grandparents, the other mothers, fathers, grandparents, and innumerable cousins—brothers and sisters—of the Lakota extended family. Home and family were special places.

I even had great-grandparents. Great-grandpa, a Santee Dakota, died when I was about three and I only vaguely recall a tall man with a booming voice. But Great-grandma lived into her nineties. Of Santee, Ponca, and English descent she told of the adventures of her white father who had come west in his teens and eventually settled in northeastern Nebraska. She told stories of starving Indians in Minnesota who had been defeated in a war with the whites. Tears were in her eyes when she told of these Indians being crammed into steamboats for a dreadful journey down the Mississippi, then up the Missouri to a place called Crow Creek. Her voice was barely audible when she told of the women and children dying of starvation and disease before they were finally settled at Santee, Nebraska. It wasn't until I was in a college history class did I realize that Grandma had been telling of the Indians' part in the 1862 Minnesota Uprising.

The child that I was did not recognize the oral tradition my Great-grandmother followed. The tone of her voice was indignant when she told about the Ponca Indians forced removal from Nebraska to Oklahoma. But there was pride when she told about Standing Bear, the Ponca Chief. Again, it was in college and reading Helen Hunt Jackson's CENTURY OF DISHONOR that I realized I knew all about the Poncas from my grandmother's oral history. Years later as an historical writer I was grateful for the insight I had from this heritage of the oral tradition.

My paternal grandmother also followed the oral tradition, but her stories were told to entertain as well as to teach. A Sicangu Teton Lakota she told about Iktomi, the trickster of Sioux Indian mythology; the White Buffalo Calf Woman; Iya, the camp eater; and many more tribal myths and legends. As an eager listening child I didn't know what they were. I thought of them as just Grandma's stories. I was surprised and disappointed to discover that the stories weren't of her own creation when I found them published in books. But some of the stories were of her own invention for I never found or heard them from any other source. Several of these I later used in my own stories for children.

My grandmothers and other older members of my family gave me the traditional education of the Lakota child. My formal education began when I was five in a Bureau of Indian Affairs Day School. I remember being carried on my father's back through the cold and blowing snow so that I wouldn't miss school. Both of my parents believed education was the path the Indian youth had to follow and school became a special place.

Mr. Miller, my teacher for six years, also pampered and spoiled me. From my later teaching experience I can imagine his delight in a child who took to reading like a bird to flying. He encouraged my fledgling flights with words—reading them and putting them together in my own sentences. He introduced me to libraries with their infinite source of knowledge and pleasure.

It was part of life on the reservation that after the sixth grade a child would be sent away from home to a boarding school. I was sent 200 hundred miles away to St. Mary's School for Indian girls, an Episcopal mission school. St. Mary's became another special place.

Besides academic subjects we girls were taught the etiquette needed to be a lady. There was piano, organ, violin, and ballet lessons. We sang Gilbert and Sullivan and danced around the maypole. We learned to eat caviar and blue cheese. We had lessons in art, classical music, and religion.

We also learned the importance of the clock and that "Indian time" had no place in a modern society. Life for an Indian was ruled by the rising and setting of the sun; the easy flow of season to season. A thing was done when it felt like the time to do it and there was no need to hurry. How contrary and frustrating to be ruled by the numbers on a clock. But we learned that we must accept the structure of an industrial world if would be a part of it. Today I still rush to be on time and feel guilty when I am late.

At St. Mary's I became aware of man's inhumanity to man. One of my teachers was Miss Suzuki who with her family had been forced to live in a Japanese-American Internment camp during World War II.

In college I discovered great gaps in math and science that St. Mary's hadn't begun to fill. But the study habits the school had instilled carried me through Algebra and Chemistry.

College was, naturally, a special place even though for the first time in my life I was an Indian. In the pampered and protected world of childhood and St. Mary's I had been only "me." In college I learned the non-Indian's version of the history of my people, of the stereotypes of the noble savage and his counterpart the lazy, drunk, and dumb Indian. I was frustrated with my inability to do anything about these view points. But there was an English instructor and a history professor who understood and encouraged me to try. Later in my writing I have tried to correct inaccuracies and dispell misconceptions about the American Indian. I try to show that there is still value in our unconcern for material possessions and that we must still lovingly care for the land and water because the earth is our mother.

My father hoped that there would always be special places for me and there have been many. These places during the formative time of youth gave direction to the path of a little girl becoming a woman.

"WOMEN"

Virginia Driving Hawk Sneve

The Dakota word for woman, common to all dialects, is **winyan.** The word for girl, however, has distinct variations; the Santee is **wicinyana;** Yankton, **wicincana;** and Teton is **wicincala.** The generally used word, "squaw," has been applied to describe women of all tribes. The word is of Algonquian origin from **Squaas.** It was used by white men in a derogatory sense to reflect their opinion of Indian women. The term "squaw man" was a disparaging description of a white man who had an Indian wife. The use of the word "squaw" is, therefore, offensive and not acceptable to Indian people.

The Dakota woman's role was less glamorous than that of the proud, beautifully decked out warrior. By the time a girl was eight years old she spent all of her time in female company, rarely seeing any males other than her father and brothers. However, a girl's brother was her protector and she learned her future wifely duties by making and decorating articles of clothing for him. In turn, the brother, when old enough, might bring his sister a horse from a successful raid.

Women made, repaired, and moved the tipi. They butchered the buffalo and other game, dressed the hides, hauled wood and water, and cared for the children. A young girl learned to do all of these things well so that she would be a good wife to a brave warrior and a good mother to his children.

Polygamy was common to the Dakota; however, the first wife was not hurt or offended when her man took other wives. She welcomed them, for additional women lightened her work load, and belonging to a family of many wives indicated that the male was wealthy, a good provider, and virile.

A Dakota woman did not consider her chores as drudgery. She was proud of her duties, and her uncomplaining performance of them showed that she was a "good" wife. Women were highly respected and although they had no active part in the government of the tribe, their opinion, especially that of elderly, wise women, was sought and heeded.

Traditionally the Dakota women did the farming, for such work was degrading for a warrior. When the Dakota, particularly the strong, nomadic Teton, were confined to reservations and told to be farmers, the male suffered a total loss of self-esteem because his role as hunter, leader, and protector was completely abolished. The women adapted to reservation life much more easily. They continued with duties similar to those of the freer life, and indeed their lot was lighter with the government issue of ready-made tents and clothing, food stuffs and cooking utensils.

Dakota women have been ignored by historians or they have been romanticized as "beautiful maidens" or "princesses." This view and the derogatory one of "squaw" is true in the few places in South Dakota which were named for women or after an incident concerning them.

Virginia Driving Hawk Sneve, "Women," from THE DAKOTA'S HERITAGE, pp. 16-17, 1973, Brevet Press, P.O. Box 1404, Sious Falls, South Dakota 57101. Reprinted by permission of the publisher and the author.

THE SOUTHERN JEWISH AMERICAN PRINCESS
(IN THE FABULOUS FIFTIES)

Arlene G. Peck

What was it like growing up as a Jewish American Princess? Specifically, what was it like as a Southern Jewish Princess during the mid-1950's when life and responsibility were different. Life in the South was slow, uncomplicated, and crime wasn't rampant. The only "grass" we knew about was what the yardman cut, and "pot" was something that people cooked in.

We were the pre-tease, before-blow dry generation who thrived on seeing and being seen and most of all, being considered "with it." Popular was the key word. Clothes were important—too important—and there were few among us who did not have a charcoal grey felt skirt with pink poodles connected by a chain, with a matching cashmere sweater set, and finished off with expensive foreign imported shoes and our ever-present, leather, collegian tweed pocketbook. We were the SUPER princesses, indulged from the womb to the tomb and we reaped the benefits of our parents' success. We were the forerunners of today's Gucci-Pucci generation, the ones who today look chic wearing their hair pulled back at the nape of the neck with a rubberband and tied with a designer scarf.

Most of all there was SORORITY. Sorority is what separated the haves and the have nots. And, as the local southern Jewery was divided between the Reformed Jews (who had their roots in Germany) the Askanizie (who arrived later from Eastern Europe, usually with less money and less education) and the Sephardic or Spanish Jew (who were a close community and usually stayed apart from the rest), so were the sororities.

When September arrived and we received a "special" invitation from one of the elite sororities, "we had arrived!" Never again would we have to worry about sitting by ourselves at the lunch table. There was a special table for these select few. For the rest of our school career we majored in "friends" and minored in "popular." Somehow, for those who didn't sit at that table where the gods favored us from their lofty heights, life went on, but nowhere near as exciting. We were the girls who never got our hair wet or went camping. Even though we might play intramural basketball, we would never, but never, sweat! Horses sweat, people perspire, but the SORORITY GIRL GLOWED! Looking cute in adorable gym outfits was the name of the game—much more than winning.

After Friday night football games, the popular "in place" to be was "The Hang-out," a drive-in restaurant located near the local college campus. Only there was it permissable to be seen without a date. There were no singles bars because only "hussys" would frequent them. Rule one was NEVER GIVE YOUR RIGHT NAME. There in the safety of our peers and fortified with a "class" ficitious name like Modine Gunch, we were flirtatious, suggestive, seductive and sexy. We were also teasers. Jeans were unheard of and we were so inhibited in those days, that we wore girdles when we didn't need them because it was unladylike to JIGGLE. In the "Gone with the Wind" tradition, a trip downtown during the daytime meant that the Southern Jewish Princess had to dress in heels and gloves. To be seen on the street smoking was for harlots only. Besides, it was more fun sitting on the floor of the girl's bathroom passing around an unfiltered cigarette. Luckily, our lungs survived high school.

Northern college men who headed South for their education were filled with mixed feelings about the Southern Jewish American Princess. True, they were spoiled and pampered, but the Southern Jewish family was hospitable and their daughters were also usually pretty. If they weren't, then along with their "coming out" party at sixteen, they would visit the plastic surgeon for their nose job. Of course, the orthodontist was doing a thriving business.

We dated at ridiculous ages. Invitations were sent out to girls who were thirteen and looked twenty. We coerced our parents into allowing the eye makeup and the high heels that to this day have crippled my toes. The standard argument was, "You've GOT to let me; EVERYBODY DOES, or EVERYBODY HAS ONE." Dates were made weeks ahead; one reason being that it was unthinkable to wear the same dress twice. It could be reconstructed, and time had to be allowed for a trip to the local seamstress where, what nature had forgotten, she would fix with ruffles and more ruffles. Even if you weren't, everyone looked well-endowed. And, it was because of those volumenous ruffles, and the layers of crinolines that were starched so they could stand alone, that anything but double dating was discouraged. It was just impossible to fit more than four people in the car. Looking back, that was probably the reason most of us returned home from the dance with our virtues intact. That, and the fact that it took half an hour to hook ourselves into our "merry widow" waist clincher bra!

Speaking of that, no sooner were we out of our training bras into the dating scene at the age of thirteen that we received our indoctrination from our mothers. There is an old joke of the Jewish grandmother who was walking her grandchildren down the street and came upon a friend who exclaimed, "Oy, your grandchildren are adorable! How old are they?" The reply was, "The lawyer is two, the doctor is four." In a sentence, this sums up our mothers' attitudes' regarding the kinds of boys who would be an acceptable Prince for their Princess. We were taught that lightning would strike if we even considered speaking more than casually to a boy who wasn't Jewish. Horror stories were told of girls who married outside the faith and every city had at least one scandal. It was as though a vacuum had swallowed them up, never to be heard from again and doomed to live alone, and, certainly, without her former southern Jewish Princess friends. Of course, conversion was acceptable because after all even Queen Esther married outside her faith. And, who could forget the love story of David and Bathsheba that was known by every Sunday school student?

I remember testing my mother's words when I arrived at college and was invited to a non-Jewish fraternity party by the captain of the football team. He called me on my "princess" phone (what else?) and I accepted . . . expecting to be struck dead before the evening was over. I went, but with the guilt feelings of a lifetime on my head.

Chris was adorable (all football players are named Chris or Jim), and as we were dancing under the magnolias (it was a southern campus), sipping Purple Passion, which was, in reality, White Lightning passed off as grape juice, I decided to find out if "they" were right. I tugged at a ruffle and casually asked, "What do you want to do when you finish school?" He looked over at me with those nordic gorgeous blue eyes and said, "Er, Ah, er, I kinda thought I'd be a coach." I spent the rest of the evening asking the other nordic types who asked me to dance, what they wanted to be and the answers ranged from working for a large corporate company to chief executive at the local bank. This was the first time in my life I found out that the boys that

I knew didn't have to be a doctor, lawyer, professional man, or go into his fathers business. WASP's didn't have a quota system and could be anything they wanted!

Southern Jewish American Princesses were accustomed to having two live-in servants, their mothers and their fathers. Until I went to college, I thought that the good fairy came into my room and put clean sheets on the bed, pressed clothes in the closet and nice meals on the table. I was so impressed when I found out that there were girls in my dorm from the North who actually sewed and ironed shirts and knew how to get clothes whiter than white. (I failed that in college.) Thats why it was so important that a Southern Jewish American Princess never married beneath her station, because then we might find ourselves with husbands who thought that we were spoiled . . . which we were!

We grew up thinking that everyone used fine cut crystal glass to keep our toothbrushes in. By seventeen, we had our first car, diamond ring and trip to Europe (chaperoned, of course). For those who followed the trend, marriage was at eighteen, to our first husbands that is.

And, today, what has happened to us "golden girls" of the fifties? We were the children of parents who were, for the most part, first-generations Americans. Their parents had fled the old country to escape the pogroms. Our parents were the products of the post-war years and were afraid to speak out about prejudice. They shut their eyes to the quota systems and "restricted" clubs and avoided facing issues that we are battling today. Because of this background, many of us have turned into stronger, or at least more vocal Jews. Our parents were afraid to speak out about the injustices lest the fears of the Holocaust happen again. Today, we know if we DON'T speak out, it COULD happen here. We are raising our children with a stronger Jewish identity and a feeling of ethnic pride. That "Special" time is gone, but it has been replaced with something that is better.

RICH IS BETTER

Helen S. Garson

Growing up is something I did awkwardly and late. My calendar years were further along than my wisdom when I set sail for the world outside the extended family, thinking the world flat and expecting to fall off the edge if I ventured too far. For a time I was convinced that I was violating the laws of the Commandments and the Commentaries of my family as I began to perceive that strangers were not invariably enemies, that there were many ways to live that were not known to my relatives, and that it was possible to be different from them. Only in maturity did I come to terms with both the pleasure and the pain of growing up female and Jewish.

My parents came from a line of small business people. On my father's side everyone was comfortable, some even wealthy. But in my mother's family it was the opposite; everyone struggled. My mother attributed the success of her in-laws to their "arriving early," which meant that unlike her Russian immigrant parents, my father's Austrian ancestors came to this country in the nineteenth century and were established before the great wave of immigration of eastern

Reprinted by permission of the author.

Jews reached this country. Although in my childhood I often sensed animosities between the families of my parents, I never thought much about these until I married the son of Russian immigrants and failed one of the tests of their clan: it was discovered that there were German Jews in my father's background. My own peculiarities—aloofness, bookishness, snobbery—were attributed to this flaw. How my own family explained the problems is more complex, but I suspect that my mother secretly shared the belief of my in-laws.

The concerns of the family in my growing up years were material and social, just as they are now, though they have been transposed to a warmer climate. Religion played almost no part in our lives, although my maternal grandmother (probably affected more by remnants of Victorian morality than by Jewish religiosity) seemed to worry a good bit about sinful children and must have been praying for us on Holy Days, when she spent long hours in the synagogue. All of the children, my cousins and I, outfitted for the occasions, were marched into the synagogue briefly on each Holy Day to receive grandmother's blessing. Hers were the only blessings we could get. Nobody else in the family attended services, neither her husband nor her sons and daughters. But holidays provided opportunities for socializing, for partying, for taking meals with aunts, uncles, cousins, and grandparents. The adults, as I remember them, had happy times, the children less so: too much food, too much wine, too much energy for too little space led to the inevitable conflicts of personality with children who saw each other only on Sundays and holidays.

Of the eleven cousins on my maternal side, two were boys. Everyone knew they were going to be successful, at something. The keen sense of competition among the adults extended to concern about the future of their male offspring. Girls were only expected to marry. In most Jewish families, even irreligious ones, boys were regarded differently from girls, and mine was like most, although I had no brothers. Girls were measured by their beauty, their manners, and their ability to accommodate. My rating was never very high. I preferred books to company, and early on the family viewed me with some trepidation, along with my mother, concerned about my consuming interest in books and sports and my lack of sociability. Every time my grandmother saw me with a book she'd cluck her tongue in disapproval. In later years I began to wonder about the description of the Jews as the "people of the Book," for in my family they would have had problems. Success for men was evaluated by the amount of money they earned and the possessions they had, and for women by "good" marriages, that is, to men of money and possessions.

Appearance was central. Even in lean times my mother saw to it that we were well clothed. No doubt she believed that elegant dresses and striking home furnishings would lure rich young men for her daughters. Holding firmly to the belief that "rich was better" she surveyed males of marriagable age more as potential providers than as interesting, intelligent people. Since my father and grandfather worked constantly—six days and nights a week, including Saturday—it was taken for granted that all men followed the same pattern; the loving husband was the man who saw to it that his wife had visible goods and household help. The failure was the man whose wife did her own housework and helped earn the living.

None of the women I knew as a child worked and there was a stigma attached to the working women. When the family gossiped about some woman's going to work, somewhere in the conversation would by the statement, ". . . and she had to go to work." The husband was at fault for the shame of it all. Because women were not supposed to work, various members of the family couldn't understand why girls should be sent to college, since college was regarded only as preparation for a job. Why spend on an education for a girl when it would prepare her for something you didn't think she should be doing? When I went to college, although by then my mother's sisters and brothers all had moved to different parts of the country, they wrote frequently and critically about "waste" and "indulgence." Not surprisingly, among all the cousins, I was the only girl who got a college education.

Why my parents were willing to have me go to college when they saw no visible good in it has always puzzled me. Perhaps it was because they had no sons, or perhaps, because they had struggled through the depression years, they saw education as a type of insurance policy, but surely they never anticipated that I would seek education beyond the undergraduate degree and become a working wife and mother. Of course, given the world in which I grew up, neither did I.

My father died before I completed my academic training. Had he lived, I imagine he would have shared my mother's mixed feelings about my life and career: pride in what I've done and concern that nobody think her daughter has to work. As to the attitude of other members of the family, whenever I have too great a sense of accomplishment, I find I can always bring myself back to earth by remembering the comment my husband's father made when I informed him of my successful dissertation defense and the subsequent granting of my doctorate. "So," said my father-in-law, "how much money will you earn now in your job?" I told him. "Well," he said, with a gesture of dismissal, "with that kind of money, better you should be a secretary."

"Chinese mother and child." By permission of Maria de Noronha (Gallman), the artist.

"NO NAME WOMAN"

Maxine Hong Kingston

"You must not tell anyone," my mother said, "what I am about to tell you. In China your father had a sister who killed herself. She jumped into the family well. We say that your father has all brothers because it is as if she had never been born.

"In 1924 just a few days after our village celebrated seventeen hurry-up weddings—to make sure that every young man who went 'out on the road' would responsibly come home—

From THE WOMAN WARRIOR: Memories of a Girlhood Among Ghosts, by Maxine Hong Kingston. Copyright © 1975, 1976 by Maxine Hong Kingston. Reprinted by permission of Alfred A. Knopf, Inc.

your father and his brothers and your grandfather and his brothers and your aunt's new husband sailed for America, the Gold Mountain. It was your grandfather's last trip. Those lucky enough to get contracts waved good-bye from the decks. They fed and guarded the stowaways and helped them off in Cuba, New York, Bali, Hawaii. 'We'll meet in California next year,' they said. All of them sent money home.

"I remember looking at your aunt one day when she and I were dressing; I had not noticed before that she had such a protruding melon of a stomach. But I did not think, 'She's pregnant,' until she began to look like other pregnant women, her shirt pulling and the white tops of her black pants showing. She could not have been pregnant, you see, because her husband had been gone for years. No one said anything. We did not discuss it. In early summer she was ready to have the child, long after the time when it could have been possible.

"The village had also been counting. On the night the baby was to be born the villagers raided our house. Some were crying. Like a great saw, teeth strung with lights, files of people walked zigzag across our land, tearing the rice. Their lanterns doubled in the disturbed blackwater, which rained away through the broken bunds. As the villagers closed in, we could see that some of them, probably men and women we knew well, wore white masks. The people with long hair hung it over their faces. Women with short hair made it stand up on end. Some had tied white bands around their foreheads, arms, and legs.

"At first they threw mud and rocks at the house. Then they threw eggs and began slaughtering our stock. We could hear the animals scream their deaths—the roosters, the pigs, a last great roar from the ox. Familiar wild heads flared in our night windows; the villagers encircled us. Some of the faces stopped to peer at us, their eyes rushing like searchlights. The hands flattened against the panes, framed heads, and left red prints.

"The villagers broke in the front and the back doors at the same time, even though we had not locked the doors against them. Their knives dripped with the blood of our animals. They smeared blood on the doors and walls. One woman swung a chicken, whose throat she had slit, splattering blood in red arcs about her. We stood together in the middle of our house, in the family hall with the pictures and tables of the ancestors around us, and looked staight ahead.

"At that time the house had only two wings. When the men came back, we would build two more to enclose our courtyard and a third one to begin a second courtyard. The villagers pushed through both wings, even your grandparents' rooms, to find your aunt's, which was also mine until the men returned. From this room a new wing for one of the younger families would grow. They ripped up her clothes and shoes and broke her combs, grinding them underfoot. They tore her work from the loom. They scattered the cooking fire and rolled the new weaving in it. We could hear them in the kitchen breaking our bowls and banging the pots. They overturned the great waist-high earthenware jugs; duck eggs, pickled fruits, vegetables burst out and mixed in acrid torrents. The old woman from the next field swept a broom through the air and loosed the spirits-of-the-broom over our heads. 'Pig.' 'Ghost.' 'Pig,' they sobbed and scolded while they ruined our house.

"When they left, they took sugar and oranges to bless themselves. They cut pieces from the dead animals. Some of them took bowls that were not broken and clothes that were not torn. Afterward we swept up the rice and sewed it back up into sacks. But the smells from the spilled preserves lasted. Your aunt gave birth in the pigsty that night. The next morning when I went for the water, I found her and the baby plugging up the family well.

"Don't let your father know that I told you. He denies her. Now that you have started to menstruate, what happened to her could happen to you. Don't humiliate us. You wouldn't like to be forgotten as if you had never been born. The villagers are watchful.''

Whenever she had to warn us about life, my mother told stories that ran like this one, a story to grow up on. She tested our strength to establish realities. Those in the emigrant generations who could not reassert brute survival died young and far from home. Those of us in the first American generations have had to figure out how the invisible world the emigrants built around our childhoods fit in solid America.

The emigrants confused the gods by diverting their curses, misleading them with crooked streets and false names. They must try to confuse their offspring as well, who, I suppose, threaten them in similar ways—always trying to get things straight, always trying to name the unspeakable. The Chinese I know hide their names; sojourners take new names when their lives change and guard their real names with silence.

Chinese-Americans, when you try to understand what things in you are Chinese, how do you separate what is peculiar to childhood, to poverty, insanities, one family, your mother who marked your growing with stories, from what is Chinese? What is Chinese tradition and what is the movies?

If I want to learn what clothes my aunt woke, whether flashy or ordinary, I would have to begin, "Remember Father's drowned-in-the-well sister?" I cannot ask that. My mother has told me once and for all the useful parts. She will add nothing unless powered by Necessity, a riverbank that guides her life. She plants vegetable gardens rather than lawns; she carries the odd-shaped tomatoes home from the fields and eats food left for the gods.

Whenever we did frivolous things, we used up energy; we flew high kites. We children came up off the ground over the melting cones our parents brought home from work and the American movie on New Year's Day—*Oh, You Beautiful Doll* with Betty Grable one year, and *She Wore a Yellow Ribbon* with John Wayne another year. After the one carnival ride each, we paid in guilt; one tired father counted his change on the dark walk home.

Adultery is extravagance. Could people who hatch their own chicks and eat the embryos and the heads for delicacies and boil the feet in vinegar for party food, leaving only the gravel, eating even the gizzard lining—could such people engender a prodigal aunt? To be a woman, to have a daughter in starvation time was a waste enough. My aunt could not have been the lone romantic who gave up everything for sex. Women in the old China did not choose. Some man had commanded her to lie with him and be his secret evil. I wonder whether he masked himself when he joined the raid on her family.

Perhaps she encountered him in the fields or on the mountain where the daughters-in-law collected fuel. Or perhaps he first noticed her in the marketplace. He was not a stranger because the village housed no strangers. She had to have dealings with him other than sex. Perhaps he worked an adjoining field, or he sold her the cloth for the dress she sewed and wore. His demand must have surprised, then terrified her. She obeyed him; she always did as she was told.

When the family found a young man in the next village to be her husband, she stood tractably beside the best rooster, his proxy, and promised before they net that she would be his forever. She was lucky that he was her age and she would be the first wife, an advantage secure now. The night she first saw him, he had sex with her. Then he left for America. She had almost forgotten what he looked like. When she tried to envision him, she only saw the black and white face in the group photograph the men had had taken before leaving.

The other man was not, after all, much different from her husband. They both gave orders; she followed. "If you tell your family, I'll beat you. I'll kill you. Be here again next week." No one talked sex, ever. And she might have separated the rapes from the rest of living if only she did not have to buy her oil from him or gather wood in the same forest. I want her fear to have lasted just as long as rape lasted so that the fear could have been contained. No drawn-out fear. But women at sex hazarded birth and hence lifetimes. The fear did not stop but permeated everywhere. She told the man, "I think I'm pregnant." He organized the raid against her.

On nights when my mother and father talked about their life back home, sometimes they mentioned an "outcast table" whose business they still seemed to be settling, their voices tight. In a commensal tradition, where food is precious, the powerful older people made wrongdoers eat alone. Instead of letting them start separate new lives like the Japanese, who could become samurais and geishas, the Chinese family, faces averted but eyes glowering sideways, hung on to the offenders and fed them leftovers. My aunt must have lived in the same house as my parents and eaten at an outcast table. My mother spoke about the raid as if she had seen it, when she and my aunt, a daughter-in-law to a different household, should not have been living together at all. Daughter-in-law lived with their husbands' parents, not their own; a synonym for marriage in Chinese is "taking a daughter-in-law." Her husband's parents could have sold her, mortgaged her, stoned her. But they had sent her back to her mother and father, a mysterious act hinting at disgraces not told me. Perhaps they had thrown her out to deflect the avengers.

She was the only daughter; her four brothers went with her father, husband, and uncles "out on the road" and for some years became western men. When the goods were divided among the family, three of the brothers took land, and the youngest, my father, chose an education. After my grandparents gave their daughter away to her husband's family, they had dispensed all the adventure and all the property. They expected her alone to keep the traditional ways, which her brothers, now among the barbarians, could fumble without detection. The heavy, deep-rooted women were to maintain the past against the flood, safe for returning. But the rare urge west had fixed upon our family, and so my aunt crossed boundaries not delineated in space.

The work of preservation demands that the feelings playing about in one's guts not be turned into action. Just watch their passing like cherry blossoms. But perhaps my aunt, my forerunner, caught in a slow life, let dreams grow and fade and after some months or years went toward what persisted. Fear at the enormities of the forbidden kept her desires delicate, wire and bone. She looked at a man because she liked the way the hair was tucked behind his ears, or she liked the question-mark line of a long torso curving at the shoulder and straight at the hip. For warm eyes or a soft voice or a slow walk—that's all—a few hairs, a line, a brightness, a sound, a pace, she gave up family. She offered us up for a charm that vanished with tiredness, a pigtail that didn't toss when the wind died. Why, the wrong lighting could erase the dearest thing about him.

It could very well have been, however, that my aunt did not take subtle enjoyment of her friend, but, a wild woman, kept rollicking company. Imagining her free with sex doesn't fit, though. I don't know any women like that, or men either. Unless I see her life branching into mine, she gives me no ancestral help.

To sustain her being in love, she often worked at herself in the mirror, guessing at the colors and shapes that would interest him, changing them frequently in order to hit on the right combination. She wanted him to look back.

On a farm near the sea, a woman who tended her appearance reaped a reputation for eccentricity. All the married women blunt-cut their hair in flaps about their ears or pulled it back in tight buns. No nonsense. Neither style blew easily into heart-catching tangles. And at their weddings they displayed themselves in their long hair for the last time. ''It brushed the backs of my knees,'' my mother tells me. ''It was braided, and even so, it brushed the backs of my knees.''

At the mirror my aunt combed individuality into her bob. A bun could have been contrived to escape into black streamers blowing in the wind or in quiet wisps about her face, but only the older women in our picture album wear buns. She brushed her hair back from her forehead, tucking the flaps behind her ears. She looped a piece of thread, knotted into a circle between her index fingers and thumbs, and ran the double strand across her forehead. When she closed her fingers as if she were making a pair of shadow geese bite, the string twisted together catching the little hairs. Then she pulled the thread away from her skin, ripping the hairs out neatly, her eyes watering from the needles of pain. Opening her fingers, she cleaned the thread, then rolled it along her hairline and the tops of her eyebrows. My mother did the same to me and my sisters and herself. I used to believe that the expression ''caught by the short hairs'' meant a captive held with a depilatory string. It especially hurt at the temples, but my mother said we were lucky we didn't have to have our feet bound when we were seven. Sisters used to sit on their beds and cry together, she said, as their mothers or their slave removed the bandages for a few minutes each night and let the blood gush into their veins. I hope that the man my aunt loved appreciated a smooth brow, that he wasn't just a tits-and-ass man.

Once my aunt found a freckle on her chin, at a spot that the almanac said predestined her for unhappiness. She dug it out with a hot needle and washed the wound with peroxide.

More attention to her looks than these pullings of hairs and pickings at spots would have caused gossip among the villagers. They owned work clothes and good clothes, and they wore good clothes for feasting the new seasons. But since a woman combing her hair hexes beginnings, my aunt rarely found an occasion to look her best. Women looked like great sea snails—the corded wood, babies, and laundry they carried were the whorls on their backs. The Chinese did not admire a bent back; goddesses and warriors stood straight. Still there must have been a marvelous freeing of beauty when a worker laid down her burden and stretched and arched.

Such commonplace loveliness, however, was not enough for my aunt. She dreamed of a lover for the fifteen days of New Year's, the time for families to exchange visits, money, and food. The plied her secret comb. And sure enough she cursed the year, the family, the village, and herself.

Even as her hair lured her imminent lover, many other men looked at her. Uncles, cousins, nephews, brothers would have looked, too, had they been home between journeys. Perhaps they had already been restraining their curiosity, and they left, fearful that their glances, like a field of nesting birds, might be startled and caught. Poverty hurt, and that was their first reason for leaving. But another, final reason for leaving the crowded house was the never-said.

She may have been unusually beloved, the precious only daughter, spoiled and mirror gazing because of the affection the family lavished on her. When her husband left, they welcomed the chance to take her back from the in-laws; she could live like the little daughter for just a while longer. There are stories that my grandfather was different from other people, "crazy ever since the little Jap bayoneted him in the head." He used to put his naked penis on the dinner table, laughing. And one day he brought home a baby girl, wrapped up inside his brown western-style greatcoat. He had traded one of his sons, probably my father, the youngest, for her. My grandmother made him trade back. When he finally got a daughter of his own, he doted on her. They must have all loved her, except perhaps my father, the only brother who never went back to China, having once been traded for a girl.

Brothers and sisters, newly men and women, had to efface their sexual color and present plain miens. Disturbing hair and eyes, a smile like no other, threatened the ideal of five generations living under one roof. To focus blurs, people shouted face to face and yelled from room to room. The immigrants I know have loud voices, unmodulated to American tones even after years away from the village where they called their friendships out across the fields. I have not been able to stop my mother's screams in public libraries or over telephones. Walking erect (knees straight, toes pointed forward, not pigeon-toed, which is Chinese-feminine) and speaking in an inaudible voice, I have tired to turn myself American-feminine. Chinese communication was loud, public. Only sick people had to whisper. But at the dinner table, where the family members came nearest one another, no one could talk, not the outcasts nor any eaters. Every word that falls from the mouth is a coin lost. Silently they gave and accepted food with both hands. A preoccupied child who took his bowl with one hand got a sideways glare. A complete moment of total attention is due everyone alike. Children and lovers have no singularity here, but my aunt used a secret voice, a separate attentiveness.

She kept the man's name to herself throughout her labor and dying; she did not accuse him that he be punished with her. To save her inseminator's name she gave silent birth.

He may have been somebody in her own household, but intercourse with a man outside the family would have been no less abhorrent. All the village were kinsmen, and the titles shouted in loud country voices never let kinship be forgotten. Any man within visiting distance would have been neutralized as a lover—"brother," "younger brother," "older brother"—one hundred and fifteen relationship titles. Parents researched birth charts probably not so much to assure good fortune as to circumvent incest in a population that has but one hundred surnames. Everybody has eight million relatives. How useless then sexual mannerisms, how dangerous.

As if it came from an atavism deeper that fear, I used to add "brother" silently to boys' names. It hexed the boys, who would or would not ask me to dance, and made them less scary and as familiar and deserving of benevolence as girls.

But, of course, I hexed myself also—no dates. I should have stood up, both arms waving, and shouted out across libraries, "Hey, you! Love me back." I had no idea, though, how to make attraction selective, how to control its direction and magnitude. If I made myself American-pretty so that the five or six Chinese boys in the class fell in love with me, everyone else—the Caucasian, Negro, and Japanese boys—would too. Sisterliness, dignified and honorable, made much more sense.

Attraction eludes control so stubbornly that whole societies designed to organize relationships among people cannot keep order, not even when they bind people to one another from childhood and raise them together. Among the very poor and the wealthy, brothers married their adopted sisters, like doves. Our family allowed some romance, paying adult brides' prices and providing dowries so that their sons and daughters could marry strangers. Marriage promises to turn strangers into friendly relatives—a nation of siblings.

In the village structure, spirits shimmered among the live creatures, balanced and held in equilibrium by time and land. But one human being flaring up into violence could open up a black hole, a maelstrom that pulled in the sky. The frightened villagers, who depended on one another to maintain the real, went to my aunt to show her a personal, physical representation of the break she had made in the "roundness." Misallying couples snapped off the future, which was to be embodied in true offspring. The villagers punished her for acting as if she could have a private life, secret and apart from them.

If my aunt had betrayed the family at a time of large grain yields and peace, when many boys were born, and wings were being built on many houses, perhaps she might have escaped such severe punishment. But the men—hungry, greedy, tired of planting in dry soil, cuckolded—and had to leave the village in order to send food-money home. There were ghost plagues, bandit plagues, wars with the Japanese, floods. My Chinese brother and sister had died of an unknown sickness. Adultery, perhaps only a mistake during good times, became a crime when the village needed food.

The round moon cakes and round doorways, the round tables of graduated size that fit one roundness inside another, round windows and rice bowls—these talismans had lost their power to warn this family of the law: a family must be whole, faithfully keeping the descent line by having sons to feed the old and the dead, who in turn look after the family. The villagers came to show my aunt and her lover-in-hiding a broken house. The villagers were speeding up the circling of events because she was too shortsighted to see that her infidelity had already harmed the village, that waves of consequences would return unpredictably, sometimes in disguise, as now, to hurt her. This roundness had to be made coin-sized so that she would see its circumference: punish her at the birth of her baby. Awaken her to the inexorable. People who refused fatalism because they could invent small resources insisted on culpability. Deny accidents and wrest fault from the stars.

After the villagers left, their lantern now scattering in various directions toward home, the family broke their silence and cursed her. "Aiaa, we're going to die. Death is coming. Death is coming. Look what you've done. You've killed us. Ghost! Dead ghost! Ghost! You've never been born." She ran out into the fields far enough from the house so that she could no longer hear their voices, and pressed herself against the earth, her own land no more. When she felt the birth coming, she thought that she had been hurt. Her body seized together. "They've hurt me too much," she thought. "This is gall, and it will kill me." With forehead and knees against the earth, her body convulsed and then relaxed. She turned on her back, lay on the ground. The black well of sky and stars went out and out and out forever; her body and her complexity seemed to disappear. She was one of the stars, a bright dot in blackness, without home, without a companion, in eternal cold and silence. An agoraphobia rose in her, speeding higher and higher, bigger and bigger; she would not be able to contain it; there would be no end to fear.

Flayed, unprotected against space, she felt pain return, focusing her body. This pain chilled her—a cold, steady kind of surface pain. Inside, spasmodically, the other pain, the pain of the child, heated her. For hours she lay on the ground, alternately body and space.

Sometimes a vision of normal comfort obliterated reality: she saw the family in the evening gambling at the dinner table, the young people massaging their elders' backs. She saw them congratulating one another, high joy on the mornings the rice shoots came up. When these pictures burst, the stars drew yet further apart. Black space opened.

She got to her feet to fight better and remembered that old-fashioned women gave birth in their pigsties to fool the jealous, pain-dealing gods, who do not snatch piglets. Before the next spasms could stop her, she ran to the pigsty, each step a rushing out into emptiness. She climbed over the fence and knelt in the dirt. It was good to have a fence enclosing her, a tribal person alone.

Laboring, this woman who had carried her child as a foreign growth that sickened her every day, expelled it at last. She reached down to touch the hot, wet, moving mass, surely smaller than anything human, and could feel that it was human after all—fingers, toes, nails, nose. She pulled it up on to her belly, and it lay curled there, butt in the air, feet precisely tucked one under the other. She opened her loose shirt and buttoned the child inside. After resting, it squirmed and thrashed and she pushed it up to her breast. It turned its head this way and that until it found her nipple. There, it made little snuffing noises. She clenched her teeth at its preciousness, lovely as a young calf, a piglet, a little dog.

She may have gone to the pigsty as a last act of responsibility: she would protect this child as she had protected its father. It would look after her soul, leaving supplies on her grave. But how would this tiny child without family find her grave when there would be no marker for her anywhere, neither in the earth nor the family hall? No one would give her a family hall name. She had taken the child with her into the wastes. At its birth the two of them had felt the same raw pain of separation, a wound that only the family pressing tight could close. A child with no descent line would not soften her life but only trail after her, ghostlike, begging her to give it purpose. At dawn the villagers on their way to the fields would stand around the fence and look.

Full of milk, the little ghost slept. When it awoke, she hardened her breasts against the milk that crying loosens. Toward morning she picked up the baby and walked to the well.

Carrying the baby to the well shows loving. Otherwise abandon it. Turn its face into the mud. Mothers who love their children take them along. It was probably a girl; there is some hope of forgiveness for boys.

"Don't tell anyone you had an aunt. Your father does not want to hear her name. She has never been born." I have believed that sex was unspeakable and words so strong and fathers so frail that "aunt" would do my father mysterious harm. I have thought that my family, having settled among immigrants who had also been their neighbors in the ancestral land, needed to clean their name, and a wrong word would incite the kinspeople even here. But there is more to this silence: they want me to participate in her punishment. And I have.

In the twenty years since I heard this story I have not asked for details nor said my aunt's name; I do not know it. People who can comfort the dead can also chase after them to hurt them further—a reverse ancestor worship. The real punishment was not the raid swiftly inflicted by the villagers, but the family's deliberately forgetting her. Her betrayal so maddened them, they saw to it that she would suffer forever, even after death. Always hungry, always needing, she would have to beg food from other ghosts, snatch and steal it from those whose living descendants give them gifts. She would have to fight the ghosts massed at crossroads for the buns a few thoughtful citizens leave to decoy her away from village and home so that ancestral spirits could feast unharassed. At peace, they could act like gods, not ghost their descent lines providing them with paper suits and dresses, spirit money, paper houses, paper automobiles, chicken, meat, and rice into eternity—essences delivered up in smoke and flames, steam and incense rising from each rice bowl. In an attempt to make the Chinese care for people outside the family, Chairman Mao encourages us now to give our paper replicas to the spirits of outstanding soldiers and workers, no matter whose ancestors they may be. My aunt remains forever hungry. Goods are not distributed evenly among the dead.

My aunt haunts me—her ghost drawn to me because now, after fifty years of neglect, I alone devote pages of paper to her, though not origamied into houses and clothes. I do not think she always means me well. I am telling on her, and she was a spite suicide, drowning herself in the drinking water. The Chinese are always very frightened of the drowned one, whose weeping ghost, wet hair hanging and skin bloated, waits silently by the water to pull down a substitute.*

LOOKING BACK

Rose Mary Prosen

> *Looking back we do not remember*
> *ourselves but the neighborhoods*
> *we lived in and the things there we knew.*
> *. . . How*
> *much we belong to the past we learn*
> *only when we have labored*
> *to survive and prevail without it.*

Richard Howard
On the United States
Considered as a Landscape

Easter. Arising at four a.m. Standing at the gas stove in the kitchen while mother curled my hair with the curling irons. Wearing a long, loose white gown and gauze wings hooked onto my back; a crown of flowers on my head; a small white basket with a long curved handle in my hands, flower petals inside to strew in the aisles at church as I and my fellow angels marched, preparing the way for the Holy Monstrance, the robed priest, the altar boys, splendid in bright red cassocks, the incense burning and swinging on its chains; the organ and choir shaking our

Rose Mary Prosen, "Looking Back" from GROWING UP SLAVIC IN AMERICA, edited by Michael Novak, © 1976. Empac! Reprinted by permission of the editor and the author. Some minor revisions have been made by the author for this anthology.

*See an excellent interpretation of this story in *Melus,* Vol. V, No. 2 (Summer, 1978) by Woon-Ping Chin Holaday entitled "From Ezra Pound to Maxine Hong Kinston: Expressions of Chinese Thought in American Literature."

souls with Easter music. Who can forget the rich poetry of church ritual from her childhood days? It is not to be forgotten; never to be forgotten; never can be.

The church full of early morning men, their grimy, calloused hands scrubbed down with Lava soap; the aroma of garlic, cigars, of perspiration, of breath, not bad but *au naturel* (baking soda was our tooth powder); the women in their flowered straw hats, wearing their one good dress, their church dress; everyone wearing Sunday shoes, shining brightly, newly heeled; the choir announcing "Christ has risen as He said! Alleluia! Alleluia!" The triple brass bells ringing, alternating; brass bells on the left of the canopied tabernacle and on the right; the clouds of incense stinging my eyes as I floated down the aisle. My sister angels and I led the whole procession; we emptied our little wooden baskets, strewing the whitesheeted center aisle with bright red and blue and yellow petals until we reached the front of the altar, where we stopped, turned, and watched the three priests ascend the steps, assisted by their altar boys, some of them, sometimes, missing a cue; whispers to Joey to move left, not right; to hold the priest's cape lower or higher.

The choir sang in Slovenian and in English, the adopted language; the language their children were learning in the church school: English, the key to success; its correct pronunciation the mark of social distinction; its usage humiliating the old people, some of them barely literate, living their lives in devotion to Our Lady of Perpetual Help, chanting their rosaries at early evening; black babushkas, black dresses, widows, their faces creased in perpetual grief, sustaining themselves in plain chant in their own language, Slovenian, its very sounds striking the dim lit Tuesday evening services with assurance, with specificity; the communal spirit of women who had lost husbands, children, friends; who had buried babies, those too-many-born in times when the only birth-control was self-control; who had washed their own dead with their own hands in their own beds; who continued to plant lettuce, carrots, tomatoes, corn, beans; to nurture plum trees, pear trees, grape vines; to preserve these personal fruits and vegetables in Mason jars for the American winter; the old ladies of the neighborhood who in their devotion to the Blessed Virgin Mary and their own home, their kitchen, their cooking, preserved more than food and a religious tradition. Out of such single-minded routines arose the hope of a better life for their children, and the strength to endure another day in the family of strangers their children sometimes became. Better to keep holy the familiar paths than to wander in the wilderness, though they had boarded the great ship which had taken them across the Big Pond to a strange land where a peasant could dress like a gentleman if he could save the dollars to buy the suit that said he was such a man. Money. They came for money; money to buy the land that would mean they were no longer tenant farmers; that they were landlords; that they could nurture their own land and pass it on to their sons and grandsons, and nobody could take the land from them without war.

Through the years, I have had my quarrels with the Church, as I have had my quarrels with the world. Wanting to be me, I needed to find out who I was. Rebellious, confused, I left my home, my church, my neighborhood, and ventured forth into the world, into Cleveland, into America, into Europe, wondering where it was I belonged. I flowed into the mainstream, but sometimes the currents were too strong for me; the questions unanswerable. I drowned, and drowned, and drowned. In the ninth grade, a boy said to me, "You talk funny." I wondered what he meant. I listened to my friends, and I did not think they "talked funny." Then, that great American experiment, the public high school, opened my ears. I heard the English language spoken as I had never heard it spoken. At that time, a time without television, the high school was the only place to hear multiple dialects. I began to hear that I did indeed pronounce my words differently, and so did my friends. I wrote a letter to a movie magazine. For twenty-five cents I could study the correct pronunciation of English words from a special publication, entitled, "How to Become an Actress." I practiced in secret, in the bathroom, of course, until I could pronounce the difficult "th" sound, which seemed the most distinctive and, therefore, the most necessary to conquer. How superior I felt when I had mastered this sound!

Of course, there were other language problems. Thanks to the Dominican nuns in our elementary school, I learned the grammar of the English language better than any professor was ever to teach it during my high school/college years. I still have those composition books where I learned to diagram sentences until I thought architecture was merely an extension of grammar! Those lessons are the lessons I myself teach today when I teach English grammar. I learned the rules of the language as I was to learn and love its sounds. Alas, however, I refused to speak Slovenian. What was a Slovenian? A hunkie. A greenhorn. A dumb Slav. "You sound like you just got off the boat," another boy had said to me once. I became ashamed that my parents spoke "funny"; that we laughed too loud; that we drank homemade wine; that our walls were wallpapered in flower patterns; that we grew our own vegetables; that my father raised chickens in our garage; that he constructed his children's beds out of scrap wood with his own hands; that he repaired all our shoes in our basement; that my mother never sat down to eat dinner with us (she cooked, served, ate when everyone was finished); that our clothes and our curtains and towels were homemade, some of them out of feed bags from the local granary; that stockings and worn clothing were never thrown away but given to my uncle who transformed them into rag rugs; that we had linoleum carpets; and, I suspect, there were other more subtle aspects of that early life which I tried to reject but cannot remember.

What was to become of me? What became of most of the girls of that neighborhood in those days? Many of them went to work in factories at fifteen—the woolen mills, the lamp works. They became factory girls, glad to have a job, then a husband. Some of them became domestics. Without specific purpose, I finished high school, not the public high school. I transferred to a Catholic high school, Notre Dame Academy, after I had saved money for tuition. I was becoming an American, but I needed to be with my own kind, the safe structured world of Catholics. The language of my birth, Slovenian, did not pass my lips as I grew into womanhood. If someone did speak to me in that language, I might respond. More often, I would not. However, by the time I was thirteen, there had been five other children born, and my parents were outnumbered. We all spoke English. Except for Slovenian prayers, English dominated my family home and, of course, the elementary school. We had become Americans. My mother, whose parents were from Slovenia, spoke both languages. My father began to learn the English language, working in a brickyard and then in the steel mill. At home, he sat with me as I read my school books. He pronounced the sentences with me, word by word. We all became Americans, reading about Dick and Jane and "Run, Spot, run."

There were no Dicks or Janes in my neighborhood; there were many Josephs and Marys. In these strange first-grade readers, the children never went to church. There were no nuns nor priests nor wine nor polkas. Mrs. Dick & Jane did not preserve tomatoes for the winter. She and her husband never argued about money. Mr. Dick & Jane never got drunk. There was no saloon in the lives of this peculiar American family. Strangest of all, there were no flowers growing in their yard. They never mentioned flowers. In our school, every spring, the children sold seed packets. Every yard, small as some of them were, was filled with several different kinds of flowers, the most outstanding being the sunflower. I loved to look at the brightly colored illustrations on the seed packets. What I know today about flowers, I learned at St. Lawrence School and in the yards of its neighborhood. Men and women, saving nickels and dimes for the insurance man, always had a nickel for a packet of seeds. It is amazing to me today to list the flowers that grew in our family yard. The variety is so numerous a reader might imagine that we had an acre of land, but we did not. We had a small city lot. In it grew marigolds, roses, lilies-of-the-valley, petunias, forget-me-nots, daffodils, geraniums, irises, nasturtiums, sweet peas, and morning glories against the wooden fence. Oh, yes, there were also glorious peonies! My parents planted and cared for all these flowers as naturally as eating and sleeping. I never once heard the word "landscaping." I was astonished to learn years later that some people actually bought full-grown flowers from a business called a "nursery" and paid a perfect stranger to dig up their yards. How strange to deny themselves the pleasure of watching a seed sprout into a beautiful blossom! Perhaps it was then I began to suspect that mine was a peasant's heritage tied to the land and the fruit thereof. Imagine raising rabbits as well as chickens in a city garage! Today, I am sure the neighbors would object. Then, the neighbors, too, had their chickens and rabbits, if only two or three. I remember the smell of chicken blood in the basement after my father had wrung a chicken's neck, then chopped off its head. Chickens do run around without their heads! No chicken today tastes like the chickens my mother cleaned and prepared for Sunday dinner. There is no chicken soup in America today like the chicken soup my mother made from our home grown chickens. Homemade noodles went with the homemade soup. My sister and I hung around the kitchen table as my mother floured the cutting board, rolled out the dough and chopped the noodles. The flour clung to our aprons and dusted the floor. Even our eyelashes fluttered flour dust. Dick and Jane's mother never made her own chicken soup. Neither did her children have the pleasure of watching her chop homemade noodles.

After food and flowers, I remember most of all music. My parents bought a used player piano and, at age seven, I signed up at the Dominican convent to take piano lessons. How proud I and my family were when I wore the blue satin blouse and red plaid skirt my mother made me for my first recital. In the basement of the church, the neighborhood gathered to see what their children had been up to all that school year. There was accordion music, of course, folk dancing, colors, dramatic recitations in Slovenian and English. Afterwards, the adults reviewed their children's performances in Slovenian, while the children reviewed themselves in English. The old folks looked on and wept. What they must have seen, I suspect, is the beginning of the end of their way of life; a discomfort more acute than age and ailing naturally bring; a discomfort that signified social change, for with money and education came social mobility. Who would respect the woman who wore her money in a little bag around her neck; who boiled bones for soup to nourish her family of eight; who took in boarders in every room in the house, including the kitchen; who boiled and laundered shirts on a washboard in her kitchen when she wasn't peeling, or canning, or baking, or ironing; who never bought a paper product because old newspapers served just as well? Who could respect her haggling ways, her sharp tongue when the Jewish peddler arrived at her door, carrying his suitcase stuffed full of life's luxuries? A penny too much was a penny wasted! Even rags had market value. On Saturdays came the horse and wagon and a skinny man who collected rags and paper. "Paper-rags! Paper-rags!"

he would shout, and the ladies of the neighborhood would hurry out, their fingers shaking as they received their pennies. What child could understand then that terrible struggle to pay the mortgage before anything; that fierce desire to own the land and a house thereon; to owe no one; to be free and clear? I certainly did not.

At the same time, a Sunday did not pass without some money being placed in the collection basket at Mass. Pennies and nickels and dimes built the church and school, the national home, and, of course, a bank. In a time when workers had meager, if any, unemployment compensation and inadequate hospitalization benefits; a time when the welfare system had yet to be defined; at such a time, a generation of men and women from Central Europe determined to survive and make a better life for their children. They did so, and in their doing, they forged steel and wove woolens, assembled lamps and mixed paint; they manned the factories of America which have made us today the most prosperous people in the history of the world. Today our garbage cans are extravagantly full. Our pets eat better than did some of our ancestors. Surely, somewhere in heaven the old ladies in black babushkas are shaking their heads at the sight of our waste.

So I remember the men and women of my neighborhood; the factory whistles, announcing the eight-hour shifts; the men in their steel-toed shoes, their blue denim clothes heavy with grease, their lunch buckets empty, giving me a piece of candy as they passed our house walking home from the mills. What were their names? One was Matt; one was Cy. My father coming home; my mother filling the bathtub with hot water; listening to Gabriel Heater's news on the radio; boiling the greasy work clothes in a copper tub in the basement; hearing the train whistle and chug; calling out to the train conductor, "Gimme some chalk." My father and I walking in the center of the tracks, picking up coal. The women in the grocery store, pointing to sides of beef, or pork, picking out that evening's meal; the sausage house where the butcher smoked his special brand of sausage; watching the blood and fat and meat chips being ground through the giant grinder into casings; the smell of sawdust on the store's floor; my mother, carrying her paper shopping bags as she walked up the street to our house; the icebox in our hallway which could hold 50 pounds of ice, although we would buy only 25 when we did buy any; the fish truck, stinking and loaded with crushed ice and Lake Erie blue pike on Fridays. Our lives had rhythm: fish on Fridays, chicken on Sundays. Saturday nights for baths. And what were vacations for? Why, painting the house, repairing the sidewalk or stairs, scrubbing, rubbing, scouring. In their entire lives, my parents never had a vacation. Yet, I do not remember self-pity. It was enough to have a sturdy, neat house and healthy children. It was more than enough. Such was their source of pride. Such was the simple life of my childhood days, or so it seems to me now.

I am beginning to feel there is gold in the dust that I sift as I write these words; a pagan spirit, beyond any language, that is my heritage, tempered by thrift and work. Of course, no one was perfect, but the strong took care of the weak. The retarded, the mad, the deformed, the illegitimate—none of these were sent away. Families cared for their own, accepting these burdens as fatalistically as rain and thunder. The drunken, the desperate, the stupid—these, too, fit into the community of workers. The old and the young and the middle-aged shared households each leaning on each as circumstances required. The Church stood at the center of all our lives, the priests burdened beyond confessionals to guide the young and console the old, to straddle two worlds, Slovenia and America; somehow, to strike a meeting ground for three generations of souls.

My generation became American. Not until I was out of high school did I begin to ask, "What is an American?" When a stranger asked me, "What is your nationality?" I always answered, "Slovenian," though I had been born in Cleveland, as had my mother and father. All my grandparents were from Slovenia. My father was to return there at the age of three when his father decided he would not make America his family's home. That grandfather died in Franz Josef's cavalry during World War I, age thirty-eight. My grandmother sent her son to America to avoid conscription and to find employment in 1922. She sold a cow to finance his ocean voyage, and sent her eldest son to Cleveland. She was never to see him again.

When my paternal grandmother died, in her eighties, a photographer recorded her village funeral. The men, and women, and children she had known all her life carried her to her churchyard grave within walking distance of her home. No automobiles. No hearse. Only people and flowers. Frances. *Frančiska*. She had lived the lonely widow's life, never to see her grandchildren, for she had sent her second son to U.S. Steel in Cleveland, also. One stayed with her. I saw her grave in 1965 in Dolensko, in the churchyard of Sts. Cosmos and Damian. I lit one candle and placed it in the earth before her tombstone. Frances, I thought, what a hard life! I remembered her letters. What were her words? I had the photographs—her deep eyes and patient frown, her gnarled hands, worker's hands. Frances, I have come to greet you! From a factory town, from the shadows of steel mills, I kneel before your tombstone. My eyes look up to see the mountains of your life—those mountains which I had described to me as a little girl form my father's memory. I felt at home. In your house I saw the same picture of St. Cecelia playing at her organ mounted on your wall—the same picture my mother had mounted on our wall. I had studied piano. I had received the family gift of music.

An ox startled me out of my reverie, and I arose and walked out of the churchyard, across the bridge, and up the path to the house that was my heritage. Two rooms. One for eating and sleeping; one for smoking meat and storing food. A sturdy house rooted to the earth, it seemed. Sleeping that night in the old house, I dreamed the songs of my childhood, songs my father had taught me; songs the children at the elementary school sang in concert every spring, directed by that great spirit, Ivan Zorman, our church musical director. Songs about mountains, horses, flowers, boys and girls, lovers, winning or losing. At dawn, I stirred and listened to the swishing sounds of workers. I got up, looked out the window and saw a man and a boy, cutting the tall grass, rhythmically, their scythes glinting in the early morning sun. It was another world. Was I awake? Yes. It was 1965, but motors had not yet invaded this village in Dolensko. Later, in the attic, I saw a spinning wheel and a few ceramic pots, used long ago by attaching to long poles. Then, they were thrust into the stove below, which was furnace as well as hearth and oven.

In one giant leap, a country peasant had become the city steel worker.* What were his dreams at night? How many mornings did he arise to walk in the dark to the mill where he earned the money to buy his bread, bread that he had once made with his own wheat? What

---

*Between 1880 and 1914, when emigration from Slovenia to America was at its peak, Slovenia was still a predominantly agricultural country. According to current statistics, only twenty percent of Slovenians are engaged in agriculture, while the remaining four-fifths derive their livelihood from industry, mining, tourism, and other non-agricultural occupations.

transformations blazed within his soul? Some men drank. The corner saloon on Friday and Saturday nights was always full—their time for psychoanalysis and their time for remembering home. Some felt displaced their whole life long, never learning English, never leaving the neighborhood, hugging their own blood, their own plot of land, living still as workers on the landlord's great estate. They knew their boundaries—the lines their children crossed and crossed. The price for bread was high.

Each Easter, I remember the blessing of the basket; the ritual meal of colored eggs, baked ham, homemade bread, fresh horseradish, sausage and homemade wine; the sparkling windows of our house, the clean curtains, floors, walls and woodwork; all of us singing for the Great Feast Day; the sidewalks and porches hosed down; the yards raked, ready for seeding; the great basso voice of Mr. Snyder in the church choir, shaking the statues, the parishioners, the very earth, stirring roots, arousing the spirits of our ancestors in that Slovenian-American village in Newburgh. In my memory, his voice stirred the winds of the Asian steppes, raised questions: who are these, my people, my soul? The Great Slavonic heart of a people dispersed and made singular through war and time and the elements; one tribe to settle in Cleveland, Ohio, to become again new men and women. I, too, am new.

MY NORWEGIAN-AMERICAN PARENTS' COURTSHIP

Thelma Jones

In urging her to marry Father, Mother's parents pointed out that being a schoolman's wife would be an education in itself. Mother found out that this was true, though scarcely in the way her parents had meant.

One of the earliest lessons she learned was that Father expected every phase of their lives to be subordinate to the current college.

On a late fall evening, Father was studying his next day's teaching assignments at the dining-room table when Mother burst in from the doctor's with an announcement. This was in Aalborg, Minnesota, where in the early 1900s Father was principal of Aalborg College as well as teacher of one-third of all the subjects offered—all for nine hundred dollars a year, or whatever part of that sum the school was able to pay.

Father had been working on his pet subject, U.S. history. He had been so entranced with Jefferson's opposition to Hamilton's doctrine of implied powers in the Constitution that he had not heard his seven-months-old first-born howling her head off in the bedroom. Nor was he now aware of Mother until she shook him. Getting lost in a book is a teacher's occupational hazard.

"Why, Thorwald," Mother exclaimed, "you haven't heard a word I've said! The doctor says I'm fine and that the new baby will probably be here the last week in May."

Thelma Jones, Chapter One from SKINNY ANGEL, 1946, McGraw-Hill Book Company. Reprinted by permission of the author.

Slowly Father returned to this world. He smiled up at Mother. She was twenty-two and, in spite of her worn clothes, in spite of the twenty pounds or so she had added since her marriage, she was blazingly beautiful. She had piles of ash-blond hair dressed in the loose pompadour of the period, high color, and features cut with exquisite delicacy and flowing smoothness. Her full mouth was literally like some half-blown rosy flower. She had then, and never lost, a child-like, blurting innocence and love of fun.

Father's smile faded. He had just realized what it was that Mother had said. He rose and leaned dramatically across the table.

"Did you say the last week in May?" he asked. "The last week in May? You can't. I won't have it. It's preposterous—utterly preposterous. Why, Alice, do you know what you are selfishly proposing to do? The last week in May is *Commencement Week!*"

Mother threw back her head and whooped with laughter. Father eyed her uncertainly. He never knew when he was being funny. Mother laboriously grafted a sense of humor onto those of her children who needed it, but she had got hold of Father too late. He was already set in a mold of professorial dignity.

It was for dignity's sake that he then wore a Vandyke beard and a gates-ajar collar. It was for dignity that his blue serge suit was kept brushed free from chalk dust and pressed almost threadbare. But no brushing could blot out the suit's shiny elbows and shiny seat. These shiny spots were the badges of Father's calling just as much as a pick and lunchpail mark the day laborer.

Father was thirty-one at this period, and he had become a handsome man. He was big and blond and full of the majesty for which he strove. Numerous women gave him tender looks. But he just thought these women were interested in the constitutional history of the U.S.A., or whatever other subject he happened to be discussing, and so he talked on and on for them. Mother never had apprehensions about other women, but that was almost the only worry she did not have.

Mother's greatest worry was making ends meet gently. They could never relax and be candidly poor as could the day laborer—who usually had the edge on them financially, anyway. No, they had to keep up a front so that the world could see the advantages of education.

Father, the visionary, built the front, and Mother, who learned to be practical so that they did not perish, propped it up. Father built the front out of owning small equities in large drafty houses—preferably on windy but imposing hilltops—in each new school town, and out of filling these houses with handsome sets of books for which Mother mailed payments year after weary year.

He also built the front out of being able to tell people almost anything they wanted to know about anything. When he told them how a certain public figure stood on the tariff question and what color socks he wore, people assumed that Father was on intimate terms with the Great. When he described minutely the fauna of Switzerland or the eating habits of remote South American tribes, they supposed that he had travelled widely. Actually, all this information that so helped to build the front came from Father's deftness with the tools of his trade: knowledge, imagination and an authoritative delivery.

And behind the front Mother learned to eke out and make over and try vinegar on the serge's shine. She practiced secret economy until she was perfect at it.

While she never took privation with a saccharine smile, she did find material for a lot of good laughs. If nothing else presented itself, she could always snipe at Father's dignity and enjoy his blank bewilderment. He never knew what hit him. Nothing—neither the poverty nor the period of success nor the sad and funny and strange burdens put upon her as a schoolman's wife—ever extinguished Mother's sassiness.

She was flip even about her secret tragedy—her weight. After her marriage she began to expand, curve after curve, like a ripe rose. She was only a shade over five feet tall and she went from 108 to 186 pounds. But just how much she gained during those first years, she did not know. In their first location, Red Deer, Nebraska, only the grocer-butcher had a scale, and Mother was too proud to ask him to weigh her—he who had weighed out so much meat for which she could not pay him. Anyway, as she pertly said, she soon became chronically pregnant and it was not fair to judge under delicate conditions.

"I'm fat but my soul is thin," she declared, with variations, again and again. "If Heaven is a place where our desires are gratified, I'll be a skinny angel. My halo will be so much too big that it'll flop around and my angelic robe will be the loud plaid I can't wear now. Yes, and ruffled. And short—up to my knees."

Just as Mother expanded in flesh so she grew in spirit under the burdens Father put upon her. Not only did she bear children over a period of nearly twenty years, but Father brought home a never-ending stream of poor or unhappy students or teachers or football players. Some of them stayed for supper and some of them stayed for years, moving with the family from college to college. Mother learned to open her house and arms with scarcely any indignation.

No student or teacher, or other person who came in prolonged contact with her, was ever the same again. How it happened neither knew, since Mother was never softly sympathetic, but soon the newest addition, willy-nilly, had ushered Mother into his inner life. There, where she had never asked to be in the first place, Mother's pretty fingers innocently strayed around her. She just couldn't help it. She began poking around, and shaping, and making changes she was sure were for the better. They almost always were, and after the first shock her victim was often grateful and loved her for the changes she had made.

Mother was pleased when she was loved—unless it was done with sentimentality, and then she was likely to turn and rend. She could not abide mawkishness. Once a girl student living with us eulogized her in the school paper. Unfortunately the girl termed her a "motherly soul." Mother confronted her in the hall, paper in hand, blue eyes snapping.

"Goodness knows I am in no position to deny my maternity" she said as she stooped to pick up a hair ribbon, a baseball bat and the current baby's rattle, "but I will not be called motherly. Motherly souls are flabby dumplings, tied in the middle with apron-strings, who meet people at doors with big pans of fresh cookies and half-witted smiles. . . . Please dustmop the dust from under your bed."

Sometimes Father had the grace to look sheepish over these presentations to Mother, but not often. He burdened himself, back-breakingly and with ardor, for the cause of education in dear old Red Deer College and her six successors. So why shouldn't Mother bear burdens, too? Indeed, why shouldn't everyone sacrifice for education, Father shouted. Education could end wars and all the bad things that come from ignorance and undisciplined minds. It could make the world rich and good.

"Give," cried Father. *"Give money to enlarge this school. Let's get the best teachers money can hire. Let's make this a four-year college, accredited. A four-year college—why, let's offer post-graduate work. Let's spread knowledge and more knowledge until there is not one uneducated person left in our country!"*

Father never understood people. Never did he learn that most people preferred the personal and immediate beefsteak to causes.

It was not, of course, because she had a presentiment that she might be sacrificed that Mother had not wanted to marry Father. He simple had not looked like fun to her. And she was utterly flabbergasted when he declared his love. She was sixteen, he twenty-five, and she scarcely knew him. He wrote a formal letter of proposal from Red Deer, across Nebraska, where he had taken his first college teaching job in the Danish church school.

In a blue gingham dress trimmed with blue ribbon bows, her heavy, pale braids woud in a knot on her neck, Mother picked up the mail at the post office after school. She opened the letter and leaned against the nearest store-front, reading and gasping. Dazed, she tried to recall just what she knew about Father.

Well, he was the young man to whom the town of Hammond, Nebraska, pointed with pride. People would boast, "Say, I knew that square-head when he couldn't even talk American, and now you'd think he'd invented the place, he knows so much about it."

Mother could just remember back to the time when her older sisters came home agog about the family of new children who had entered school that day. They were Norwegian and they were even blonder than the Danish farmers west of town. The biggest boy's name was Thorwald. They all had white, absolutely *white* hair, and pink and white faces, and they blacked their shoes. No Hammond child wasted time blacking shoes; if the streets were not dust to your uppers, they were mud. But the five Norwegian children kept right on blacking theirs.

They were peculiar in other ways, too. There was quite a mystery about the mother. Few people had seen her at all—and that in a small town! Mother's fat little twin brothers had seen her, though. They reported that she didn't dress like the Danish farm women, who wore cloths over their heads, and men's shoes. Instead she was small and neat, dressed in black. And when she had looked out suddenly from her window and seen the twins peeking around the bushes, her blue eyes were fierce and hooded, like hawk's eyes—caged hawk's eyes.

Her husband said that she was ailing, but the twins heard that the truth was—of all things—that she hated this country and thought it crude. She would not neighbor, and she would not learn English, or even allow it spoken in her home. She kept her mind turned back upon Frederickshald, Norway, where she had sat in her parlor doing fine embroidery and chatting in French with other ladies, while the maids passed the coffee and cake.

Mother knew the Norwegian father a little. He worked in the hardware store. He was a quiet, little, pink-cheeked man who laughed along with other people when he made mistakes in his broken mixture of Norwegian, French and English. The twins said that back in Norway he had been a sea captain and an owner of two sailing vessels—barks—besides. For a long time he had kept hoping that steamships were a passing fad, but when they snapped up all the good paying fr ight and he was given increasingly poorer cargoes, he had to face facts. One thing he knew: he would never learn to operate the *fordömte* stinkpotters.

In his desperation he thought of the Missouri River. With the Mississippi, it was the longest river in the world; certainly they could use a good skipper there. He was halfway across the United States before he learned that the Missouri was in no large way navigable.

He got off the train at Hammond, Nebraska, started a small hardware store, and sent for his family. The store failed because he and his customers could not understand each other. After that he worked in and out of the hardware store already established there, as glazier, tinsmith and carpenter. A sailor could do anything with his hands. He seemed content enough. But every few months he put down his tools and walked out of town on the railroad tracks. Maybe he took a bottle along. Maybe the waving bluestem reminded him of the ocean. Anyway, the twins ran all the way back to town to tell what they had seen the time they followed him.

There he stood on the tracks, the meek little handy-man, surrounded by grass like waves of water, roaring in Norwegian. He sounded as though he were commanding people, and swearing at them. And he held his hands queerly before him as though turning a ship's wheel.

But Mother knew that Thorwald, the son of these two, cast no nostalgic looks backward. He was so crazy about the United States, the *idea* of the United States, that he would button-hole people in order to talk about it. Most of them, born blessed, did not know what the shouting was all about.

Mother recalled that the very first time she had really noticed him, he was talking about the United States. He was giving the high school graduation address, and she, aged eleven, was there giggling with her chum. She looked up at this tall, gawky fellow with the intense manner and the inch-high white hair, and stopped her tittering and whispering, bewitched by his mouth. It opened and words poured out, more and more words, with no time out for breath, and no wavering. It was a perfectly wonderful sight.

And then the summer before the letter came, when he was home from teaching, he had asked to call. Mother had been startled into saying "Yes"—but only that once. He spent the evening lecturing to her on the Battle of Gettysburg.

As he wound up the first day of the battle, Mother, wriggling and unhappy, broke in to ask if he would care for a game of tiddledy-winks.

"Oh, yes," said Father politely, passing on to Gettysburg's second day.

At the close of the second day, Mother tried again. "How interesting! Shall we sing? I have some new songs."

"Yes, indeed!" Father sprang to his feet.

Mother loved singing almost as much as she did laughing. She went to the piano and began in her beautiful soprano:

"Apple blossoms, falling soft on you and me—"

Father tried that much in a sheepish monotone, then, eyes brightening, he said, "You know, Alice, it was on the third morning of Gettysburg, in the blazing heat, that Meade counterattacked. . . ."

Mother gave up and sat down quietly on the sofa. As she watched the words flow from Father's mouth, she thought of the song made from Tennyson's *The Brook*. Being reminded of fitting songs at unfitting times was Mother's most embarrassing habit.

Mentally she hummed:

"I chatter, chatter, as I flow
To join the brimming river,
For men may come and men may go
But I go on forever."

"Dear God," she silently prayed, "don't let me bust out loud with it!" Fighting the song down, she exploded into whoops of laughter. She clapped her hands over her mouth and doubled up. Father, who had been counting the Gettysburg dead, stared in horror.

And yet he wanted to marry her. Out there against the store-front, Mother read his letter again. His esteem for her was great, he wrote, and he believed his future to be rosy. He was now earning seven hundred dollars a year—well, not exactly, since he was paid in school orders cashable at five per cent discount—but this was a situation he trusted would soon clear up. He felt he had every reasonable expectation of earning nine hundred within a few years. He hoped that she would allow him to speak to her father.

There was a postscript, not labored like the body of the letter: *Alice, you are always laughing!* That touched Mother. She wanted to cry, but she was afraid, too. And, perversely, she wanted to giggle. She scudded down the street and burst into her father's one-story law office.

Her father swung around from his roll-top desk. He was a heavy-set bald man, coatless, in fine, homemade white shirt and lawn tie. He was the shrewdest lawyer in that part of Nebraska, and his face was always a stern deadpan, but Mother knew he would do anything for her.

"Papa," she wailed, "Papa help!"

He helped her write a letter that was kind but which held out no hope.

Two years later Father wrote another letter of proposal.

"Take him, Alice," entreated her mother over a lapful of the linen-bosomed shirts she delighted to make her menfolk.

"Take him," echoed her father. "Living with Thorwald will be as good as finishing college." He gave a rumbling sigh.

Hard times had come and caught him with only the first three of his seven children through school. Mother, the middle child, could not go back to the university for her junior year. This hurt him.

Nor was that all. When Mother stepped off the train at the end of her sophomore year, he looked at her and his heart lurched. She had become a raving, tearing little beauty. Not a young fellow in town but would be after her, and not one of them was worth the powder to blow him up. The good ones, the hard-working, ambitious young men, went to the cities where there were more opportunities. Those that were left were mostly country boys who aspired to nothing more than clerking in the local feed-and-grain store. Mother's parents had waited, braced, for developments.

Mother straightaway had picked out a handsome young man named Charlie Wells. Charlie had liquid black eyes, a fine singing voice, and he was fun. He worked in the livery stable. What's more, all he wanted to do was work in the livery stable. But Mother and he laughed continually at the same things, and sang duets in the Presbyterian choir. They never dared look at each other in choir—and especially at funerals—for fear something would start them off in stifled, agonized laughter. How Mother loved him. He was always a perfect gentleman, walking her out with a square, brown hand under her elbow.

In July a rumor blew around the square along with the dust. A common girl in the town was going to have a baby, and she meant to name Charlie as the father. Mother's heart nearly burst with indignation. No one knew better than she just how clean Charlie was.

One night she woke with a start, thinking that she had heard Charlie's voice. She had, for he was downstairs talking with her father. She tiptoed to the head of the star is in her nightie, pale braids swinging. She could see them by the front door, her father's bald head close to Charlie's dear, dark one.

Her father said, "If you had told me that you were one of those who might have been responsible for the girl's condition, Charlie, I wouldn't have touched your case. I'd have advised you to get out of town at once. But as it is, we'll fight. . . . Goodnight."

Mother leaned, trembling, against the wall, her throat aching with love and with joy at Charlie's manliness.

The next morning the fat little twin brothers were late for breakfast. They came in red and gasping, slid into their chairs and speared pancakes.

"Guess what," one of them panted. "Charlie Wells—"

"Yes?" Mother was instantly alert.

"You boys may leave the table and wash," ordered their father sternly.

They returned, splashed with water. "Charlie Wells—" one of them began.

"Have you said grace?" their mother demanded.

They bowed their dripping heads. When they raised them again, Mother, who was writhing, said, "Yes, you were saying about Charlie?"

"He's lit out," cried the boys in unison. "Musta hopped the midnight train."

"May I please leave the table?" Mother asked faintly.

Father's second proposal came two months later. Mother's parents believed it was the perfect solution.

"Take him, dear," her mother repeated, pleading. "Such a fine, clean boy."

"Boy!" Mother echoed bitterly. Father was twenty-seven—falling to pieces.

"You'd please us, Alice," her father said.

"All right," said Mother, pale-lipped, "I'll take him."

She tramped upstairs and dropped across her white iron bed, weeping over the unbearableness of marrying without love.

But as the wedding plans thickened, Mother's spirits rose. Her trousseau was lovely—all the fine cambric underwear in sets. She liked her ring—a slender sword bent in a circle, the hilt studded with diamond chips. And Father took only one shy peck of a kiss when he delivered it.

She began to look forward to his letters. He wrote ardently of the house he was having built. So impressive-looking it was, two stories, crowning four acres of hill, and it would cost less that eight hundred dollars for everything. ("Less than eight hundred dollars!" Mother's father lifted a dubious eyebrow. "Something wrong some place.") And Thorwald was furnishing the house. It would be all ready for Mother to step into.

And then at the wedding reception, her stiff, white satin gown sweeping out in sixteen gores from the nineteen inches of her waistline, Mother had a joyous thought. Father had spoken glowingly of the Red Deer buildings, students and faculty. Of course it would be on a slightly smaller scale, but why shouldn't her life at Red Deer be just like her life at the university—everybody rambling across the campus, jollying each other, and singing around pianos? Why hadn't she thought of this before? Mother tilted back her lovely little head and gave Father a smile so dazzling that he blushed pink as the bridesmaids' roses.

THE RENT MONEY IN THE GARBAGE PAIL AND OTHER TENEMENT MEMORIES

Dorothy Friedman

This is the story of an old tenement built in the late 1880s to house the Jewish immigrants who were coming to New York City in large clusters, clinging to the same vine of poverty and huddling together. In the early 1930s 12 families lived in that house. They were bonded to each other not only by poverty and trouble, but also by love; yes, a great deal of love. This is a love story.

Mrs. Newman's voice was a robust echo in the damp hallway; it resounded like a fist banging the high notes on the piano.

"Annie, Annie, send Dvadela down. I'm heating water for Rosie, they'll bathe together."

Mama was removing the newspaper on the shelves, gummy with undernourished and dead roaches. Before she could answer Mrs. Newman, I pulled my threadbare nightgown from the drawer. Once it had been fluffy and pink and belonged to Bessie Goldberg, who lived on the third floor.

"Could I, could I, Mama?"

"All right, all right, but don't slide down the banisters."

Mrs. Newman lived one flight down on the first floor. I walked past the first section of banister and slid down the second. The door was open for me. Warm, wonderful Sabbath odors were coming from the apartment: gefilte fish, chalunt, potato kugel.

"At least he makes a living," Mrs. Newman would shrug.

He was Mr. Newman, a dour, unwelcoming man who worked for a pipe manufacturer. Evenings he sat, stared straight ahead and smoked his pipe. He expected prompt service.

"Talk to him, talk to the wall, it's the same," complained Mrs. Newman. She was plump and pretty as a tomato and loved a good joke.

But now it was hours before he would be getting home. Rosie and I spashed in the water and sailed the soap until Mrs. Newman carried us out of the tub, wrapped in big towels, and sat up on the kitchen table. First she combed Rosie's hair, which was fine and coiled like little yellow ribbons. Then gently she combed the tangles out of mine. "Black, curly bushes you got, like your father," she said.

She carried me on her right arm and a pot of chalunt in her left hand. On such nights we ate, Papa, Mama and my 3-year-old sister Etala, a year younger than I.

The depression which was clawing its way into every apartment seemed to start in our home. There were never green seltzer bottles standing guard outside our door. Papa had no trade. That was the title of our misery.

Next door to us lived a frail old couple, known as Tante Pessimira and Uncle Shlama. They were mostly supported by their son, the doctor. We would wander into their apartment for cookies and seltzer mixed with chocolate syrup, sometimes large hunks of chicken schmaltz on

Dorothy Friedman, "The Rent Money in the Garbage Pail and Other Tenement Memories" from the *Daily News,* August 28, 1977. Reprinted by permission of the author. (I am grateful to my mother, Fanny Stettner, for sending me the newspaper story.)

matzos. Uncle Shlama tuned violins and the walls were covered with them. When I'd hear him tune them, I'd fantasize some exquisite creature locked away inside and crying out in a sweet voice to be set free.

At 10 each morning the junk peddler came around with his horse and wagon. He rang a large cowbell and sang in a forceful baritone, "Old clothes, old rags, old newspapers, old springs, old junk."

As the train rumbled overhead his horse would nervously raise his front legs and whinny. The peddler waited for our mothers to come down with their newspapers and whatever rags they had saved. The open wagon was piled high with neat stacks of junk. When he went off, they'd walk up the stairs a few pennies the richer.

Around noontime someone, male or female, would come to sing in the courtyard. The singing was often beautiful and the women were touched, so the precious pennies would drift down rolled in small packets of paper.

The street to the right of us was Dumont Ave. Up on the corner was PS 109. From the unguarded conversation of the neatly-heeled, silk-stockinged teachers I learned early that I belonged to "those foreigners on Sackman St." Most of our parents had European accents. Unconsciously I picked up the WASP snobbery. I was proud of Papa's Bostonian speech and Mama's London upbringing, bleak as it was.

On the left we were bordered by Livonia Ave. Here the elevated trains struggled noisily hour after hour.

On a nearby corner was the drugstore. As the Depression deepened, gangs formed and made that drugstore their headquarters. Often late at night there were shootouts with opposing gangs, and in the morning the muddied gutters ran red with blood. The gangs called themselves the Protective Merchants Association and harassed the neighborhood businessmen. One of the gang lived in our house, Danny Silverman. His family had the only phone. His mother was a deeply troubled woman who lived in constant fear for her son's life.

On another corner was the Livonia Avenue Movies. For five cents two people could get in. After school long lines formed down the block. Up and down the line the question was "Who's got three cents, I got two?"

The cashier's cage was in a large room, always noisy, always filled with baby carriages and umbrellas, always slushy and dirty from snow or rain. Often during the most exciting part of the movie—a train bearing down on the hero or a horse running wildly with the heroine—a big sign, "Baby crying" would flash across the screen. Then there was the rush and bustle of at least half a dozen mothers who ran out to check which baby needed diapering or a bottle. Sometimes Mrs. Blum, who had no children, would take me. I loved to sit in the dark and listen to the piano. The piano player would produce thunder and lightning during the hair-raising scenes or play high, thin, wailing notes as the tears rolled copiously from the heroine's eyes.

The walk home was short but exciting too. We would cross over to the candy store at our corner. Mrs. Blum would buy me a large chocolate bar with words imprinted in the chocolate. I would suck at it slowly and watch the letters disappear. Outside, a man without legs sold pencils. Mrs. Blum would drop a penny in his cup, but she never took a pencil. We'd stop at the laundry and I'd flatten my nose against the glass. The little Chinese girl inside would ape me while her father ironed a shirt.

Then I'd stop at the store where the gypsies lived. There were no curtains on the storefront. Inside I could see a round table and chairs and a crib. The ladies were the most beautiful I'd ever seen. They wore long colorful dresses, and sometimes they would come to the door to beckon us in with a "Come, I'll tell you your fortune." I was anxious to go in, but Mrs. Blum was unfriendly to them and she'd walk me off hurriedly.

When I grew older, I learned that Mr. Blum frequented the gypsy store for his own reasons.

We kids roamed freely from apartment to apartment. It was as if we had the same mothers. What goodies there were we shared. In good weather we'd play in the backyard where frightened rodents jumped out from uncovered garbage cans. The cats were my constant companions, often my only ones. Every now and then the health department put a "contagious" sign on the door of a playmate, and I'd know she had either scarlet fever or whooping cough, some such malady, and it would be a long time before she or he joined me again.

Now and then a couple of the women would have a *braggis*. That was a falling out. Then the group of them would get together in the hallway or in an apartment. They would insist that the two women confront each other. They would do so in high excited voices, then they'd cry. Soon they'd kiss and say, "All right, all right; I'm not mad any more."

Once I got sick and Mrs. Newman came up to put bancus on me. Bancus were small glass cups filled with flame in some mysterious manner and applied to the chest and back. I got better immediately, a sort of faith healing. If that didn't help, you needed a doctor.

Once a month the landlady came to collect the rent. She was a tall, thin woman with waxy fingers that drummed incessantly on the round oak table in the front room. Mama was always nervous when she came. My sister and I would tiptoe about with the index finger to our lips. Mama would rush about to bring her the ink. She'd make out a receipt with fancy swirls. Often we'd been to Tante Beckie's house the week before to get the $15. I liked going there. Tante Beckie had a big back yard with sunflowers, a hammock and grownup double swing. The marshes were close by and sometimes nanny goats would walk up to me. But Mama always cried when we went there. I wondered why.

I'll never forget one April Fools' Day when the landlady came for the rent. She sat drumming her fingers as usual while Mama searched in the closet for the rent money. She could only find $5; a $10 bill was missing. She searched and cried until finally the landlady, pince-nez glasses at the tip of her long, thin nose, rose to her full height and said, "I'll be back tomorrow; I'm sure you'll have it then."

When Mrs. Goldberg dropped in and saw Mama crying she joined in the search. One by one the neighbors learned what was happening and joined in. There was thunder and lightning, and the tiny apartment was crowded with women searching through closets, taking down pots and pans and dishes, going through the clothing, moving aside mattresses, but it was no use. The money was gone. By this time the rain was beating angry fists against the windows. Mrs. Rosen, who hardly ever spoke up, said shyly, "Annie, maybe you threw it out when you changed the paper."

Tearfully Mama agreed.

"So what are we waiting for?" Mrs. Goldberg responded. "In two hours they'll collect the garbage."

En masse they filed down the stairs, out into the lashing rain, and marched into the alley. Systematically they turned over every one of the three huge garbage cans. Then down on their hands and knees they went. My sister and I did the same. They searched and cursed the landlady. She was *chaza* (pig's lard); she would take the roof from over our heads; she had no heart. It rained and rained and Mama wept. Hair dripping like wet shoestrings, noses, eyes and chins flowing, we knelt there, and went through every bit of moldy, rotting, water-soaked garbage, every tiny bit of paper.

Suddenly Mrs. Rosen began to cry and rock in ecstasy: "I found it, I found it!"

There it was, intact, rolled up, wet and filthy, a real $10 bill.

Mama kissed her and cried; she kissed Mama and cried. Soon everybody was kissing everybody else and crying, "Gutzidanken, Gutzidanken, they'll have a roof over their heads, Gutzidanken." Then they remembered us children. "Inside, inside, you'll get pneumonia, God forbid."

The ladies on the ground floor ran in and got towels and briskly dried us. "Dry up fast, fast, we must bless God."

For weeks Mrs. Rosen was the heroine. Over and over she was made to tell how she found it. "It was a miracle. . . ."

Finally, we were moving. Where we would go we would get a free apartment. In exchange Mama would wash hallways, and Papa would stoke furnaces and take out heavy vats of garbage. The neighbors brought us sandwiches, cookies, nuts and fruits. Mama cried, "How can I leave all of you?"

"Maybe it's for the best," they said, "maybe." Then they cried some more.

As the moving van pulled out, they stood there waving handkerchiefs. From the van we called, "Goodby, goodby." For a short distance I could see the handkerchiefs hanging in the air like white pigeons, limp and still for a moment in time. The El roared overhead, and I sensed a world fast disappearing.

AN ANCIENT HERITAGE IN A NEW WORLD

Maria B. Frangis

My father and mother emigrated from southern Greece to America in the early 1900's.

My father, the only child of a widowed mother, left his small village at the age of twenty-two during a peak immigration wave to America from Greece, in order to better his lot in the new world. For so many young Greek males, this was the only hope for providing much-needed financial help to family members left behind . . . relief for weary parents trying to work a stubborn soil, dowry money to help sisters marry according to the Greek custom, ticket money for brothers, cousins or uncles to join those who had already blazed a trail in the land of opportunity.

My father was sent to a friend from his same village who had settled in South Carolina.

Reprinted by permission of the author.

"Greek Orthodox Cathedral of the Annunciation," Atlanta, Georgia. By permission of Mike Balsamides.

Like so many of his unskilled counterparts, with little formal education, and with no knowledge of English, he went into the restaurant business. Most immigrants started out in the kitchen, learning the food business quickly and moving to ownership of their own luncheonette or diner very soon. When I was born my father was half owner of a large, established restaurant.

My mother, from a large family of eight girls and three boys, accompanied an older sister to America after the sister's marriage to a Greek immigrant who had done well enough in Ohio to return to Greece for a bride, a prevalent practice of the time. My mother was sent along to help keep her sister from feeling homesick, being the first to leave the bosom of the family for such a faraway place.

The marriage of my mother and father was arranged through a relative of my father's, and in 1923, the wedding took place in Ohio. Arranged marriages were the standard procedure, since meeting, dating, and marrying for love were simply not the Greek system. In my parents' case, the union turned out to be a happy one, and they settled in South Carolina where I was born in 1930, the youngest of three daughters.

My sisters and I grew up in a large two-story frame house on Main Street in the deep South. Our childhood was typically small-town southern USA, with the difference that we were second generation Greek-Americans in a household where two languages were spoken and where close ties with family, with the Greek Orthodox Church, and with the old country were taken for granted. It seemed as if we were forever in the post office mailing New York Exchange Checks or big boxes of clothing to the relatives in Greek villages.

We took a family trip to Greece when I was three years old, some of which, startingly, I can recall. In fact, twenty years later when I visited Greece again, I was able to pick out my mother's home in her little village on the Ionian Sea where she was born and where we had stayed those many years before, a moving experience.

My recollections of my deceased father, are of a pragmatic, conservative, self-educated business man who spoke excellant English with little of accent except for, uniquely, a slight southern one. He read avidly and was a close observor of the political scene. Aristotle had described man as political creature, and certainly, there is hardly a Greek throughout history who has not reveled in politics.

I can remember my father taking time away from his restaurant to walk me to our State Capitol grounds to see President Franklin Delano Roosevelt, and how proud I felt to be there. And I can see him conscientiously exercising his right to vote and making certain that my mother did also, after marking the newspaper ballot for her, so she'd know exactly what to do in the voting booth.

My mother, a strong, independent and more social person than my father, had most of the responsibility for our upbringing. While she had worked in a millinery shop before her marriage, she assumed the traditional role of wife, mother, homemaker. Generally in Greek households, the male was breadwinner and reigned supreme. Woman's work was in the home.

With little formal education, my mother struggled with the language, learned to drive a car, and adjusted to southern customs, even southern cooking, for along with our Greek cuisine, we grew up eating cornbread, black-eyed peas, and grits.

My mother loved the kitchen and out of it, in a seemingly never-ending stream, would come home-baked bread, pastitsio (a meat and macaroni casserole), meat and rice stuffed grapevine leaves, the rich and luscious nut and honey dripping Greek pastries, and delicious little cheese and spinach mixture hor d'oevres wrapped in filo dough which is a thin pastry much like strudel. Even today, with my sisters and I married and in our own homes, the good food from my mother's kitchen to our own homes help keep our Greek traditions alive.

Namedays, which Greeks celebrate as much and sometimes more than birthdays, were always occasions for much cooking and baking. On the day of the patron saint for whom one might be named, for instance St. Demetrius on October 26 which was my father's nameday and which my mother always made into an occasion, there was open house for friends and relatives, the strains of lively Greek music from the phonograph, Greek folk dancing in a line with hands joined and participated in by young and old alike, much revelry and a veritable orgy of eating.

Easter, the highest religious holiday of the year, was another busy time for housewives. Families and friends again gathered. Traditionally, eggs were died red, a lamb was baked (in more recent years on an open spit outside), pastries and a sweet Easter bread, or tsoureki, prepared. "Christos Anesti" or "Christ is Risen" would be the greeting when eggs were cracked. "Alethos Anesti" or "He is Risen Indeed" would come the reply.

I have rich memories of namedays and Easters in our home. I see my mother, always a little too stout for her own good, elbow deep in flour, pressured to the limits to get everything ready, receiving her joy from watching her family and friends about her.

I also have fond memories of my mother during the time she was preparing herself to acquire her citizenship papers, my sisters and I quizzing her to make certain she had all the answers just right. "How many members in the House of Representatives? How many in the Senate? Repeat the preamble to the Constitution, the pledge of allegiance to the flag." And her rendition of "God Bless America" in her broken English and with a voice slightly off key will remain with me forever.

So growing up Greek-American in the 30's and 40's was tradition rich and deeply cultural. And it was also cloistered and church bound.

All friendships, social contacts and activities were geared to the Greek community and within the framework of the Greek Orthodox Church, the hub of community life. Twice a week, after "American" school, we attended an afternoon Greek school at the church where we studied the language and culture of our heritage. We sang in the church choir and participated in church youth organizations or in the youth segments of a Greek national fraternal order known as AHEPA (American Hellenic Educational Progressive Association).

My sisters and I were expected to date and to marry Greek. This held a great deal more strictly for girls that it did for boys, although any marriage by male or female outside the faith was always considered a potential catastrophe or falling away. This was largely due to the fact that ethnic survival in America seemed to depend on keeping as many of us as possible within the fold, and mixed marriages constituted a threat. Converts fit in uneasily and were viewed suspiciously. There was always the possibility they could influence the Greek mate over to a non-Greek lifestyle.

Today, with third and fourth generations Greek Americans on the scene, their roots firmly planted in America, with the complexion of the church no longer that of an immigrant church, and with more and more mixed marriages being performed every day, the whole tone and attitude has changed. Converts to the faith are graciously accepted and often make the best Greek Orthodox. This is because they are not only instructed in a new faith by the priest through special teaching sessions followed by the sacrament of Christmation (confirmation), but they also willingly embrace a whole new culture and way of life, and they work hard at understanding and appreciating what the Greek-Orthodox born to it all often takes for granted.

In the 30's and 40's, however, to be ethnic was to be foreign and therefore different and in many cases unacceptable. The emphasis was on assimilation, on not looking or acting Greek. Girls dyed their hair blonde to look more "American." Second generation children shrank back when their first generation parents rattled off Greek in public and heads turned to stare.

For myself, I was not pained by my ethnic origin as much as I felt restricted by it. I yearned to be a girl scout and to go to summer camp, two things never permitted lest I become "too Americanized." This meant I might make too many non-Greek friends, adopt their lifestyle, and break my ethnic ties. I would be "lost" to my family, my parish, my community. It must be remembered that the emphasis of first generation parents was on trying to maintain the Greek heritage in a vastly non-Greek world. Our numbers, therefore, must not be allowed to dwindle.

My struggle was to break out a little, if I could, from my safe, secure, and altogether familiar Greek cacoon. I made many non-Greek friends in school and threw myself into being a good student and in participating in extra-curricular activities, editing my high school newspaper and annual. This was my way of assuring acceptance, but it also exposed me to that world beyond where there were sororities where I spend the night parties with girl friends, hayrides, football dates, weekends at the beach—all permissible if they were with Greek boys, Greek girls and Greek chaperones, but definitely off limits otherwise. Some of my contemporaries would "sneak out" with non-Greek dates and to non-Greek parties, but this was something which I couldn't bring myself to do.

I was one of the few girls in my Greek community who went away to college, spending four years at a girls' school in Virginia, recommended by a favorite teacher, in a city where there was no Greek community or church. I wanted the opportunity to broaden my horizons, to spread my wings without ever really desiring to fly the nest completely. I am grateful to my parents and to my sisters who intervened in my behalf (they finished the University in our hometown) for the opportunity to do so. Although my roommate was a Greek-American girl from Indiana (we were matched up by the school) and therefore "safe" from my parents' viewpoint, I still learned how to adjust, to survive and even to thrive in a non-Greek atmosphere.

Again, I poured my energies into my studies and into campus activities. Social contacts were still with Greek boys from surrounding campuses, but there were a few forays with the forbidden, and I made an amazing discovery. I could go out with non-Greek boys and not feel somehow threatened. I could actually enjoy them without worrying that I might marry one and thus disturb my family. At the same time, I realized that there were cultural differences and that, on a lifetime basis, I would be happiest with a boy of my own background and upbringing. I was simple more comfortable, more in tune with the Greeks.

Being away from home taught me something else . . . how to value my ethnicity. The girls at school loved the boxes of Greek delicacies (koularakia, baklava along with occasional chocolate chip cookies) that my mother piled me with for four years. They urged my roommate and me to teach them Greek phrases, some nice and some not so nice, and to Greek folk dance. We were different, but it was a difference the others were interested in and wanted to learn more about. We knew another language, we had another culture, we were somehow richer in experience. The Greek heritage was ancient, noble much of western civilization was influenced by it. We were a link in a greatness that stretched far back into the dawn of history. My parents' urgings through all the growing up years, ''Be proud, be proud,'' echoes in my ears while away at college, and I woke up one morning thinking, ''They were right, it's all true.''

So my college experience was invaluable not only in building my confidence and independence, but in revealing that I wanted to maintain my dual heritage because I loved it and was proud, and not because it was imposed through parental pressure.

After graduation, in the working world where I spent some years in radio, in television, in publishing and as a free-lance writer, I realized even more that I could be happy and accept my Greek world and at the same time, comfortable and not threatened outside of it. I was able to move smoothly from the homes and gatherings of school and work friends to the familiar surroundings of family and parish.

I married Greek just as my parents had hoped perhaps because I consciously limited my social contacts to the Greek world. My husband grew up in Athens, Greece, and came to America to finish his education, so his childhood experiences were different from mine. (He knew war and poverty and occupation.)

In any case, we are in agreement about bringing up our two sons in a far broader atmosphere that the narrowly confined one of my youth. They are learning how to straddle the two cultures which they inhabit. They are involved beyond their parish community as well as within it, hopefully wearing their dual heritage lightly and naturally, and feeling their uniqueness as something special and not something strange.

Today, high value is placed on one's roots, one's sense of place and belonging, on tradition and on heritage. America no longer wants to be a melting pot but rather a mosiac, where all the individual pieces help to make up the whole. To be ethnic is to be all right. We've come a long way from the 30's and 40's, and it feels good to be here with the best of both worlds.

TANGLED VINES, THORNS, AND FLOWERS: THE FAMILY*

"Polish Family," approximately 1905. The mother sewed all the clothing by hand. The family migrated to the United States during the 1920's, settling in New York. By permission of Fanny Stettner from a family album. She is standing behind her brother in the picture.

And the Lord God Said: "It is not good that the man should be alone; I will make a fitting helper for him."

Genesis 2:18

*I am indebted to Lyn Lifshin who edited a collection of mother and daughter poems entitled *Tangled Vines* (Beacon Press, Boston, MA), © 1978. Her title was used, in part, here.

MY GRANDMOTHER THE WASP

Doras Reed Benbow

I was brought up by my grandmother who till the day she died in 1945 still wore steel ribbed corsets, high laced shoes, Queen Mary hats that rode on the top of her head to make her look taller (she was only 5'—but her stature was 10'). I was shocked and amazed when I met my husband's grandmother for the first time because she was dressed in the latest fashion with silk stockings, jacket dress, etc. "Is this a *grandmother?*" I wondered.

Grandmother Reed was a Connecticut Yankee. There were only two classes of people: the rich and the poor. We were no doubt middle class, but she never admitted to anything in the middle, to her things were either black or white, never gray. Gray meant mediocrity. She stood tall and it wasn't the steel corset that helped her, it was the steel in her backbone. It was the steel in her code of life. Just as a thing was black or white, so was it right or wrong—no in between.

She was left a widow in her early 50's. I was close to four years old at the time. The brownstone house in New Haven was filled with people when my grandfather died. My mother had just remarried and being young, was living at home. My Uncle Harold was living at home. My Great-grandmother Clinton was in and out. To top it off, there were at least three contemporaries of my mother whom my grandmother had taken in when their mother died.

I never saw my grandmother do any housework. Somehow it got done. She was forever "on the go"—and I went with her most of the time. She took me to church suppers where they stood me on a chair to recite a poem composed by Miss Wetmore (I still remember "The Indian Maid") which was my first brush with poetry! I later had to take elocution lessons and piano lessons hating every minute of it. But if it hadn't been for grandma's push, I would not be where I am today. I know that sounds trite but it is true. She herself was tone deaf with little education.

Grandma had a steel corset code. One rib was poked into me at an early age. I had been in the attic dressing up and put on a pair of glasses which I found in a bureau drawer. I came downstairs to show off.

"Where did you get those glasses?" asked Grandma.

"I found them on the floor," I replied.

"You took them from the drawer!"

I admitted the truth and she grabbed me, giving me a swat someplace. I was too shocked to realize where.

"Don't ever lie to me again!" "I can't stand a liar," she declared vehemently. Then she sat me down and gave me a piece of pie.

I never forgot that scene. It was the one and only time Grandma ever hit me. The lesson never had to be repeated. I passed that philosophy on to my two sons. Grandma always said, "Tell me the truth and I'll stick by you through thick and thin but I will not help a liar."

There was another steel rib to the corset that poked me. Grandma believed in keeping her word. "A man's word is his bond," she pronounced.

Reprinted by permission of the author.

"Aristocratic lady." By permission of Maria de Noronha
(Gallman), the artist.

It was at this point that I realized what had been my bulwark throughout the vicissitudes of life. It was my grandmother. And the core of her security was in herself and God.

However, since Grandma was a WASP, so was God. Of course, the term was not singled out because it was taken for granted. Anybody who was somebody was naturally white, Anglo-Saxon, and Protestant. Grandma was a great church-goer. She was at heart and mind an Episcopalian but that didn't stop her from attending other churches to see what was going on—like full immersion at the Baptist Church—or "holy rolling" at the Church of the Nazarene. She drew the line at the Catholic Church even though that denomination is very close to the Episcopalian one. Grandma felt that Catholics were not to be trusted. All that "mumbo jumbo" she would call it and ignore it until my Uncle Harold married a Catholic girl. My grandmother was displeased at first but not for long because she treated my aunt so much like a Protestant that she finally became one and joined my grandmother's church.

Grandma was a WASP. I was one, too, then. Through my heritage I had to remain a WAS but the P has left forever, for I have known all religions and been a part of them. My friends have come from all the branches of one Tree of Life and I am part of them, also. God has been with me and this knowledge through my grandmother's tutelage has put the steel in my backbone. But, Gram, who is now living in one of the many mansions promised her by Jesus, has learned that He is not a WASP.

CANUCK

Camille Lessard

Camille Lessard (1883-1972) was born and educated in Sainte-Julie-de-Megantic, Québec. After three years of teaching, she immigrated to Lewiston, Maine in 1904, worked in local textile mills, and later accompanied her family to Edmonton, Alberta, where she headed the French section of the municipal library. After serving as a postal official in St. Louis, Missouri, she became a colonization agent for a major southern railroad—the first woman to secure this position, a post she held for seven years. During and after these wanderings, she remained a regular contributor to **Le Messager,** *a French-language newspaper of Lewiston, Maine, which first published her novel,* **Canuck,** *in serial form in 1934. Mademoiselle Lessard—later Madame Camille Lessard-Bissonnette—was also editor of the Women's Pages for* **La Patrie,** *a popular Montreal newspaper. She spent her final years in California and died in Long Beach in 1972.*

Canuck is a short novel depicting the immigration of a French-Canadian family to the United States, the family's painful transition from a rural lifestyle to an urban industrial setting, its nostalgia for the countryside and folkways of Quebec. The main characters are Vital Labranche, his wife and their three children, most notably Victoria ("Vic"), the strong-willed mature eighteen-year-old daughter. The following excerpt, the novel's fourth chapter, entitled "Vic's Revolt," illustrates an economic aspect of the cultural conflict faced by countless immigrants. Drawn to this country by dreams of prosperity, Vital Labranche has unwittingly succumbed to excessive greed, exploiting his wife and children for the sole sake of personal gain.

His greed is exacerbated by the atmosphere of generalized materialism he finds in his adopted country. He would doubtless proceed on this course, were it not for Vic's improbable, daring revolt, a major factor in his eventual transformation from greedy despot to generous provider.

It should be stressed that the daughter's dramatic break with a strong tradition of filial obedience is most unusual in Franco American literature. One might argue that we have here an example of the keen French critical sense, ever ready to surface, combined with the explosiveness of a young woman belonging to an ethnic group frequently referred to as "the Latins of the North."

Note: The translation is based on the 1936 edition of the novel, published in volume form by Editions Le Messager, Lewiston, Maine.

"VIC'S REVOLT"

Translated by Armand B. Chartier

One day, a cloud burst which was to bring about a chain of circumstances destined to alter completely the course of life for all members of the Labranche family. Labranche and his wife were always the first to return home from work unless they stopped at the grocery store for provisions. Their looms being on the ground floor, near the exit close to the gate, as soon as the looms began to slow down—a sign that it was time to leave—the two spouses were outside almost immediately and they would then hurry home.

Vic would come a few minutes afterward, for she not only had to go down three long staircases, but she also had to cross the entire length of the mill before reaching the gates. Finally Maurice would arrive, invariably a good fifteen minutes later than the rest of the family, since he worked in a distant shop. One evening, as the girl opened the door, she heard her father raging, while her mother and Besson were crying.

"Now then," Vic asked, "what is it this time? Our lives are miserable enough without having these angry scenes every day. What happened?"

"It's that Maurice," said Labranche. "Without asking my permission, he changed factories and, because of this, he's going to lose half a day's pay."

"Did he switch to a better-paying job?"

"Yes, but he should have spoken to me about it," insisted Labranche. "I learned about it from the others. If I had known, I could have arranged for him to change jobs without losing that half-day's pay."

"His intentions were good," Vic pleaded. "I'm almost certain that if he hadn't acted as he did, someone else would have taken advantage of it to get a better job. Before getting angry and causing us grief, wait and see what Maurice has to say about all this."

"Yes, take his side again," Labranche fumed. "What do you care if your father works his heart out in a factory, so long as Maurice has his way! Maurice comes before me, I suppose?

"Vic's Revolt," from CANUCK by Camille Lessard, translated by Armand B. Chartier. (I am indebted to my colleague, Armand B. Chartier, in the Department of Languages at the University of Rhode Island/Kingston for this translation.)

I'm going to show you, once again, who is boss here, Maurice or myself! I'm waiting for him, and he's going to get the best spanking he's ever had in his life.''

These last words had upon Vic the effect of a charge of dynamite exploding hinges. Her eyes on fire, her nostrils flaring, her lips deathly pale, she walked boldly toward her father and declared: "If you dare touch Maurice tonight, my room will be empty tomorrow."

"Your room will never be empty," Labranche shouted. "If you leave, the police will bring you back here without your being very proud of yourself! You know, even though you're eighteen years old, I still have rights on you!!"

"Yes, you have rights on me," replied Vic, losing all reserve and all respect, "but I dare you to enforce those very rights! Have the police take me away if you wish, but I'll keep the seat warm for you in the paddy wagon and I'll make sure you get to use it! Don't forget that you committed a criminal act by forcing Maurice to work in the mills instead of sending him to school like you should have! You passed him off for a fifteen-year old in order to exploit the health, the sweat and the blood of this child—to your advantage! What do you suppose the police would say if I informed them of this? Whatever happens as far as I am concerned, you had better leave the police alone! You can ruin Maurice's future and his health. . . . You can hasten Besson's death by forcing us to live in a hole, thus depriving him of fresh air and sunshine—so that you can keep adding to your savings account! . . . You can go on making a martyrdom out of my mother's life! . . . In a word, you can go on starving all of us, but believe me, leave the American police alone! . . . If you had worked half as hard on your farm as you're doing here in the mills, you would never have been forced to leave your farm! . . . The work in the fields and in the stables was done by Maman and by me, as soon as I was big enough, and yet I wasn't very old! . . . And while that was going on, you were riding around in a buggy or in a carriole, or playing cards and running amuck! . . . When you'd come home, if we hadn't finished all the heavy work, there would be hellish scenes! . . . And during one of those scenes, you even dared strike Maman because we weren't able to repair one of the fences, and the animals had gone over to the neighbor's! . . . Hitting Maman, whose little finger is more worthy than your entire person! . . . Maman and I are quite willing to go on helping you so that as soon as possible you can go back to laying down the law in the stores of the village whence we came, but believe me, it's better that you not lay a hand on Maurice tonight!'' . . .

Labranche, his eyes out of their sockets as if he were about to have an apoplectic fit, fell into a chair, floored by the unforeseen violence of the attack. Vic, without adding a word, turned on her heels, crossed the boys' bedroom and shut herself up in her own room.

A door opens and closes. . . . It must be Maurice arriving. . . . Angry words. . . . A meek voice vainly trying to make itself heard. . . . Doorhinges squeaking, and a boy who throws himself weeping onto his bed. . . . It's indeed Maurice, followed by Besson speaking to him softly, between sighs. . . . Vic would like to go console the children, but she fears another scene if her father were to open the bedroom door. She waits. A chair is pushed back, shoes are flung, a door slams shut. Her father must have gone off to his card game at the neighbor's. Vic tiptoes through the boys' room and, as an extra precaution, she looks through the keyhole. Her father has indeed left, and she hears her mother sighing. Opening the door, she says: "Maman, come here."

The mother, her back rounded, her eyes red, her lips trembling, comes murmuring: "My God, how steep is Thy Calvary for me!" Vic bends down toward the sobbing boys and, her forehead against their heads, whispers: "Don't cry any more, we're going to talk."

Madame Labranche collapses on the foot of the bed and Besson, shaken by a horrible fit of coughing, throws himself into her arms. Vic puts her arm around Maurice's shoulder and draws him toward her. For a few minutes the girl sits staring at the quilt bedspread, in order to give everyone time to settle down, then, in a hollow voice, she begins speaking to the three unhappy people: "I've been weighing things very carefully for the past hour and I've understood that the only way to help you is for me to leave! . . . Just think. Right now I'm earning twenty dollars per week and that, along with the rest of the money coming into the house, is still not enough to allow us to live decently. We're dressed like paupers and we live like outcasts in the bleakest and poorest part of Lowell! On Sundays, we must beg so that each one of us can get ten cents for Mass! We must cry and beg to get a two-cent stamp to mail a letter! We're not allowed to go for a walk, because walking wears out the soles of our shoes! Our windows have no curtains, our floors have no carpets and Besson can't even get cough syrup! . . . My leaving would be the only way I could help you. I work next to a young girl by the name of Vaillancourt who lives five minutes from here. Her mother is a widow and, consequently, there are no men in the house to . . . make life miserable! . . . She had a boarder who paid three dollars per week and who recently got married. Madame Vaillancourt would probably take me in at the same rate. I could share her daughter's bedroom. Having my money at my disposal, I could buy medicine for Besson and books for Maurice. Little by little, I could find a way of buying clothes for you, Maman, as well as for the boys. From whatever is left, I would take a bit for clothing for myself and put the balance into the bank for Maurice's college education. This child *must* get an education, and I'm the only one in a position to help him. Don't worry about Father sending the police after me: he'll be much too afraid that I'll denounce him because of Maurice's age. He has always broken whatever would not bend under his tyrannical will, it's time he learn that one can escape from him. If I stay here, I can do absolutely nothing for you. In order to help you, I must go."

"But, my poor child, what if you were sick?" Madame Labranche moaned.

"Why should I be sick? And if I were, you wouldn't be far; moreover, I would be with good people, they wouldn't let me die without taking care of me. I could see Maurice every evening on my way home from work, and, if Father were to go out on Saturday or Sunday, all of you could come to see me, it wouldn't be far away. I don't want you to cry. . . . The operation is very hard, but it has to be done if we all want to be saved. Look at me: I feel brave . . . don't take my courage away from me. . . . Tonight, I'm going to put my few rags into a bag and tomorrow I'll send for them after reaching an agreement with Madame Vaillancourt. Tomorrow evening, the scene Father will make, when he learns I've left, will not be the happiest . . . but you'll see that it won't be long. Little by little he'll calm down, for he'll understand that he's through goading us, spurring us, whipping us on, as if we were animals. . . ."

LULLABY

Leslie Silko

The sun had gone down but the snow in the wind gave off its own light. It came in thick tufts like new wool—washed before the weaver spins it. Ayah reached out for it like her own babies had, and she smiled when she remembered how she had laughed at them. She was an old woman now, and her life had become memories. She sat down with her back against the wide cottonwood tree, feeling the rough bark on her back bones; she faced east and listened to the wind and snow sing a high-pitched Yeibechei song. Out of the wind she felt warmer, and she could watch the wide fluffy snow fill in her tracks, steadily, until the direction she had come from was gone. By the light of the snow she could see the dark outline of the big arroyo a few feet away. She was sitting on the edge of Cebolleta Creek, where in the springtime the thin cows would graze on grass already chewed flat to the ground. In the wide deep creek bed where only a trickle of water flowed in the summer, the skinny cows would wander, looking for new grass along winding paths splashed with manure.

Ayah pulled the old Army blanket over her head like a shawl. Jimmie's blanket—the one he had sent to her. That was a long time ago and the green wool was faded, and it was unraveling on the edges. She did not want to think about Jimmie. So she thought about the weaving and the way her mother had done it. On the tall wooden loom set into the sand under a tamarack tree for shade. She could see it clearly. She had been only a little girl when her grandma gave her the wooden combs to pull the twigs and burrs from the raw, freshly washed wool. And while she combed the wool, her grandma sat beside her, spinning a silvery strand of yarn around the smooth cedar spindle. Her mother worked at the loom with yarns dyed bright yellow and red and gold. She watched them dye the yarn in boiling black pots full of beeweed petals, juniper berries, and sage. The blankets her mother made were soft and woven so tight that rain rolled off them like birds' feathers. Ayah remembered sleeping warm on cold windy nights, wrapped in her mother's blankets on the hogan's sandy floor.

The snow drifted now, with the northwest wind hurling it in gusts. It drifted up around her black overshoes—old ones with little metal buckles. She smiled at the snow which was trying to cover her little by little. She could remember when they had no black rubber overshoes; only the high buckskin leggings that they wrapped over their elk-hide moccasins. If the snow was dry or frozen, a person could walk all day and not get wet; and in the evenings the beams of the ceiling would hang with lengths of pale buckskin leggings, drying out slowly.

She felt peaceful remembering. She didn't feel cold any more. Jimmie's blanket seemed warmer than it had ever been. And she could remember the morning he was born. She could remember whispering to her mother who was sleeping on the other side of the hogan, to tell her it was time now. She did not want to wake the others. The second time she called to her, her mother stood up and pulled on her shoes; she knew. They walked to the old stone hogan together, Ayah walking a step behind her mother. She waited alone, learning the rhythms of the pains while her mother went to call the old woman to help them. The morning was already

Leslie Silko, "Lullaby" from the *Chicago Review,* Vol. 26, No. 1, 1974. Reprinted with permission of the author.

"Indian woman." This ninety-one year old Salish woman of the
Flathead Reservation in Montana shows the weathered effects of a
rugged, hard life. By permission of the Bureau of Indian Affairs.

warm even before dawn and Ayah smelled the bee flowers blooming and the young willow growing at the springs. She could remember that so clearly, but his birth merged into the births of the other children and to her it became all the same birth. They named him for the summer morning and in English they called him Jimmie.

It wasn't like Jimmie died. He just never came back, and one day a dark blue sedan with white writing on its doors pulled up in front of the boxcar shack where the rancher let the Indians live. A man in a khaki uniform trimmed in gold gave them a yellow piece of paper and told them that Jimmie was dead. He said the Army would try to get the body back and then it would be shipped to them; but it wasn't likely because the helicopter had burned after it crashed. All of this was told to Chato because he could understand English. She stood inside the doorway holding the baby while Chato listened. Chato spoke English like a white man and he spoke Spanish too. He was taller than the white man and he stood straighter too. Chato didn't explain why; he just told the military man they could keep the body if they found it. The white man looked bewildered; he nodded his head and he left. Then Chato looked at her and shook his head. "Goddamn," he said in English, and then he told her "Jimmie isn't coming home anymore," and when he spoke, he used the words to speak of the dead. She didn't cry then, but she hurt inside with anger. And she mourned him as the years passed, when a horse fell with Chato and broke his leg, and the white rancher told them he wouldn't pay Chato until he could work again. She mourned Jimmie because he would have worked for his father then; he would have saddled the big bay horse and ridden the fence lines each day, with wire cutters and heavy gloves, fixing the breaks in the barbed wire and putting the stray cattle back inside again.

She mourned him after the white doctors came to take Danny and Ella away. She was at the shack alone that day when they came. It was back in the days before they hired Navajo women to go with them as interpreters. She recognized one of the doctors. She had seen him at the children's clinic at Canoncito about a month ago. They were wearing khaki uniforms and they waved papers at her and a black ball point pen, trying to make her understand their English words. She was frightened by the way they looked at the children, like the lizard watches the fly. Danny was swinging on the tire swing in the elm tree behind the rancher's house, and Ella was toddling around the front door, dragging the broomstick horse Chato made for her. Ayah could see they wanted her to sign the papers, and Chato had taught her to sign her name. It was something she was proud of. She only wanted them to go, and to take their eyes away from her children.

She took the pen from the man without looking at his face and she signed the papers in three different places he pointed to. She stared at the ground by their feet and waited for them to leave. But they stood there and began to point and gesture at the children. Danny stopped swinging. Ayah could see his fear. She moved suddenly and grabbed Ella into her arms; the child squirmed, trying to get back to her toys. Ayah ran with the baby toward Danny; she screamed for him to run and then she grabbed him around the chest and carried him too. She ran south into the foothills of juniper trees and black lava rock. Behind her she heard the doctors running, but they had been taken by surprise, and as the hills became steeper and the cholla cactus were thicker, they stopped. When she reached the top of the hill, she stopped too to listen in case they were circling around her. But in a few minutes she heard a car engine start and they drove away. The children had been too surprised to cry while she ran with them. Danny was shaking and Ella's little fingers were gripping Ayah's blouse.

She stayed up in the hills for the rest of the day, sitting on a black lava boulder in the sunshine where she could see for miles all around her. The sky was light blue and cloudless, and it was warm for late April. The sun warmth relaxed her and took the fear and anger away. She lay back on the rock and watched the sky. It seemed to her that she could walk into the sky, stepping through clouds endlessly. Danny played with little pebbles and stones, pretending they were birds, eggs and then little rabbits. Ella sat at her feet and dropped fistfuls of dirt into the breeze, watching the dust and particles of sand intently. Ayah watched a hawk soar high above them, dark wings gliding; hunting or only watching, she did not know. The hawk was patient and he circled all afternoon before he disappeared around the high volcanic peak the Mexicans call Guadalupe.

Late in the afternoon, Ayah looked down at the gray boxcar shack with the paint all peeled from the wood; the stove pipe on the roof was rusted and crooked. The fire she had built that morning in the oil drum stove had burned out. Ella was asleep in her lap now and Danny sat close to her, complaining that he was hungry; he asked when they would go to the house. "We will stay up here until your father comes," she told them, "because those white men were chasing us." The boy remembered then and he nodded at her silently.

If Jimmie had been there he could have read those papers and explained to her what they said. Ayah would have known, then, never to sign them. The doctors came back the next day and they brought a BIA policeman with them. They told Chato they had her signature and that was all they needed. Except for the kids. She listened to Chato sullenly; she hated him when he told her it was the old woman who died in the winter, spitting blood; it was her old grandma who had given the children this disease. "They don't spit blood," she said coldly, "The whites lie." She held Ella and Danny close to her, ready to run to the hills again. "I want a medicine man first," she said to Chato, not looking at him. He shook his head. "It's too late now. The policeman is with them. You signed the paper." His voice was gentle.

It was worse than if they had died: to lose the children and to know that somewhere, in a place called Colorado, in a place full of sick and dying strangers, her children were without her. There had been babies that died soon after they were born, and one that died before he could walk. She had carried them herself, up to the boulders and great pieces of the cliff that long ago crashed down from Long Mesa; she laid them in the crevices of sandstone and buried them in fine brown sand with round quartz pebbles that washed down from the hills in the rain. She had endured it because they had been with her. But she could not bear this pain. She did not sleep for a long time after they took her children. She stayed on the hill where they had fled the first time, and she slept rolled up in the blanket Jimmie had sent her. She carried the pain in her belly and it was fed by everything she saw: the blue sky of their last day together and the dust and pebbles government car, but because he had taught her to sign her name. Because it was like the old ones always told her about learning their language or any of their ways: it endangered you. She slept alone on the hill until the middle of November when the first snows came. Then she made a bed for herself where the children had slept. She did not lay down beside Chato again until many years later, when he was sick and shivering and only her body could keep him warm. The illness came after the white rancher told Chato he was too old to work for him any more, and Chato and his old woman should be out of the shack by the next afternoon because the rancher had hired new people to work there. That had satisfied her. To see how the white man repaid Chato's years of loyalty and work. All of Chato's fine-sounding English talk didn't change things.

II

It snowed steadily and the luminous light from the snow gradually diminished into the darkness. Somewhere in Cebolleta a dog barked and other village dogs joined with it. Ayah looked in the direction she had come, from the bar where Chato was buying the wine. Sometimes he told her to go on ahead and wait; and then he never came. And when she finally went back looking for him, she would find him passed out at the bottom of the wooden steps to Azzie's Bar. All the wine would be gone and most of the money too, from the pale blue check that came to them once a month in a government envelope. It was then that she would look at his face and his hands, scarred by ropes and the barbed wire of all those years, and she would think 'this man is a stranger'; for 40 years she had smiled at him and cooked his food, but he remained a stranger. She stood up again, with the snow almost to her knees, and she walked back to find Chato.

It was hard to walk in the deep snow and she felt the air burn in her lungs. She stopped a short distance from the bar to rest and readjust the blanket. But this time he wasn't waiting for her on the bottom step with his old Stetson hat pulled down and his shoulders hunched up in his long wool overcoat.

She was careful not to slip on the wooden steps. When she pushed the door open, warm air and cigarette smoke hit her face. She looked around slowly and deliberately, in every corner, in every dark place that the old man might find to sleep. The barowner didn't like Indians in there, especially Navajos, but he let Chato come in because he could talk Spanish like he was one of them. The men at the bar stared at her, and the bartender saw that she left the door open wide. Snow flakes were flying inside like moths and melting into a puddle on the oiled wood floor. He motioned at her to close the door, but she did not see him. She held herself straight and walked across the room slowly, searching the room with every step. The snow in her hair melted and she could feel it on her forehead. At the far corner of the room, she saw red flames at the mica window of the old stove door; she looked behind the stove just to make sure. The bar got quiet except for the Spanish polka music playing on the jukebox. She stood by the stove and shook the snow from her blanket and held it near the stove to dry. The wet wool smell reminded her of new-born goats in early March, brought inside to warm near the fire. She felt calm.

In past years they would have told her to get out. But her hair was white now and her face was wrinkled. They looked at her like she was a spider crawling slowly across the room. They were afraid; she could feel the fear. She looked at their faces steadily. They reminded her of the first time the white people brought her children back to her that winter. Danny had been shy and hid behind the thin white woman who brought them. And the baby had not known her until Ayah took her into her arms, and then Ella had nuzzled close to her as she had when she was nursing. The blonde woman was nervous and kept looking at a dainty gold watch on her wrist. She sat on the bench near the small window and watched the dark snow clouds gather around the mountains; she was worrying about the unpaved road. She was frightened by what she saw inside too: the strips of venison drying on a rope across the ceiling and the children jabbering excitedly in a language she did not know. So they stayed for only a few hours. Ayah watched the government car disappear down the road and she knew they were already being weaned from these lava hills and from this sky. The last time they came was in early June, and Ella stared at her the way the men in the bar were now staring. Ayah did not try to pick her up; she smiled at her instead and spoke cheerfully to Danny. When he tried to answer her, he could not seem to remember and he spoke English words with the Navajo. But he gave her a scrap of paper that he had found somewhere and carried in his pocket; it was folded in half, and he shyly looked up at her and said it was a bird. She asked Chato if they were home for good this time. He spoke to the white woman and she shook her head. "How much longer," he asked, and she said she didn't know; but Chato saw how she stared at the box car shack. Ayah turned away then. She did not say good-bye.

III

She felt satisfied that the men in the bar feared her. Maybe it was her face and the way she held her mouth with teeth clenched tight, like there was nothing anyone could do to her now. She walked north down the road, searching for the old man. She did this because she had the blanket, and there would be no place for him except with her and the blanket in the old adobe barn near the arroyo. They always slept there when they came to Cebolleta. If the money and the wine were gone, she would be relieved because then they could go home again; back to the old hogan with a dirt roof and rock walls where she herself had been born. And the next day the old man could go back to the few sheep they still had, to follow along behind them, guiding them into dry sandy arroyos where sparse grass grew. She knew he did not like walking behind old ewes when for so many years he rode big quarter horses and worked with cattle. But she wasn't sorry for him; he should have known all along what would happen.

There had not been enough rain for their garden in five years; and that was when Chato finally hitched a ride into the town and brought back grown boxes of rice and sugar and big tin cans of welfare peaches. After that, at the first of the month they went to Cebolleta to ask the postmaster for the check; and then Chato would go to the bar and cash it. They did this as they planted the garden every May, not because anything would survive the summer dust, but because it was time to do this. And the journey passed the days that smelled silent and dry like the caves above the canyon with yellow painted buffaloes on their walls.

IV

He was walking along the pavement when she found him. He did not stop or turn around when he heard her behind him. She walked beside him and she noticed how slowly he moved now. He smelled strong of woodsmoke and urine. Lately he had been forgetting. Sometimes he called her by his sister's name and she had been gone for a long time. Once she had found him wandering on the road to the white man's ranch, and she asked him why he was going that way; he laughed at her and said "you know they can't run that ranch without me," and he walked on determined, limping on the leg that had been crushed many years before. Now he looked at her curiously, as if for the first time, but he kept shuffling along, moving slowly along the side of the highway. His gray hair had grown long and spread out on the shoulders of the long overcoat. He wore the old felt hat pulled down over his ears. His boots were worn out at the toes and he had stuffed pieces of an old red shirt in the holes. The rags made his feet look like little animals up to their ears in snow. She laughed at his feet; the snow muffled the sound of her laugh. He stopped and looked at her again. The wind had quit blowing and the snow was falling straight down; the southeast sky was beginning to clear and Ayah could see a star.

"Let's rest awhile," she said to him. They walked away from the road and up the slope to the giant boulders that had tumbled down from the red sandrock mesa throughout the centuries of rainstorms and earth tremors. In a place where the boulders shut out the wind, they sat down with their backs against the rock. She offered half of the blanket to him and they sat wrapped together.

The storm passed swiftly. The clouds moved east. They were massive and full, crowding together across the sky. She watched them with the feeling of horses—steely blue-gray horses startled across the sky. The powerful haunches pushed into the distances and the tail hairs streamed white mist behind them. The sky cleared. Ayah saw that there was nothing between her and the stars. The light was crystalline. There was no shimmer, no distortion through earth haze. She breathed the clarity of the night sky; she smelled the purity of the half moon and the stars. He was lying on his side with his knees pulled up near his belly for warmth. His eyes were closed now, and in the light from the stars and the moon, he looked young again.

She could see it descend out of the night sky: an icy stillness from the edge of the thin moon. She recognized the freezing. It came gradually, sinking snow flake by snow flake until the crust was heavy and deep. It had the strength of the stars in Orion, and its journey was endless. Ayah knew that with the wine he would sleep. He would not feel it. She tucked the blanket around him, remembering how it was when Ella had been with her; and she felt the rush so big inside her heart for the babies. And she sang the only song she knew to sing for babies. She could not remember if she had ever sung it to her children, but she knew that her grandmother had sung it and her mother had sung it:

> *The earth is your mother,*
> * she holds you.*
> *The sky is your father,*
> * he protects you.*
> *sleep,*
> *sleep,*
> *Rainbow is your sister,*
> * she loves you.*
> *The winds are your brothers,*
> * they sing to you.*
> *sleep,*
> *sleep,*
> *We are together always*
> *We are together always*
> *There never was a time*
> *when this*
> *was not so.*

MY FATHER'S WAR

Anne Webster

If General George was father of
our country, my father was big chief
on the home front. The Army looked
past his straight back as they
5   listened to his murmuring heart.
When they wouldn't let him join
their war, he went down to the muddy
Chattahoochee and sat quietly,
waiting that subtle pull on the line.

10   One day each week he spent howing
his yardful of corn, tinting his skin
with red clay and sun. At night
my father crept on mocassined feet,
his obsidian eyes gleaming as he
15   searched the house for firewater.
He fought his way through jobs
like land mines, each one growing
more treacherous. Sometimes he lay
in the mud for days, his fatigues
20   decorated with permanent stains.

My uncle, the colonel, cried
when my father's body declared
war on itself. But my father sat
on the river bank and smiled,
25   ignoring the rocket burst of cancer
in his head. The water soaked into
his feet, made lakes of his lungs.
Dreaming of fast ponies and scalps,
he slid under the swift current.

Reprinted from *The Sunstone Review,* Vol. 6, No. 2, 1977. Reprinted with permission of the editor. (I am grateful to my colleague, Robert E. Wood, in the English Department at Georgia Tech for suggesting that I include this poem.)

HER LIFE

Esta Seaton

This is the picture that keeps forming in my mind:
my young mother, barely seventeen,
cooking their Kosher dinner on the coal stove
that first winter in Vermont,
5   and my father, mute in his feelings
except when he shouted,
eating to show his love.

Forty years later her blue eyes would grow cold
with the shock of those grey rooms
10   and the babies one after another
and the doctor who said
"If you don't want any more children
move out of the house."

EXPLANATION

Esta Seaton

"Neurotic?" my mother repeated.
"Well, we called it nervous.
Your Aunt Reba, she was nervous;
Always scrubbing the walls."
5   Scrubbing and scrubbing so
    the walls would shine.

And cried. She cried a lot.
And quickly, at a trifle.
"Nervous," my Uncle Louie
10   used to say,
Shrugging his shoulders.
Shrugging and shrugging his shoulders
    while his wife wept brine.

That wasn't all. There were the others.
15   Cousins and brothers, screaming and
    shouting.
"Families were like that," explained
    my mother.
But it was nothing
20   "Not," came her calm appraisal,
"like people nowadays."

Esta Seaton, "Explanation," from *The Minnesota Review,* Vol. II, No. 2, Winter, 1962. Reprinted by permission of the author.

WHATEVER HE DID HAD FLOURISH

Jeanne Wakatsuki Houston and James D. Houston

Farewell to Manzanar by Jeanne Wakatsuki Houston and James D. Houston is the true story of a Japanese American family during the Second World War. Jeanne was seven years old in 1942 when her family was uprooted from their home and sent to live at Manzanar internment camp, with 10,000 other Japanese Americans.

From FAREWELL TO MANZANAR by Jeanne Wakatsuki Houston and James D. Houston. Copyright © 1973 by Jeanne Wakatsuki Houston and James D. Houston. Reprinted by permission of Houghton Mifflin Company.

In addition to searchlight towers and armed guards, Manzanar included cheerleaders, Boy Scouts, baton twirling lessons and a dance band called The Jive Bombers who played all the popular songs except the nation's number one hit: "Don't Fence Me in."

Chapter Six gives insight into how one spirited Japanese American family attempted to survive the indignities of forced detention and how a native-born American girl discovered what it is like to spend several years behind barbed wire in the United States. Her devotion and love for her complex father are clearly delineated in this selection, revealing his reasons for coming to America and his pride.

That cane Papa brought back with him he had carved and polished himself in North Dakota. When his limp went away he continued to use it. He didn't need to. He like it, as a kind of swagger stick, such as military officers sometimes use. When he was angry he would wield it like the flat of a sword, whacking out at his kids or his wife or his hallucinations. He kept that cane for years, and it served him well. I see it now as a sad, homemade version of the samurai sword his great-great-grandfather carried in the land around Hiroshima, at a time when such warriors weren't much needed anymore, when their swords were both their virtue and their burden. It helps me understand how Papa's life could end at a place like Manzanar. He didn't die there, but things finished for him there, whereas for me it was like a birthplace. The camp was where our life lines intersected.

He was the oldest son in a family that had for centuries been of the samurai class. He used to brag that they had owned more land than you could cross on horseback in a single day. By the time he was born, in 1887, they weren't warriors any longer. Japan was in the throes of that rapid, confusing metamorphosis from a feudal to an industrial nation, which began when Commodore Perry's black-hulled armada steamed into Tokyo Bay and forced the Japanese to open their ports and cities to western trade.

Papa's grandfather was a judge, at one point a magistrate for the small, lovely island of Miya-jima. He had four children, including one son, Papa's father. His three daughters were among the first women in Japan to receive university degrees. One daughter married an army general who for a time governed Formosa, and it was this uncle-general who encouraged Papa to enroll in a military school.

As far as everyone could see he was preparing for a career in the navy. Then, at seventeen, he abruptly dropped out. His favorite aunt lent him some money, and a short time later he bought passage on a ship bound for the Hawaiian Islands. That was the last anyone in Japan saw or heard of him.

In those days he was a headstrong idealist. He was spoiled, the ways eldest sons usually are in Japan, used to having his way, and he did not like what he saw happening to the family. Ironically, it foreshadowed just the sort of thing he himself would be faced with later on: too many children and not enough money. His father's first wife bore five children. When she died, he remarried and four more came along. His father, who had been a public official, ended up running a "teahouse" in Hiroshima—something like a cabaret. It was a living, but Papa wanted no part of this. In the traditional Japanese class system, samurai ranked just below nobility; then came farmers and those who worked the land. Merchants ranked fourth, below the farmers. For Papa, at seventeen, it made no difference that times were hard; the idea of a teahouse was an insult to the family name. What's more, their finances were in such a state that even as eldest son there was almost nothing for him to look forward to. The entire area around Hiroshima, mainly devoted to agriculture, was suffering a severe depression. In 1886 Japan had for the first time allowed its citizens to emigrate, and thousands from his district had already left the country in search of better opportunities. Papa followed them.

He reached Honolulu in 1904, with a letter of introduction to a cousin who taught school on Oahu. Papa used to tell the story of his first stroll through town, just off the boat and wanting to stretch his legs before looking up his relatives. He came across a sign outside a building that said in three languages WORKERS WANTED. Proud that he could read the English as well as the Japanese, he figured he'd have an edge over anyone else applying. He was feeling cocky anyway on this first day in the new world, seventeen years old and a little money burning in his pocket. He stepped into a men's shop a few doors down and bought himself a new suit, a new shirt, a new tie, a new hat—everything he'd seen the most prosperous men along the street wearing. He changed clothes in the store, then went to see about that job.

He followed arrows from the sign to the back of the building, where he found a yard full of half-dressed Chinese and Japanese field hands waiting in line to apply for work in the sugar cane. His disdain for them was met with laughter. They looked at him as if he were a maniac, pointing with derision at his dandy's outfit. He rushed back to the street, cursing, dismayed, humilitated, heading for the safety of his cousin's.

A few weeks later he was introduced to a vacationing American, a lawyer from Idaho who offered to pay his passage to the states and provide room and board in exchange for three years' work as a houseboy. Papa accepted. It looked better than sweating in the fields, which was how most of his countrymen were making their new start. And one imagines that the American mainland glittered for him the way it did for all those entrepreneurs and pilgrims and runaways and adventurers who crossed the Atlantic and the Pacific hoping to carve out a piece of it for themselves.

In Idaho he worked as a valet, a cook, a chauffeur, a mechanic, a general handyman. He learned to roast turkeys and to drive a Pierce-Arrow sedan, and he perfected the English he had begun to learn before he left Japan.

In all, he spent five years with this family. Then his patron helped him enter the University of Idaho as an undergraduate, aiming toward a law degree. Papa used to joke that if hadn't met Mama he might have ended up a senator.

"She was too pretty," her brother Charlie once said. "Ko couldn't leave her alone. She was the only Japanese girl in the whole northwest worth looking at. I think there were two others around in those days, and they were both so skinny they could hide behind cornstalks."

Mama's father came from a family of stonecutters around Niigata, on the inner coast of northern Japan. But she was born in Hawaii where her father had come to do the backbreaking work Papa luckily avoided—a three-year labor contract on a sugar-cane plantation, ten hours a day, six days a week, for twelve dollars and fifty cents a month. Completing that, he worked his way to the mainland and set out with his three sons to find a piece of land. They settled in the rich farm country around Spokane, in eastern Washington. In 1906 Mama and Granny joined them there. Granny was thirty then, Mama was ten. They sailed into San Francisco Bay on the morning after the earthquake and spent their first three days in America sitting offshore watching the city go up in flames.

Her family had high hopes for Mama. She was their only daughter. In those days Japanese women on the mainland were rare, one for every seven or eight Japanese men. Most men had to go back to Japan to find a woman, or take their chances on a "picture bride." Mama was worth a lot, and before she finished high school they had promised her to the upright son of a well-to-do farmer in the territory.

She met Papa early one summer morning at a wholesale market where her family sold produce. Papa was unloading trucks and wagonloads of vegetables. She was seventeen, small, buxom, with a classically round face of a kind much admired among Japanese. He was twenty-five, a sometime law student who spent his summers working around Spokane. He liked to shoot pool in his spare time, he played cards and dressed like a man from a much flashier part of the country. He was also pitching for a semipro baseball team called *Nippon*. We have a picture of him down on one knee for the team photo, in the front row, his mitted left hand resting on the other knee, his thick hair loose, his eyes showing a cocky confidence. His lean jaw bulges slightly, as if holding a small plug of tobacco, in the manner of Ty Cobb, whose style was the one to imitate about that time.

Mama's parents were terrified when they saw him coming. He not only led what seemed to them a perilously fast life; he also borrowed money. The story goes that he once asked Mama to borrow as much as she could from Granny. All Granny had at the time was a five-dollar bill. She gave it to Mama, who passed it on to Papa, who then came stalking into the kitchen, stiff-backed, glaring scornfully at Granny. He was insulted. "It's not enough," he said. "Five dollars. I need more than five dollars. If that's all you've got, I'd rather have nothing!" And he threw the bill into the fire.

The first time Mama ran away with him, her brothers came looking for her, brought her back to the family farm, and locked her in a second-story room. Mama was so desolate, her oldest brother Charlie couldn't stand it. He leaned a ladder up to her window, forced the latch and let her out.

That time they got away, got married, and made it down to Salem, Oregon, where Papa cooked in a restaurant and she worked as a nurse and dietician until my oldest brother was born, in 1916.

After that she had a child about every two years, nine in the next eighteen, and Papa kept moving, looking for the job, or the piece of land, or the inspiration that would make him his fortune and give him the news he hoped all his life he would one day be able to send back to his relatives: *Wakatsuki Ko made it big in America and has restored some honor to his family's name.*

Education mattered a great deal to him. In later years he would brag to us that he "went to law school" and imply that he held some kind of degree from a northern university. It's true that everywhere he stopped he'd be helping a friend through one legal squabble or another—an immigration problem, a repossessed fishing boat. He worked for the government at one point, translating legal documents. But as badly as he wanted us to believe it, he never did finish law school. Who knows why? He was terribly proud, sometimes absurdly proud, and he refused to defer to any man. Maybe, in training for that profession in those years before the First World War, he saw ahead of him prejudices he refused to swallow, humiliations he refused to bear.

On the other hand, his schooling was like almost everything else he tried. For all his boasts and high intentions, he never quite finished anything he set out to do. Something always stopped him: bad luck, a racial barrier, a law, his own vanity or arrogance or fear of losing face.

For a couple of years he tried lumberjacking in Seattle. We have another old photo, this one from the twenties, that shows him standing on a railroad siding, with his boots spread wide, one hand in his jeans pocket and the other holding a wide-brim hat flung high in boisterous greeting—a Nipponese frontiersman with the pine forests rising behind him.

In Oregon he learned a little dentistry (a skill he later put to good use at Manzanar, where he made dozens of dentures free of charge). He tried farming there too. The alien land laws prevented him from owning property, but he could lease the land, or make a tenancy deal and work it.

A few years before I was born he had settled the family on a twenty-two-acre farm near Watsonville, California, raising apples, strawberries, and a few vegetable crops. He was making good money, living in a big Victorian house, and it looked as if he'd found his castle at last. But his luck didn't hold. The well went dry. Thirty years after sailing away from a financial dead end and the remnants of a once-noble family in Japan, he found himself in the middle of America's Depression and on the move again, with eight kids and a wife this time, working his way down the California coast picking prunes, peaches, Brussels sprouts, sending his children into the orchards like any migrant worker's family, hoping their combined earnings would leave a little left over after everyone was fed and the cars gassed up for the next day's search for work.

Just before I was born he leased another piece of land, in Inglewood, outside Los Angeles, and farmed again, briefly. Then, deciding land was too risky for investing either time or money, he turned to the ocean, started fishing out of Santa Monica, and did well enough at it through the late thirties that by December of 1941 he had those two boats, *The Waka* and *The Nereid,* a lease on that beach house in Ocean Park, and a nearly new Studebaker he had made a down payment on two weeks before Pearl Harbor was attacked.

The start of World War II was not the climax to our life in Ocean Park. Pearl Harbor just snipped it off, stopped it from becoming whatever else lay ahead. Papa might have lost his business anyway—who knows—sunk his boat perhaps, the way Woody almost sank one off Santa Monica a few years later, when he motored into the largest school of mackerel he'd ever seen, got so excited hauling in the fish he let them pile up on deck, and didn't notice water slipping through the gunwale slits and into the hold until the bow went under.

If any single event climaxed those prewar years, it was, for me at least, the silver wedding anniversary we celebrated in 1940. Papa was elegant that day, in a brand-new double-breasted worsted suit, with vest and silk tie and stickpin. He was still the dude, always the dude, no matter what, spending more money on his clothes than on anything else. Mama wore a long, crocheted, rose-colored dress. And I see them standing by our round dining room table, this time heaped not with food but with silver gifts—flatware, tureens, platters, trays, gravy bowls, and brandy snifters. The food was spread along a much larger table, buffet style, in glistening abundance—chicken teriyaki, pickled vegetables, egg rolls, cucumber and abalone salad, the seaweed-wrapped rice balls called *sushi,* shrimp, prawns, fresh lobster, and finally, taking up what seemed like half the tablecloth, a great gleaming roast pig with a bright red apple in its mouth.

A lot of in-laws were there, and other Japanese families, and Papa's fishing cronies, a big Portuguese named Goosey who used to eat small hot yellow peppers in one big bite, just to make me laugh, and an Italian named Blackie, with long black sideburns and black hair slicked straight back, wearing black and white shoes and a black suit with white pinstripes. These two were his drinking buddies, as flushed now as Papa was from the hot sake that was circulating and the beer and whiskey.

Papa announced that it was time to carve the pig. We all stood back to make a wide half circle around that end of the table. He had supervised the roasting, now he was going to show us how you cut up a pig. When he knew everyone was watching this—we were his audience, this dining room his theater—he lifted a huge butcher's cleaver, and while Goosey and Blackie, trying not to giggle, held each side of a long cutting board beneath its neck, Papa chopped the head off in two swift, crunching strokes. All the men cheered the sons, the carousers. The women sucked in their breath and murmured. Three more strokes and Papa had the animal split—two sides of roast pork steaming from within. With serious face and a high-held, final flick he split each side in half, quartering the pig. Then he set the cleaver down, stepped back, reached behind him without looking for a towel one of my sisters somehow had there waiting, and as he wiped his hands he said imperiously to his sons, "Cut it up. You girls, bring the platters here. Everybody wants to eat."

That's how I remember him before he disappeared. He was not a great man. He wasn't even a very successful man. He was a poser, a braggart, and a tyrant. But he had held onto his self-respect, he dreamed grand dreams, and he could work well at any task he turned his hand to: he could raise vegetables, sail a boat, plead a case in small claims court, sing Japanese poems, make false teeth, carve a pig.

Whatever he did had flourish. Men who knew him at Fort Lincoln remember him well. They were all Issei, and he was one of the few fluent in Japanese and English. Each morning the men would gather in their common room and he would read the news aloud, making a performance of it by holding the American paper in front of him and translating into Japanese on the spot, orating the news, altering his voice to suit the senator, the general, or the movie star.

Papa worked as an interviewer there, helping the Justice Department interview other Isseis. He almost became an alcoholic there on rice wine the men learned to brew in the barracks. And somehow, during the winter of '42, both of his feet were frostbitten. No one quite knows how. Papa never talked about that to anyone after he got back. But it isn't difficult to imagine. He arrived from Long Beach, California, at the beginning of January, in a country where cattle often freeze to death, and he was of course a prisoner of war.

"GOODBYE AND GOOD LUCK"

Grace Paley

I was popular in certain circles, says Aunt Rose. I wasn't no thinner then, only more stationary in the flesh. In time to come, Lillie, don't be surprised—change is a fact of God. From this no one is excused. Only a person like your mama stands on one foot, she don't notice how big her behind is getting and sings in the canary's ear for thirty years. Who's listening? Papa's in the shop. You and Seymour, thinking about yourself. So she waits in a spotless kitchen for a kind word and thinks—poor Rosie. . . .

Poor Rosie! If there was more life in my little sister, she would know my heart is a regular college of feelings and there is such information between my corset and me that her whole married life is a kindergarten.

Nowadays you could find me any time in a hotel, uptown or downtown. Who needs an apartment to live like a maid with a dustrag in the hand, sneezing? I'm in very good with the bus boys, it's more interesting than home, all kinds of people, everybody with a reason. . . .

And my reason, Lillie, is a long time ago I said to the forelady, "Missus, if I can't sit by the window, I can't sit." "If you can't sit, girlie," she says politely, "go stand on the street corner." And that's how I got unemployed in novelty wear.

For my next job I answered an ad which said: "Refined young lady, medium salary, cultural organization." I went by trolley to the address, the Russian Art Theater of Second Avenue where they played only the best Yiddish plays. They needed a ticket seller, someone like me, who likes the public but is very sharp on crooks. The man who interviewed me was the manager, a certain type.

Immediately he said: "Rosie Lieber, you surely got a build on you!"

"It takes all kinds, Mr. Krimberg."

"Don't misunderstand me, little girl," he said. "I appreciate, I appreciate. A young lady lacking fore and aft, her blood is so busy warming the toes and the finger tips, it don't have time to circulate where it's most required."

Everybody likes kindness. I said to him: "Only don't be fresh, Mr. Krimberg, and we'll make a good bargain."

We did: Nine dollars a week, a glass of tea every night, a free ticket once a week for Mama, and I could go watch rehearsals any time I want.

My first nine dollars was in the grocer'.s hands ready to move on already, when Krimberg said to me, "Rosie here's a great gentleman, a member of this remarkable theater, wants to meet you, impressed no doubt by your big brown eyes."

And who was it, Lillie? Listen to me, before my very eyes was Volodya Vlashkin, called by the people of those days the Valentino of Second Avenue. I took one look, and I said to myself: Where did a Jewish boy grow up so big? "Just outside Kiev," he told me.

How? "My mama nursed me till I was six. I was the only boy in the village to have such health."

"My goodness, Vlashkin, six years old! She must have had shredded wheat there, not breasts, poor woman."

"My mother was beautiful," he said. "She had eyes like stars."

He had such a way of expressing himself, it brought tears.

To Krimberg, Vlashkin said after this introduction: "Who is responsible for hiding this wonderful young person in a cage?"

"That is where the ticket seller sells."

"So, David, go in there and sell tickets for a half hour. I have something in mind in regards to the future of this girl and this company. Go, David, be a good boy. And you, Miss Lieber, please, I suggest Feinberg's for a glass of tea. The rehearsals are long. I enjoy a quiet interlude with a friendly person."

So he took me there, Feinberg's, then around the corner, a place so full of Hungarians, it was deafening. In the back room was a table of honor for him. On the tablecloth embroidered by the lady of the house was "Here Vlashkin Eats." We finished one glass of tea in quietness, out of thirst, when I finally made up my mind what to say.

"Mr. Vlashkin, I saw you a couple of weeks ago, even before I started working here, in *The Sea Gull.* Believe me, if I was that girl, I wouldn't look even for a minute on the young bourgeois fellow. He could fall out of the play altogether. How Chekhov could put him in the same play as you, I can't understand."

"You liked me?" he asked, taking my hand and kindly patting it. "Well, well, young people still like me . . . so, and you like the theater too? Good. And you, Rose, you know you have such a nice hand, so warm to the touch, such a fine skin, tell me, why do you wear a scarf around your neck? You only hide your young, young throat. These are not olden times, my child, to live in shame."

"Who's ashamed?" I said, taking off the kerchief, but my hand right away went to the kerchief's place, because the truth is, it really was olden times, and I was still of a nature to melt with shame.

"Have some more tea, my dear."

"No, thank you, I am a samovar already."

"Dorfmann!" he hollered like a king. "Bring this child a seltzer with fresh ice!"

In weeks to follow I had the privilege to know him better and better as a person—also the opportunity to see him in his profession. The time was autumn; the theater full of coming and going. Rehearsing without end. After *The Sea Gull* flopped *The Salesman from Istanbul* played, a great success.

Here the ladies went crazy. On the opening night, in the middle of the first scene, one missus—a widow or her husband worked too long hours—began to clap and sing out, "Oi, oi, Vlashkin." Soon there was such a tumult, the actors had to stop acting. Vlashkin stepped forward. Only not Vlashkin to the eyes . . . a younger man with pitch-black hair, lively on restless feet, his mouth clever. A half a century later at the end of the play he came out again, a gray philosopher, a student of life from only reading books, his hands as smooth as silk. . . . I cried to think who I was—nothing—and such a man could look at me with interest.

Then I got a small raise, due to he kindly put in a good word for me, and also for fifty cents a night I was given the pleasure together with cousins, in-laws, and plain stage-struck kids to be part of a crowd scene and to see like he saw every single night the hundreds of pale faces waiting for his feelings to make them laugh or bend down their heads in sorrow.

The sad day came, I kissed my mama goodbye. Vlashkin helped me to get a reasonable room near the theater to be more free. Also my outstanding friend would have a place to recline away from the noise of the dressing rooms. She cried and she cried. "This is a different way of living, Mama," I said. "Besides, I am driven by love."

"You! You, a nothing, a rotten hole in a piece of cheese, are you telling me what is life?" she screamed.

Very insulted, I went away from her. But I am goodnatured—you know fat people are like that—kind, and I thought to myself, poor Mama . . . it is true she got more of an idea of life than me. She married who she didn't like, a sick man, his spirit already swallowed up by God. He never washed. He had an unhappy smell. His teeth fell out, his hair disappeared, he got smaller, shriveled up little by little, till goodbye and good luck he was gone and only came to Mama's mind when she went to the mailbox under the stairs to get the electric bill. In memory of him and out of respect for mankind, I decided to live for love.

Don't laugh, you ignorant girl.

Do you think it was easy for me? I had to give Mama a little something. Ruthie was saving up together with your papa for linens, a couple knives and forks. In the morning I had to do piecework if I wanted to keep by myself. So I made flowers. Before lunch time every day a whole garden grew on my table.

This was my independence, Lillie dear, blooming, but it didn't have no roots and its face was paper.

Meanwhile Krimberg went after me too. No doubt observing the success of Vlashkin, he thought, "Aha, open sesame. . . ." Others in the company similar. After me in those years were the following: Krimberg I mentioned. Carl Zimmer, played innocent young fellows with a wig. Charlie Peel, a Christian who fell in the soup by accident, a creator of beautiful sets. "Color is his middle name," says Vlashkin, always to the point.

I put this in to show you your fat old aunt was not crazy out of loneliness. In those noisy years I had friends among interesting people who admired me for reasons of youth and that I was a first-class listener.

The actresses—Raisele, Marya, Esther Leopold—were only interested in tomorrow. After them was the rich men, producers, the whole garment center; their past is a pincushion, future the eye of a needle.

Finally the day came, I no longer could keep my tact in my mouth. I said: "Vlashkin, I hear by carrier pigeon you have a wife, children, the whole combination."

"True, I don't tell stories. I make no pretense."

"That isn't the question. What is this lady like? It hurts me to ask, but tell me, Vlashkin . . . a man's life is something I don't clearly see."

"Little girl, I have told you a hundred times, this small room is the convent of my troubled spirit. Here I come to your innocent shelter to refresh myself in the midst of an agonized life."

"Ach, Vlashkin, serious, serious, who is this lady?"

"Rosie, she is a fine woman of the middle classes, a good mother to my children, three in number, girls all, a good cook, in her youth handsome, now no longer young. You see, could I be more frank? I entrust you, dear, with my soul."

It was some few months later at the New Year's ball of the Russian Artists Club, I met Mrs. Vlashkin, a woman with black hair in a low bun, straight and too proud. She sat at a small table speaking in a deep voice to whoever stopped a moment to converse. Her Yiddish was perfect, each word cut like a special jewel. I looked at her. She noticed me like she noticed everybody, cold like Christmas morning. Then she got tired. Vlashkin called a taxi and I never saw her again. Poor woman, she did not know I was on the same stage with her. The poison I was to her role, she did not know.

Later on that night in front of my door I said to Vlashkin, "No more. This isn't for me. I am sick from it all. I am no home breaker."

"Girlie," he said, "don't be foolish."

"No, no, goodbye, good luck," I said. "I am sincere."

So I went and stayed with Mama for a week's vacation and cleaned up all the closets and scrubbed the walls till the paint came off. She was very grateful, all the same her hard life made her say, "Now we see the end. If you live like a bum, you are finally a lunatic."

After this few days I came back to my life. When we met, me and Vlashkin, we said only hello and goodbye, and then for a few sad years, with the head we nodded as if to say, "Yes, yes, I know who you are."

Meanwhile in the field was a whole new strategy. Your mama and your grandmama brought around—boys. Your own father had a brother, you never even seen him. Ruben. A serious fellow, his idealism was his hat and his coat. "Rosie, I offer you a big new free happy unusual life." How? "With me, we will raise up the sands of Palestine to make a nation. That is the land of tomorrow for us Jews." "Ha-ha, Ruben, I'll go tomorrow then." "Rosie!" says Ruben. "We need strong women like you, mothers and farmers." "You don't fool me, Ruben, what you need is dray horses. But for that you need more money." "I don't like your attitude, Rose." "In that case, go and multiply. Goodbye."

Another fellow: Yonkel Gurstein, a regular sport, dressed to kill, with such an excitable nature. In those days—it looks to me like yesterday—the youngest girls wore undergarments like Battle Creek, Michigan. To him it was a matter of seconds. Where did he practice, a Jewish boy? Nowadays I suppose it is easier, Lillie? My goodness, I ain't asking you nothing—touchy, touchy. . . .

Well, by now you must know yourself, honey, whatever you do, life don't stop. It only sits a minute and dreams a dream.

While I was saying to all these silly youngsters "no, no, no," Vlashkin went to Europe and toured a few seasons . . . Moscow, Prague, London, even Berlin—already a pessimistic place. When he came back he wrote a book, you could get from the library even today, *The Jewish Actor Abroad*. If someday you're interested enough in my lonesome years, you could read it. You could absorb a flavor of the man from the book. No, no, I am not mentioned. After all, who am I?

When the book came out I stopped him in the street to say congratulations. But I am not a liar, so I pointed out, too, the egotism of many parts—even the critics said something along such lines.

"Talk is cheap," Vlashkin answered me. "But who are the critics? Tell me, do they create? Not to mention," he continues, "there is a line in Shakespeare in one of the plays from the great history of England. It says, 'Self-loving is not so vile a sin, my liege, as self-neglecting.'

This idea also appears in modern times in the moralistic followers of Freud. . . . Rosie, are you listening? You asked a question. By the way, you look very well. How come no wedding ring?"

I walked away from this conversation in tears. But this talking in the street opened the happy road up for more discussions. In regard to many things. . . . For instance, the management—very narrow-minded—wouldn't give him any more certain young men's parts. Fools. What youngest man knew enough about life to be as young as him?

"Rosie, Rosie," he said to me one day, "I see by the clock on your rosy, rosy face you must be thirty."

"The hands are slow, Vlashkin. On a week before Thursday I was thirty-four."

"Is that so? Rosie, I worry about you. It has been on my mind to talk to you. You are losing your time. Do you understand it? A woman should not lose her time."

"Oi, Vlashkin, if you are my friend, what is time?"

For this he had no answer, only looked at me surprised. We went instead, full of interest but not with our former speed, up to my new place on Ninety-fourth Street. The same pictures on the wall, all of Vlashkin, only now everything painted red and black, which was stylish, and new upholstery.

A few years ago there was a book by another member of that fine company, an actress, the one that learned English very good and went uptown—Marya Kavkaz, in which she says certain things regarding Vlashkin. Such as, he was her lover for eleven years, she's not ashamed to write this down. Without respect for him, his wife and children, or even others who also may have feelings in the matter.

Now, Lillie, don't be surprised. This is called a fact of life. An actor's soul must be like a diamond. The more faces it got the more shining is his name. Honey, you will no doubt love and marry one man and have a couple kids and be happy forever till you die tired. More than that, a person like us don't have to know. But a great artist like Volodya Vlashkin . . . in order to make a job on the stage, he's got to practice. I understand it now, to him life is like a rehearsal.

Myself, when I saw him in *The Father-in-law*—an older man in love with a darling young girl, his son's wife, played by Raisele Maisel—I cried. What he said to this girl, how he whispered such sweetness, how all his hot feelings were on his face . . . Lillie, all this experience he had with me. The very words were the same. You can imagine how proud I was.

So the story creeps to an end.

I noticed it first on my mother's face, the rotten handwriting of time, scribbled up and down her cheeks, across her forehead back and forth—a child could read—it said, old, old, old. But it troubled my heart most to see these realities scratched on Vlashkin's wonderful expression.

First the company fell apart. The theater ended. Esther Leopold died from being very aged. Krimberg had a heart attack. Marya went to Broadway. Also Raisele changed her name to Roslyn and was a big comical hit in the movies. Vlashkin himself, no place to go, retired. It said in the paper, "an actor without peer, he will write his memoirs and spend his last years in the bosom of his family among his thriving grandchildren, the apple of his wife's doting eye."

This is journalism.

We made for him a great dinner of honor. At this dinner I said to him, for the last time, I thought, "Goodbye, dear friend, topic of my life, now we part." And to myself I said further: Finished. This is your lonesome bed. A lady what they call fat and fifty. You made it personally. From this lonesome bed you will finally fall to a bed not so lonesome, only crowded with a million bones.

And now comes? Lillie, guess.

Last week, washing my underwear in the basin, I get a buzz on the phone. "Excuse me, is this the Rose Lieber formerly connected with the Russian Art Theater?"

"It is."

"Well, well, how do you do, Rose? This is Vlashkin."

"Vlashkin! Volodya Vlashkin?"

"In fact. How are you, Rose?"

"Living, Vlashkin, thank you."

"You are all right? Really, Rose? Your health is good? You are working?"

"My health, considering the weight it must carry, is first-class. I am back for some years now where I started, in novelty wear."

"Very interesting."

"Listen, Vlashkin, tell me the truth, what's on your mind?"

"My mind? Rosie, I am looking up an old friend, an old warmhearted companion of more joyful days. My circumstances, by the way, are changed. I am retired, as you know. Also I am a free man."

"What? What do you mean?"

"Mrs. Vlashkin is divorcing me."

"What come over her? Did you start drinking or something from melancholy?"

"She is divorcing me for adultery."

"But, Vlashkin, you should excuse me, don't be insulted, but you got maybe seventeen, eighteen years on me, and even me, all this nonsense—this daydreams and nightmares—is mostly for the pleasure of conversation alone."

"I pointed all this out to her. My dear, I said, my time is past, my blood is as dry as my bones. The truth is, Rose, she isn't accustomed to have a man around all day, reading out loud from the papers the interesting events of our time, waiting for breakfast, waiting for lunch. So all day she gets madder and madder. By nighttime a furious old lady gives me my supper. She has information from the last fifty years to pepper my soup. Surely there was a Judas in that theater, saying every day, 'Vlashkin, Vlashkin, Vlashkin . . .' and while my heart was circulating with his smiles he was on the wire passing the dope to my wife."

"Such a foolish end, Volodya, to such a lively story. What is your plans?"

"First, could I ask you for dinner and the theater—uptown, of course? After this . . . we are old friends. I have money to burn. What your heart desires. Others are like grass, the north wind of time has cut out their heart. Of you, Rosie, I recreate only kindness. What a woman should be to a man, you were to me. Do you think, Rosie, a couple of old pals like us could have a few good times among the material things of this world?"

My answer, Lillie, in a minute was altogether. "Yes, yes, come up," I said. "Ask the room by the switchboard, let us talk."

So he came that night and every night in the week, we talked of his long life. Even at the end of time, a fascinating man. And like men are, too, till time's end, trying to get away in one piece.

"Listen, Rosie," he explains the other day. "I was married to my wife, do you realize, nearly half a century. What good was it? Look at the bitterness. The more I think of it, the more I think we would be fools to marry."

"Volodya Vlashkin," I told him straight, "when I was young I warmed your cold back many a night, no questions asked. You admit it, I didn't make no demands. I was softhearted. I didn't want to be called Rosie Lieber, a breaker up of homes. But now, Vlashkin, you are a free man. How could you ask me to go with you on trains to stay in strange hotels, among Americans, not your wife? Be ashamed."

So now, darling Lillie, tell this story to your mama from your young mouth. She don't listen to a word from me. She only screams, "I'll faint, I'll faint." Tell her after all I'll have a husband, which, as everybody knows, a woman should have at least one before the end of the story.

My goodness, I am already late. Give me a kiss. After all, I watched you grow from a plain seed. So give me a couple wishes on my wedding day. A long and happy life. Many years of love. Hug Mama, tell her from Aunt Rose, goodbye and good luck.

THE POWER OF PRAYER

Elizabeth Cullinan

Nothing in their lives was natural any longer—that was what it amounted to. Nothing that touched them did not take on a certain kind of strangeness.

That morning, the cold woke Aileen. She raised her head from the pillow and held it stiffly, straining her neck. Her eyes and her ears, her arms and legs and stomach—particularly her stomach—all were involved in the act of listening. There was no sound in the house, nothing but silence. A car passed. Three blocks away, on South Street, a bus went by. Aileen fell back onto her face, burrowing into the pillow and under the covers, tunneling down into softness and warmth.

"It's ten of seven," her mother said from the doorway. She stood there a moment, almost as though she were not quite sure what her next move should be, and then, when she saw Aileen push back the covers, she left.

The house was full of winter, the accumulated stuffiness of the long, cold months. Aileen stepped out of bed, picked up her underwear, and went out into the hall, looking neither to the left nor to the right, as though this were a strange house and she a timid guest. Safely inside the bathroom, she turned the big old-fashioned key in the lock; avoiding the face that looked out at her from the mirror, she ran the scalding hot and cloudy cold water, dipping her facecloth in one and then the other and rubbing it with a sliver of soap. She washed her face carelessly but gave great attention to the cleaning of her teeth, using a long ribbon of toothpaste and brushing hard, as though they would never be clean enough to suit her. Not taking any notice of her body (she was too thin, they told her—thin as a rail, skin and bones), she put on her underwear, threw her pajama coat about her shoulders, left the bathroom, and went over to her parents' bedroom. The bed was empty, and only one pillow had been slept on. The door of the spare room yawned upon a bed that hadn't been slept in at all.

So he hadn't come home; her father hadn't come home.

Feeling more at ease, she went back to her room and took a navy serge jumper and gray cotton blouse from their hanger. When she put on this drab uniform, the material fell into pleats where none were called for, and the sash went twice around her waist. (Too thin, she thought; too thin, too thin.) She combed her hair carefully, and left the room to begin the long descent through the house.

The kitchen, dining room, and furnace room were on the first floor, which was not quite as low as a basement but low enough to make it cold and damp and dark there. The second floor consisted of a front porch and two adjacent parlors separated by brocade portieres. When Aileen came to the first parlor, where, the day before, she had left her school hat, she looked in and then sucked in a great breath of horror. There, fully dressed, his coat over him, his mouth open, sleeping deeply, snoring lightly, lay her father.

The wild scream of the teakettle rose and immediately was cut off. Aileen stepped back and closed the parlor door. The second flight of stairs was dark and crooked. At the bottom she stood perfectly still, listening to the silence that seemed about to break the house apart, and then she walked down the narrow hall and looked through the little diamond-shaped window in the upper part of the door. Her mother was sitting at the kitchen table. She held a glass of tomato juice in one hand; the other supported her head. Aileen went in and put her hand on her mother's back. Without looking up, Mrs. Driscoll took Aileen's other hand, rubbing her thumb over it and pressing the fingers between her own.

Aileen produced the words that the occasion demanded but that were, today, such a bad joke. "Happy birthday."

On the first Friday of every month at the Academy of St. Monica, Mass in honor of the Sacred Heart was celebrated in the school auditorium for the benefit of the students, the nuns having already attended their own service in the small chapel on the second floor of the convent. For most of the girls, this meant getting up half an hour earlier, leaving the house without eating, and spending the rest of the day in a state that was not dizziness, nor hunger, nor headache, nor nausea, but seemed to draw upon all of these and was in no way alleviated by the sweet bun and container of milk that the nuns distributed after Mass by way of breakfast.

Aileen had missed the seven-o'clock bus, and was the only girl from St. Monica's on the seven-fifteen. She would be late for Mass, she thought, as she fell into an empty seat. Damp air blew in through the open window, and Aileen could feel the curl leaving the ends of her hair. She raised her hands to her head to protect it, and rested her elbows on the stack of books that were balanced so carefully—first the loose-leaf, then the health book, then the thick English readings, and next to it the smaller grammar and Latin and algebra texts. As they rode up the slope of South Street, between the rows of frame houses, Aileen began to go over the story around which was built her first year of high school: My father doesn't come home. . . .

The windows of the houses did not blink. The blinds were not flicked shut.

He doesn't come home until very late and sometimes not at all. I'd almost rather he *didn't* come at all, because then there isn't a quarrel. When there's a quarrel, they don't ever seem to remember me. It doesn't matter to them that I can hear the things they say. Sometimes I have to cover my ears.

The bus entered Main Street, but the sight of the stores did not distract her.

It started when he left his job at the insurance company, she went on. My uncle built two apartment houses, and he made my father the manager of one. He was going to manage the other, too—after a while—and then they were supposed to build some more together. They were going to be partners, and we were going to be very well fixed. But instead, just the opposite happened. We never have enough money, and we're way in debt. The thing is, she added, almost ashamed to be telling herself, my father goes to horse races. And he drinks. And my mother says there may be some woman. . . .

After she had admitted those facts, she went over them again, but they were still hard to believe. Those were things she had heard people joke about—drinking, and gambling, and the other. They weren't things that happened; they weren't more powerful than love in a family, and a happy life. . . . My mother thinks we should leave him, she went on, entering the next phase of the story. Maybe she's right. I don't know. I'm only fourteen. And he's my father. . . . Waves of self-pity began to rise inside her—high wave after high wave. Only fourteen, she cried to herself. I'm only fourteen and my father doesn't come home.

The bus passed Jessup Park, where two flocks of pigeons, rising into the air, began to drift over the trees in wide, separate circles; then, they merged and flew together. Aileen's arms were stiff from holding her hair in place, and so she drew them down. The damage was done. It was already quite straight. As she watched the birds' exact, aimless flight, the force of her own unhappiness gradually seemed to diminish and, almost calmly, she thought, If my mother gets a separation, there'll only be one signature on my report card. Mid-terms are next month. Everyone will know.

Beyond the next corner was St. Monica's. Aileen stood up and, trying to balance herself and the books, pulled the cord and started toward the rear exit. She jumped from the bus, then ran hard through the iron gates, under the arch of St. Augustine, up the hill, past the statue of the Sacred Heart that spread its arms in welcome, past the summerhouse at the top of the hill, and over to the school building.

As the heavy door crashed behind her, the warning bell rang from the auditorium ahead. Aileen slipped into one of the back rows and dropped to her knees on the stone floor just as the priest bent over the altar. The three long bells of the Consecration rang. Make him come home tonight, Aileen said again and again, as though concentration itself were successful prayer. I beg of You. I plead with You. Make him come home. Make home come home. *Tonight.*

A finger drummed sharply on Aileen's shoulder. Sister Alphonsus Liguori stood over her, holding out a scrap of thick net veiling. "Where is your uniform hat, Miss Driscoll?" the nun whispered.

Freshman Latin was the first class of Sister Alphonsus Liguori's day—the very worst time and the very least challenging subject, as far as she was concerned. On First Fridays the hour was almost more than she could endure. The girls who were not dozing were overexcited. The brash ones became reckless, the quiet ones dazed. The bright grew cocky and the slow seemed to come to a standstill. Sister Alphonsus waited outside the room until the class had filed in, and then she entered, hoping, as she always did, that the noise would automatically cease but it continued.

"Please, class," she said, tapping the bell that stood by her right hand. "The period has begun." She raised her hand to her forehead, waiting for the girls to follow the gesture. "In the name of the Father . . ." she began.

Until the year before, Sister Alphonsus had taught poetry at the College of St. Cecilia, which was near Ossining, and her work there had been remarkably successful. It was seldom that her students came away without at least honorable mention in any contests they entered.

However, she became, quite suddenly, subject to dizzy spells. She would have to leave a class and go to her room. Naturally, as she was first to recognize, the girls' work suffered. Sister Alphonsus' family was wealthy. Her brother wanted to send her to some convent abroad for a period of rest, and went so far as to draft a letter to the Mother Superior of the eastern province, but Sister Alphonsus decided against the plan. "I have taken the vow of poverty," she wrote him, "and it must now take me wherever it will."

She was sent to the Order's House of Rest on the tip of Long Island, and after a year there returned to teaching but on a different level. Mother General had decided that high school Latin would not be such a strain on Sister Alphonsus. The little girls required a much less strenuous program—their minds were less demanding. Sister would find them charming, and it would be in the nature of a homecoming for her to be stationed in Queens—just across the river from New York City, where she had grown up.

Elmhurst was not, of course, the world into which Sister Alphonsus Liguori had been born, and the little girls were, she soon discovered, timid or brazen, hostile or indifferent, dull or hypersensitive, but they had yet to show her their charm. Where was innocence, she wondered time and again. Where were the open hearts and honest faces she had known as a girl? Sister Alphonsus was certainly no advocate of cosmetics for the young, and yet, as she looked at the rows of drab faces before her, she remembered that a little lipstick had always heightened the features of the older girls' faces. But these children—so unattractive, so intractable—what was *she* to do with them? She held her long, thin fingers pointed up in the attitude of prayer, then she drew her *Latin: The First Year* toward her and opened it to the third trial of Hercules. "In the words of the poet Vergil," she began, " '*Arma virumque cano,*' or 'I sing of arms and the man.' " It would do them no harm to encounter ahead of time what waited for a few (a very few) in Latin IV. "The assignment for today was, I believe, 'Hercules and Cacus.' Will everyone turn to page one hundred and fifty-seven, please?" Sister Alphonsus ran her hands over the glossy pages, pressing them down. "Ellen Gleason," she called. "Would you read for us the passage beginning with line three hundred and seventy-two?"

A tall girl with badly blemished skin stood up and began haltingly, " 'Leander,' he cried, hitting himself a blow to the forehead."

"One moment, Ellen." The nun ran her finger along the inside of her coif. "We must bear in mind, young ladies, a fact which I notice is in constant danger of slipping away from us—that is, that the Romans spoke as intelligently and as fluently in their language as we do in ours. Now, we wouldn't say today that someone hit himself a blow to the forehead, would we?" Sister Alphonsus realized, too late, that perhaps the gesture itself was eccentric. "Moreover," she went on, "we are dealing with literature, which is even more refined than ordinary speech. I think that a more accurate translation of the line, Ellen, would be, ' "Leander," he cried, smiting his forehead.' " She looked around at the class and saw a piece of paper fall to the floor and a hand reach down to retrieve it. Oh, the furtiveness of adolescence, she thought with despair.

"Will the young lady behind Miss Gleason be good enough to bring me the piece of paper she's holding?"

Sister Alphonsus watched Aileen Driscoll rise and come forward. It was always the bright students, she thought. That was the pity of it. Mixing with the bold ones, wasting their intelligence in proving themselves no better than the rest. "May I have the note?" the nun asked, holding out her hand to receive the scrap of loose-leaf paper. Sister Alphonsus opened it with great dignity. "Ha, ha," she read, "look who's singing of arms and men." She folded the note and tucked it up her sleeve. "Perhaps you could manage to come and see me, Aileen, at three o'clock, after your last class?"

"I have glee club, Sister."

"Well, immediately *after* that I should like you to report here to me." Sister Alphonsus wondered if the girl were going to burst into tears. Her eyes seemed quite terrified. But then again, the nun remembered, they could be callous enough when they wanted. "May I remind you, class," she said, "that this is a short period, to begin with. Please to waste no more of my time."

The sounds of the dispersing glee club were left behind as Aileen walked past the empty classrooms toward the one that was Sister Alphonsus Liguori's. The light of the overcast day threw the palest of shadows on the wide corridor, and the quiet of the cloister seemed to be seeping over into the school. The academy had been tacked onto what was once the strictly cloistered Convent of St. Monica, and the floor of the school wing sloped at the junction of the two parts. Aileen coasted down the slight grade and, looking up as she came to the door, saw the thin, waxen face of Sister Alphonsus Liguori.

"I wonder, Aileen," said the nun, "that you can't put your high spirits to some better uses than those you find at present." When she spoke, her eyebrows rose slightly as her face strained against the bandaging of her coif.

Aileen followed her into the room and waited while the nun stepped onto the platform and settled herself at the desk as though for class. With her waxen fingers, she folded back the wide sleeves of her habit. "The only excuse I can find for your actions of this morning is the one Our Lord Jesus Christ once offered on behalf of *His* detractors—that you knew not what you did." Sister Alphonsus thrust her chin out over the stiff white shelf beneath it. "*Do* you have any idea what this message involves?" She held out the note.

It didn't involve her, Aileen thought. She hadn't sent it, only received it.

"Since you don't seem to know whether you do or not, let me ask you another question. Can you tell me what is meant by sacrilege?"

"Destroying something that belongs to God," Aileen said.

"Can you give me an example?"

"Stealing a chalice, Sister?"

"That would be an instance, though a rather uncommon one. Wouldn't you say that nuns and priests belong to God more truly than any other person does? More truly, certainly, than a chalice?"

"Yes, Sister," said the girl. She often found it difficult to associate the nuns—their complicated clothes, their sweet smell of hand lotion, and the clatter of their rosary beads—with anything in her own mortal existence.

"Well, in view of this, do you realize how far more serious a remark of this sort is?" Holding the note between her first and second fingers, Sister Alphonsus Liguori wagged it in the air. "You see, it isn't my feelings alone that are involved. It's of little importance how this makes *me* feel. Look up, please, Aileen, when I speak to you." The nun pressed the tips of her fingers together. "It is your own immortal soul that is at stake."

Tears filled Aileen's eyes. She held her arm in front of her face.

"I'm gratified to see that you seem to recognize your error. That, of course, is the first step toward atonement." In the face of what might be genuine remorse, the nun was troubled. "Have you a handkerchief?" she asked.

Aileen shook her head.

Sister Alphonsus took an immaculate, perfectly folded linen square from some secret pocket in the skirt of her habit and held it out to Aileen. "The danger with *feelings* of penitence," she began kindly, "is that we allow them to take the place of those actions that are its true manifestation." She looked away while the girl blew her nose. "I know you're sorry for this insult, but now you must prove it. First of all, I should like to know, if you can tell me, why you're so ashamed."

Suddenly it seemed to Aileen that the story that lay in readiness ought to be told. She was no ordinary offender. She came from a broken home. That was important. It made all the difference. "My father—" she began, but the words took her breath away. She had to stop.

Sister Alphonsus gave a short, discouraged sigh. "I'm afraid I don't see what your father has to do with it," she said. It was the deviousness of high school children that she detested most, and she had learned to be always on guard against it. "Well?"

Balanced on that narrow ledge hundreds of feet above the nun's upturned face, Aileen turned and crawled back to safety. "He's sick, Sister," she said. It couldn't be spoken about—not now, not ever.

Sister Alphonsus Liguori removed a speck of lint from the gaping jaw of her great sleeve. "I'm sorry to hear that," she said. "Is it a serious illness?"

"Yes, Sister."

"And is he in the hospital?"

"No, he's home."

"Just what seems to be the trouble?"

"They don't know, Sister."

"No diagnosis?" The nun raised her eyebrows, pushing her forehead into fold after fold of shining skin.

"Not yet."

"How long has he been stricken?"

"About six months."

"Six months and no diagnosis." The nun clicked her tongue. After all, it made no difference just now whether the father were sick or not. Her responsibility, in any case, was clear—contrite enough a moment ago, the child had now turned rather sullen. "Well, Aileen, it's a great pity that your father is unwell, and I hope he recovers quickly. I shall remember him in my prayers. But for the moment we must put this aside and return to our original purpose. Three times today you have offended against the virtue of reverence. You were late for Mass, your head was uncovered, and then this. Do you pray often?''

"Some.'' Aileen looked toward the gray-and-brown landscape outside. The rain had come. Against the background of the building she could see the first light drops.

"Not enough, I imagine. Like most of us, you probably don't spend nearly enough time at prayer. And so, instead of asking that you tell me whether or not you are the author of this message, and, if you're not, who is—instead of giving you a lesson to learn, and keeping you here for an hour—I'm going to have you accompany me to chapel, where you will please say a rosary in petition for an understanding of this important virtue of reverence. In addition,'' she added, "you might offer up the time for the swift recovery of your father.''

The chapel was empty except for a nun who knelt before the altar with her arms outstretched in the form of a cross. Everything glittered or shone or was stiff and crisp, as though the nuns vied among themselves in the polishing of the sacred vessels. Sister Alphonsus blessed herself with holy water and turned to Aileen. "I leave you on your honor,'' she whispered, and then left.

Aileen knelt down in the second pew from the rear, and as she made the sign of the cross saw the penitent nun sway, then recover and straighten her position. Against the virtuosity of that prayer, she felt cheap and dishonorable, for what did she ever offer God but selfish petitions? She never prayed as the nuns recommended, for the missionaries, or the conversion of Russia, for the souls in Purgatory, or the poor and oppressed of the world. She asked nothing but favors for herself, and each time one was granted, she produced another—more difficult, more urgent. She leaned back against the bench, with her elbows on the pew in front. "Let me be reverent,'' she tried now, but the prayer flew off as she thought it. There was only one thing she could ask, one thing to pray about. She would have to take the chance. "Just this once,'' she said, "and I'll promise not to beg again. But let him come home tonight. Please, let him come home.''

They waited dinner until seven-thirty. That was the far edge of their endurance—beyond that they could not hope. The two of them had learned how to pick their way through those long evenings of sadness, and the fact that it was Mrs. Driscoll's birthday did not interfere with their usual pattern but, instead, made the pattern more important. They ate fried fillet of sole with mashed potatoes that had stuck to the pot and string beans that were overcooked, too. Then, from a pound cake, Mrs. Driscoll cut one piece for Aileen and a sliver for herself, and while the girl ate away at hers, Mrs. Driscoll opened the flat package Aileen had put at her place. When she drew out the silk scarf, she began to cry, wiping her eyes with it.

Aileen stared across the table. All her feelings were pity and rage; all her thoughts were desperate. She wanted to rip the scarf in two and throw it away.

"What are we going to do?'' moaned Mrs. Driscoll.

"If only there were something we could get him interested in—something we could all do together.''

"What?'' said her mother. "All he cares about is horse racing.''

"Maybe *that*,'' Aileen said. "We could get him to take *us*.''

"Why should I lower myself?''

"It might work.''

"It wouldn't be worth it."

The pity and rage became loyalty. "We could try." He was her father. He *was* worth it. "And we could keep a lot of liquor in the house. Then he wouldn't have to go out."

"I always had such high ideals," Mrs. Driscoll said.

"It's going to be all right soon," Aileen said. She could never keep her mother interested in solutions; the trouble itself absorbed and distracted her. "It can't last," she added. "It has to stop sometime." She did feel that very strongly.

They did the dishes and then went upstairs, shutting off the lights behind them as though they were destroying clues. Only the hall lamp was left burning, to shed a pale orange light on the porch door and the staircase behind it. At the top of the last flight, Aileen kissed her mother. On a stand attached to the opposite wall was a statue of the Infant of Prague, dressed in real robes of taffeta and velvet, his tiny hand raised in a blessing. Perhaps He was the one she should have prayed to, Aileen thought. God had so many aspects, how could you choose among them—the Father, the Son, or the Holy Ghost; Jesus on the cross, Christ the King, transfigured and radiant, or the Sacred Heart, opening his chest for all to see the bleeding heart. "I think you ought to take a pill," she told her mother.

"I must. If I don't get some sleep I'll be physically unable to go on."

"Good night," Aileen said. She didn't mention the birthday; she would not have the tears start again. In her room she took off the uniform and, instead of putting on her bathrobe, got out her good outfit—a short black velveteen jacket and full blue tweed skirt—and put that on. Going over to the mirror, she ran the comb through her long hair—her very straight hair—and then began to pin it up. He had forgotten the birthday, she thought. That was it. When he remembered, he would realize what a terrible thing that was—so terrible that nothing could possibly ever be so bad again. When her hair was all pinned up, she took it down to try it another way—in a soft roll over each ear. If things could never again be this bad, they would have to get better. Her father, was, after all, not as bad as some fathers, who were terribly strict and unfair. Sometimes, when she listened to him talking to people or watched the way he smoked a cigarette, she was very proud that he was her father; she loved him very much then. And besides he knew just how to make her laugh, and he had always been very kind. Aileen put the last pin in the right-hand bun, then looked straight at herself. He would be kind again. She would love him again.

She was feeling confident and almost easy when she heard the car door slam in front of the house. She went to the window and saw her father come up the path, bending against the rain but walking steadily. Her chest began to burn with unhappiness, and the bones of her back and shoulders seemed intensely painful to her. Oh, she thought, what a way to answer the prayer, God—to let him come home early, but not early enough!

The front door was shut hard, and Aileen heard him go downstairs. He would be checking the back door and the gas stove; even now he was very careful about those things. She listened as he began traveling up through the old house, putting out the hall light, moving on toward where she was. Well, she wouldn't notice him. She didn't have to. She went back to her dresser and picked up the hand mirror to look at the back of her hair. The part was crooked, and strands that were too short to be folded in with the buns hung untidily around her neck. It was not right, she saw. Not right at all.

He had climbed the second flight of stairs. He was there at the top of the house now, and she heard him coming toward her room. He pushed the door open gently.

"Well, if it isn't Aileen," he said and smiled at her.

She would not be won by teasing. "Hello," she said quietly. She put down the hand mirror and, turning to the mirror on the dresser, seeing him and herself there, began to unpin the rolls over her ears. Wronged, waiting to be allowed to forgive, her feelings were suspended.

"Is your mother in bed?" he asked.

"Yes," Aileen said. She looked full at him and saw that he hadn't been drinking; there wasn't even that excuse.

"Asleep already?" His voice was mocking, and seemed to include her in the mockery.

"She took a pill." He had just forgotten. But she would not tell him. She would not be the one to accuse him. She was his daughter. She was only fourteen.

With his dark hooded eyes still on her, he yawned, then spoke gravely and, so it seemed, deliberately, as though they were discussing serious matters that would be important to her later on when she was older, when she was a woman. "How was the birthday?" he asked her.

"TO THE READER"

Mary McCarthy

I was born in Seattle in 1912, the first of four children. My parents had met at a summer resort in Oregon, while my mother was a coed at the University of Washington and my father, a graduate of the University of Minnesota, was in the Washington Law School. His father, J.H. McCarthy, had made a fortune in the grain-elevator business in Duluth and Minneapolis, before that, the family had been farmers in North Dakota and, before that, in Illinois. Originally, some generations back, the McCarthys had settled in Nova Scotia, the story is that they had emigrated for religious reasons and not because of the potato famine. In any case, according to legend, they became "wreckers," a common species of land pirate, off the Nova Scotia coast, tying lanterns at night to their sheep on the rocky cliffs to simulate a beaconing port and lure ships to their destruction, for the sake of plunder, or, as it is sometimes told, for the sake of the salvage contract. Plunder would be more romantic, and I hope that was it. By the time I knew them, the McCarthys had become respectable. Nevertheless, there was a wild strain in the family. The men were extraordinarily good-looking, dark and black-browed as pirates, with very fair skin and queer lit-up grey-green eyes, fringed by the "McCarthy eyelashes," long, black, and thick. There was an oddity in the hair pigmentation: my grandfather McCarthy was white by the time he was twenty, and my father was grey at the same age. The women were pious and plain. My grandmother, Elizabeth Sheridan, looked like a bulldog. Her family, too, had originally settled in Canada, whence they had come down to Chicago.

All her sons, as if to be ornery, married pretty wives, and all married Protestants. (Her daughter, my aunt Esther, married a widower named Florence McCarthy who, freakishly, was not a Catholic either.) My mother, Therese Preston, always called "Jess" or "Jessie," was a beautiful, popular girl with an attractive, husky singing voice, the daughter of a prominent Seattle lawyer who had a big house overlooking Lake Washington. His family came originally from Vermont, of old New England stock. Harold Preston had run for United States senator and been defeated, as I always heard it, by "the interests." As state senator, he framed the first Workmen's Compensation Act passed in the United States, an act that served as a model for the workmen's compensation laws later enacted throughout the Union. He was supposed to have had a keen legal brain and was much consulted by other lawyers on points of law. He was president of the state and the city Bar Associations. He did not aspire to a judgeship, the salaries, even on the highest level, were too low, he used to say, to attract the most competent men. In professional and business circles in Seattle, his name was a byword for honesty.

The marriage between my mother and my father was opposed by both sides of the family, partly on religious grounds and partly because of my father's health. He had a bad heart, the result, I was told as a child, of playing football, and the doctors had warned him that he might die at any moment. The marriage took place, despite the opposition. It was a small wedding, with chiefly family present, in the house over the lake. My father survived seven years (during which my mother had four children and several miscarriages), but he was never very well. Nor did he make any money. Though he had a law office in the Hoge Building and a shadowy partner, he spent most of his time at home, often in bed, entertaining us children.

It sounds like a gloomy situation, yet in fact it was very gay. My mother's parents were in a state of constant apprehension that she was going to be left a young widow with a handful of children to take care of, but my mother and father seemed to be completely carefree. They were very much in love, everyone agrees, and money never worried my father. He had an allowance of eight or nine hundred dollars a month from his father, and my mother had a hundred from hers. In spite of this, they were always in debt, which was my father's fault. He was a recklessly extravagant man, who lay in bed planning treats and surprises. The reader will hear later of my little diamond rings and my ermine muff and neckpiece. I remember, too, beauty pins, picnics in the back yard, Easter egg hunts, a succession of birthday cakes and ice-cream molds, a glorious May basket my father hung on my doorknob, a hyacinth plant, parties with grab bags and fish ponds, the little electric stove on which my mother made us chocolate and cambric tea in the afternoons. My mother had a strain of extravagance in her family, too. But it was my father who insisted on turning everything into a treat. I remember his showing me how to eat a peach by building a little white mountain of sugar and then dipping the peach into it. And I remember his coming home one night with his arms full of red roses for my mother, and my mother's crying out, "Oh, Roy!" reproachfully because there was no food for dinner. Or did someone tell me this story? If we went without dinner while we were waiting for the monthly allowance, it cannot have happened often, our trouble, on the contrary, was upset stomachs due to "fancy" food, or so I am told—I have no recollection of this myself or of all the enemas and purges we are supposed to have taken. I do remember that we could not keep maids or nurses, those that stayed longest were a raw, red, homely Irishwoman with warts on her hands, the faithful Gertrude, whom I disliked because she was not pretty, and a Japanese manservant who was an artist with the pastry bag.

My father, I used to maintain, was so tall that he could not get through a door without bending his head. This was an exaggeration. He was a tall man, but not remarkably so, as I can see from pictures, like all the McCarthy men, he had a torso that was heavy-boned and a little too long for his legs. He wore his gray hair in a pompadour and carried a stick when he walked. He read to me a great deal, chiefly Eugene Field and fairy tales, and I remember we heard a nightingale together, on the boulevard, near the Sacred Heart convent. But there are no nightingales in North America.

My father was a romancer, and most of my memories of him are colored, I fear, by an untruthfulness that I must have caught from him, like one of the colds that ran round the family. While my grandfather Preston was preternaturally honest, there was mendacity, somewhere, in the McCarthy blood. Many of my most cherished ideas about my father have turned out to be false. There was the legend of his football prowess. For years I believed, and repeated, that he had been captain of the Minnesota football team, but actually it was only a high-school team in Minneapolis. I suppose I must have got this impression from the boasts of my grandmother McCarthy. For years I believed that he was a Deke at college, but I think it was really Delta Upsilon. His gold watch, saved for my brother Kevin, turned out to be plated—a great disappointment. He was at the head of his class in law school, so I always heard, but I do not think this was true. As for the legend that he was a brilliant man, with marked literary gifts, alas, I once saw his diary. It was a record of heights and weights, temperatures and enemas, interspersed with slightly sententious "thoughts," like a schoolboy's, he writes out for himself, laboriously, the definitions of an atheist and an agnostic.

All the same, there was a romantic aura surrounding him, a certain mythic power that made people want to invent stories about him. My grandmother Preston, for instance, who was no special partisan of his, told me that on our fatal journey from Seattle to Minneapolis, my father drew a revolver on the train conductor, who was threatening to put our sick family off somewhere in North Dakota. I wrote this, and the reader will find it, in the memoir titled "Yonder Peasant, Who Is He?" But my uncle Harry, who was on the train, tells me that this never happened. My father, he says, was far too sick to draw a gun on anybody, and who would have told my grandmother, except my uncle Harry himself, since he and his wife were the only adult survivors of our party? Or did my grandmother hear it from some other passenger, on his way east during the great flu epidemic?

My last clear personal recollection of my father is one of sitting beside him on that train trip and looking out the window at the Rocky Mountains. All the rest of the party, as my memory sees it, are lying sick in bed in their compartments or drawing rooms, and I am feeling proud of the fact that my father and I, alone and still well, are riding upright in the Pullman car. As we look up at the mountains, my father tells me that big boulders sometimes fall off them, hitting the train and killing people. Listening, I start to shake and my teeth to chatter with what I think is terror but what turned out to be the flu. How vivid all this is in my mind! Yet my uncle Harry says that it was he, not my father, who was sitting with me. Far from being the last, my father was the first to fall ill. Nor does Uncle Harry recall talking about boulders.

It is the case of the gold watch, all over again. Yet how could I have mistaken my uncle for my father?

"My mother is a Child of Mary," I used to tell other children, in the same bragging spirit that I spoke of my father's height. My mother, not long after her marriage, was converted to

Catholicism and though I did not know what a Child of Mary was (actually a member of a sodality of the Ladies of the Sacred Heart), I knew it was something wonderful from the way my mother spoke of it. She was proud and happy to be a convert, and her attitude made us feel that it was a special treat to be a Catholic, the crowning treat and privilege. Our religion was a present to us from God. Everything in our home life conspired to fix in our minds the idea that we were very precious little persons, precious to our parents and to God, too, Who was listening to us with loving attention every night when we said our prayers. "It gave you a basic complaisancy," a psychoanalyst once told me (I think he meant "complacency"), but I do not recall feeling smug, exactly. It was, rather, a sense of wondering, grateful privilege. Later, we heard a great deal about having been spoiled by our parents, yet we lacked that discontent that is the real mark of the spoiled child, to us, our existence was perfect, just the way it was.

My parents' death was brought about by a decision on the part of the McCarthy family. They concluded—and who can blame them?—that the continual drain of money, and my father's monthly appeals for more, had to stop. It was decided that our family should be moved to Minneapolis, where my grandfather and grandmother could keep an eye on what was happening and try to curb my father's expenditures.

At this point, I must mention a thing that was told me, only a few years ago, by my uncle Harry, my father's younger brother. My father, he confided, was a periodical drunkard who had been a family problem from the time of his late teens. Before his marriage, while he was still in Minnesota, a series of trained nurses had been hired to watch over him and keep him off the bottle. But, like all drunkards, he was extremely cunning and persuasive. He eluded his nurses or took them with him (he had a weakness for women, too) on a series of wild bouts that would end, days or weeks later, in some strange Middle Western city where he was hiding. A trail of bad checks would lead the family to recapture him. Or a telegram for money would eventually reveal his whereabouts, though if any money was sent him, he was likely to bolt away again. The nurses having proved ineffective, Uncle Harry was summoned home from Yale to look after him, but my father evaded him also. In the end, the family could no longer handle him, and he was sent out West as a bad job. That was how he came to meet my mother.

I have no idea whether this story is true or not. Nor will I ever know. To me, it seems improbable, for I am as certain as one can be that my father did not drink when I was a little girl. Children are sensitive to such things, their sense of smell, first of all, seems sharper than other people's, and they do not like the smell of alcohol. They are also quick to notice when anything is wrong in a household. I do recall my father's trying to make some homemade wine (this must have been just before Prohibition was enacted) out of some grayish-purple bricks that had been sold him as essence of grape. The experiment was a failure, and he and my mother and their friends did a good deal of laughing about "Roy's wine." But if my father had been a dangerous drinker, my mother would not have laughed. Moreover, if he was a drinker, my mother's family seem not to have known it. I asked my mother's brother whether Uncle Harry's story could possibly be true. His answer was that it was news to him. It is just possible, of course, that my father reformed after his marriage, which would explain why my mother's family did not know of his habits, though as Uncle Harry pointed out, rather belligerently: "You would think they could have looked up their future son-in-law's history." Periodical drunkards, however, almost never reform, and if they do, they cannot touch wine. It remains a mystery, an eerie and troubling one. Could my father have been drinking heavily when he came home with those red roses, for my mother, in his arms? It is a drunkard's appeasing gesture, certainly, lordly and off- balance. Was that why my mother said, "Oh, Roy!"?

If my father was a sort of remittance man, sent out West by his family, it would justify the McCarthys, which was, of course, Uncle Harry's motive in telling me. He felt I had defamed his mother, and he wanted me to understand that, from where she sat, my father's imprudent marriage was the last straw. Indeed, from the McCarthy point of view, as given by Uncle Harry, my father's marriage was just another drunkard's dodge for extracting money from his father, all other means having failed. My mother, "your lovely mother," as Uncle Harry always calls her, was the innocent lure on the book. Perhaps so. But I refuse to believe it. Uncle Harry's derelict brother, Roy, is not the same person as my father. I simply do not recognize him.

Uncle Harry was an old man, and rather far gone in his cups himself, when he made these charges, which does not affect the point, however—in fact, might go to substantiate it. An uncanny resemblance to my father had come out in him with age, a resemblance that had not existed when he was young: his white bair stood up in a pompadour, and he had the same gray-green, electric eyes and the same animal magnetism. As a young man, Uncle Harry was the white hope of the family, the boy who went east to school, to Andover and Yale, and made a million dollars before he was thirty. It was in this capacity, of budding millionaire and family impresario, that he entrained for Seattle, in 1918, together with his pretty, social wife, my aunt Zula, to superintend our move to Minneapolis. They put up at the New Washington Hotel, the best hotel in those days, and, as my grandmother Preston told it, they brought the flu with them.

We were staying at the hotel, too, since our house had been vacated—a very unwise thing, for the first rule in an epidemic is to avoid public places. Indeed, the whole idea of traveling with a sick man and four small children at the height of an epidemic seems madness, but I see why the risk was taken from an old Seattle newspaper clipping, preserved by my great-grandfather Preston: "The party left for the East at this particular time in order to see another brother, Lewis McCarthy [Louis], who is in the aviation service and had a furlough home." This was the last, no doubt, of my father's headstrong whims. I remember the grave atmosphere in our hotel suite the night before we took the train. Aunt Zula and the baby were both sick, by this time, as I recall it, and all the adults looked worried and uncertain. Nevertheless, we went ahead, boarding the train on a Wednesday, October 30. A week later, my mother died in Minneapolis; my father survived her by a day. She was twenty-nine, he was thirty-nine (a nice difference in age, my grandmother always said).

I sometimes wonder what I would have been like now if Uncle Harry and Aunt Zula had not come on, if the journey had never been undertaken. My father, of course, might have died anyway, and my mother would have brought us up. If they had both lived, we would have been a united Catholic family, rather middle class and wholesome. I would probably be a Child of Mary. I can see myself married to an Irish lawyer and playing golf and bridge, making occasional retreats and subscribing to a Catholic Book Club. I suspect I would be rather stout. And my brother Kevin—would he be an actor today? The fact is, Kevin and I are the only members of the present generation of our family who have done anything out of the ordinary, and our relations at least profess to envy us, while I do not envy them. Was it a good thing, then, that our parents were "taken away," as if by some higher design? Some of my relations philosophize to this effect, in a somewhat Panglossian style. I do not know myself.

Possibly artistic talent was already dormant in our heredity and would have come out in any case. What I recall best about myself as a child under six is a passionate love of beauty, which was almost a kind of violence. I used to get cross with my mother when she screwed her hair up on top of her head in the mornings, I could not bear that she should not be beautiful all the time. My only criterion for judging candidates who presented themselves to be our nursemaids was good looks, I remember importuning my mother, when I was about five, to hire one called Harriet—I liked her name, too—and how the world, for the first time, seemed to me cruel and inexplicable, when Harriet, who had been engaged, never materialized. She must have had a bad character, my mother said, but I could not accept the idea that anyone beautiful could be bad. Or rather, "bad" seemed to me irrelevant when put beside beauty, just as the faithful Gertrude's red warts and her ugly name made me deaf to anything alleged to me about her kindness. One of the great shocks connected with the loss of my parents was an aesthetic one, even if my guardians had been nice, I should probably not have liked them because they were so unpleasing to look at and their grammar and accents were so lacking in correctness. I had been rudely set down in a place where beauty was not a value at all. "Handsome is as handsome does," my grandmother McCarthy's chauffeur, Frank, observed darkly, when my uncle Louis married an auburn-haired charmer from New Orleans. I hated him for saying it, it was one of those cunning remarks that throw cold water on life.

The people I was forced to live with in Minneapolis had a positive gift for turning everything sour and ugly. Even our flowers were hideous: we had golden glow and sickly nasturtiums in our yerd. I remember one Good Friday planting sweet peas for myself next to the house, and I believe they actually blossomed—a personal triumph. I had not been an especially pretty child (my own looks were one of my few early disappointments), but, between them, my guardians and my grandmother McCarthy turned me into such a scarecrow that I could not look at myself in the mirror without despair. The reader will see in the photographs that follow the transformation effected in me. It was not only the braces and the glasses but a general leanness and sallowness and lankness.

Looking back, I see that it was religion that saved me. Our ugly church and parochial school provided me with my only aesthetic outlet, in the words of the Mass and the litanies and the old Latin hymns, in the Easter lilies around the altar, rosaries, ornamented prayer books, votive lamps, holy cards stamped in gold and decorated with flower wreaths and a saint's picture. This side of Catholicism, much of it cheapened and debased by mass production, was for me, nevertheless, the equivalent of Gothic cathedrals and illuminated manuscripts and mystery plays. I threw myself into it with ardor, this sensuous life, and when I was not dreaming that I was going to grow up to marry the pretender to the throne of France and win back his crown with him, I was dreaming of being a Carmelite nun, cloistered and penitential, I was also much attracted by an order for fallen women called the Magdalens. A desire to excel governed all my thoughts, and this was quickened, if possible, by the parochial-school methods of education, which were based on the competitive principle. Everything was a contest, our schoolroom was divided into teams, with captains, for spelling bees and other feats of learning, and on the playground we organized ourselves in the same fashion. To win, to skip a grade, to get ahead—the nuns' methods were well adapted to the place and time, for most of the little Catholics of our neighborhood were children of poor immigrants, bent on bettering themselves and also on surpassing the Protestants, whose children went to Whittier, the public school. There was no idea of equality in the parochial school, and such an idea would have been abhorrent to me, if it had existed, equality, a sort of brutal cutting down to size, was what I was treated to at home. Equality was a species of unfairness which the good sisters of St. Joseph would not have tolerated.

I stood at the head of my class and I was also the best runner and the best performer on the turning poles in the schoolyard, I was the best actress and elocutionist and the second most devout, being surpassed in this by a blond boy with a face like a saint, who sat in front of me and whom I loved, his name, which sounds rather like a Polish saint's name, was John Klosick. No doubt, the standards of the school were not very high, and they gave me a false idea of myself, I have never excelled at athletics elsewhere. Nor have I ever been devout again. When I left the competitive atmosphere of the parochial school, my religion withered on the stalk.

But in St. Stephen's School, I was not devout just to show off, I felt my religion very intensely and longed to serve God better than anyone else. This, I thought, was what He asked of me. I lived in fear of making a poor confession or of not getting my tongue flat enough to receive the Host reverently. One of the great moral crises of my life occurred on the morning of my first Communion. I took a drink of water. Unthinkingly, of course, for had it not been drilled into me that the Host must be received fasting, on the penalty of mortal sin? It was only a sip, but that made no difference, I knew. A sip was as bad as a gallon, I could not take Communion. And yet I had to. My Communion dress and veil and prayer book were laid out for me, and I was supposed to lead the girls' procession, John Klosick, in a white suit, would be leading the boys'. It seemed to me that I would be failing the school and my class, if, after all the rehearsals, I had to confess what I had done and drop out. The sisters would be angry, my guardians would be angry, having paid for the dress and veil. I thought of the procession without me in it, and I could not bear it. To make my first Communion later, in ordinary clothes, would not be the same. On the other hand, if I took my first Communion in a state of mortal sin, God would never forgive me, it would be a fatal beginning. I went through a ferocious struggle with my conscience, and all the while, I think, I knew the devil was going to prevail: I was going to take Communion, and only God and I would know the real facts. So it came about: I received my first Communion in a state of outward holiness and inward horror, believing I was damned, for I could not imagine that I could make a true repentance—the time to repent was now, before committing the sacrilege, afterward, I could not be really sorry for I would have achieved what I had wanted.

I suppose I must have confessed this at my next confession, scarcely daring to breathe it, and the priest must have treated it lightly: my sins, as I slowly discovered, weighed heavier on me than they did on my confessors. Actually, it is quite common for children making their first Communion to have just such a mishap as mine: they are so excited on that long-awaited morning that they hardly know what they are doing, or possibly the very taboo on food and water and the importance of the occasion drive them into an unconscious resistance. I heard a story almost identical with mine from Ignazio Silone. Yet the despair I felt that summer morning (I think it was Corpus Christi Day) was in a certain sense fully justified: I knew myself, how I was and would be forever, such dry self-knowledge is terrible. Every subsequent moral crisis of my life, moreover, has had precisely the pattern of this struggle over the first Communion, I have battled, usually without avail, against a temptation to do something which only I knew was bad, being swept on by a need to preserve outward appearances and to live up to other people's expectations of me. The heroine of one of my novels, who finds herself pregnant, possibly as the result of an infidelity, and is tempted to have the baby and say nothing to her husband, is in the same fix, morally, as I was at eight years old, with that drink of water inside me that only I knew was there. When I supposed I was damned, I was right—damned, that is, to a repetition or endless re-enactment of that conflict between excited scruples and inertia of will.

I am often asked whether I retain anything of my Catholic heritage. This is hard to answer, partly because my Catholic heritage consists of two distinct strains. There was the Catholicism I learned from my mother and from the simple parish priests and nuns in Minneapolis, which was, on the whole, a religion of beauty and goodness, however imperfectly realized. Then there was the Catholicism practiced in my grandmother McCarthy's parlor and in the home that was made for us down the street—a sour, baleful doctrine in which old hates and rancors had been stewing for generations, with ignorance proudly stirring the pot. The difference can be illustrated by an incident that took place when I stopped off in Minneapolis, on my way to Vassar as a freshman, in 1929. In honor of the occasion, my grandmother McCarthy invited the parish priest to her house, she wanted him to back up her opinion that Vassar was "a den of iniquity." The old priest, Father Cullen, declined to comply with her wishes and, ignoring his pewholder's angry interjections, spoke to me instead of the rare intellectual opportunities Vassar had in store for me.

Possibly Father Cullen was merely more tactful than his parishioner, but I cannot forget my gratitude to him. It was not only that he took my grandmother down a peg. He showed largeness of spirit—a quality rare among Catholics, at least in my experience, though false magnanimity is a common stock in trade with them. I have sometimes thought that Catholicism is a religion not suited to the laity, or not suited, at any rate, to the American laity, in whom it seems to bring out some of the worst traits in human nature and to lend them a sort of sanctification. In the course of publishing these memoirs in magazines, I have received a great many letters from the laity and also from priests and nuns. The letters from the laity—chiefly women—are all alike, they might almost have been penned by the same person, I have filed them under the head of "Correspondence, Scurrilous." They are frequently full of misspellings, though the writers claim to be educated, and they are all, without exception, menacing. "False," "misrepresentation," "lying," "bigotry," "hate," "poison," "filth," "trash," "cheap," "distortion"—this is the common vocabulary of them all. They threaten to cancel their subscriptions to the magazine that published the memoir, they speak of a "great many other people that you ought to know feel as I do," i.e., they attempt to constitute themselves a pressure group. Some demand an answer. One lady writes: "I am under the impression that the Law forbids this sort of thing."

In contrast, the priests and nuns who have written me, apropes the same memoirs, strike a note that sounds almost heretical. They are touched, many of them say, by my "sincerity"; some of the nuns are praying for me, they write, and the priests are saying masses. One young Jesuit tells me that he has thought of me when he visited Forest Ridge Convent in Seattle and looked over the rows of girls: "I see that the startling brilliance of a slim orphan girl was fairly matched with fiery resolve and impetuous headlong drive. Nor was it easy for her those days. I suppose I should be thinking that technically you are an apostate, in bad standing, outside the gate. . . ." An older priest writes me that I am saved whether I know it or not: "I do not suggest to you where you will find your spiritual home—but that you will find it—of that I am certain—the Spirit will lead you to it. Indeed for me you have already found it, although you still must seek it." A Maryknoll nun invites me to visit her mission. None of these correspondents feels obliged to try to convert me, they seem to leave that to God to worry about. Some of them have passed through a period of doubt themselves and write me about that, to show their understanding and sympathy. Each of the letters has its own individuality. The only point of uniformity is that they all begin: "Dear Mary."

I am grateful to these priests and nuns, grateful to them for existing. They must be a minority, though they would probably deny it, even among the clergy. The idea that religion is supposed to teach you to be good, an idea that children have, seems to linger on, like a sweet treble, in their letters. Very few people appear to believe this any more, it is utterly out of style among fashionable neo-Protestants, and the average Catholic perceives no connection between religion and morality, unless it is a question of someone else's morality, that is, of the supposed pernicious influences of books, films, ideas, on someone else's conduct.

From what I have seen, I am driven to the conclusion that religion is only good for good people, and I do not mean this as a paradox, but simply as an observable fact. Only good people can afford to be religious. For the others, it is too great a temptation—a temptation to the deadly sins of pride and anger, chiefly, but one might also add sloth. My grandmother McCarthy, I am sure, would have been a better woman if she had been an atheist or an agnostic. The Catholic religion, I believe, is the most dangerous of all, morally (I do not know about the Moslem), because, with its claim to be the only true religion, it fosters that sense of privilege I spoke of earlier—the notion that not everyone is lucky enough to be a Catholic.

I am not sorry to have been a Catholic, first of all for practical reasons. It gave me a certain knowledge of the Latin language and of the saints and their stories which not everyone is lucky enough to have. Latin, when I came to study it, was easy for me and attractive, too, like an old friend, as for the saints, it is extremely useful to know them and the manner of their martyrdom when you are looking at Italian painting, to know, for instance, that a tooth is the emblem of Saint Apollonia, patron of dentistry, and that Saint Agnes is shown with a lamb, always, and Saint Catherine of Alexandria with a wheel. To read Dante and Chaucer or the English Metaphysicals or even T. S. Eliot, a Catholic education is more than a help. Having to learn a little theology as an adult in order to understand a poem of Donne or Crashaw is like being taught the Bible as Great Literature in a college humanities course; it does not stick to the ribs. Yet most students in America have no other recourse than to take these vitamin injections to make good the cultural deficiency.

If you are born and brought up a Catholic, you have absorbed a good deal of world history and the history of ideas before you are twelve, and it is like learning a language early, the effect is indelible. Nobody else in America, no other group, is in this fortunate position. Granted that Catholic history is biased, it is not dry or dead, its virtue for the student, indeed, is that it has been made to come alive by the violent partisanship which inflames it. This partisanship, moreover, acts as a magnet to attract stray pieces of information not ordinarily taught in American schools. While children in public schools were studying American history, we in the convent in the eighth grade were studying English history down to the time of Lord Palmerston; the reason for this was, of course, that English history, up to Henry VIII was Catholic history, and, after that, with one or two interludes it became anti-Catholic history. Naturally, we were taught to sympathize with Bloody Mary (never called that in the convent), Mary Queen of

Scots, Philip of Spain, the martyr Jesuits, Charles I (married to a Catholic princess), James II (married first to a Protestant and then to Mary of Modena), the Old Pretender, Bonnie Prince Charlie, interest petered out with Peel and Catholic Emancipation. To me, it does not matter that this history was one-sided (this can always be remedied later), the important thing is to have learned the battles and the sovereigns, their consorts, mistresses, and prime ministers, to know the past of a foreign country in such detail that it becomes one's own. Had I stayed in the convent, we would have gone on to French history, and today I would know the list of French kings and their wives and ministers, because French history, up to the Revolution, was Catholic history, and Charlemagne, Joan of Arc, and Napoleon were all prominent Catholics.

Nor is it only a matter of knowing more, at an earlier age, so that it becomes a part of oneself, it is also a matter of feeling. To care for the quarrels of the past, to identify oneself passionately with a cause that became, politically speaking, a losing cause with the birth of the modern world, is to experience a kind of straining against reality, a rebellious nonconformity that, again, is rare in America, where children are instructed in the virtues of the system they live under, as though history had achieved a happy ending in American civics.

So much for the practical side. But it might be pointed out that to an American educator, my Catholic training would appear to have no utility whatever. What is the good, he would say, of hearing the drone of a dead language every day or of knowing that Saint Ursula, a Breton princess, was martyred at Cologne, together with ten thousand virgins? I have shown that such things proved to have a certain usefulness in later life—a usefulness that was not, however, intended at the time, for we did not study the lives of the saints in order to look at Italian painting or recite our catechism in order to read John Donne. Such an idea would be atrocious blasphemy. We learned those things for the glory of God, and the rest, so to speak, was added to us. Nor would it have made us study any harder if we had been assured that what we were learning was going to come in handy in later life, any more than children study arithmetic harder if they are promised it will help them later on in business. Nothing is more boring to a child than the principle of utility. The final usefulness of my Catholic training was to teach me, together with much that proved to be practical, a conception of something prior to and beyond utility ("Consider the lilies of the field, they toil not, neither do they spin"), an idea of sheer wastefulness that is always shocking to non-Catholics, who cannot bear, for example, the contrast between the rich churches and the poor people of southern Europe. Those churches, agreed, are a folly, so is the life of a dirty anchorite or of a cloistered, non-teaching nun— unprofitable for society and bad for the person concerned. But I prefer to think of them that way than to imagine them as an investment, shares bought in future salvation. I never really liked the doctrine of Indulgences—the notion that you could say five Hail Marys and knock off a year in Purgatory. This seemed to me to belong to my grandmother McCarthy's kind of Catholicism. What I liked in the Church, and what I recall with gratitude, was the sense of mystery and wonder, ashes put on one's forehead on Ash Wednesday, the blessing of the throat with candles on St. Blaise's Day, the purple palls put on the statues after Passion Sunday, which meant they were hiding their faces in mourning because Christ was going to be crucified, the ringing of the bell at the Sanctus, the burst of lilies at Easter—all this ritual, seeming slightly strange and having no purpose (except the throat-blessing), beyond commemoration of a Person Who had died a long time ago. In these exalted moments of altruism the soul was fired with reverence.

Hence, as a lapsed Catholic, I do not trouble myself about the possibility that God may exist after all. If He exists (which seems to me more than doubtful), I am in for a bad time in the next world, but I am not going to bargain to believe in God in order to save my soul. Pascal's wager—the bet he took with himself that God existed, even though this could not be proved by reasoning—strikes me as too prudential. What had Pascal to lose by behaving as if God existed? Absolutely nothing, for there was no counter-Principle to damn him in case God didn't. For myself, I prefer not to play it so safe, and I shall never send for a priest or recite an Act of Contrition in my last moments. I do not mind if I lose my soul for all eternity. If the kind of God exists Who would damn me for not working out a deal with Him, then that is unfortunate. I should not care to spend eternity in the company of such a person.

POLKA

A Memorial Tribute for my Mother and Father

Rose Barle, 1908-1955
Joseph Prosen, 1903-1976

Rose Mary Prosen

They are dancing a polka in heaven.
Their eyes are as bright as they were.
The music is sweet.
They are light on their feet.
There is swinging and stomping.
No hearts weak from pounding.
They are air, they are space, they are sound.

The stars are alarmed in their presence.
The silence regroups in its space.
He is young. She is too.
They are their dream come true.
There is laughing and talking.
No brains worn from thinking.
They are light, they are right, they are true.

The children are feasting at Christmas.
Their thoughts are robust as good wine.
They are old. They are young.
They are six who have found:
There is living and dying.
No hands free from working.
They are his, they are hers, they are theirs.

The city is not what it is thinking.
The houses disguise what it knew:
One plot soaked with life.
A tavern's delight:
There is eating and drinking.
No mouth dry from planning.
It is job, it is home, it is world.

The neighbors are naturally guessing.
Their fears are displayed. They are brief.
There are tears. There are words.
A requiem mass:
There is mourning and mourning.
No eye wet for nothing.
They are live, they are sick, they are new.

The priests are announcing a blessing.
Their words are *rejoice! There is peace!*
The music is minor.
The flowers are festive.
There is sighing and singing.
No one free from his memory.
All are grave, all are slow, all are dear.

Is life less than our bones will make it?
Is it less than our hearts can withstand?
There is clamor and hope.
There is silence and loss.
There is stirring and storing.
No feast without killing.
It is green, it is gray, it is gold.

I hope there are polkas in heaven—
Johann Strauss and his brothers divine,
Accordian bands, the best Viennese hands,
Beer and sausage supreme and pastries of cream.
Oom pa pa! Oom pa pa!
No death without life.
It is once, it is come, it is gone.

CHRONICLE, 1931-1945

Rose Mary Prosen

JULY, 1977

I open the steel ribs of my red umbrella.
It is not yet midnight. The shower of warm rain
Is welcome. The humidity is high: 97. Summer
Hangs. I sigh. My thoughts stray. The black
Sidewalk glitters, unreels frame after frame:

1

I am a little girl. I am wearing a white veil.
It is my First Holy Communion. It is my first
Love affair: Jesus. I adore Him. Every morning
Thereafter, I awake to receive Him. I am happy.

2

My mother makes my dresses. She lines our bureau
Drawers with sachet. She cooks dinner. My father
Gets first choice of the soup meat. My mother
Eats last, always. My sister and I feel proud,
Though she resents my shadow. I am older,
I will be the oldest of six children.

3

There is a Depression. My parents argue about
Money. Beggars come to our door. I do not
Understand their eyes. On the first floor
Of our two-family house, a child dies. There are
Seven brothers and sisters in those four rooms.
The family buys a small white coffin. I do not
Cry. I am alert.

4

I am at my grandmother's house, sleeping in a
Small room upstairs. The walls are whitewashed.
A door from the bedroom opens into the attic.
I am afraid. In our house on the next street
My brother is being born in the front bedroom.
My Aunt Sophie is assisting at the birth. My
Father is happy. He is passing out cigars:
It's a boy! This time, it lives. The decision
Is made: he will be a priest. My mother has a
Shrine to St. Anthony in her bedroom. My brother
is named Anthony. He is special.

5

There is a War declared by the President.
The people love him. Roosevelt will save us.
We collect tinfoil and cans. A second brother
Is born. My father is deferred to work seven days
A week as a defense worker in the steel mill. He
Is happy. He is making more money than he has ever
Made. For four years he comes home only to sleep
And eat. My brothers do not know him. They are
Devoted to my mother who loves them deeply.

6

My sister Margaret is born. The War goes on.
I stay home from school in February to take care
Of the house while my mother is in St. Ann's Hospital.
Two boys from school come to visit me during lunchtime.
I do not open the door. We talk through the chain.
The neighborhood spies tell my father about the visit.
I am indifferent. I am happy to have a new dress:
It is light blue cotton with bright red carnations.
I ordered it from the Sears catalogue. My sister
Margaret is adorable. I am stuck with much of the
Housework. My sister Irma and I split the chores.
The boys are special.

7

I graduate from the eighth grade at St. Lawrence
School. I make a pale blue cotton dress for myself
On the old sewing machine. There are twenty pleats
Across the front of the blouse. My mother does not
Come to the graduation. I am too proud to complain
Or cry. There is a party. That summer my father
Buys a brick house in a different neighborhood.
We will have four bedrooms. The War will be over;
V-E Day. V-J Day. Kathy will be born in November,
One month prematurely. My mother hemorrhages. I
See the bloody bed. I call for an ambulance. My
Father spends every night at the hospital. In ten
Years my mother will die from leukemia. That year
I begin to menstruate. I defy my parents. I want
Independence. My mother throws water into my face.
I will be fourteen.

***

The sidewalk ends. It is late. I close my red
umbrella and step inside my apartment building.
It is still raining, a soft, warm rain. I am tired.
I will sleep.

A POEM FOR OLGA

Rose Mary Prosen

Olga, I don't know you,
but I know how it is
to talk to the stonecutter.
I know his voice.

I know how it is
to walk through the same rooms:
to hear no voice,
and yet always to hear the same voice.

I have looked at the sunrise
for so many years.
I have noticed the flowers.
Lately, I have been thinking
that maybe the sunflower
in my father's old garden
was meant to remind us

that those whom we hold
are never ours, but,
for a while are rooted
and have their place
in the sun. We water
and watch. Our children
pick up the seeds.

THE CREMONA VIOLIN

(After E.T.A. Hoffmann's story)

Lisel Mueller

Two red spots on Antonia's cheeks
gave early warning. So her father-lover,
swearing that she should never
sing again, took down the violin
Amati or perhaps Guarneri made,
as proxy for her voice.

Evenings he played, doors shut to company.
Then her breath rose, eyes glistened, muscles tensed
until, fatigued, she took
a low bow and cried out,
"I never was better, father;
how well you make me sing!"

Priceless to him, those evenings with his daughter
whom neither the world nor another lover
should ever claim again.
Now that she was his instrument,
he learned new subleties of playing,
new ways of tenderness.

From *Dependencies,* © 1965. Reprinted by permission of The University of North Carolina Press.

And killed her with that playing. Her flawed chest
could not abide love's labor. When she died
he broke the singing body into bits,
and hung a cypress wreath
where it had been, and danced
a dance of death, his black crape flying.

Synopsis of *Antonia's Song* from E.T.A. Hoffmann's story (the inspirational source for "The Cremona Violin" by Lisel Mueller.)*

A young law student comes to the town of H. and becomes acquainted with the eccentric Councillor Krespel. He learns that K. has a young woman living with him—Antonia—but their exact relationship is not known. The townspeople tell a curious story about Krespel and Antonia; the night he brought her to his house she sang ravishingly, but since then nobody has ever heard her sing again.

The young man manages to win K's trust and becomes a frequent guest at his house, where he also meets Antonia. K. builds and collects violins, especially valuable old ones which he takes apart to study them. There is one, however, that he has not destroyed; he occasionally plays it for A. The young man is determined to hear A. sing, and one night he almost manages to get her so involved in a conversation about music that she is ready to open her mouth when K. grabs him and pushes him out of the house. He is so mortified that he leaves town.

Two years later he returns on business and comes just as Antonia is being buried. He is convinced that the death is K's fault and seeks him out, accusing him of a crime. K is at first almost amused by this accusation, but then he tells the young lawyer his story. A. was his daughter, the result of a marriage to a famous Italian singer. The marriage had always been kept a secret and was not particularly happy, since the lady had a vile temper. After a particularly unpleasant scene K. leaves her, before the child is even born. He never saw his daughter, although he remained in touch with her mother. In the meantime A. becomes a famous singer herself. After the mother dies, K. goes to get her. The first time he hears the girl sing he realizes—from two red spots on her cheeks—that she is subject to a rare disease which would kill her within a few months if she continued to sing. He asks her never to sing again and she promises that she won't—the exception being that one night he brings her home. A. is devoted to her father and follows all his wishes. Occasionally she asks him to play that one violin for her, since its tone reminds her of her own voice.

One night K. imagines that he hears somebody play the piano in the living room and recognizes the touch of a young composer whom A. once loved. Then A. starts to sing. K. is

*I am grateful to Heidi Rockwood in the Modern Language Department at Georgia Tech for her synopsis of the Hoffmann story. Professor Rockwood's contribution to this anthology entitled "The Best of Two Worlds" is in Unit Ten: *The Immigrant Experience.*

A more detailed analysis of "Antonia's Song" from *Tales of Hoffman* can be found in a work by this same title edited by Christopher Lazare, A.A. Wyn (New York, 1946), pp. 116-138. I am grateful to Eddie Minchew, my former student at Georgia Tech, for suggesting this book.

unable to move and finally faints at the sight of A. and the young man embracing in a halo of blazing light. When he finally awakens he rushes to A's room and finds her lying dead on her bed. Her favorite violin is broken.

"MORE LIGHT"

(Words attributed to Goethe on his deathbed)

For my father

Lisel Mueller

He, too, went down on occasion,
touched land on the pitch-black bottom
of fish that can do without eyes,
tangled with spiny and slimy life,
with creatures all greedy feelers,
all sting, strike, suction,
unknown to moonlight. There must have been times
when there seemed no end to coral gardens
and the imperturbable waving of sea fans
while clamor he had not thought possible
pressed on his eardrums its rhythms
of rancorless lust. To think,
when he pleasure-sailed on the Adriatic
—August afternoons—
atop a mirror that gave of nothing
but his sure, shaved face
and an indestructible sky,
how thin that surface, how impudent!
Salons, of course, and claret and ladies with taste;
walks and sonatas and careful conversations
that could be printed verbatim;
unflinching eyes and a statesman's profile:
but there was restless Werther
and hell-bent, curious Faust.
He must have been there, gone back
to explore the secret canals
of succulent sponges, to drift
by the faint luminescence of stripes,

From *Dependencies,* © 1965. Reprinted by permission of The University of North Carolina Press.

to let his conscience slip off
in the subleties of the dark.
But always the clean, sharp hurt
of remembered sunlight pulled him
clear of a mermaid's breast
toward a place where men try to prove
by courtesy and equations
and by occasional mercy
that there are lovelier creatures
and more delicate pearls.

A VERY SPECIAL PET

Nicholasa Mohr

*Nicholasa Mohr's **El Bronx Remembered** describes the barrio of New York City's South Bronx during the decade of 1946-1956 where, in the kitchen, Joncrofo the chicken lived under the sink and Mami sang sweet, nostalgic songs about Puerto Rico, a beautiful green island far away from the inner city. The short story selected for this anthology is from that work, A National Book Award nominee.*

The Fernández family kept two pets in their small five-room apartment. One was a large female alley cat who was a good mouser when she wasn't in heat. She was very large and had a rich coat of grey fur with black stripes and a long bushy tail. Her eyes were yellow and she had long white whiskers. Her name was Maríalu.

If they would listen carefully to what Maríalu said, Mrs. Fernández assured the children, they would hear her calling her husband Raúl.

"Raúl . . . Raúl . . . this is Maríalu . . . Raúl . . . Raúl . . . this is Maríalu," the children would sing loudly. They all felt sorry for Maríalu, because no matter how long and hard she howled, or how many times she ran off, she could never find her real husband, Raúl.

The second pet was not really supposed to be a pet at all. She was a small, skinny white hen with a red crest and a yellow beak. Graciela and Eugenio Fernández had bought her two years ago, to provide them with their eight children with good fresh eggs.

Her name was Joncrofo, after Graciela Fernández's favorite Hollywood movie star, Joan Crawford. People would repeat the hen's name as she pronounced it, "Joncrofo la gallina."

Joncrofo la gallina lived in the kitchen. She had one foot tied with a very long piece of twine to one of the legs of the kitchen sink. The twine was long enough for Joncrofo to wander all over the kitchen and even to hop onto the large window with the fire escape. Under the sink Mrs. Fernández kept clean newspapers, water, and cornmeal for the hen, and a wooden box lined with some soft flannel cloth and packing straw. It was there that they hoped Joncrofo would lay her eggs. The little hen slept and rested there, but perhaps because she was nervous, she had never once laid an egg.

Graciela and Eugenio Fernández had come to the Bronx six years ago and moved into the small apartment. Except for a trip once before to the seaport city of Mayagüez in Puerto Rico, they had never left their tiny village in the mountains. To finance their voyage to New York, Mr. and Mrs. Fernández had sold their small plot of land, the little livestock they had, and their wooden cabin. The sale had provided the fare and expenses for them and their five children. Since then, three more children had been born. City life was foreign to them, and they had to learn everything, even how to get on a subway and travel. Graciela Fernández had been terribly frightened at first of the underground trains, traffic, and large crowds of people. Although she finally adjusted, she still confined herself to the apartment and seldom went out.

She would never complain; she would pray at the small altar she had set up in the kitchen, light her candles, and murmur that God would provide and not forget her and her family. She was proud of the fact that they did not have to ask for welfare or home relief, as so many other families did.

"Papi provides for us. We are lucky and we have to thank Jesus Christ," she would say, making the sign of the cross.

Eugenio Fernández had found a job as a porter in one of the large buildings in the garment center in Manhattan. He still held the same job, but he hoped to be promoted someday to freight-elevator operator. In the meantime, he sold newspapers and coffee on the side, ran errands for people in the building, and was always available for extra work. Still, the money he brought home was barely enough to support ten people.

"Someday I'm gonna get that job. I got my eye on it, and Mr. Friedlander, he likes me . . . so we gotta be patient. Besides the increase in salary, my God!—I could do a million things on the side, and we could make a lotta money. Why I could . . ." Mr. Fernández would tell his family this story several times a week.

"Oh, wow! Papi, we are gonna be rich when you get that job!" the children would shriek.

"Can we get a television when we get rich, Papi?" Pablito, the oldest boy, would ask, Nellie, Carmen, and Linda wanted a telephone.

"Everybody on the block got a telephone but us." Nellie, the oldest girl, would speak for them.

The younger children, William, Olgita, and Freddie, would request lots of toys and treats. Baby Nancy would smile and babble happily with everybody.

"We gonna get everything and we gonna leave El Bronx," Mr. Fernández would assure them. "We even gonna save enough to buy our farm in Puerto Rico—a big one! With lots of land, maybe a hundred acres, and a chicken house, pigs, goats, even a cow. We can plant coffee and some sugar, and have all the fruit trees—make a lotta money. Why I could . . ." Mr. Fernández would pause and tell the children all about the wonderful food they could eat back in his village. "All you need to get the farm is a good start."

"We gonna take Joncrofo, right?" the kids would ask. "And Maríalu? Her too?"

"Sure," Mr. Fernández would say good-naturedly, "even Raúl, her husband, when she finds him, eh?" He would wink, laughing. "And Joncrofo don't have to be tied up like a prisoner no more—she could run loose."

It was the dream of Graciela and Eugenio Fernández to go back to their village as owners of their own farm, with the faith that the land would provide for them.

This morning Mrs. Fernández sat in her kitchen, thinking that things were just not going well. Now that the holidays were coming and Christmas would soon be here, money was scarcer than ever and prices were higher than ever. Things had been hard for Eugenio Fernández; he was still working as a porter and lately had been sick with a bad throat. They had not saved one cent toward their farm. In fact, they still owed the dry-goods salesman for the kitchen curtains and two bedspreads; even insurance payments were long overdue. She wanted to find a job and help out, but there were still three small preschool children at home to care for. Lately, she had begun to worry; it was hard to put meat on the table.

Graciela Fernández sighed, looking about her small, clean kitchen, and caught sight of Joncrofo running frantically after a stray cockroach. The hen quickly jerked her neck and snapped up the insect with her beak. In spite of all the fumigation and daily scrubbing, it seemed there was always a cockroach or two in sight. Joncrofo was always searching for a tasty morsel—spiders, ants, even houseflies. She was quick and usually got her victim.

The little white hen had a wicked temper and would snap at anyone she felt was annoying her. Even Maríalu knew better; she had a permanent scar on her right ear as a result of Joncrofo's sharp yellow beak. Now the cat carefully kept her distance.

In spite of Joncrofo's cantankerous ways, the children loved her. They were proud of her because no one else on the block had such a pet. Whenever other children teased them about not having a television, the Fernández children would remind them that Joncrofo was a very special pet. Even Baby Nancy would laugh and clap when she saw Joncrofo rushing toward one of her tiny victims.

For some time now, Mrs. Fernández had given up any hope of Joncrofo producing eggs and had also accepted her as a house pet. She had tried everything: warm milk, fresh grass from the park, relining the wooden box. She had even consulted the spiritualist and followed the instructions faithfully, giving the little hen certain herbs to eat and reciting the prayers; and yet nothing ever worked. She had even tried to fatten her up, but the more Joncrofo ate, it seemed, the less she gained.

After thinking about it for several days, this morning Graciela Fernández reached her decision. Tonight, her husband would have good fresh chicken broth for his cold, and her children a full plate of rice with chicken. This silly hen was really no use alive to anyone, she concluded.

It had been six long years since Mrs. Fernández had killed a chicken, but she still remembered how. She was grateful that the older children were in school, and somehow she would find a way to keep the three younger ones at the other end of the apartment.

Very slowly she got up and found the kitchen cleaver. Feeling it with her thumb, she decided it should be sharper, and taking a flat stone, she carefully sharpened the edge as she planned the best way to finish off the hen.

It was still quite early. If she worked things right, she could be through by noontime and have supper ready before her husband got home. She would tell the children that Joncrofo flew away. Someone had untied the twine on her foot and when she opened the window to the fire escape to bring in the mop, Joncrofo flew out and disappeared. That's it, she said to herself, satisfied.

The cleaver was sharp enough and the small chopping block was set up on the kitchen sink. Mrs. Fernández bent down and looked Joncrofo right in the eye. The hen stared back without any fear or much interest. Good, thought Mrs. Fernández, and she walked back into the apartment where Olgita, Freddie, and Baby Nancy were playing.

"I'm going to clean the kitchen, and I don't want you to come inside. Understand?" The children looked at her and nodded. "I mean it—you stay here. If I catch you coming to the kitchen where I am cleaning, you get it with this," she said, holding out her hand with an open palm, gesturing as if she were spanking them. "Now, I'm going to put the chair across the kitchen entrance so that Baby Nancy can't come in. O.K.?" The children nodded again. Their mother very often put one of the kitchen chairs across the kitchen entrance so the baby could not come inside. "Now," she said, "you listen and you stay here!" The children began to play, interested only in their game.

Mrs. Fernández returned to the kitchen, smoothed down her hair, readjusted her apron, and rolled up her sleeves. She put one of the chairs across the threshold to block the entrance, then found a couple of extra rags and old newspapers.

"Joncrofo," she whispered and walked over to the hen. To her surprise, the hen ran under the sink and sat in her box. Mrs. Fernández bent down, but before she could grab her, Joncrofo jumped out of her box and slid behind one of the legs of the kitchen sink. She extended her hand and felt the hen's sharp beak nip one of her fingers. "Ave Maria!" she said, pulling away and putting the injured finger in her mouth. "O.K., you wanna play games. You dumb hen!"

She decided to untie the twine that was tied to the leg of the sink and then pull the hen toward her. Taking a large rag, she draped it over one hand and then, bending down once more, untied the twine and began to pull. Joncrofo resisted, and Mrs. Fernández pulled. Harder and harder she tugged and pulled, at the same time making sure she held the rag securely, so that she could protect herself against Joncrofo's sharp beak. Quickly she pulled, and with one fast jerk of the twine, the hen was up in the air. Quickly Mrs. Fernández draped the rag over the hen. Frantically, Joncrofo began to cackle and jump, flapping her wings and snapping her beak. Mrs. Fernández found herself spinning as she struggled to hold on to Joncrofo, who kept wriggling and jumping. With great effort, Joncrofo got her head loose and sank her beak into Mrs. Fernández's arm. In an instant she released the hen.

Joncrofo ran around the kitchen cackling loudly, flapping her wings and ruffling her feathers. The hen kept an eye on Mrs. Fernández, who also watched her as she held on to her injured arm. White feathers were all over the kitchen; some still floated softly in the air.

Each time Mrs. Fernández went toward Joncrofo, she fled swiftly, cackling even louder and snapping wildly with her beak.

Mrs. Fernández remained still for a moment, then went over to the far end of the kitchen and grabbed a broom. Using the handle, he began to hit the hen, swatting her back and forth like a tennis ball. Joncrofo kept running and trying to dodge the blows, but Mrs. Fernández kept landing the broom each time. The hen began to lose her footing, and Mrs. Fernández vigorously swung the broom, hitting the small white hen until her cackles became softer and softer. Not able to stand any longer, Joncrofo wobbled, moving with slow jerky movements, and dropped to the floor. Mrs. Fernández let go of the broom and rushed over to the hen. Grabbing her by the neck, she lifted her into the air and spun her around a few times, dropping her on the floor. Near exhaustion, Mrs. Fernández could hear her own heavy breathing.

"Mami . . . Mamita. What are you doing to Joncrofo?" Turning, she saw Olgita, Freddie, and Baby Nancy staring at her wide-eyed. "Ma . . . Mami . . . what are you doing to Joncrofo?" they shouted and began to cry. In her excitement, Mrs. Fernández had forgotten completely about the children and the noise the hen had made.

"Oooo . . . is she dead?" Olgita cried, pointing. "Is she dead?" She began to whine.

"You killed Joncrofo, Mami! You killed her. She's dead." Freddie joined his sister, sobbing loudly. Baby Nancy watched her brother and sister and began to cry too. Shrieking, she threw herself on the floor in a tantrum.

"You killed her! You're bad, Mami. You're bad," screamed Olgita.

"Joncrofo . . . I want Joncrofo. . . ." Freddie sobbed. "I'm gonna tell Papi," he screamed, choking with tears.

"Me too! I'm gonna tell too," cried Olgita. "I'm telling Nellie, and she'll tell her teacher on you," she yelled.

Mrs. Fernández watched her children as they stood looking in at her, barricaded by the chair. Then she looked down at the floor where Joncrofo lay, perfectly still. Walking over to the chair, she removed it from the entrance and before she could say anything, the children ran to the back of the apartment, still yelling and crying.

"Joncrofo. . . . We want Joncrofo. . . . You're bad . . . you're bad. . . ."

Mrs. Fernández felt completely helpless as she looked about her kitchen. What a mess! she thought. Things were overturned, and there were white feathers everywhere. Feeling the tears coming to her eyes, she sat down and began to cry quietly. What's the use now? She sighed and thought, I should have taken her to the butcher. He would have done it for a small fee. Oh, this life, she said to herself, wiping her eyes. Now my children hate me. She remembered that when she was just about Olgita's age she was already helping her mother kill chickens and never thought much about slaughtering animals for food.

Graciela Fernández took a deep breath and began to wonder what she would do with Joncrofo now that she was dead. No use cooking her. They won't eat her, she thought, shaking her head. As she contemplated what was to be done, she heard a low grunt. Joncrofo was still alive!

Mrs. Fernández reached under the sink and pulled out the wooden box. She put the large rag into the box and placed the hen inside. Quickly she went over to a cabinet and took out an eyedropper, filling it with water. Then she forced open Joncrofo's beak and dropped some water inside. She put a washcloth into lukewarm water and washed down the hen, smoothing her feathers.

"Joncrofo," she cooed softly, "cro . . . cro . . . Joncrofita," and stroked the hen gently. The hen was still breathing, but her eyes were closed. Mrs. Fernández went over to the cupboard and pulled out a small bottle of rum that Mr. Fernández saved only for special occasions and for guests. She gave some to Joncrofo. The hen opened her eyes and shook her head, emitting a croaking sound.

"What a good little hen," said Mrs. Fernández. "That's right, come on . . . come, wake up, and I'll give you something special. How about if I get you some nice dried corn? . . . Come on." She continued to pet the hen and talk sweetly to her. Slowly, Joncrofo opened her beak and tried to cackle, and again she made a croaking sound. Blinking her eyes, she sat up in her box, ruffled her feathers, and managed a low soft cackle.

"Is she gonna live, Mami?" Mrs. Fernández turned and saw Olgita, Freddie, and Baby Nancy standing beside her.

"Of course she's going to live. What did you think I did, kill her? Tsk, tsk . . . did you really think that? You are all very silly children," she said, and shook her finger at them. They stared back at her with bewilderment, not speaking. "All that screaming at me was not nice." She went on, "I was only trying to save her. Joncrofo got very sick, and see?" She held up the eyedropper. "I had to help her get well. I had to catch her in order to cure her. Understand?"

Olgita and Freddie looked at each other and then at their mother.

"When I saw that she was getting sick, I had to catch her. She was running all around, jumping and going crazy. Yes." Mrs. Fernández opened her eyes and pointed to her head, making a circular movement with her right index finger. "She went cuckoo! If I didn't stop her, Joncrofo would have really killed herself," she said earnestly. "So I gave her some medicine— and now. . . ."

"Is that why you got her drunk, Mami?" interrupted Olgita.

"What?" asked Mrs. Fernández.

"You gave her Papi's rum . . . in the eyedropper. We seen you," Freddie said. Olgita nodded.

"Well," Mrs. Fernández said, "that don't make her drunk. It . . . it . . . ah . . . just calms her down. Sometimes it's used like a medicine."

"And makes her happy again?" Olgita asked. "Like Papi? He always gets happy when he drink some."

"Yes, that's right. You're right. To make Joncrofo happy again," Mrs. Fernández said.

"Why did she get sick, Mami, and go crazy?" asked Freddie.

"I don't know why. Those things just happen," Mrs. Fernández responded.

"Do them things happen on the farm in Puerto Rico?"

"That's right," she said. "Now let me be. I gotta finish cleaning here. Go on, go to the back of the house; take Baby Nancy . . . go on."

The children left the kitchen, and Mrs. Fernández barricaded the entrance once more. She picked up the box with Joncrofo, who sat quietly blinking, and shoved it under the sink. Then she put the cleaver and the chopping board away. Picking up the broom, she began to sweep the feathers and torn newspapers that were strewn all about the kitchen.

In the back of the apartment, where the children played, they could hear their mother singing a familiar song. It was about a beautiful island where the tall green palm trees swayed under a golden sky and the flowers were always in bloom.

BERYL

Lyn Lifshin

My father in his
sister's dark house
chanting like a
Jew, Candles,
5   Friday wine

Everything there has a
peculiar heavy
richness
flushed cheeks and
10   velvet, amber shawls
A fat smell of praying

In Vermont in
rooms plain grey and
wooden
15   I remember his sitting

those nights without
a word and
how he stood in the park,
listening to chestnuts dropping.
20   But not much else

only just now
I'm saying
Beryl, his
sleek Hebrew name,
25   I didn't even know
I knew it

Is that what he
wanted back

or what?

From BLACK APPLES by Lyn Lifshin, The Crossing Press, Trumansburg, New York. Reprinted by permission of the author. (I am grateful to Samuel Bogorad for suggesting that I use Ms. Lifshin's work in my anthology, and also to Larry Rubin, my colleague in the English Department at Georgia Tech, for helping me make the selections. "Seder" and "Never the City's Name" can be found in Unit Seven, RELIGION AND RITUAL and Unit Ten, THE IMMIGRANT EXPERIENCE, respectively.)

WE WISE CHILDREN

Teruko Ogata Daniel

    Sawayo Ono was wearing dark glasses again! Excitedly we clawed and scrambled over each other trying to peek through the bedroom curtains at our next door neighbor. Laboriously, slowly, she knelt on one knee, reached into the oval straw laundry basket and grasped a pillow case, stopped for a rest, and then placing her left hand on her knee once again raised herself sluggishly. Three long clotheslines spanned the dusty yard reaching from the back of the house to the back of the outdoor stairway leading to the porch and backdoor of the second story house. The prolonged difficulty of each of her moves soon bored us and we one by one fell backwards on the beds thinking the same thoughts. . . .

    It was bad enough that she, Sawayo Ono, a married woman of nine children and pushed a clothes hangar, then a knitting needle deep into her insides trying to get rid of a tenth child. This

Reprinted by permission of the author.

we have heard whispered at the Fourth of July picnic by mothers in our Japanese community as they sliced sushi, arranged delicate pink slices of sashimi on lettuce covered platters, and plopped pop bottles of Orange Nesbitt next to the children's paper plates set on picnic tables fluttering beneath sibilant, rustling locust trees at the Volunteer City Park.

She came to eastern Washington state as a picture bride betrothed to Tadashi Ono, a strong but somewhat uncomplicated railroad hand popular among his Japanese co-workers. Sawayo had quickly established a reputation for being moody, difficult, vindictive, and unpredictable. True, she was educated, bright, and attractive; nevertheless, she could have been less proud and patronizing toward her unschooled but hardworking husband. Women resented her blunt dislike of the Japanese community while men feared her biting tongue and contempt for manly accomplishments.

When her first born son drowned at the age of nine in the Columbia River while joyriding on a raft in the company of a white boy, and his remains were delivered to her in a tin container some six weeks later, she denied it was Harry, her son.

"How can you say such a thing? How can you tell without looking at him?" everyone asked, shocked by her rejection. But she didn't answer. She continued obstinately to refuse to claim Harry's remains. "Can't you see? The tin box belongs to the white boy's parents!" Sawayo insisted. Later, after her husband had purchased a lot in the cemetery and painstakingly erected a monument of river stones and mortar, she still stubbornly rejected the truth. On the day of the funeral, county officials brought her a tattered remnant of the plaid shirt Harry had worn that fateful day. It was a shirt she had sewn for him herself. It had been discovered some eighty miles downstream during the course of the search for the other boy whose body was yet unfound. Then and only then did she appear to accept part of the truth, clutching the plaid shreds to her breasts with white knuckles, vacant eyed and half mad with grief. "Can't you see? you have the wrong boy here," she moaned as she stood outside the ring of husband, sons and daughters, and friends gathered about the graveside.

Seven years later when her third son, frail, introverted, and solitary began coughing and running a temperature each morning and late afternoon, the women whispered he would soon die of tuberculosis. It was then that Sawayo refused to attend or participate in the annual New Year's celebration and Japanese School Program, scornfully dismissing it as a gathering of gossiping women and drunken men interested only in spreading malicious lies about her son. Tadashi Ono's failure to control his wife's behavior rocked the community. Excited buzzing swept the women as reports circulated how Tadashi had soundly thrashed Sawayo causing her to take to bed. His loss of face was graciously unmentioned by sympathetic party goers.

Now she had done it again: raged at her husband and seven sons for their failure to gather promptly for mealtimes. Last, she had refused to read the Japanese printed paper delivered in yesterday's mail to her husband after dinner. Maddened by her continual dissatisfactions and airs, Tadashi Ono had grabbed a coal shovel, tripped her when she tried to flee out of the kitchen, struck several murderous blows with the shovel upon her shoulders, flung the coal shovel aside, and then stomped her in the ribs and attacked her with his fists.

So there she was—wearing dark glasses to conceal her blackened eyes. Swollen faced, bruised, and pain ridden she lurched then lunged, falling upon the clotheslines, pinning the flapping pillow cases and sheets. We peeked and then huddled in a circle atop the bed, whispering wisely, and remarked, "That Sawayo! Why can't she be like other mothers and quit causing her family such embarrassment?"

"THE WAYS/THE WAY IT IS" NINE POEMS

Nila Northsun

I. WHAT GRAMMA SAID ABOUT HOW SHE CAME TO THE RESERVATION

> i guess i'll tell you how we came here
> when i was a young girl my
> family lived in duck valley
> my older sister was supposed to get married
> 5   to this young man
> but they waited
> then he saw me &
> liked me better
> but she was older &
> 10   was supposed to marry first
>
> one day he rode up to the house
> i was outside hanging clothes
> he scooped me up on the horse
> & ran away with me
> 15   that is how we got married
>
> we had to move away
> we came here to fallon
> we were the first ones here
> it became the palute-shoshoni reservation
> 20   that is how we came here

II. WHAT GRAMMA SAID ABOUT HER GRANDPA

> he was white grandpa
> his name jim butler
> he's good irish man
> he was nice talk our
> 5   language
> big man with moustache
> boss of town
> tonopah
> he found silver mine
> 10   we still on reservation they
> come tell us 'your grandpa
> found mine' so
> we move to tonopah

Nila Northsun, "The Ways/The Way It Is," from DIET PEPSI, NACHO CHEESE published by Duckdown Press, P.O. Box 996, Carpinteria, Calif. Reprinted by permission of the author.

15   he say 'buy anything you want
      don't buy just little things
      don't just buy candy
      buy something big'
      that's what he used to say
20   4th of july he make
      a great long table
      put sheet over it
      then put all kinds of food on it
      he say 'get your plate &
25   help yourselves'
      he fed all the indians
      he was good man
      but then
      he marry white woman
30   & we go back to reservation

"Two Pima women, Grandmother and granddaughter." By permission of Helga Teiwes, Arizona State Museum, University of Arizona.

III. WHAT GRAMMA SAID ABOUT HER KIDS

when i asked 'gramma why did you have so many kids?'

     oh, i don't know
     maybe because i wanted my mother-in-law
     to like me
5   i had babies
     but they were all girls
     1 2 3 4 5 6 7 8 9 10 11
     eleven girls
     after each one was born
10   mother-in-law would come to visit
     when she'd leave she'd look at all
     the dresses hanging on the clothes line
     shake her head & say
     'when are a pair of pants going to hang up there?'
15   she said this after every visit
     finally
     number 12 was a boy
     & i stopped having kids
     by then
20   mother-in-law was dead

IV. WHAT GRANDPA SAID

     he never said much
     roaming the mountains & desert
     in the daytime looking for precious rocks
     maybe he'd find a silver mine
5   on hot summer days gramma laid
     on a bed under one of the trees
     she'd visit with my mother in the shade
     drinking kool-aid
     smoking salems
10   talking indian
     we made mud pies
     dozens & dozens of mud pies
     take an old pan or jar
     sift dirt thru a piece of screen to weed out
15   twigs & chicken-shit
     and HO!
     perfect mud pie batter
     we'd make little ones
     big ones long ones

20   all kinds of mud pies
       they'd cook up fast in the sun
       when evening started to come
       so did the mosquitoes &
       we all went into the house
25   grandpa would come home
       with a new bag of rocks
       yellow ones
       blue ones brown ones
       all kinds of rocks
30   but he never said much about them
       or anything else

V. WHAT HAPPENED TO GRANDPA

       he was in his early 70's
       still had coal black hair
       when we came to visit from the coast
       we'd bring him a crab he loved crabs
5   gramma didn't like the taste
       or the smell
       after she'd gone to bed
       he'd sit in the kitchen
       under the bare lightbulb
10   & as gently as he could
       crack the shell
       he & my father would visit
       during these late crab-eating hours
       talking about prospecting he loved prospecting

15   one night
       gramma & grandpa were watching
       lawrence welk on t.v.
       grandpa was tapping his foot to
       the music he loved the lawrence welk show
20   but in the middle of a lively polka
       his foot stopped tapping

VI. WHAT GRAMMA SAID AFTER

even after grandpa died
he came to visit gramma
while she slept &
stroked her hair waking
5   her up
—go away
i am trying to sleep—
she pretended she was mad
she was afraid
10   —go away—
made him mad
& he shook the dishes in the cupboard
—stop that
I am trying to sleep—
15   but he kept on stroking
& shaking

moving her bed
from the bedroom to the living room
was the way
20   she finally slept

VII. WHAT GRAMMA SAID LATE AT NIGHT

we would whisper from our beds
'gramma tell us stories'
we all slept in the big living room
my cousin
5   us 3 kids
& gramma
she slept in the living room
now that grandpa died
'gramma tell us stories'
10   she would begin in indian
'no no tell us in english'
sometimes she would
sometimes she wouldn't
my cousin would translate
15   sometimes she would say indian words
if the english ones embarassed her
quithup for shit
bee-zhees for tits
moobee-ship for snot
20   late at night
she'd whisper back from her bed

VIII. WHAT GRAMMA SAID IN THE LAST STORY

'gramma tell us stories'
she whispered something in indian
'cousin what did she say'
all she said was she shook the bed
5   'gramma tell us more'
but that was all
she had no more stories to tell
'ask your mother
she can tell you more'

IX. THE WAY & THE WAY THINGS ARE (FOR GRAMMA)

gramma thinks about her grandchildren:
they're losing the ways
don't know how to talk indian
don't understand me when
5   i ask for tobacco
don't know how to skin a rabbit
sad sad
they're losing the ways

but gramma
10   you told your daughters to
marry white men
told them they would have
nicer houses
fancy cars
15   pretty clothes
could live in the city

gramma your daughters did
they couldn't speak indian anymore
how could we grandchildren learn
20   there are no rabbits to
skin in the city
we have no gramma there to
teach us the ways

you were still on the reservation
asking somebody anybody
25   please
get me tobacco

NIKKI-ROSA

Nikki Giovanni

childhood remembrances are always a drag
if you're Black
you always remember things like living in Woodlawn
with no inside toilet
5   and if you become famous or something
they never talk about how happy you were to have your mother
all to yourself and
how good the water felt when you got your bath from one of
those big tubs that folk in chicago barbecue in
10   and somehow when you talk about home
it never gets across how much you
understood their feelings
as the whole famiiy attended meetings about Hollydale
and even though you remember
15   your biographers never understand
your father's pain as he sells his stock
and another dream goes
and though you're poor it isn't poverty that
concerns you
20   and though they fought a lot
it isn't your father's drinking that makes any difference
but only that everybody is together and you
and your sister have happy birthdays and very good christmasses

and I really hope no white person ever has cause to write
25   about me because they never understand Black love is Black
wealth and they'll probably talk about my hard childhood
and never understand that all the while I was quite happy

THE CLASSROOM AND BEYOND

"Two girls in a school playground." Editor's photograph.

Give me a fish and I eat for a day
Teach me to fish and I eat for a lifetime.

Author and origins unknown.

"FOR DIMES AND QUARTERS"

Monica Krawczyk

Antosia, living in her little four-room house, often dreamed about the whole world. Her big blue eyes sparkled with every new idea, every new thing that came to her. In the old country her mother had often reminded her, "Antosia, be not too bold, for curiosity is the first step to hell. Look what happened to Eve and her apple." When Antosia was leaving her mother's side to venture with her man and their two children into the wilds of America, her mother warned her with a threat in her voice, "Antosia, you are such a crazy one to see . . . to know everything. Just stay home and take care of your man and your children."

She did. But on Sunday she went to church, and after mass she lingered to speak with Zosia Krukowska, who no longer wore old-country shawls. Instead, she paraded a hat with huge red roses. Antosia shook her head. She could not go "downtown" buying new things. No money to spare. She just had to stay at home.

Once a year in early September she felt great joy in making a visit to Columbia School to enroll one of her children in kindergarten. She would comb her thick brown hair and roll it on the back of her head. She would take out her freshly ironed white shawl, and standing before a small wall mirror, she would carefully place it over her head and tie it under her chin. She smiled with the excitement of the visit to school. "Miss Cook," she had said on her last visit, "Today I bring my Jozka. Ah, such a nice big building. I like if I myself come to school. Always I want to learn." Miss Cook laughed. "Why not? We have night school for mothers and fathers, like you." Antosia shrugged her shoulders. "Ah, yes, my man no like if I go. Children small, lots of work." And the curious one that she was, she still hoped and dreamed that some day she would learn to know more of the big new world.

One sunny day in November, Miss Cook called after school, leading Jozka by the hand. Antosia was pleased, for her floor had been neatly scrubbed, there were clean stiffly-ironed curtains to the windows, and there was a row of six loaves of warm good-smelling bread on the table.

"Good afternoon, Mrs. Milewski," Miss Cook greated.

Antosia pulled out a chair, brushed it quickly, and smiling, said, "Miss Cook, I am glad . . . you come to my house."

"Indeed, I am happy too," Miss Cook responded. "What a nice home, clean, comfortable." And after a few remarks about Jozka's progress in kindergarten, she said, "I came to ask if you could find someone to help my mother clean her house."

Antosia was surprised. "I? Find someone?" In the next moment she asked, right out, "Miss Cook, how you like if I come?"

"That would be wonderful, Mrs. Milewski," said Miss Cook. "Mother would be delighted with you . . ." Miss Cook gave her the address and the name of the street car.

Antosia closed the door carefully, and reflected dizzily on this new thing.

She liked Miss Cook's mother, a kind and patient old lady, wearing a black, snug-fitting dress, with a dainty white collar at her neck. And Miss Cook's house was a castle, like in the old country. She saw the sun streaming through tall, wide windows to floors that shone like glass. Chairs with graceful legs were upholstered in heavy flowered brocade. And when Antosia walked over the thick, soft rugs in deep wine colors, she laughed. Like a queen she felt.

But most of all Antosia enjoyed cleaning the library. It was a room full of books, on every shelf from the floor to the ceiling. To Antosia a book was a most precious thing, like her own prayer book. Otherwise, how could she ever say the many beautiful thoughts to God. Books were stories. She lingered in the room with a feeling of admiration, of awe. She handled each book tenderly as she wiped away every speck of harmful dust.

Going home that day she thought of how fortunate she was, for besides living in Miss Cook's home for the seven hours that day, she received good pay for her work. She must not put the money in her purse where it would get mixed with the everyday cash for bread and salt. It must go for something special, something that she could not afford to buy with her man's shoe-mending money.

One day an idea came into her mind. She could save the money for a gift, something new, like a reward for her husband, who each day went into his little shoe shop, and for hours upon hours bent over his work, tearing off old soles and heels from shoes, and sewing and hammering on new ones. Besides, for three evenings a week he went to night school to learn to speak English. Yes, he deserved the reward.

Ah, how she, too, would have liked to have gone to night school, the curious one that ever she was! But her man always objected. "A woman's place is in the home." Still Antosia was not content.

One evening, she said to her husband, "Bring your book home and show it to me. Maybe I could learn, too."

Milewski, a tall, pale, worried man, looked at her with displeasure. "With everything you want to get mixed up," he said. "Better you just watch the kettles on the stove."

By chance one day, Antosia came across her man's book when she was taking coats out of the tall wardrobe for an airing. A bright red book it was, and not very large. During the day after this, in her spare moments, she would sit with Jozef's book in her hand, looking at the words made up of letters that were like the Polish ones in her prayer book, but strangely put together. Smiling, she tried to give them sound.

It was during one such lesson that a loud knock came upon the quiet of the kitchen. Antosia opened the door to a man with a huge book under his arm. He was smooth-shaven and tall, with a good face. He stood with his hat raised.

"Good afternoon, Mrs. Milewski," he greeted cheerfully. "May I come in?" he asked. "I have something to show you."

Antosia liked his manner, her smile gave him a friendly welcome.

Immediately he saw the little red book in her hand. "I see you like to read, Mrs. Milewski," he praised. "I, too, have a book, a big one, with a lot of pictures. May I show it to you? Just sit where you are." Had this agent come with a rug or a brush, Antosia would have said quickly, "No, no, Mister, I do not buy. No money." But a book, one even larger than any in Miss Cook's house—that was another matter.

He picked up Milewski's reader. "Some one goes to night school?"

"Yes, my man," Antosia told him, and added hurriedly, "I learn too, in day time."

"You are wise," he said. "Now this book that I have will help your husband learn his lessons, and you, too. Your children also. I see the little coats and sweaters on the hooks."

"Yes, we got four children. I like if it help my man, and my boys, Franek and Kazek. Girls, they study good."

"Excellent for all of them," he went on. "Every subject, about everything you can think of. And you know what else?" Like the magician bringing out his best trick, he said with emphasis, "A story of every country . . . in the whole world!"

Antosia listened wide-eyed. She asked quickly, "Is there story about Poland, too?"

"Oh, yes." He turned the pages and ran his finger down the index. "Here it is—Poland. Pages and pages about it."

To Antosia it seemed like a miracle. "In that one book?" she asked. "Show me pages, please."

"Not in this volume," he explained. "There are thirty-six such books." Antosia felt hot, her heart pounded. Thirty-six books. . . . He must have the wrong house.

"You don't have to buy them, Mrs. Milewski." He was sitting beside her now, like her man sometimes did, and speaking slowly. "You see, this is a new company. We can deliver all thirty-six books to your house, on trial, to see if you like them. You can keep them as long as you like, while you are trying them out."

"You mean . . . for nothing I try them?" Antosia asked, and was sorry in the next moment that she had asked, for who in this world would give her something for nothing?

"Almost for nothing," he said. "And think of having the story of the world right in your house."

Antosia nodded. She remembered the delight, the wonder she had felt in Miss Cook's library. Then her face dropped.

The salesman must have guessed her thoughts. "You need to pay only two dollars do, and then one dollar or so a month."

Antosia thought hard. Always she sought advice from her man in money matters, like buying a new stove on payment, or an extra bed for her growing children. But Jozef's mind was already heavy with payments on the house, and sick and worried with the three-times-a-week night school. She must not trouble him. Unless, like a flash it came to her mind, it could be out of the extra special savings she had hid away for a gift for her man. The books, to be sure, would be a reward for Jozef! For the children! For herself—for the whole house!

At once once she said, "I pay the two dollars." She went to the reed cheat quickly, and with trembling fingers took out the money. What better use could she make of her savings. . . .

The books came. The truck had backed up to the front door of the house, and two men carried them in heavy boxes, grunting under their weight.

From his shoe shop next door, Milewski ran in. "Some mistake, not?" he asked Antosia.

The men brushed past him to the front room where Antosia directed, and the first box slid to the floor with a heavy thud.

Milewski stood in one spot, pale, his eyes burning with anger. After the men were barely out, he demanded, "What the devil is in there?"

Antosia smiled nervously and touched the first box. "Books."

Like a thunderclap the words struck Milewski. "Are you crazy? Books are not bread. They cost money. . . ."

At first Antosia wanted to walk away. This gift had not come at a good moment. She would have liked them to come when she was alone. Once they had been arranged in their place on the table against the wall, they would have looked alive, like those in Miss Cook's house. Now the books were nailed in a box and her man was making war upon them. She stood still, her hands pinching her apron. She was completely crushed.

"There must be a hundred of them," Milewski stormed. "And who will read them? The children have books at school. I already pay taxes for them. What craziness got into your head? Remember," he shouted, "I do not pay a cent!" He walked out slamming the door.

Her man's words rumbled through her head until it ached. Truly, she was out of her mind. Books cost money, and there were other needs—the clothes wringer needed fixing, Franek had to have new shoes, there was the new dress she wanted to buy for Manka for the school program. But thirty-six books in her house! Suddenly her mouth tightened in determination. The books would be paid from her savings.

Antosia waited anxiously for the children coming from school. Franek was the first to see the boxes. "What's in there? Can I open them? Can I have the boxes?"

"There are many books," Antosia said, as though it were a promise of great joy.

Franek scowled. "Books! What for?" With hammer in hand, he attacked the job of prying the boxes open.

"Careful," Antosia warned, "so you do not hurt them."

Franek laughed. "You can't hurt books."

Manka ran in, the oldest of her children, and eagerly pulled out the first book. "*Mamo,* are these ours? How wonderful! Just look at them. All kinds of topics for my studies. *Mamo,* it's like a library right in our house!"

Little Jozka appeared, with a jumping rope in her hand, and quickly leaned over Manka to see the book. "Oh, Mamo, a whole bunch of pictures to draw. This will be my book."

Kazek was stepping into his overalls, always in a hurry to be out of the house.

"Look at one book, Kazek," Antosia urged. He, too, needed the learning—so wild and rough he was, so full of life.

"Mom, the boys are waiting," Kazek's even teeth sparkled as he talked. "I'm pitcher today," he boasted, patting her hand lovingly. "Honest, I got to go." Like a flash he was out.

"*Mamo,* where did you get them?" Manka asked.

Antosia smiled a little, her husband's slamming of the door still a shadow on her mind. "The books are a present . . . for the whole family," she said. Silently she prayed, "They will all come to them in time."

From this day each morning after the family left, Antosia was down on her knees in the front room, looking over the books, studying the pictures, giving sound to the words. Sometimes she stayed with them so long that the bread dough was running out of the pan, or her lunch was late, or beds had gone unmade. She scolded herself, "Curiosity, woman, will bring you trouble. And the books are here to stay. . . ." It seemed she never could have enough of them.

In the evenings, both Manka and Jozka were quick to reach for a book, and Antosia was pleased and proud that the books were in use.

When Kazek brought his six-weeks report card one day, Antosia frowned. "Kazek, I know the marks would be higher if you studied out of these big books."

"Mom, I learn in school," he said.

"Not enough," Antosia told him. "Try these books."

"Wait till it's winter and too cold out. I'm getting a paper route, too, so I won't have much time. Honest, Mom, the kids are waiting. Say, where's my ball and bat? I left it right here."

Such a one that Kazek was. But Antosia would remind him, let come the first cold day.

Late that same evening, before Milewski had returned from night school, and the others were asleep, Franek was sitting in his father's chair, waiting to talk to his mother. It struck Antosia this moment how much he looked like his father, in his growing up. His blue eyes were wide and soft, his brown hair combed back from his forehead. Something was on his mind.

"Mom, why did you buy all those books?" he asked.

"I thought you would like them, Franek," Antosia said. "From these books you can learn the ways of men. A few years yet and you will be among them, working for your bread."

"I don't like books. For that money I would have liked something else," Franek said.

Antosia's heart ached for this big boy. "What, Franek, would you like for the money?" she asked warmly, putting down her mending.

"Well, Jimmie has some chickens to sell. I would like to raise chickens and I could earn some money selling eggs."

Antosia was not surprised. Franek had his own ideas. She remembered his rabbits and pigeons. He would have no books stuffed into his head.

Franek went on, "Jimmie's family is moving to Wisconsin, so he's got to sell them quick. Two dollars for the six chickens. And you know what else," his eyes were shining with excitement, "his mother says I can have their chicken coop, too. For nothing. Only I have to take it apart. Then I can build my own coop. You know how I learned when I helped Pa build his shoe shop."

Antosia laughed with tears in her eyes. All this planning in Franek's head. He knew what he wanted. And he had a way with growing things! "Franek, tomorrow I will give you the money for the chickens."

"But the books. . . ."

"Miss Cook will have to find me one more cleaning place. Now to bed."

Milewski, for whom the books were meant especially, had not mentioned them since the day they had arrived. In addition to his little red reader, he now carried two other books, one about law, and the other about the constitution of this country.

One evening Antosia, mending Kasek's stockings, watched her man as he sat at the table studying out of his book.

"Tell me, Jozef, what is it you study now?"

He did not answer. Antosia continued her sewing and the room became very still.

Suddenly the book fell out of Jozef's tired hands and his eyes were shut in sleep. His head slowly dropped to his arms on the table. An hour later Antosia helped him to bed, and wondered how he could ever get to the thirty-six books. . . .

The next day Antosia was surprised when a letter came addressed to Mrs. A. Milewski, looking suspiciously like a bill. As soon as Manka came from school, Antosia said, "Read it, Manka, please."

"It says here," Manka read slowly, "for thirty-six books . . . encyclopedia set . . . one hundred fifty-eight dollars."

Antosia put her hand to her face as if someone had struck her. She sat down with a heavy sigh. She recalled the clean-shaven, polite man with all his promises. A bill for one-hundred fifty-eight dollars . . . a punishment for her!

After supper, when she was alone with her man she showed him the bill. Now he must know about it.

"All the time I knew it," Jozef said. "You get nothing . . . for nothing."

He said much more, his eyes flashing angrily at her. "One hundred fifty-eight dollars! You are crazy. From where can we get so much money?"

Antosia took the words to herself calmly and penitently. "You are right," she told him.

The next morning it rained. Today she could not look at the books. They were cold, reminding her only of her great worry. She stacked the breakfast dishes, put on her coat and hurried to school to see Miss Cook.

"I come today for help." Antosia told her story quickly. "I can't pay so much money!" she asserted. "What should I do?"

Miss Cook looked at the bill. "Those are splendid books," she said. "Your family should have them."

"I like to keep them," Antosia said, "but only my man works, fixing shoes. We have expenses, for children, for house, insurance. Sometimes extra, like chickens for Franek or for doctor. Not enough money," she shrugged her shoulders helplessly.

"The children could help when they start working," Miss Cook suggested.

"No, no! My man cannot sleep nights with worry."

"It's true, it is hard," Miss Cook sympathized. "You really don't have to keep the books. Just write and tell them."

"Miss Cook, please, you be so kind and write me letter. Say, thank you very much for trial. . . ."

That evening, as soon as the lamp was lit, Antosia cleared the table and sat to it. This night she must look at the books for the last time.

Jozef had gone to bed, and Franek had not yet come in—he was locking up his chickens. Kazek was sewing on his baseball and both Manka and Jozka were absorbed in the books.

Antosia said to Manka, "Have you finished your studying?"

"No, but I have time until next week. What is it, *Mamo?*"

"Bring out the book that has the story about Poland."

Manka soon opened to the pages and showed Antosia the pictures.

"God give those people health," Antosia said, "for making such nice books. Now see, a *chatka* with a stork on the roof of it. This old, old wooden church could be the one from my village. See this *teatr* building in Warsaw, the *Wawel* in Krakow. And the flag of Poland. . . ." Her throat choked with tears.

"Let me read you the story, *Mamo,*" Manka offered.

She read in a clear young voice, slowly, without hesitation, about the land that Antosia had come from, about all her people, their ideals, traditions, their customs.

A tender loneliness came over Antosia. She was back in Poland, a little girl in her full, wide skirts, picking buttercups in the meadow with the sweet, stirring song of the *slowik* overhead; she was at the carnival dance, with Jozef swinging her in a lively *krakoviak* and whispering sweet words into her ear; she thought of the day when the two of them spoke brief words of parting to their parents, and went forth, far away, to a free land. . . .

Antosia listened intently. How good it was that Manka could read Jozef's and her story now, here, in the language of the free land, of the country that was theirs.

"Copy the address of the company, so you may some day buy these books." Her voice shook as she said, "Soon the truck comes to take them away."

"*Mamo,* no, no!" Manka cried. "We need them. All my lessons. . . ."

Jozka was alarmed. "We won't let them take the books," she said, standing up to the door as if to block the way this moment.

Now Kazek, too, was aroused. "Mom, why do you let them go?" he asked.

Franek walked in. "What's all the noise?"

"Sh . . ." Antosia tried to quiet them. "So you do not awaken Father. The bill came yesterday, for one hundred fifty-eight dollars! The books have to go!"

"How about on payments," Kazek suggested. "I've got a paper route now. I can pay fifty cents or a dollar."

Franek spoke up. "I already talked to the manual training teacher about making a nice bookcase for 'em."

"There, see *Mamo?*" Manka was enthusiastic. "I can help, too, watching the kids for the Canfields. We'll all pitch up our dimes and quarters."

Antosia was delighted as with the taste of milk and honey. Her children knew what was good; her children, all of them, wanted to help save the books.

Two days went by, and no truck arrived. Three days, four, and then on the fifth, there was the knock, cheerful, not heavy-knuckled like that of a truck man.

It really frightened Antosia, for all these days she had been moving about her house with a heavy heart.

She opened the door, and there he was, smooth-shaven, smiling, his hat raised. "How do you do, Mrs. Milewski," he said. "May I come in?"

Antosia stepped back, her face tense with anger. What could he want now, the deceiver! Should she slam the door in his face?

He was rustling a paper. "It's about this letter. . . ."

"I told Miss Cook to write it," Antosia said coldly.

"Yes, I know. You have had the books a while now and that's why I came. I want to know what you think of them?"

"I?" she looked at him, unbelieving. With some hesitation, she said, "I like them very much." Seeing his smile broaden, she added, "And my children, too, like them."

"Then you keep them," he said, emphatically. Before she had a chance to protest, he went on, "Look, how much can you pay a month?"

"You mean. . . ."

"Yes, I mean you should keep the books. Can you pay," he was doing some figuring in a little black notebook, "say three or four or five dollars a month? You get it paid up sooner, that's all. Or, just the two dollars we agreed. We know you're honest."

The gates of heaven were open again and Antosia's heart nearly burst with joy. She wanted to take his hand in hers. "Mister," she said, "you are a good man. How would it be . . . I pay you every month?" On her fingers she counted her children's dimes and quarters; then, after a moment's hesitation, she said, "I pay you every month just how much I can!"

"Very fine, very fine," he told her.

Antosia hardly heard his words. To her, it was a real wonder—the books would remain in her house.

SEE HOW THEY RUN

Mary Elizabeth Vroman

*Mary Elizabeth Vroman became the first black woman accepted as a member of the Screen Writers Guild when this short story "See How They Run" was made into a movie, **Bright Road**, in 1953.*

A bell rang. Jane Richards squared the sheaf of records decisively in the large Manila folder, placed it in the right-hand corner of her desk, and stood up. The chatter of young voices subsided, and forth-three small faces looked solemnly and curiously at the slight young figure before them. The bell stopped ringing.

I wonder if they're as scared of me as I am of them. She smiled brightly.

"Good morning, children, I am Miss Richards." As if they don't know—the door of the third-grade room had a neat new sign pasted above it with her name in bold black capitals; and anyway, a new teacher's name is the first thing that children find out about on the first day of school. Nevertheless, she wrote it for their benefit in large white letters on the blackboard.

"I hope we will all be happy working and playing together this year." *Now why does that sound so trite?* "As I call the roll will you please stand, so that I may get to know you as soon as possible, and if you like you may tell me something about yourselves, how old you are, where you live, what your parents do, and perhaps something about what you did during the summer."

Seated, she checked the names carefully. "Booker T. Adams."

Booker stood, gangling and stoop-shouldered; he began to recite tiredly, "My name is Booker T. Adams, I'se ten years old." *Shades of Uncle Tom!* "I live on Painter's Path." He paused, the look he gave her was tinged with something very akin to contempt. "I didn't do nothing in the summer," he said deliberately.

"Thank you, Booker." Her voice was even. "George Allen." *Must remember to correct that stoop. . . . Where is Painter's Path? . . . How to go about correcting those speech defects? . . . Go easy, Jane, don't antagonize them. . . . They're clean enough, but this is the first day. . . . How can one teacher do any kind of job with a load of forty-three? . . . Thank heaven the building is modern and well built even though it is overcrowded, not like some I've seen—no potbellied stove.*

"Sarahlene Clover Babcock." *Where do these names come from? . . . Up from slavery. . . . How high is up?* Jane smothered a sudden desire to giggle. Outside she was calm and poised and smiling. Clearly she called the names, listening with interest, making a note here and there, making no corrections—not yet.

She experienced a moment of brief inward satisfaction: *I'm doing very well, this is what is expected of me* . . . Orientation to Teaching . . . Miss Murray's voice beat a distant tattoo in her memory. Miss Murray with the Junoesque figure and the moon face. . . . "The ideal teacher personality is one which, combining in itself all the most desirable qualities, expresses itself with quiet assurance in its endeavor to mold the personalities of the students in the most desirable patterns." . . . Dear dull Miss Murray.

She made mental estimates of the class. *What a cross section of my people they represent,* she thought. *Here and there signs of evident poverty, here and there children of obviously well-to-do parents.*

"My name is Rachel Veronica Smith. I am nine years old. I live at Six-oh-seven Fairview Avenue. My father is a Methodist minister. My mother is a housewife. I have two sisters and one brother. Last summer mother and daddy took us all to New York to visit my Aunt Jen. We saw lots of wonderful things. There are millions and millions of people in New York. One day we went on a ferryboat all the way up the Hudson Rover—that's a great big river as wide as this town, and—"

The children listened wide-eyed. Jane listened carefully. *She speaks good English. Healthy, erect, and even perhaps a little smug. Immaculately well dressed from the smoothly braided hair, with two perky bows, to the shiny brown oxford. . . . Bless you, Rachel, I'm so glad to have you.*

"—and the buildings are all very tall, some of them nearly reach the sky."

"Haw-haw"—this from Booker, cynically.

"Well, they are too." Rachel swung around, fire in her eyes and insistence in every line of her round, compact body.

"Ain't no buildings as tall as the sky, is dere, Miz Richards?"

Crisis No. 1. Jane chose her answer carefully. *As high as the sky . . . musn't turn this into a lesson in science . . . all in due time.* "The sky is a long way out, Booker, but the buildings in New York are very tall indeed. Rachel was only trying to show you how very tall they are. In fact, the tallest building in the whole world is in New York City."

"They call it the Empire State Building," interrupted Rachel, heady with her new knowledge and Jane's corroboration.

Booker wasn't through. "You been dere, Miz Richards?"

"Yes, Booker, many times. Someday I shall tell you more about it. Maybe Rachel will help me. Is there anything you'd like to add, Rachel?"

"I would like to say that we are glad you are our new teacher, Miss Richards." Carefully she sat down, spreading her skirt with her plump hands, her smile angelic.

Now I'll bet me a quarter her reverend father told her to say that. "Thank you, Rachel."

The roll call continued. . . . Tanya, slight and pinched, with the toes showing through the very white sneakers, the darned and faded but clean blue dress, the gentle voice like a tinkling bell, and the beautiful sensitive face. . . . Boyd and Lloyd, identical in their starched overalls, and the slightly vacant look. . . . Marjorie Lee, all of twelve years old, the well-developed body moving restlessly in the childish dress, the eyes too wise, the voice too high. . . . Joe Louis, the intelligence in the brilliant black eyes gleaming above the threadbare clothes. *Lives of great men all remind us—Well, I have them all . . . Frederick Douglass, Franklin Delano, Abraham Lincoln, Booker T., Joe Louis, George Washington. . . . What a great burden you bear, little people, heirs to all your parents' stillborn dreams of greatness. I must not fail you.* The last name on the list . . . C.T. Young. Jane paused, small lines creasing her forehead. She checked the list again.

"C.T., what is your name? I only have your initials on my list."

"Dat's all my name, C.T. Young."

"No, dear, I mean what does C.T. stand for? Is it Charles or Clarence?"

"No'm, jest C.T."

"But I can't put that in my register, dear."

Abruptly Jane rose and went to the next room. Rather timidly she waited to speak to Miss Nelson, the second-grade teacher, who had the formidable record of having taught all of sixteen years. Miss Nelson was large and smiling.

"May I help you, dear?"

"Yes, please. It's about C.T. Young. I believe you had him last year."

"Yes, and the year before that. You'll have him two years too."

"Oh? Well, I was wondering what name you registered him under. All the information I have is C.T. Young."

"That's all there is, honey. Lots of these children only have initials."

"You mean . . . can't something be done about it?"

"What?" Miss Nelson was still smiling, but clearly impatient.

"I . . . well . . . thank you." Jane left quickly.

Back in Room 3 the children were growing restless. Deftly Jane passed out the rating tests and gave instructions. Then she called C.T. to her. He was as small as an eight-year-old, and hungry-looking, with enormous guileless eyes and a beautifully shaped head.

"How many years did you stay in the second grade, C.T.?"

"Two."

"And in the first?"

"Two."

"How old are you?"

" 'Leven."

"When will you be twelve?"

"Nex' month."

And they didn't care . . . nobody ever cared enough about one small boy to give him a name.

"You are a very lucky little boy, C.T. Most people have to take the name somebody gave them whether they like it or not, but you can choose your very own."

"Yeah?" The dark eyes were belligerent. "My father named me C.T. after hisself, Miz Richards, and dat's my name."

Jane felt unreasonably irritated. "How many children are there in your family, C.T.?"

" 'Leven."

"How many are there younger than you?" she asked.

"Seven."

Very gently. "Did you have your breakfast this morning, dear?"

The small figure in the too-large trousers and the too-small shirt drew itself up to full height. "Yes'm, I had fried chicken, and rice, and coffee, and rolls, and oranges too."

Oh, you poor darling. You poor proud lying darling. Is that what you'd like for breakfast?

She asked, "Do you like school, C.T.?"

"Yes'm," he told her suspiciously.

She leafed through the pile of records. "Your record says you haven't been coming to school very regularly. Why?"

"I dunno."

"Did you eat last year in the lunchroom?"

"No'm."

"Did you ever bring a lunch?"

"No'm, I eats such a big breakfast, I doan git hungry at lunchtime."

"Children need to eat lunch to help them grow tall and strong, C.T. So from now on you'll eat lunch in the lunchroom"—an afterthought: *Peraps it's important to make him think I believe him*— "and from now on maybe you'd better not eat such a big breakfast."

Decisively she wrote his name at the top of what she knew to be an already too-large list. "Only those in absolute necessity," she had been told by Mr. Johnson, the kindly, harassed principal. "We'd like to feed them all, so many are underfed, but we just don't have the money." Well, this was absolute necessity if she ever saw it.

"What does your father do, C.T.?"

"He work at dat big factory cross-town, he make plenty money, Miz Richards." The record said "unemployed."

"Would you like to be named Charles Thomas?"

The expressive eyes darkened, but the voice was quiet. "No'm."

"Very well." Thoughtfully Jane opened the register; she wrote firmly: *C.T. Young.*

October is a witching month in the Southern United States. The richness of the golds and reds and browns of the trees forms an enchanted filigree through which the lilting voices of children at play seem to float, embodied like so many nymphs of Pan.

Jane had played a fast-and-furious game of tag with her class and now she sat quietly under the gnarled old oak, watching the tireless play, feeling the magic of the sun through the leaves warmly dappling her skin, the soft breeze on the nape of her neck like a lover's hands, and her own drowsy lethargy. *Paul, Paul my darling . . . how long for us now?* She had worshiped Paul Carlyle since they were freshmen together. On graudation day he had slipped the small circlet of diamonds on her finger. . . . "A teacher's salary is small, Jane. Maybe we'll be lucky enough to get work together, then in a year or so we can be married. Wait for me, darling, wait for me!"

But in a year or so Paul had gone to war, and Jane went out alone to teach. . . . Lansing Creek—one year . . . the leaky roof, the potbellied stove, the water from the well. . . . Maryweather Point—two years . . . the tight-lipped spinster principal with the small, vicious face and the small, vicious soul. . . . Three hard, lonely years and then she had been lucky.

The superintendent had praised her. "You have done good work, Miss—ah—Jane. This year you are to be placed at Centertown High—that is, of course, if you care to accept the position."

Jane had caught her breath. Centertown was the largest and best equipped of all the schools in the county, only ten miles from home and Paul—for Paul had come home, older, quieter, but still Paul. He was teaching now more than a hundred miles away, but they went home every other week end to their families and each other. . . . "Next summer you'll be Mrs. Paul Carlyle, darling. It's hard for us to be apart so much. I guess we'll have to be for a long time till I can afford to support you. But, sweet, these little tykes need us so badly." He had held her close, rubbing the nape of the neck under the soft curls. "We have a big job, those of us who teach," he had told her, "a never-ending and often thankless job, Jane, to supply the needs of these kids who lack so much."

They wrote each other long letters, sharing plans and problems. She wrote him about C.T. "I've adopted him, darling. He's so pathetic and so determined to prove that he's not. He learns nothing at all, but I can't let myself believe that he's stupid, so I keep trying."

"Miz Richards, please, ma'am." Tanya's beautiful amber eyes sought hers timidly. Her brown curls were tangled from playing, her cheeks a bright red under the tightly-stretched olive skin. The elbows jutted awkwardly out of the sleeves of the limp cotton dress, which could not conceal the finely chiseled bones in their pitiable fleshlessness. As always when she looked at her, Jane thought, *What a beautiful child!* So unlike the dark, gaunt, morose mother, and the dumpy, pasty-faced father who had visited her that first week. A fairy's changeling. *You'll make a lovely angel to grace the throne of God, Tanya! Now what made me think of that?*

"Please, ma'am, I'se sick."

Gently Jane drew her down beside her. She felt the parchment skin, noted the unnaturally bright eyes. *Oh, dear God, she's burning up!* "Do you hurt anywhere, Tanya?"

"My head, ma'am, and I'se so tired." Without warning she began to cry.

"How far do you live, Tanya?"

"Two miles."

"You walk to school?"

"Yes'm."

"Do any of your brothers have a bicycle?"

"No,m."

"Rachel!" *Bless you for always being there when I need you.* "Hurry, dear, to the office and ask Mr. Johnson please to send a big boy with a bicycle to take Tanya home. She's sick."

Rachel ran.

"Hush now, dear, we'll get some cool water, and then you'll be home in a little while. Did you feel sick this morning?"

"Yes'm, but Mot Dear sent me to school anyway. She said I just wanted to play hooky."

Keep smiling, Jane. Poor, ambitious, well-meaning parents, made bitter at the seeming futility of dreaming dreams for this lovely child . . . willing her to rise above the drabness of your own meager existence . . . too angry with life to see that what she needs most is your love and care and right now medical attention.

Jane bathed the child's forehead with cool water at the fountain. *Do the white schools have a clinic? I must ask Paul. Do they have a lounge or a couch where they can lay one wee sick head? Is there anywhere in this town free medical service for one small child . . . born black?*

The boy with the bicycle came. "Take care of her now, ride slowly and carefully, and take her straight home. . . . Keep the newspaper over your head, Tanya, to keep out the sun, and tell your parents to call the doctor." But she knew they wouldn't—because they couldn't!

The next day Jane went to see Tanya.

"She's sho' nuff sick, Miz Richards," the mother said. "She's always been a puny child, but this time she's took real bad, throat's all raw, talk all out of her haid las' night. I been using a poultice and some herb brew but she ain't got no better."

"Have you called a doctor, Mrs. Fulton?"

"No'm, we cain't afford it, an' Jake, he doan believe in doctors nohow."

Jane waited till the tide of high bright anger welling in her heart and beating in her brain had subsided. When she spoke, her voice was deceptively gentle. "Mrs. Fulton, Tanya is a very sick little girl. She is your only little girl. If you love her, I advise you to have a doctor to her, for if you don't . . . Tanya may die."

The wail that issued from the thin figure seemed to have no part in reality.

Jane spoke hurriedly. "Look, I'm going into town, I'll send a doctor out. Don't worry about paying him. We can see about that later." Impulsively she put her arms around the taut, motionless shoulders. "Don't you worry, honey, it's going to be all right."

There was a kindliness in the doctor's weatherbeaten face that warmed Jane's heart, but his voice was brusque. "You sick, girl? Well?"

"No, sir, I'm not sick." *What long sequence of events has caused even the best of you to look on even the best of us as menials?* "I'm a teacher at Centertown High. There's a little girl in my class who is very ill. Her parents are very poor. I came to see if you would please go to see her."

He looked at her, amused.

"Of course I'll pay the bill, doctor," she added hastily.

"In that case . . . well . . . where does she live?"

Jane told him. "I think it's diphtheria, doctor."

He raised his eyebrows. "Why?"

Jane sat erect. *Don't be afraid, Jane! You're as good a teacher as he is a doctor, and you made an A in that course in childhood diseases.* "High fever, restlessness, sore throat, headache, croupy cough, delirium. It could, of course, be tonsillitis or scarlet fever, but that cough—well, I'm only guessing, of course," she finished lamely.

"Hmph." The doctor's face was expressionless. "Well, we'll see. Have your other children been inoculated?"

"Yes, sir. Doctor, if the parents ask, please tell them that the school is paying for your services."

This time he was wide-eyed.

The lie haunted her. She spoke to the other teachers about it the next day at recess. "She's really very sick, maybe you'd like to help?"

Mary Winters, the sixth-grade teacher, was the first to speak. "Richards, I'd like to help, but I've got three kids of my own, and so you see how it is?"

Jane saw.

"Trouble with you, Richards, is you're too emotional." This from Nelson. "When you've taught as many years as I have, my dear, you'll learn not to bang your head against a stone wall. It may sound hardhearted to you, but one just can't worry about one child more or less when one has nearly fifty."

The pain in the back of her eyes grew more insistent. "I can," she said.

"I'll help, Jane," said Marilyn Andrews, breathless, bouncy newlywed Marilyn. "Here's two bucks. It's all I've got, but nothing's plenty for me." Her laughter pealed echoing down the hall.

"I've got a dollar, Richards"—this from mousy, severe little Miss Mitchell—"though I'm not sure I agree with you."

"Why don't you ask the high-school faculty?" said Marilyn. "Better still, take it up in teachers' meeting."

"Mr. Johnson has enough to worry about now," snapped Nelson. *Why, she's mad,* thought Jane, *mad because I'm trying to give a helpless little tyke a chance to live, and because Marilyn and Mitchell helped.*

The bell rang. Wordlessly Jane turned away. She watched the children troop in noisily, an ancient nursery rhyme running through her head:

> *Three blind mice, three blind mice,*
> *See how they run, see how they run,*
> *They all ran after the farmer's wife,*
> *She cut off their tails with a carving knife.*
> *Did you ever see such a sight in your life*
> *As three blind mice?*

Only this time, it was forty-three mice. Jane giggled. *Why, I'm hysterical,* she thought in surprise. *The mice thought the sweet-smelling farmer's wife might have bread and a wee bit of cheese to offer poor blind mice, but the farmer's wife did't like poor, hungry, dirty blind mice. So she cut off their tails. Then they couldn't run anymore, only wobble. What happened then? Maybe they starved, those that didn't bleed to death. Running round in circles. Running where, little mice?*

She talked to the high-school faculty, and Mr. Johnson. Altogether she got eight dollars.

The following week she received a letter from the doctor:

Dear Miss Richards:

I am happy to inform you that Tanya is greatly improved, and with careful nursing will be well enough in about eight weeks to return to school. She is very frail, however, and will require special care. I have made three visits to her home. In view of the peculiar circumstances, I am donating my services. The cost of the medicines, however, amounts to the sum of $15. I am referring this to you as you requested. What a beautiful child!

Yours sincerely,
Jonathan H. Sinclair, M.D.

P.S. She had diphtheria.

Bless you forever and ever, Jonathan H. Sinclair, M.D. For all your long Southern heritage, "a man's a man for a' that . . . and a' that!"

Her heart was light that night when she wrote to Paul. Later she made plans in the darkness. *You'll be well and fat by Christmas, Tanya, and you'll be a lovely angel in my pageant. . . . I must get the children to save pennies. . . . We'll send you milk and oranges and eggs, and we'll make funny little get-well cards to keep you happy.*

But by Christmas Tanya was dead!

The voice from the dark figure was quiet, even monotonous. "Jake an' me, we always work so hard, Miz Richards. We didn't neither one have no schooling much when we was married—folks never had much money, but we was happy. Jake, he tenant farm. I tuk in washing—we plan to save and buy a little house and farm of our own someday. Den the children come. Six boys, Miz Richards—all in a hurry. We both want the boys to finish school, mebbe go to college. We try not to keep them out to work the farm, but sometimes we have to. Then come Tanya. Just like a little yellow rose she was, Miz Richards, all pink and gold . . . and her voice like a silver bell. We think when she grow up an' finish school she take voice lessons—be like Marian Anderson. We think mebbe by then the boys would be old enough to help. I was kinda feared for her when she get sick, but then she start to get better. She was doing so well, Miz Richards. Den it get cold, an' the fire so hard to keep all night long, an' eben the newspapers in the cracks doan keep the win' out, an' I give her all my kivver; but one night she jest tuk to shivering an' talking all out her haid—sat right up in bed, she did. She call your name onc't or twice, Miz Richards, then she say, 'Mot Dear, does Jesus love me like Miz Richards say in Sunday school?' I say, 'Yes, honey'. She say, 'Effen I die will I see Jesus?' I say, 'Yes, honey, but you ain't gwine die'. But she did, Miz Richards . . . jest smiled an' laid down—jest smiled an' laid down."

It is terrible to see such hopeless resignation in such tearless eyes. . . . One little mouse stopped running. . . . *You'll make a lovely angel to grace the throne of God, Tanya!*

Jane did not go to the funeral. Nelson and Rogers sat in the first pew. Everyone on the faculty contributed to a beautiful wreath. Jane preferred not to think about that.

C.T. brought a lovely potted rose to her the next day. "Miz Richards, ma'am, do you think this is pretty enough to go on Tanya's grave?"

"Where did you get it, C.T.?"

"I stole it out Miz Adams' front yard, right out of that li'l' glass house she got there. The door was open, Miz Richards, she got plenty, she won't miss this li'l' one."

You queer little bundle of truth and lies. What do I do now? Seeing the tears blinking back in the anxious eyes, she said gently, "Yes, C.T., the rose is nearly as beautiful as Tanya is now. She will like it."

"You mean she will know I put it there, Miz Richards? She ain't daid at all?"

"Maybe she'll know, C.T. You see, nothing that is beautiful ever dies as long as we remember it."

So you loved Tanya, little mouse? The memory of her beauty is yours to keep now forever and always, my darling. Those things money can't buy. They've all been trying, but your tail isn't off yet, is it, brat? Not by a long shot. Suddenly she laughed aloud.

He looked at her wonderingly. "What you laughing at, Miz Richards?"

"I'm laughing because I'm happy, C.T.," and she hugged him.

Christmas with its pageantry and splendor came and went. Back from the holidays, Jane had an oral English lesson.

"We'll take this period to let you tell about your holidays, children."

On the weekends that Jane stayed in Centertown she visited different churches, and taught in the Sunday schools when she was asked. She had tried to impress on the children the reasons for giving at Christmastime. In class they had talked about things they could make for gifts, and ways they could save money to buy them. Now she stood by the window, listening attentively, reaping the fruits of her labors.

"I got a doll and a doll carriage for Christmas. Her name is Gladys, and the carriage has red wheels, and I got a tea set and—"

"I got a bicycle and a catcher's mitt."

"We all went to a party and had ice cream and cake."

"I got—"

"I got—"

"I got—"

Score one goose egg for Jane. She was suddenly very tired. "It's your turn, C.T." *Dear God, please don't let him lie too much. He tears my heart. The children never laugh. It's funny how polite they are to C.T. even when they know he's lying. Even that day when Boyd and Lloyd told how they had seen him take food out of the garbage cans in front of the restaurant, and he said he was taking it to some poor hungry children, they didn't laugh. Sometimes children have a great deal more insight than grownups.*

C.T. was talking. "I didn't get nothin' for Christmas, because mamma was sick, but I worked all that week before for Mr. Bondel what owns the store on Main Street. I ran errands an' swep' up an' he give me three dollars, and so I bought mamma a real pretty handkerchief an' a comb, an' I bought my father a tie pin, paid a big ole fifty cents for it too . . . an' I bought my sisters an' brothers some candy an' gum an' I bought me this whistle. Course I got what you give us, Miz Richards" (she had given each a small gift) "an' mamma's white lady give us a whole crate of oranges, an' Miz Smith what lives nex' door give me a pair of socks. Mamma she was so happy she made a cake with eggs an' butter an' everything, an' then we ate it an' had a good time."

Rachel spoke wonderingly. "Didn't Santa Claus bring you anything at all?"

C.T. was the epitome of scorn. "Ain't no Santa Claus," he said and sat down.

Jane quelled the age-old third-grade controversy absently, for her heart was singing. *C.T. . . . C.T., son of my own heart, you are the bright new hope of a doubtful world, and the gay new song of a race unconquered. Of them all—Sarahlene, sole heir to the charming stucco home on the hill, all fitted for gracious living; George, whose father is a contractor; Rachel, the minister's daughter; Angela, who has just inherited ten thousand dollars—of all of them who got, you, my dirty little vagabond, who have never owned a coat in your life, because you say you don't get cold; you, out of your nothing, found something to give, and in the dignity of giving found that it was not so important to receive. . . . Christ Child, look down in blessing on one small child made in Your image and born black!*

Jane had problems. Sometimes it was difficult to maintain discipline with forty-two children. Busy as she kept them, there were always some not busy enough. There was the conference with Mr. Johnson.

"Miss Richards, you are doing fine work here, but sometimes your room is a little . . . well—ah—well, to say the least, noisy. You are new here, but we have always maintained a record of having fine discipline here at this school. People have said that it used to be hard to tell whether or not there were children in the building. We have always been proud of that. Now take Miss Nelson. She is an excellent disciplinarian." He smiled. "Maybe if you ask her she will give you her secret. Do not be too proud to accept help from anyone who can give it, Miss Richards."

"No, sir, thank you, sir, I'll do my best to improve, sir." *Ah, you dear, well-meaning, shortsighted, round, busy little man. Why are you not more concerned about how much the children have grown and learned in these past four months than you are about how much noise they make? I know Miss Nelson's secret. Spare not the rod and spoil not the child. Is that what you want me to do? Paralyze these kids with fear so that they will be afraid to move? afraid to question? afraid to grow? Why is it so fine for people not to know there are children in the building? Wasn't the building built for children?* In her room Jane locked the door against the sound of the playing children, put her head on the desk, and cried.

Jane acceded to tradition and administered one whipping. Booker had slapped Sarahlene's face because she had refused to give up a shiny little music box that played a gay little tune. He had taken the whipping docilely enough, as though used to it; but the sneer in his eyes that had almost gone returned to haunt them. Jane's heart misgave her. *From now on I positively refuse to impose my will on any of these poor children by reason of my greater strength.* So she had abandoned the rod in favor of any other means she could find. They did not always work.

There was a never-ending drive for funds. Jane had a passion for perfection. Plays, dances, concerts, bazaars, suppers, parties followed one on another in staggering succession.

"Look here, Richards," Nelson told her one day, "it's true that we need a new piano, and that science equipment, but, honey, these drives in a colored school are like the poor: with us always. It doesn't make too much difference if Suzy forgets her lines, or if the ice cream is a little lumpy. Cooperation is fine, but the way you tear into things you won't last long."

"For once in her life Nelson's right, Jane," Elise told her later. "I can understand how intense you are because I used to be like that; but, pet, Negro teachers have always had to work harder than any others and till recently have always got paid less, so for our own health's sake we have to let up wherever possible. Believe me, honey, if you don't learn to take it easy, you're going to get sick.''

Jane did. Measles!

"Oh, no," she wailed, "not in my old age!" But she was glad of the rest. Lying in her own bed at home, she realized how very tired she was.

Paul came to see her that weekend, and sat by her bed and read aloud to her the old classic poems they both loved so well. They listened to their favorite radio programs. Paul's presence was warm and comforting. Jane was reluctant to go back to work.

What to do about C.T. was a question that daily loomed larger in Jane's consciousness. Watching Joe Louis' brilliant development was a thing of joy, and Jane was hard pressed to find enough outlets for his amazing abilities. Jeannette Allen was running a close second, and even Booker, so long a problem, was beginning to grasp fundamentals, but C.T. remained static.

"I always stays two years in a grade, Miz Richards," he told her blandly. "I does better the second year."

"Do you *want* to stay in the third grade two years, C.T.?"

"I don't keer." His voice had been cheerful.

Maybe he really is slow, Jane thought. But one day something happened to make her change her mind.

C.T. was possessed of an unusually strong tendency to protect those he considered to be poor or weak. He took little Johnny Armstrong, who sat beside him in class, under his wing. Johnny was nearsighted and nondescript, his one outstanding feature being his hero-worship of C.T. Johnny was a plodder. Hard as he tried, he made slow progress at best.

The struggle with multiplication tables was a difficult one, in spite of all the little games Jane devised to make them easier for the children. On this particular day there was the uneven hum of little voices trying to memorize. Johnny and C.T. were having a whispered conversation about snakes.

Clearly Jane heard C.T.'s elaboration. "Man, my father caught a moccasin long as that blackboard, I guess, an' I held him while he was live right back of his ugly head—so."

Swiftly Jane crossed the room. "C.T. and Johnny, you are supposed to be learning your tables. The period is nearly up and you haven't even begun to study. Furthermore, in more than five months you haven't even learned the two-times table. Now you will both stay in at the first recess to learn it, and every day after this until you do."

Maybe I should make up some problems about snakes, Jane mused, *but they'd be too ridiculous. . . . Two nests of four snakes—Oh, well, I'll see how they do at recess.* Her heart smote her at the sight of the two little figures at their desks, listening wistfully to the sound of the children at play, but she busied herself and pretended not to notice them. Then she heard C.T.'s voice:

"Lissen, man, these tables is easy if you really want to learn them. Now see here. Two times one is two. Two times two is four. Two times three is six. If you forgit, all you got to do is add two like she said."

"Sho' nuff, man?"

"Sho'. Say them with me . . . two times one—" Obediently Johnny began to recite. Five minutes later they came to her. "We's ready, Miz Richards."

"Very well. Johnny, you may begin."

"Two times one is two. Two times two is four. Two times three is. . . . Two times three is—"

"Six," prompted C.T.

In sweat and pain, Johnny managed to stumble through the two-times table with C.T.'s help.

"That's very poor, Johnny, but you may go for today. Tomorrow I shall expect you to have it letter perfect. Now it's your turn, C.T."

C.T.'s performance was a fair rival to Joe Louis's. Suspiciously she took him through in random order.

"Two times nine?"

"Eighteen."

"Two times four?"

"Eight."

"Two times seven?"

"Fourteen."

"C.T., you could have done this long ago. Why didn't You?"

"I dunno. . . . May I go to play now, Miz Richards?"

"Yes, C.T. Now learn your three-times table for me tomorrow."

But he didn't, not that day, or the day after that, or the day after that. . . . *Why doesn't he? Is it that he doesn't want to? Maybe if I were as ragged and deprived as he I wouldn't want to learn either.*

Jane took C.T. to town and bought him a shirt, a sweater, a pair of dungarees, some underwear, a pair of shoes, and a pair of socks. Then she sent him to the barber to get his hair cut. She gave him the money so he could pay for the articles himself and figure up the change. She instructed him to take a bath before putting on his new clothes, and told him not to tell anyone but his parents that she had bought them.

The next morning the class was in a dither.

"You seen C.T.?"

"Oh, boy ain't he sharp!"

"C.T., where'd you get them new clothes?"

"Oh, man, I can wear new clothes any time I feel like it, but I can't be bothered with being a fancypants all the time like you guys."

C.T. strutted in new confidence, but his work didn't improve.

Spring came in its virginal green gladness and the children chafed for the out-of-doors. Jane took them out as much as possible on nature studies and excursions.

C.T. was growing more and more mischievous, and his influence began to spread throughout the class. Daily his droll wit became more and more edged with impudence. Jane was at her wit's end.

"You let that child get away with too much, Richards," Nelson told her. "What he needs is a good hiding."

One day Jane kept certain of the class in at the first recess to do neglected homework, C.T. among them. She left the room briefly. When she returned C.T. was gone.

"Where is C.T.?" she asked.

"He went out to play, Miz Richards. He said couldn't no ole teacher keep him in when he didn't want to stay."

Out on the playground C.T. was standing in a swing, gently swaying to and fro, surrounded by a group of admiring youngsters. He was holding forth.

"I gets tired of stayin' in all the time. She doan pick on nobody but me, an' today I put my foot down. 'From now on', I say, 'I ain't never goin' to stay in, Miz Richards'. Then I walks out." He was enjoying himself immensely. Then he saw her.

"You will come with me, C.T." She was quite calm except for the telltale veins throbbing in her forehead.

"I ain't comin'." The sudden fright in his eyes was veiled quickly by a nonchalant belligerence. He rocked the swing gently.

She repeated, "Come with me, C.T."

The children watched breathlessly.

"I done told you I ain't comin', Miz Richards." His voice was patient, as though explaining to a child. "I ain't . . . comin' . . .a . . . damn . . . tall!"

Jane moved quickly, wrenching the small but surprisingly strong figure from the swing. Then she bore him bodily, kicking and screaming, to the building.

The children relaxed and began to giggle. "Oh, boy! Is he goin' to catch it!" they told one another.

Panting, she held him, still struggling, by the scruff of his collar before the group of teachers gathered in Marilyn's room. "All right, now *you* tell me what to do with him!" she demanded. "I've tried everything." The tears were close behind her eyes.

"What'd he do?" Nelson asked.

Briefly she told them.

"Have you talked to his parents?"

"Three times I've had conferences with them. They say to beat him."

"That, my friend, is what you ought to do. Now he never acted like that with me. If you'll let me handle him, I'll show you how to put a brat like that in his place."

"Go ahead," Jane said wearily.

Nelson left the room, and returned with a narrow but sturdy leather thong. "Now, C.T."—she was smiling, tapping the strap in her open left palm—"go to your room and do what Miss Richards told you to."

"I ain't gonna, an' you can't make me." He sat down with absurd dignity at a desk.

Still smiling, Miss Nelson stood over him. The strap descended without warning across the bony shoulders in the thin shirt. The whip became a dancing demon, a thing posssssed, bearing no relation to the hand that held it. The shrieks grew louder. Jane closed her eyes against the blurred fury of a singing lash, a small boy's terror, and a smiling face.

Miss Nelson was not tired. "Well, C.T.?"

"I won't. Yer can kill me but I *won't!*"

The sounds began again. Red welts began to show across the small arms and through the clinging sweat-drenched shirt.

"Now will you go to your room?"

Sobbing and conquered, C.T. went. The seated children stared curiously at the little procession. Jane dismissed them.

In his seat C.T. found pencil and paper.

"What's he supposed to do, Richards?"

Jane told her.

"All right, now write!"

C.T. stared at Nelson through swollen lids, a curious smile curving his lips. Jane knew suddenly that come hell or high water, C.T. would not write. *I musn't interfere. Please, God, don't let her hurt him too badly. Where have I failed so miserably? . . . Forgive us our trespasses.* The singing whip and the shrieks became a symphony from hell. Suddenly Jane hated the smiling face with an almost unbearable hatred. She spoke, her voice like cold steel.

"That's enough, Nelson."

The noise stopped.

"He's in no condition to write now anyway."

C.T. stood up. "I hate you. I hate you all. You're mean and I hate you." Then he ran. No one followed him. *Run, little mouse!* They avoided each other's eyes.

"Well, there you are," Nelson said as she walked away. Jane never found out what she meant by that.

The next day C.T. did not come to school. The day after that he brought Jane the fatal homework, neatly and painstakingly done, and a bunch of wild flowers. Before the bell rang, the children surrounded him. He was beaming.

"Did you tell yer folks you got a whipping, C.T.?"

"Naw! I'd 'a' only got another."

"Where were you yesterday?"

"Went fishin'. Caught me six cats long as your haid, Sambo."

Jane buried her face in the sweet-smelling flowers. *Oh, my brat, my wonderful resilient brat. They'll never get your tail, will they?*

It was seven weeks till the end of term when C.T. brought Jane a model wooden boat.

Jane stared at it. "Did you make this? It's beautiful, C.T."

"Oh, I make them all the time . . . an' airplanes an' houses too. I do 'em in my spare time," he finished airily.

"Where do you get the models, C.T.?" she asked.

"I copies them from pictures in the magazines."

Right under my nose . . . right there all the time, she thought wonderingly. "C.T., would you like to build things when you grow up? Real houses and ships and planes?"

"Reckon I could, Miz Richards," he said confidently.

The excitement was growing in her. "Look, C.T. You aren't going to do any lessons at all for the rest of the year. You're going to build ships and houses and airplanes and anything else you want to."

"I am, huh?" He grinned. "Well, I guess I wasn't goin' to get promoted nohow."

"Of course, if you want to build them the way they really are, you might have to do a little measuring, and maybe learn to spell the names of the parts you want to order. All the best contractors have to know things like that, you know."

"Say, I'm gonna have real fun, huh? I always said lessons wussent no good nohow. Pop say too much study eats out yer brains anyway."

The days went by. Jane ran a race with time. The instructions from the model companies arrived. Jane burned the midnight oil planning each day's work:

Learn to spell the following words: ship, sail, steamer—boat, anchor, airplane wing, fly.

Write a letter to the lumber company, ordering some lumber.

The floor of our model house is ten inches wide and fourteen inches long. Multiply the length by the width and you'll find the area of the floor in square inches.

Read the story of Columbus and his voyages.

Our plane arrives in Paris in twenty-eight hours. Paris is the capital city of a country named France across the Atlantic Ocean.

Long ago sailors told time by the sun and the stars. Now, the earth goes around the sun—

Work and pray, work and pray!

C.T. learned. Some things vicariously, some things directly. When he found that he needed multiplication to plan his models to scale, he learned to multiply. In three weeks he had mastered simple division.

Jane bought beautifully illustrated stories about ships and planes. He learned to read.

He wrote for and received his own materials.

Jane exulted.

The last day! Forty-two faces waiting anxiously for report cards. Jane spoke to them briefly, praising them collectively, and admonishing them to obey the safety rules during the holidays. Then she passed out the report cards.

As she smiled at each childish face, she thought, *I've been wrong. The long arm of circumstance, environment, and heredity is the farmer's wife that seeks to mow you down, and all of us who touch your lives are in some way responsible for how successful she is. But you aren't mice, my darlings. Mice are hated, hunted pests. You are normal, lovable children. The knife of the farmer's wife is double-edged for you because you are Negro children, born mostly in poverty. But you are wonderful children, nevertheless, for you wear the bright protective cloak of laughter, the strong shield of courage, and the intelligence of children everywhere. Some few of you may indeed become as the mice—but most of you shall find your way to stand fine and tall in the annals of men. There's a bright new tomorrow ahead. For every one of us whose job it is to help you grow that is insensitive and unworthy there are hundreds who daily work that you may grow straight and whole. If it were not so, our world could not long endure.*

She handed C.T. his card.

"Thank you, ma'am."

"Aren't you going to open it?"

He opened it dutifully. When he looked up, his eyes were wide with disbelief. "You didn't make no mistake?"

"No mistake, C.T. You're promoted. You've caught up enough to go to the fourth grade next year."

She dismissed the children. They were a swarm of bees released from a hive. "'By, Miss Richards." . . . "Happy holidays, Miss Richards."

C.T. was the last to go.

"Well, C.T.?"

"Miz Richards, you remember what you said about a name being important?"

"Yes, C.T."

"Well, I talked to mamma, and she said if I wanted a name it would be all right, and she'd go to the courthouse about it."

"What name have you chosen, C.T.?" she asked.

"Christopher Turner Young."

"That's a nice name, Christopher," she said gravely.

"Sho'nuff, Miz Richards?"

"Sure enough, C.T."

"Miz Richards, you know what?"

"What, dear?"

"I love you."

She kissed him swiftly before he ran to catch his classmates.

She stood at the window and watched the running, skipping figures, followed by the bold mimic shadows. *I'm coming home, Paul. I'm leaving my forty-two children, and Tanya there on the hill. My work with them is finished now.* The laughter bubbled up in her throat. *But Paul, oh Paul. See how straight they run!*

THE PROPER THING TO SAY, TO DO AND TO WEAR

Ann C. Hooper

I spent my childhood in a large, southern city where my family lived comfortably in an academic and cultured environment. Our economic status enabled us to avoid much of the humiliation caused by segregation. Summer vacations were spent in northern cities; we traveled by plane or in Pullman drawing rooms. My father tipped redcaps who took us directly to our train accommodations, thus allowing a swift passage through the colored entrance and waiting room. Because of the crowded conditions and other inequities at the only black high school, my parents decided to send me to an exclusive boarding school in a nearby state, seeking for me the best that was available at the time. I was twelve years old, and the year was 1944.

The founder and president of this exclusive school was a dynamic black woman, educated in a large New England school system. Her philosophy was to teach black boys and girls how to be cultured, how to act like refined white people—how to be acceptable in white society. She frequently said in her lengthy addresses to the student body, "I look in the mirror at myself and say, 'There is nothing black about me but the color of my skin. I am as cultured and refined as any white person'. "It's all right," she used to say, "for a white woman to smoke in public because white women have arrived." Since black women hadn't arrived in her opinion, smoking in public was gross. When I did smoke, I never smoked in public. I was not sure whether I had arrived or not.

Reprinted by permission of the author.

Ivy covered buildings and yellow cottages nestled among the trees created a New England atmosphere where amidst many rules and regulations, we were taught "The Proper Thing to Say, to Do and to Wear," the title of one of the president's publications. Responding courteously to adults was the first lesson learned upon arrival. We were commanded to say "Yes, Mrs. So and So, or No, Mr. So and So." Never were we to reply to an adult with a simple "yes" or "no." Proper dress in or out of the dormitory was rigorously enforced. To this day, I have never left my bedroom without being fully clothed or wearing a housecoat, always remembering that being in the dormitory hall improperly clad was an infraction costing one demerit. Fifteen demerits meant expulsion. Furthermore, we were required to wear a hat, gloves, and stockings (no socks) on our infrequent shopping trips to town on the rickety school bus. The same dress was required for our train trips home. There is no doubt, however, that proper dress in public was necessary for a black person to be treated with respect at that time.

Mealtime comprised a most important aspect of our development. The girls entered the dining hall through one door and the boys another. Complete silence was the rule. We had to be standing behind our chairs before the outside bell stopped ringing. Then the student headwaiter signaled the pianist to strike the beginning chord and we all sang the grace. The boys helped the girls to be seated, and we were ready to dine at very properly set tables. First of all, we placed our half-folded napkins across our laps. Student waiters, well versed in the art of serving, brought the food. The dietician patrolled the aisles between the tables watching for flaws in our table manners. She would not hesitate to tell us to keep one hand in our lap, to place our knife across the top of the plate, not to lean back in the chair, to cut no more than three pieces of meat at a time, or to talk in conversational tones. We ate family style at tables of ten, with a student host and hostess at each end. The hostess served a plate which was passed to her right down to the host who served what was at his end, and then the plate was passed on down to the person sitting to the left of the hostess. No one could start eating until everyone was served. Every meal was filled with ceremony. When the meal was over, the headwaiter made announcements, and we filed out silently. After the evening meal, the whole student body sang "Now the Day Is Over" or "Day Is Dying in the West." All eyes had to be closed while the evening hymn was sung. Failure to have them closed resulted in a reprimand. This was intended to put us in a thoughtful mood, ready for the study period which lasted until 9:30 P.M.

The president realized the importance of high morale and esprit de corps in a boarding school environment. Several times a month, jollification was held after the evening meal. The pianist went to the piano, and the jollification leaders circulated between the tables clapping their hands while we sang pep songs such as "The Marine Hymn," "Anchors Aweigh," or "Pack Up Your Troubles." Certain girls led us in yells or cheers for the basketball coach and team before or after games, to welcome a guest, or to greet the president upon her return from a speaking tour, and on other occasions. We always recognized accomplishments by students and teachers.

Once a month, there was a formal dinner. Boys wore navy blue suits, and girls wore long dresses. After the usual meal, we sang songs such as "Just a Song at Twilight" or "There's a Long, Long Trail Awinding." There was usually a program which consisted of poems, recitations, and musical selections. I can remember being part of a quartet that sang "Red Sails in the Sunset." The school choir gave its first rendition of "Battle Hymn of the Republic" at a formal dinner. Everyone who had a birthday during that month sat at a special table where they had a special dessert. The rest of us didn't have to sit in our assigned seats either. Eating with our closest friends enhanced this "gala" affair.

Moreover, the Literary Society convened once a month. The program, was usually devoted to one author. There were musical selections which ranged from the boys' quartet singing "Sleep Kentucky Babe" to "Sylvia" by the girls' ensemble.

A tea was held once a month in the living room of the president's cottage, class by class. Properly attired, we recited such poems as "Snowbound" by Whittier and Longfellow's "Hiawatha." Piano selections played on the president's grand piano included numbers by Chopin, Bach, Beethoven, and Schumann—the usual recital numbers. Most of the girls took piano lessons. Such games as "The Moon Is as Round as a Cheese" and "I pass these Scissors to You Crossed" were played. The trick of the first game was to recite the ditty while making a circle with the left hand. The trick of the latter game entailed passing scissors with the ankles crossed and receiving them with the ankles uncrossed. "Fruit Basket" or other similar alphabet games were played, all reminiscent of Mme de Rambouillet's salon.

Every student was required to appear on a program. The annual declamation contest was primarily for students who had not participated in a program during the year. Seven or eight students sat in a semi-circle on the stage, each coming to the podium for his or her speech. The talks came from a dog earred book belonging to the English teacher. The topics resembled those of Aesop's fables; each speech had a moral at the beginning or the end. The chairman of the judging committee, which was made up of faculty and staff, announced the first, second, and third place winners at the end of the program.

Sunday school in the chapel, followed by church across the highway, began our Sundays. There was a student Sunday school superintendent and a secretary. After singing "Stand Up, Stand Up for Jesus," "O, Worship the King" or a similar hymn, the student body went to various classrooms where the day's lesson was discussed. On reassembling, the secretary counted the collection and a banner was placed in the aisle adjacent to the class that donated the most money. The white frame church across the highway was a typical rural church in appearance. However, the service was quiet and refined. The minister, who was associated with the school, gave an intellectual sermon. The church choir, composed of select members of the school choir, led the hymns and rendered special seections by Handel, Bach, and the usual secular composers. A Negro spiritual was sung while collection was taken up and when communion was served. Occasionally, the dietician or a member of the community would add a verse to a spiritual. This was the only "soulful" element about our otherwise sophisticated service. This, too, underlines the stark contrast between the school and the rural community surrounding it.

Each holiday was celebrated by a traditional program attended by people from the community and neighboring towns, featuring the renowned choir and musical selections sung by the whole student body. The entire school rehearsed on Friday mornings. We were especially adept at singing Negro spirituals such as "Ain't Gonna Study War No More," "Couldn't Hear Nobody Pray," and "Wade in the Water." Our repertoire was endless. When the board of trustees (composed of affluent white men) met, our singing brought tears to their eyes, inspiring them to make generous contributions. This was the purpose of our singing. We could be convened at a moment's notice to sing for any visitor who was a potential benefactor. The president would call the student soloist to come down to the front of the chapel, and she would direct the singing for the visitors who usually sat on the stage.

The work ethic took priority in our development. We did all of the cleaning and maintenance. Every student had duty work in one of the buildings, on the grounds or in the dining hall. Duty work in the buildings ranged from cleaning the glass panels in the hall doors, to mopping the bathroom. Working in the pantry was the most sought after job by the girls. This meant that it wasn't necessary to return directly to the dormitory after meals and that the opportunity might arise to converse with the waiters. The positions of headwaiter, supervisor of the pantry, and supervisor of the school building janitors were prestigious and coveted, going to students with the most leadership ability. On the other hand, formal academic studies did not occupy top priority, there always being a lack of teachers with proper credentials. Even at that time, well-qualified teachers preferred urban areas, and the president treated the staff like children too. However, since the word "education" is derived from the Latin word "to draw out," one can say with certainty that we were totally educated through this regime.

During the school day, no one was allowed to return to the dormitory because we were all supposed to be in one place or the other. Going back and forth was discouraged. The girls, however, were allowed to return at lunch time on certain days when a change was necessary. Ostensibly, to keep track of the girls who entered the dorm, it was required that each girl sign the period book which was kept in the matron's office. It resembled a ledger, and a quick glance confirmed the regularity or lack of regularity of every girl. During my five years' tenure, no girl had to skip this monthly signing-in ritual because of pregnancy.

One day, the president announced that a student was coming from Nigeria, West Africa. We eagerly awaited her arrival. As soon as she deplaned, she was rushed to a beauty parlor where her natural hair was straightened. Therefore, when she arrived on campus, she didn't look exactly as we had expected. Although her natural hairstyle was a part of her culture, it was not an acceptable coiffure at that time in our milieu. Keeping our hair straightened, curled, and in a becoming style occupied an inordinate amount of our time. If this student brought native garb or jewelry, she never felt inclined to wear it in our midst. No one evidenced great interest in her Nigerian culture either.

We were a select group, all the children of affluent people. In retrospect, our discipline problems were minor compared to those of high schools of today. Furthermore, we were well mannered upon our arrival at this school. However, in the struggle for civil rights, becoming acceptable in white society sometimes had to be carried to the extreme. Emphasis on refinement, on keeping property clean and well kept, and on proper dress and decorum in private or in public was all a part of the battle for equality. Learning how to stand up and speak or perform in front of an audience was useful, and no doubt enabled some of us to open doors previously closed. I will never regret the years that I spent at this school; I will always cherish the friendships that I formed there. My only regret is that the president did not live until the day when it is no longer necessary to deny black heritage. Now she would be able to say, "My skin is black, and I am proud of it." No longer does the American life style, coupled with the melting pot syndrome, pressure anyone into being ashamed of her color or kinky hair. However, as I look back over this experience, it becomes more and more evident that although many aspects of our training were exaggerated, they basically were fundamental things which enable people to get along with each other in a pluralistic society—in any society.

GRANDMOTHER SKOGLUND'S ADVICE TO LYNG AND THE UNIVERSITY EXPERIENCE

Borghild Dahl

Borghild Dahl's **Homecoming** *focuses upon the warm family life of a high spirited girl whose parents had migrated from Norway to Minnesota and of her dreams and ambitions in the new-world environment providing freedom and educational opportunities for her where they would not have existed for a woman in Norway at that time. Excerpts from chapter four and chapter five of the book describe the strong will and wisdom of Grandmother Skoglund as she compares economic possibilities for young people in Norway and in America.*

After the boys had left, Grandmother Skoglund and Lyng's mother and Lyng sat chatting. Lyng's mother was in excellent spirits. She told about an outing she and some other young people had had at their chalet in the mountains of Norway.

"It was the first time Markus told me he loved me," she said blushing. "What a time we did have!"

"How would you like a cup of coffee and a sugar lump?" Lyng suggested after a little. "The jug is still warm."

She rinsed out three cups and filled them with coffee and passed cream and sugar.

"You spoil all of us," Grandmother Skoglund said contentedly.

It was cool and pleasant under the big tree. Already long shadows had begun to stretch down over the green knoll.

"Now I am going to tell you about something wonderful that happened to me yesterday," Lyng said.

Her mother looked at her inquiringly. Grandmother Skoglund leaned forward.

"Yes," Lyng said. "I've been promoted at the Emporium. Mr. Cotton called me up to his office. He said that, beginning Monday, I am to be taken on permanently as a regular clerk at the store, and I'm to get the same salary as the others who have been working there for years. Isn't that wonderful?"

Lyng's mother set her cup down so hard that the coffee spilled and soaked into the cake on her plate. "No daughter of mine is going to spend her life clerking in a store," she said. "Do you suppose for a minute I would have allowed you to start working at the Emporium last spring, if I hadn't been sure you would eventually come to your senses? That you would realize you were out of your own class, working side by side with the rabble? Your father and I didn't leave everything that was dear to us back in Norway and come to this huge, unfriendly, foreign land only to have humiliation heaped on the heads of our children."

"Humiliation? Why, Mother, it's a promotion. Viola Ryan, the other cash girl, would give her right arm for the chance I'm getting. And she's worked there much longer than I have."

"Then why do you suppose this man—Mr. Cotton—why do you suppose he picked you out especially for this grand job you're telling us about? What do you suppose that other cash girl will say about the two of you behind your backs?"

"Mother, you have no right to insinuate—"

"Lyng," Grandmother Skoglund interrupted quietly. "Let's not spoil this day with an argument. We were having such a beautiful time."

"But I have to talk about this now," Lyng insisted. "Mr. Cotton expects me to start tomorrow morning."

"Last spring when you asked permission to work there," Lyng's mother said, "you made it clear that all you wanted was to earn money enough to buy clothes so that you would look like every other girl your age. Although, as I told you then, why this should give you so much satisfaction is beyond me."

"Mother, you have been saying lately how slow things are getting at the shop. Suppose some day there won't be any work for you up there? Can't you understand how important it is for me to have a steady job at a nice place like the Emporium?"

"It isn't a nice place and you know it. Lyng, you are not going to work at that store after the fifteenth of September."

"What do you want me to do then? Sit at home and eat off you?"

"No, you are going to the University of Minnesota."

Lyng set her cup down on the cloth that had served as their table. "Mother, even you ought to know that is impossible."

"Why is it impossible? Ever since your father died—it's thirteen years now—have you lacked anything? Haven't you had a roof over your head and a clean bed to sleep in and three nourishing meals a day?"

"It isn't fair to you, Mother. Nor to Grandmother Skoglund. She hasn't been at all well lately and—"

"Lyng," Grandmother Skoglund pleaded again. Then she sat up straight. "Your mother is right. You must go to the university."

Lyng stared at her unbelievingly. "Not you, too, Grandmother Skoglund. Surely you understand how hard it has been."

"Of course, I do. So does your mother, only sometimes you two don't seem to understand each other. It has made it nice for all of us, Lyng, the way you have brought home money this summer. But being a clerk isn't going to get you anywhere. That is what your mother is trying to tell you."

"If I'm a clerk, we'll at least live."

Grandmother Skoglund moved closer to Lyng. "If your father could have been with us today, he would have sided with your mother and me. Hard as he had to work as a newcomer in this country, trying to make both ends meet, he was always studying. 'Learn so you can earn,' he repeated over and over. 'In America even the poorest peasant can do both, if he has the will.'" Grandmother Skoglund had been speaking Norwegian, but this last she quoted in her halting English. Then, reverting to the Norwegian, she went on, "For years he kept going to that school for Norwegian boys that Mr. Skurdalsvold had in his barn. Your father didn't have the money to buy his own books so he rented the ones he needed from Mr. Skurdalsvold, and you should have seen how he pored over them. He took them along when he went to work so he could study on the streetcar or any spare minute he might have at noon. And no matter how late he returned from work and how tired he was, out came the books again before he went to bed. Oh, your father certainly believed in learning.''

For several minutes no one said anything. From the lake came the putting of the gasoline launches and the shrill whistle of the coal steamer.

Grandmother Skoglund raised her eyes to Lyng's. "Surely," she said, "you who are born in America and have had the advantage of growing up in this wonderful country, know better than to throw away your birthright."

There was a long silence.

Grandmother Skoglund laid her hand on Lyng's arm. "Lyng," she said so softly that it was almost a whisper, "if I ask you to do it for my sake, won't you go to the university?"

Lyng stirred uneasily. In all her life, Grandmother Skoglund had never asked a favor of her.

"If I do, how are we going to manage?"

Grandmother Skoglund smiled. "We must all work together. You, Reidun, if you expect Lyng to continue at school, must do your share." Lyng's mother opened her mouth as if to speak, but Grandmother Skoglund continued. "Oh, I don't mean about yourself, Reidun. It's about the boys. I have felt for some time that they should contribute something toward the upkeep of the household."

"They worked over at their aunts' yesterday," Lyng's mother said. "Remember, they are still growing and need plenty of rest."

"Markus worked from the time he could manage the sheep and the cattle," Grandmother Skoglund said. "He couldn't have been more than nine years old at the time. It will do Haakon good to realize that he is going to have to work for a living. And being busy will help to keep Kristian out of mischief."

"Haakon works hard at school," Lyng's mother insisted. "He brings home good marks."

"So does Kristian," Grandmother Skoglund siad. "At least they aren't bad. But when Lyng was much younger than the boys are now, she was expected to help with the work at home."

"What could the boys do?" Lyng's mother demanded.

"Bert Fleming always has jobs," Lyng said. "He's had a paper route for years, and now he works at the macaroni factory over on Franklin Avenue on Saturdays."

"Haakon isn't strong enough to work at a factory," Lyng's mother said.

Lyng stood up. "All right," she said. "I'll go back to school on one condition. That Haakon and Kristian get some kind of work, and that you, Mother, will promise not to coddle them and let them quit when the going gets a little hard."

"Of course, the boys will get jobs and be told they are expected to make good," Grandmother Skoglund said. "You won't have to worry about them, Lyng. They're fine boys, both of them." With difficulty she got to her feet. "I'm as stiff and bent as a corkscrew," she said laughing and brushing off the back of her dress. "I'm not used to sitting on the ground these days." She looked at the sun. "It's really getting late. We ought to start for home."

Lyng put her arm around Grandmother Skoglung's waist and drew her closer. Then she leaned down and touched Grandmother Skoglund's cheek with her own. In the whole world there was no one she loved quite as much as Grandmother Skoglund.

. . .

Lyng leaned on the banister and pulled herself up the steps leading to the main reading room of the university library. When she reached the top, she stopped to rest. She might as well give up. For a month now she had been under the load of trying to attend the university and help at home, and she had done a poor job of both.

She had known from the start that it couldn't be done. She should have had more backbone than to give in. But when Grandmother Skoglund begged her, as a special favor, it hadn't been easy to refuse her. If Grandmother Skoglund were to express an earnest desire to fly to the moon, Lyng supposed she would do her best to help her to get there.

But this afternoon Lyng knew she was facing an impossible situation. Her long paper in rhetoric was due tomorrow and so far she had done nothing except select a topic. She had chosen to write on Alfred the Great because he belonged to the history of England. Miss Scherf, the rhetoric teacher, only had to mention a person or an event that had figured in American history and up went a dozen hands. Lyng wouldn't risk revealing her ignorance by venturing to write on anything American.

Perhaps she should have talked the matter over with Miss Scherf and found out about all these extra-curricular activities required of a teacher. But she had done all she could to maintain a high standard of scholarship and help with the work at home. If she had attempted anything more, she would failed in the two most important things. No, it was useless to have any regrets over what couldn't be helped. She must concentrate instead on what to do now.

It would be best for the present not to mention the bad news she had received to anyone. Until school closed the family wouldn't expect her to have secured a position. If she was no closer to having one by that time, she would try to take definite steps.

But although Lyng tried to remain optimistic, she worried. Her silence at meals and her lack of appetite did not escape the sharp notice of Grandmother Skoglund.

"You go at things too hard, *Vesla-mi,*" she told Lyng. "Remember that there will be days after both you and I are gone."

In spite of Lyng's protests, Grandmother Skoglund did the entire housecleaning during the month of May all by herself.

"Do you think I would let you graduate from the university with the house as dirty as it is after the soot and smoke of the winter?" she demanded.

"But the graduation exercises will take place on the university campus," Lyng said.

"I've never known a fine-feathered bird to have flown from a filthy nest," Grandmother Skoglund told her. "I can always smell from the clothes of a person what kind of a home he comes from, no matter how fine he may try to make himself look. Besides, I have invited Gunara and Tallette to come over for a bit after the exercises, and I don't want the girls to think their mother is getting so old she can't keep up with them."

"Grandmother Skoglund, you are hopeless," Lyng laughed.

Lyng's mother, too, was busy preparing for the great event. She made a black taffeta suit for herself out of an evening gown she had bought from one of the customers of the shop, and the result was astounding. No lady with a fortune at her command could have looked smarter than Lyng's mother did after it was finished. Her mother also made a summer coat for Grandmother Skoglund from material she brought home from the shop, and a pretty black-and-white mercerized print dress was a present from Tante Gunara and Tante Tallette. Lyng's mother wanted to sew a dress for Lyng, but she refused this offer at once.

"You have more than enough to do as it is," Lyng said. "And I've already made plans for what I shall wear at the graduation exercises—a plain white, ready-made cotton skirt and one of my white shirtwaists. They won't show much under my gown anyway."

"I hope the university isn't making an old maid of you," Lyng's mother sighed.

At last the day of Lyng's graduation arrived, and the morning was cool but clear. Grandmother Skoglund came out of her room all ready for the celebration. Her starched petticoats rustled under her mercerized black-and-white dress and there was the slightest suggestion of a squeak from her new oxfords. Her fine white hair lay in soft ringlets around her face.

"You look positively beautiful," Lyng said, leaning down and kissing her.

Grandmother Skoglund beamed. "I do feel dressed up," she admitted.

The three of them, Lyng and her mother and Grandmother Skoglund, started out in good time for the commencement exercises. They boarded the streetcar on Riverside Avenue and changed for the Interurban on Seven Corners. Grandmother Skoglund pressed her face against the window as the streetcar crossed the Washington Avenue Bridge.

"You Tom Lowry, you Tom Lowry! What a man you were," Grandmother Skoglund exclaimed. "Crisscrossing the city with steel lines and sending cars over them without the help of horses or steam engines—way out to Lake Minnetonka and on the water itself, and now over the mighty Mississippi on this high bridge!"

On the campus, groups of cap-and-gowned men and women were already assembled in front of various buildings.

"It looks like they're going to have several graduations here today," Grandmother Skoglund remarked wonderingly. "I didn't know there were so many big schools so close together."

"All this is the campus of the University of Minnesota," Lyng explained to her. "These are students from the various departments who are assembling and will later join the main line of march."

"You mean that for four years you have been going into all these buildings?" Grandmother Skoglund asked.

"Oh, no. Not all of them. Most of my classes were in that long narrow building over there called Folwell Hall, but I worked a lot in the white building which houses the main library. And I had classes in a few of the others."

"No wonder the Americans put out great people, sending them to such gigantic institutions!" Grandmother Skoglund exclaimed. In the distance, the band was playing the *Star Spangled Banner*. Tears rolled down Grandmother Skoglund's cheeks. "It is all too beautiful," she said. "If only Markus could be with us today, how proud he would have been." Suddenly she dried her tears, and a worried expression appeared on her face. "Do you suppose we'll ever find Gunara and Tallette in this huge place?"

"Oh, yes," Lyng assured her. "They are going directly to the Armory where the exercises are being held. We made arrangements that whoever gets there first would save seats for the others. Hattie is coming with them. She and Clifford live only two blocks from their place since he has been working in the Ramsey County Clerk's office. You remember Clifford Best, don't you, Grandmother Skoglund? He and Hattie went together all through high school and were married almost two years ago. Hattie's mother went over to St. Paul yesterday and brought the baby back with her so Hattie could come today. But we'd better get started ourselves. Seats can't be saved too long, and I'll have to join my class and be ready to march."

After Lyng had taken her place in the line formed in front of the Library, she felt happier than she had for months. She was one of these fortunate people assembled here on the campus to receive a degree from this mighty institution. She had worked faithfully for the degree and no one could take it away from her. Maybe those extra-curricular activities which the secretary had stressed as so important would make it difficult for her to secure a position at first. But she would hound that secretary so hard and so consistently that in sheer self-defense, she would have to get her something. Once she had a chance to teach, she would make good. She'd see to that.

The line started to move. On the corner, outside the School of Mines, it was joined by another line. As it advanced across the campus, it grew longer and longer. Then the faculty and distinguished guests in black academic robes and brilliantly colored hoods took their places at the head of the procession. The band was playing *Hail Minnesota* as Lyng and her partner passed through the entrance to the Armory. The immense structure was crowded, with people standing along the walls.

As Lyng sat surrounded by hundreds of students who were graduating with her, she thought how silly she had been to let her fear of failing to get a job blur her appreciation of the privilege of getting an education. How happy and proud Grandmother Skoglund was today, basking in the reflected glory of her achievement. Even her mother, who certainly did not admire most things American, had the good sense to know the value of a degree from the University of Minnesota. Well, she was through with being a baby, allowing herself to sink into a mire of self-pity.

After the ceremonies were over, Lyng found her mother and Grandmother Skoglund and her aunts and Hattie waiting for her outside the Armory.

Hattie put her arms around Lyng and kissed her. "I was so proud of being your friend, Lyng, when I saw you marching into the Armory that I could have squealed."

Grandmother Skoglund asked at once to be allowed to read what was printed on Lyng's diploma. Lyng untied the maroon and gold bow and unrolled the parchment. Grandmother Skoglund held it in both hands.

"I was right," she said, giving it back to Lyng.

"About what, Grandmother Skoglund?"

"That the president himself signed it. Your mother said she didn't think he would have time, there being so many young people graduating."

Lyng smiled. "It wouldn't have been legal otherwise."

"It must be grand to be carrying around in your head all you've learned over here," Hattie said. "But then I'd never have had the stamina to keep at the grind for four long years. Our family always does things that bring immediate results."

"Let's go home," Lyng's mother suggested. "We can talk there."

"I'll have to go now," Hattie said. "Clifford's coming home early from the office tonight and I promised him a chicken dinner. I do want to wish you lots of luck, Lyng, and I hope you get a perfectly grand teaching job. Only don't be too hard on your students. Most people aren't as smart as you."

"Thanks, Hattie," Lyng said, laughing. "I won't."

Lyng's mother had started down the walk.

Grandmother Skoglund hesitated. "If—if it wouldn't be asking too much, do you suppose anyone would mind, if I could see just one more of the buildings over here? They do look so beautiful."

"Of course not," Lyng said. "It didn't occur to me that you would care to. I've been coming here for four years and I take it for granted. I think you should be interested most in Shevlin Hall. That building is just for girls to rest in and enjoy themselves and even to eat their lunches there."

"I'd love to see that," Tante Tallette said. "Imagine having a building for just that."

The bridal wreath was in full bloom and there were luxuriant clusters of it bordering both sides of the walk. When the five of them reached the east entrance, Grandmother Skoglund turned back and gazed at the white bushes admiringly.

"The Americans are so richly blessed with everything," she said.

She was even more impressed with the large living room in the center of Shevlin Hall. "Who'd ever think of putting a balcony in a living room?" she exclaimed. "And what elegant upholstered furniture! No wonder things are turning out so fine for you, Lyng, going four years to such a wonderful school. I think I'll take this chair over by the window. Then I can enjoy all the beauty, both inside and outside, at the same time." As she sat down, a look of surprise came over her face. "Why, Lyng," she asked, "are they really so backward here that they still have fireplaces? Even in Rendalen in Norway they heat with stoves these days. I should think a place like this would have central heating, as we have in our church and Gunara and Tallette have in their rooming house over in St. Paul."

"It's only another of the inconsistencies of the Americans," Lyng's mother said. "They do have central heating here. But they have a fireplace for decoration."

"Think of all the wood and ashes they have to carry for such a big one," Grandmother Skoglund sighed.

"I'm sure this is the proudest day of Mother's life," Tante Tallette told Lyng in an aside.

A fresh wave of anxiety took possession of Lyng. If the family knew what the secretary of the Placement Bureau had said, would they have the same feeling of pride? The very first thing in the morning, she would go to the office and let the secretary know in no uncertain terms that she expected the Placement Bureau to help her secure a position. She had as much a right to this service as a student with a whole list of extra-curricular activities opposite her name.

As soon as the family arrived home, Grandmother Skoglund put on her Hardanger embroidered apron and, with Lyng's help, set the food she had already prepared on the table. There was fresh homemade rye bread with hard-boiled eggs and anchovies, cream pudding that only had to be reheated, cold waffles covered with raspberry jam that had been saved from last year's canning for the occasion, tiny cakes that Grandmother Skoglund usually baked only for Christmas, and, of course, cups and cups of steaming coffee.

"I wanted to clear out the parlor for the day and give a nice party," Lyng's mother apologized to Tante Gunara and Tante Tallette, "but Lyng wouldn't hear of it. She said it would make too much work, and you two were the only ones she cared to have come anyway. I can see how she is taking on already the casual attitude toward life that is so American. Why, in Norway, if Father did nothing more than take atrip down to Kristiania, we gave a party on his arrival home that continued for several days. Everything was so festive there."

"Wait until Lyng finds herself a husband up in the town where she is going to teach," Grandmother Skoglund said.

"Then we'll celebrate for a week."

Lyng wet her dry lips with more coffee.

When the meal was almost over, Grandmother Skoglund disappeared into the pantry. She returned carrying a layer cake with four tall candles burning on top of it.

"You don't mean to say you have taken up American baking?" Tante Tallette exclaimed.

Lyng read the letters that circled the rim of the cake. They spelled the words, "Lyng Skoglund, Bachelor of Arts."

"Why, Grandmother Skoglund, how did you know?" Lyng exclaimed.

Grandmother Skoglund's eyes twinkled. "Some of the rest of us have been getting a few crumbs of this Yankee education, too, you see. I saw by your diploma that I got it all right. I had an excuse all ready so I could look at it and make sure."

One of the candles stood in the center of the letter "F," another in an "S," still another in "J," and the fourth candle in another "S." "That must stand for Freshman, Sophomore, Junior, and Senior," Lyng said. "How ever did you think of doing all this?"

"I hoped you would understand," Grandmother Skoglund beamed. "And I want you to know that the pins holding the candles on the cake are perfectly clean. I took one of your long hatpins, Reidun, down to the blacksmith shop on Ninth Street, and I had the blacksmith cut it into four pieces and file off both ends to a sharp point. Then I boiled the pins for an hour before I stuck them into the cake."

Lyng's mother gave Lyng a small package. It contained a silver teaspoon. On the end of the handle was a replica in miniature of the statue in Loring Park of Norway's great violinist, Ole Bull. In the bowl of the spoon were carved his name and the dates when he lived, 1810-1880. "Hans Englestad had many of them made for the Seventeenth of May celebration last year," Lyng's mother explained. "He had a few left, so I got this one real cheap. I thought it would be so nice for Lyng to have something Norwegian in her hope chest."

"It's pretty," Lyng said, trying to hide her indifference. Why had her mother been so insistent on her preparing herself to make a good living by attending the university, if she had her mind set on an early marriage for her? If only her mother had been practical enough to buy something she could use now. She could think of a hundred things she needed.

"Gunara, have you told Lyng about the present we bought for her?" Tante Tallette asked.

"No, you do it. You picked it out."

"We got a suitcase for you, Lyng," Tante Tallette said. "A substantial one, but not too heavy. We thought it would come in handy when you leave for your teaching job next fall."

"How thoughtful of you!" Lyng exclaimed. "I have been wondering how I would take my possessions along with me. Not that I have many. But one needs something."

"We would have brought it over today except that it would have been a nuisance lugging it all morning over at the university," Tante Gunara said.

"Tell her about the trunk," Tante Tallette said.

"Oh, that isn't really a present. One of our roomers who was going away was behind with his rent, so he left us his trunk. Later on he planned to move to Alaska, and he didn't want to be bothered with it. He came over and took the things he wanted, and we were stuck with the trunk. Tallette has scrubbed and aired it. While it isn't elegant, it is sturdy and will give you good service. And the lock is good."

"I'm sure Lyng will appreciate that," Grandmother Skoglund said. "And now I'm going to cook a fresh pot of coffee and we'll all have another cup."

"You can see now, Lyng," her mother remarked, "how nice it would have been to retire to the parlor for that."

"I like the kitchen better than any room in this house," Tante Gunara siad emphatically.

After Tante Gunara and Tante Tallette were gone, Grandmother Skoglund stifled a yawn. "I don't believe I have ever been so tired," she said sheepishly. "But then I've never been so happy either. Not even the day Markus was born."

The following morning Lyng set out for the university. When she arrived at the office of the Placement Bureau, she found the secretary alone. She was wearing the same gray outfit, and her straight hair, damp from sweat, looked more stringy than ever.

"I came to find out what you are doing about securing a position for me," Lyng said.

"We have nothing for you," the secretary replied.

"I have the right to be given the opportunity to apply for one, just as much as any of the others," Lyng said.

"That may be. But it would be useless for us to have you apply for a position which we knew, beforehand, you wouldn't stand a chance of getting. We had a call for a teacher this morning, but we recommended someone else for the position."

"I'll be back tomorrow," Lyng said curtly and left.

The next morning she started out earlier from home, but this time too the secretary told her that the openings which had come in were already given out to others. Lyng received similar responses to her inquiries for two more days. On the third morning she stood outside the locked door of the office of the Placement Bureau waiting for the secretary to arrive.

"This is getting to be a little too much," the secretary said, as soon as she saw Lyng. Both her voice and her manner were angry.

"That is exactly what I am beginning to think," Lyng said. "And since it is impossible for you to have checked over the notices this morning, I am asking you to describe them to me and let me be the judge of whether I am equipped to apply for one of them."

The secretary, who went through the mail while Lyng stood close by, finally looked up and said, "Here is a position for which you might apply." She handed Lyng a letter written in long hand. It was a request for someone to teach high school subjects in a town called New Stavanger. The salary was fifty-five dollars a month for a nine-month term.

"You see that a girl of Scandinavian heritage is preferred," the secretary said. "It's the only position that's come in so far that I think you would have a chance of getting."

"I see there is no mention made of extra-curricular activities, if that is what you mean," Lyng said.

The secretary's face became a deep red. "Do you want to apply for it or not?" she asked.

"I'll apply right away," Lyng said, "although I had certainly expected something better. I have never even heard of this town before."

The secretary consulted a map. "It's in the northwestern part of the state," she said. The population is listed as six hundred."

"Next year, after I've had experience, I'll be back here for a real position."

Lyng wrote to New Stavanger that afternoon, and, a week later, in a long white envelope, came a contract to teach there the following year. Lyng received it with mixed emotions. She did not look forward to spending nine months in such a small and obviously uninteresting town, and she had hoped to be placed in a community that did not have a predominantly Scandinavian population. But it was a position, and she would be making her living. Moreover, students in a small town needed a good teacher as much and perhaps more than those with the advantages of a large city. And she would do her best. Perhaps in another year, she might hope to secure a really good position.

To Lyng's surprise, both her mother and Grandmother Skoglund were much pleased over her contract.

"In a town that size, you will be the queen of all the social affairs of the season," her mother said. "And with twenty working days a month at the salary they are offering you, you will be earning two and a half dollars a day. That is two and a half times as much as you would have been getting at the Emporium now. Aren't you glad I insisted on your attending the university?"

"But I'll be staying away from home and will be having expenses that I wouldn't have had at the Emporium."

"A bird never learned to fly staying in the nest," Grandmother Skoglund said drily. Then she put her hand on Lyng's shoulder. "To think, *Vesla-mi,* you are the first member of our family to be holding the high position of a teacher. What a milestone this would have been in Markus' life!"

"The people in New Stavanger must be lovely," Lyng's mother went on. "The very name of New Stavanger shows that they are Norwegian. And to think they frown on dancing and cardplaying and liquor so much that they make mention of it in your contract. Lyng, if I had chosen the position for you myself, I couldn't have found one that met more completely with my approval."

TOUSSAINT

Ntozake Shange

Ntozake Shange's choreopoem, "For Colored Girls Who Have Considered Suicide, When the Rainbow Is Enuf" opened on Broadway in September of 1976 after a successful run at the New York Shakespeare Festival's off-Broadway Public Theatre. The show consists of seven girls, all dressed alike but in different colors, singing, dancing and living the poems of Ntozake Shange who was one of the seven performers. In little over an hour without an intermission, the women provide a searing, joyful, tribute to black women in America, their tragedies and triumphs as women and as blacks.

The excerpt chosen reveals the ethnic pride and complex personality of a young schoolgirl, the lady in brown. (St. Louis, 1955)

> *The lady in brown enters from up
> stage right.*

   Lady in brown
de library waz right down from de trolly tracks
cross from de laundry-mat
thru de big shinin floors & granite pillars
ol st. louis is famous for
i found toussaint
but not til after months uv
cajun katie/pippi longstockin
christopher robin/eddie heyward & a pooh bear
in the children's room
only pioneer girls & magic rabbits
& big city white boys
i knew i waznt sposedta
but i ran inta the ADULT EADING ROOM
   & came across

    TOUSSAINT

     my first blk man
(i never counted george washington carver
cuz i didnt like peanuts)
    still
TOUSSAINT waz a blk man a negro like my mama say
who refused to be a slave
& he spoke french
& didnt low no white man to tell him nothin
   not napolean
   not maximillien
   not robespierre

TOUSSAINT L'OUVERTURE
waz the beginnin uv reality for me
in the summer contest for
who colored child can read
15 books in three weeks
i won & raved abt TOUSSAINT L'OUVERTURE
at the afternoon ceremony
waz disqualified
   cuz Toussaint
      belonged in the ADULT READING ROOM
         & i cried
& carried dead Toussaint home in the book
he waz dead & livin to me
cuz TOUSSAINT & them
they held the citadel gainst the french
wid the spirits of ol dead africans from outta the ground
TOUSSAINT led they army of zombies
walkin cannon ball shootin spirits to free Haiti
& they waznt slaves no more

     TOUSSAINT L'OUVERTURE
became my secret lover at the age of 8
i entertained him in my bedroom
widda flashlight under my covers
way inta the night/we discussed strategies
how to remove white girls from my hopscotch games
& etc.
TOUSSAINT
waz layin in bed wit me next to raggedy ann
the night i decided to run away from my
   integrated home
      integrated street
         integrated school
1955 waz not a good year for lil blk girls

Toussaint said 'lets go to haiti'
i said 'awright'
& packed some very important things in a brown paper bag
so i wdnt haveta come back
then Toussaint & i took the hodiamont streetcar
to the river
last stop
only 15¢

cuz there waznt nobody cd see Toussaint cept me
& we walked all down thru north st. louis
where the french settlers usedta live
in tiny brick houses all huddled together
wit barely missin windows & shingles uneven
wit colored kids playin & women on low porches sippin beer

i cd talk to Toussaint down by the river
like this waz where we waz gonna stow away
on a boat for new orleans
& catch a creole fishin-rig for port-au-prince
then we waz just gonna read & talk all the time
& eat fried bananas
   we waz just walkin & skippin past ol drunk men
when dis ol young boy jumped out at me sayin
'HEY GIRL YA BETTAH COME OVAH HEAH N TALK TO ME'
well
i turned to TOUSSAINT (who waz furious)
& i shouted
'ya silly ol boy
ya bettah leave me alone
or TOUSSAINT'S gonna get yr ass'
de silly ol boy came round de corner laughin all in my face
'yellah gal
ya sure must be somebody to know my name so quick'
i waz disgusted
& wanted to get on to haiti
widout some tacky ol boy botherin me
still he kept standin there
kickin milk cartons & bits of brick
tryin to get all in my business
     i mumbled to L'OUVERTURE 'what shd I do
finally
i asked this silly ol boy

'WELL WHO ARE YOU?'
he say
'MY NAME IS TOUSSAINT JONES'
well
i looked right at him
those skidded out cordoroy pants
a striped teashirt wid holes in both elbows
a new scab over his left eye
& i said

    'what's yr name again'
he say
'i'm toussaint jones'
'wow
i am on my way to see
TOUSSAINT L'OUVERTURE in HAITI
are ya any kin to him
he dont take no stuff from no white folks
& they gotta country all they own
& there aint no slaves'
that silly ol boy squinted his face all up
'looka heah girl
i am TOUSSAINT JONES
& i'm right heah lookin at ya
& i dont take no stuff from no white folks
ya dont see none round heah do ya?'
& he sorta pushed out his chest
then he say
'come on lets go on down to the docks
& look at the boats'
i waz real puzzled goin down to the docks
wit my paper bag & my books
i felt TOUSSAINT L'OUVERTURE sorta leave me
& i waz sad
til i realized
TOUSSAINT JONES waznt too different
from TOUSSAINT L'OUVERTURE
cept the ol one waz in haiti
& this one wid me speakin english & eatin apples
yeah.
toussaint jones waz awright wit me
no tellin what all spirits we cd move
down by the river
st. louis 1955   hay wait.

  The lady in brown exits into the stage right volm.

FOR RITA KOHN

Marina Rivera

Paper flowers because you chose me
for something hard, above all
the white faces, made me leader
with the blond. I gave you
5   roses, one dozen paper roses
boxed to hold in your hands.
You wanted to hold me, too small,
too tight a knot that only slips
off and catches somewhere else.
10   Like the bird held only because
stunned, the eyes warm for a moment.
There is no neck, no visible spine.
I give you past all these years,
again I give you paper roses
15   because they are cheap *and* beautiful
because you were only one of these,
teaching what I learn slowly.

"Two friends in a garden." By permission
of Harriett Warshaw, the artist.

From *Sobra,* 1977, p. 18. Casa Editorial, Chapbook Number Six, West Coast Print Center, Berkeley, Calif. Reprinted by permission of the author. (See Ms. Rivera's poem "Chon" in Unit Five, EXPLOITATION IN HUMAN RELATIONSHIPS.)

THE LESSON

Toni Cade Bambara

Back in the days when everyone was old and stupid or young and foolish and me and Sugar were the only ones just right, this lady moved on our block with nappy hair and proper speech and no makeup. And quite naturally we laughed at her, laughed the way we did at the junk man who went about his business like he was some big-time president and his sorry-ass horse his secretary. And we kinda hated her too, hated the way we did the winos who cluttered up our parks and pissed on our handball walls and stank up our hallways and stairs so you couldn't halfway play hide-and-seek without a goddamn gas mask. Miss Moore was her name. The only woman on the block with no first name. And she was black as hell, cept for her feet, which were fish-white and spooky. And she was always planning these boring-ass things for us to do, us being my cousin, mostly, who lived on the block cause we all moved North the same time and to the same apartment then spread out gradual to breathe. And our parents would yank our heads into some kinda shape and crisp up our clothes so we'd be presentable for travel with Miss Moore, who always looked like she was going to church, though she never did. Which is just one of things the grownups talked about when they talked behind her back like a dog. But when she came calling with some sachet she'd sewed up or some gingerbread she'd made or some book, why then they'd all be too embarrassed to turn her down and we'd get handed over all spruced up. She'd been to college and said it was only right that she should take responsibility for the young ones' education, and she not even related by marriage or blood. So they'd go for it. Specially Aunt Gretchen. She was the main gofer in the family. You got some ole dumb shit foolishness you want somebody to go for, you send for Aunt Gretchen. She been screwed into the go-along for so long, it's a blood-deep natural thing with her. Which is how she got saddled with me and Sugar and Junior in the first place while our mothers were in a la-de-da apartment up the block having a good ole time.

So this one day Miss Moore rounds us all up at the mailbox and it's puredee hot and she's knockin herself out about arithmetic. And school suppose to let up in summer I heard, but she don't never let up. And the starch in my pinafore scratching the shit outta me and I'm really hating this nappy-head bitch and her goddamn college degree. I'd much rather go to the pool or to the show where it's cool. So me and Sugar leaning on the mailbox being surly, which is a Miss Moore word. And Flyboy checking out what everybody brought for lunch. And Fat Butt already wasting his peanut-butter-and-jelly sandwich like the pig he is. And Junebug punchin on Q.T.'s arm for potato chips. And Rosie Giraffe shifting from one hip to the other waiting for somebody to step on her foot or ask her if she from Georgia so she can kick ass, preferably Mercedes'. And Miss Moore asking us do we know what money is, like we a bunch of retards. I mean real money, she say, like it's only poker chips or monopoly papers we lay on the grocer. So right away I'm tired of this and say so. And would much rather snatch Sugar and go to the Sunset and terrorize the West Indian kids and take their hair ribbons and their money too. And Miss Moore files that remark away for next week's lesson on brotherhood, I can tell. And finally I say we oughta get to the subway cause it's cooler and besides we might meet some cute boys. Sugar done swiped her mama's lipstick, so we ready.

So we heading down the street and she's boring us silly about what things cost and what our parents make and how much goes for rent and how money ain't divided up right in this country. And then she gets to the part about we all poor and live in the slums, which I don't feature. And I'm ready to speak on that, but she steps out in the street and hails two cabs just like that. Then she hustles half the crew in with her and hands me a five-dollar bill and tells me to calculate 10 percent tip for the driver. And we're off. Me and Sugar and Junebug and Flyboy hangin out the window and hollering to everybody, putting lipstick on each other cause Flyboy a faggot anyway, and making farts with our sweaty armpits. But I'm mostly trying to figure how to spend this money. But they all fascinated with the meter ticking and Junebug starts laying bets as to how much it'll read when Flyboy can't hold his breath no more. Then Sugar lays bets as to how much it'll be when we get there. So I'm stuck. Don't nobody want to go for my plan, which is to jump out at the next light and run off to the first bar-b-que we can find. Then the driver tells us to get the hell out cause we there already. And the meter reads eighty-five cents. And I'm stalling to figure out the tip and Sugar say give him a dime. And I decide he don't need it bad as I do, so later for him. But then he tries to take off with Junebug foot still in the door so we talk about his mama something ferocious. Then we check out that we on Fifth Avenue and everybody dressed up in stockings. One lady in a fur coat, hot as it is. White folks crazy.

"This is the place," Miss Moore say, presenting it to us in the voice she uses at the museum. "Let's look in the windows before we go in."

"Can we steal?" Sugar asks very serious like she's getting the ground rules squared away before she plays. "I beg your pardon," say Miss Moore, and we fall out. So she leads us around the windows of the toy store and me and Sugar screamin, "This is mine, that's mine, I gotta have that, that was made for me, I was born for that," till Big Butt drowns us out.

"Hey, I'm goin to buy that there."

"That there? You don't even know what it is, stupid."

"I do so," he says punchin on Rosie Giraffe. "It's a microscope."

"Whatcha gonna do with a microscope, fool?"

"Look at things."

"Like what, Ronald?" ask Miss Moore. And Big Butt ain't got the first notion. So here go Miss Moore gabbing about the thousands of bacteria in a drop of water and the somethinor-other in a speck of blood and the million and one living things in the air around us is invisible to the naked eye. And what she say that for? Junebug go to town on that "naked" and we rolling. Then Miss Moore ask what it cost. So we all jam into the window smudgin it up and the price tag say $300. So then she ask how long'd take for Big Butt and Junebug to save up their allowances. "Too long," I say. "Yeh," adds Sugar, "outgrown it by that time." And Miss Moore say no, you never outgrow learning instruments. "Why, even medical students and in-terns and," blah, blah, blah. And we ready to choke Big Butt for bringing it up in the first damn place.

"This here costs four hundred eighty dollars," say Rosie Giraffe. So we pile up all over her to see what she pointin out. My eyes tell me it's a chunk of glass cracked with something heavy, and different-color inks dripped into the splits, then the whole thing put into a oven or something. But for $480 it don't make sense.

"That's a paperweight made of semi-precious stones fused together under tremendous pressure," she explains slowly, with her hands doing the mining and all the factory work.

"So what's a paperweight?" asks Rosie Giraffe.

"To weigh paper with, dumbbell," say Flyboy, the wise man from the East.

"Not exactly," say Miss Moore, which is what she say when you warm or way off too. "It's to weigh paper down so it won't scatter and make your desk untidy." So right away me and Sugar curtsy to each other and then to Mercedes who is more the tidy type.

"We don't keep paper on top of the desk in my class," say Junebug, figuring Miss Moore crazy or lyin one.

"At home, then," she say. "Don't you have a calendar and a pencil case and a blotter and a letter-opener on your desk at home where you do your homework?" And she know damn well what our homes look like cause she nosys around in them every chance she gets.

"I don't even have a desk," say Junebug. "Do we?"

"No. And I don't get no homework neigher," says Big Butt.

"And I don't even have a home," say Flyboy like he do at school to keep the white folks off his back and sorry for him. Send this poor kid to camp posters, is his specialty.

"I do," says Mercedes. "I have a box of stationery on my desk and a picture of my cat. My godmother bought the stationery and the desk. There's a big rose on each sheet and the envelopes smell like roses."

"Who wants to know about your smelly-ass stationery," say Rosie Giraffe fore I can get my two cents in.

"It's important to have a work area all your own so that. . . ."

"Will you look at this sailboat, please," say Flyboy, cuttin her off and pointin to the thing like it was his. So once again we tumble all over each other to gaze at this magnificent thing in the toy store which is just big enough to maybe sail two kittens across the pond if you strap them to the posts tight. We all start reciting the price tag like we in assembly. "Handcrafted sailboat of fiberglass at one thousand one hundred ninety-five dollars."

"Unbelievable," I hear myself say and am really stunned. I read it again for myself just in case the group recitation put me in a trance. Same thing. For some reason this pisses me off. We look at Miss Moore and she lookin at us, waiting for I dunno what.

"Who'd pay all that when you can buy a sailboat set for a quarter at Pop's, a tube of glue for a dime, and a ball of string for eight cents? It must have a motor and whole lot else besides," I say. "My sailboat cost me about fifty cents."

"But will it take water?" say Mercedes with her smart ass.

"Took mine to Alley Pond Park once," say Flyboy. "String broke. Lost it. Pity."

"Sailed mine in Central Park and it keeled over and sank. Had to ask my father for another dollar."

"And you got the strap," laugh Big Butt. "The jerk didn't even have a string on it. My old man wailed on his behind."

Little Q.T. was staring hard at the sailboat and you could see he wanted it bad. But he too little and somebody'd just take it from him. So what the hell. "This boat for kids. Miss Moore?"

"Parents silly to buy something like that just to get all broke up," say Rosie Giraffe.

"That much money it should last forever," I figure.

"My father'd buy it for me if I wanted it."

"Your father, my ass," say Rosie Giraffe getting a chance to finally push Mercedes.

"Must be rich people shop here," say Q.T.

"You are a very bright boy," say Flyboy. "What was your first clue?" And he rap him on the head with the back of his knuckles, since Q.T. the only one he could get away with. Though Q.T. liable to come up behind you years later and get his licks in when you half expect it.

"What I want to know is," I says to Miss Moore though I never talk to her, I wouldn't give the bitch that satisfaction, "is how much a real boat costs? I figure a thousand'd get you a yacht any day."

"Why don't you check that out," she says, "and report back to the group?" Which really pains my ass. If you gonna mess up a perfectly good swim day least you could do is have some answers. "Let's go in," she say like she got something up her sleeve. Only she don't lead the way. So me and Sugar turn the corner to where the entrance is, but when we get there I kinda hang back. Not that I'm scared, what's there to be afraid of, just a toy story. But I feel funny, shame. But what I got to be shamed about? Got as much right to go in as anybody. But somehow I can't seem to get hold of the door, so I step away for Sugar to lead. But she hangs back too. And I look at her and she looks at me and this is ridiculous. I mean, damn, I have never ever been shy about doing nothing or going nowhere. But then Mercedes steps up and then Rosie Giraffe and Big Butt crowd in behind and shove, and next thing we all stuffed into the doorway with only Mercedes squeezing past us, smoothing out her jumper and walking right down the aisle. Then the rest of us tumble in like a glued-together jigsaw done all wrong. And people lookin at us. And it's like the time me and Sugar crashed into the Catholic church on a dare. But once we got in there and everything so hushed and holy and the candles and the bowin and the handkerchiefs on all the drooping heads, I just couldn't go through with the plan. Which was for me to run up to the alter and do a tap dance while Sugar played the nose flute and messed around in the holy water. And Sugar kept givin me the elbow. Then later teased me so bad I tied her up in the shower and turned it on and locked her in. And she'd be there till this day if Aunt Gretchen hadn't finally figured I was lyin about the boarder takin a shower.

Same thing in the store. We all walkin on tiptoe and hardly touchin the games and puzzles and things. And I watched Miss Moore who is steady watchin us like she waitin for a sign. Like Mama Drewery watches the sky and sniffs the air and takes note of just how much slant is in the bird formation. Then me and Sugar bump smack into each other, so busy gazing at the toys, 'specially the sailboat. But we don't laugh and go into our fat-lady bump-stomach routine. We just stare at that price tag. Then Sugar run a finger over the whole boat. And I'm jealous and want to hit her. Maybe not her, but I sure want to punch somebody in the mouth.

"Watcha bring us here for, Miss Moore?"

"You sound angry, Sylvia. Are you mad about something?" Givin me one of them grins like she tellin a grown-up joke that never turns out to be funny. And she's lookin very closely at me like maybe she plannin to do my portrait from memory. I'm mad, but I won't give her that satisfaction. So I slouch around the store bein very bored and say, "Let's go."

Me and Sugar at the back of the train watchin the tracks whizzin by large then small then gettin gobbled up in the dark. I'm thinkin about this tricky toy I saw in the store. A clown that somersaults on a bar then does chin-ups just cause you yank lightly at his leg. Cost $35. I could see me askin my mother for a $35 birthday clown. "You wanna who that costs what?" she'd say, cocking her head to the side to get a better view of the hole in my head. Thirty-five dollars could buy new bunk beds for Junior and Gretchen's boy. Thirty-five dollars and the whole household could go visit Granddaddy Nelson in the country. Thirty-five dollars would pay for the rent and the piano bill too. Who are these people that spend that much for performing clowns and $1,000 for toy sailboats? What kinda work they do and how they live and how come we ain't in on it? Where we are is who we are, Miss Moore always pointin out. But it don't necessarily have to be that way, she always adds then waits for somebody to say that poor people have to wake up and demand their share of the pie and don't none of us know what kind of pie she talkin about in the first damn place. But she ain't so smart cause I still got her four dollars from the taxi and she sure ain't gettin it. Messin up my day with this shit. Sugar nudges me in my pocket and winks.

Miss Moore lines us up in front of the mailbox where we started from, seem like years ago, and I got a headache for thinkin so hard. And we lean all over each other so we can hold up under the draggy-ass lecture she always finishes us off with at the end before we thank her for borin us to tears. But she just looks at us like she readin tea leaves. Finally she say, "Well, what did you think of F.A.O. Schwartz?"

Rosie Giraffe mumbles, "White folks crazy."

"I'd like to go there again when I get my birthday money," says Mercedes, and we shove her out the pack so she has to lean on the mailbox by herself.

"I'd like a shower. Tiring day," say Flyboy.

Then Sugar surprises me by sayin, "You know, Miss Moore, I don't think all of us here put together eat in a year what that sailboat costs." And Miss Moore lights up like somebody goosed her. "And?" she say, urging Sugar on. Only I'm standin on her foot so she don't continue.

"Imagine for a minute what kind of society it is in which some people can spend on a toy what it would cost to feed a family of six or seven. What do you think?"

"I think," say Sugar pushing me off her feet like she never done before, cause I whip her ass in a minute, "that this is not much of a democracy if you ask me. Equal chance to pursue happiness means an equal crack at the dough, don't it?" Miss Moore is besides herself and I am disgusted with Sugar's treachery. So I stand on her foot one more time to see if she'll shove me. She shuts up, and Miss Moore looks at me, sorrowfully I'm thinkin. And somethin weird is goin on, I can feel it in my chest.

"Anybody else learn anything today?" lookin dead at me. I walk away and Sugar has to run to catch up and don't even seem to notice when I shrug her arm off my shoulder.

"Well, we got four dollars anyway," she says.

"Uh hunh."

"We could go to Hascombs and get half a chocolate layer and then go to the Sunset and still have plenty money for potato chips and ice cream sodas."

"Uh hunh."

"Race you to Hascombs," she say.

We start down the block and she gets ahead which is O.K. by me cause I'm goin to the West End and then over to the Drive to think this day through. She can run if she want to and even run faster. But ain't nobody gonna beat me at nuthin.

"THE ETHNIC CHILD AND THE CLASSROOM EXPERIENCE"

Betty Smith

*Betty Smith (1904-1972) born and raised in Williamburg, Brooklyn, a community of first and second generation immigrants, attained fame for her best seller **A Tree Grows in Brooklyn** (1943), a Literary Guild selection and made into a film. The book sold almost four million copies and was translated into sixteen languages and appeared in a musical version on Broadway.*

At eighteen, after an early marriage and already a mother, Ms. Smith entered college and embarked upon a successful writing career. She once said: "Brooklyn is a town of dark mystery and violent passions and gentle ways. There are astonishing customs and rituals of living hidden away from the outsider and known only to Brooklyn people." That was the Brooklyn of Francie Nolan, a sensitive Irish-American girl growing up in a multi-ethnic neighborhood at the turn of the century.

School days went along. Some were made up of meanness, brutality and heartbreak; others were bright and beautiful because of Miss Bernstone and Mr. Morton. And always, there was the magic of learning things.

Francie was out walking one Saturday in October and she chanced on an unfamiliar neighborhood. Here were no tenements or raucous shabby stores. There were old houses that had been standing there when Washington maneuvered his troops across Long Island. They were old and decrepit but there were picket fences around them with gates on which Francie longed to swing. There were bright fall flowers in the front yard and maple trees with crimson and yellow leaves on the curb. The neighborhood stood old, quiet, and serene in the Saturday sunshine. There was a brooding quality about the neighborhood, a quiet deep, timeless, shabby peace. Francie was as happy as though, like Alice, she had stepped through a magic mirror. She was in an enchanted land.

She walked on further and came to a little old school. Its old bricks glowed garnet in the late afternoon sun. There was no fence around the school yard and the school grounds were grass and not cement. Across from the school, it was practically open country—a meadow with goldenrod, wild asters and clover growing in it.

Francie's heart turned over. This was it! This was the school she wanted to go to. But how could she get to go there? There was a strict law about attending the school in your own district. Her parents would have to move to that neighborhood if she wanted to go to that school. Francie knew that mama wouldn't move just because *she* felt like going to another school. She walked home slowly thinking about it.

She sat up that night waiting for papa to come home from work. After Johnny had come home whistling his "Molly Malone" as he ran up the steps, after all had eaten of the lobster, caviar, and liverwurst that he brought home, mama and Neeley went to bed. Francie kept papa company while he smoked his last cigar. Francie whispered all about the school in papa's ear. He looked at her, nodded, and said, "We'll see tomorrow."

"You mean we can move near that school?"

"No, but there has to be another way. I'll go there with you tomorrow and we'll see what we can see."

Francie was so excited she couldn't sleep the rest of the night. She was up at seven but Johnny was still sleeping soundly. She waited in a perspiration of impatience. Each time he sighed in his sleep, she ran in to see if he was waking up.

He woke about noon and the Nolans sat down to dinner. Francie couldn't eat. She kept looking at papa but he made her no sign. Had he forgotten? Had he forgotten? No, because while Katie was pouring the coffee, he said carelessly,

"I guess me and the prima donna will take a little walk later on."

Francie's heart jumped. He had not forgotten. He had not forgotten. she waited. Mama had to answer. Mama might object. Mama might ask why. Mama might say she guessed she'd go along too. But all mama said was, "All right."

Francie did the dishes. Then she had to go down to the candy store to get the Sunday paper; then to the cigar store to get papa a nickel Corona. Johnny had to read the paper. He had to read every column of it including the society section in which he couldn't possibly be interested. Worse than that, he had to make comments to mama on every item he read. Each time he'd put the paper aside, turn to mama and say, "Funny things in the papers nowadays. Take this case," Francie would almost cry.

Four o'clock came. The cigar had long since been smoked, the paper lay gutted on the floor, Katie had tired of having the news analyzed and had taken Neeley and gone over to visit Mary Rommely.

Francie and papa set out hand in hand. He was wearing his only suit, the tuxedo and his derby hat and he looked very grand. It was a splendid October day. There was a warm sun and a refreshing wind working together to bring the tang of the ocean around each corner. They walked a few blocks, turned a corner and were in this other neighborhood. Only in a great sprawling place like Brooklyn could there be such a sharp division. It was a neighborhood peopled by fifth and sixth generation Americans, whereas in the Nolan neighborhood, if you could prove *you* had been born in America, it was equivalent to a Mayflower standing.

Indeed, Francie was the only one in her classroom whose parents were American-born. At the beginning of the term, Teacher called the roll and asked each child her lineage. The answers were typical.

"I'm Polish-American. My father was born in Warsaw."

"Irish-American. Me fayther and mither were born in County Cork."

When Nolan was called, Francie answered proudly: "I'm an American."

"I *know* you're American," said the easily exasperated teacher. "But what's your nationality?"

"American!" insisted Francie even more proudly.

"Will you tell me what your parents are or do I have to send you to the principal?"

"My parents are American. They were born in Brooklyn."

All the children turned around to look at a little girl whose parents had *not* come from the old country. And when Teacher said, "Brooklyn? Hm. I guess that makes you American, all right," Francie was proud and happy. How wonderful was Brooklyn, she thought, when just being born there automatically made you an American!

Papa told her about this strange neighborhood: how its families had been Americans for more than a hundred years back; how they were mostly Scotch, English and Welsh extraction. The men worked as cabinet makers and fine carpenters. They worked with metals: gold, silver and copper.

He promised to take Francie to the Spanish section of Brooklyn some day. There the men worked as cigar-makers and each chipped in a few pennies a day to hire a man to read to them while they worked. And the man read fine literature.

They walked along the quiet Sunday street. Francie saw a leaf flutter from a tree and she skipped ahead to get it. It was a clear scarlet with an edging of gold. She stared at it, wondering if she'd ever see anything as beautiful again. A woman came from around the corner. She was rouged heavily and wore a feather boa. She smiled at Johnny and said,

"Lonesome, Mister?"

Johnny looked at her a moment before he answered gently,

"No, Sister."

"Sure?" she inquired archly.

"Sure," he answered quietly.

She went her way. Francie skipped back and took papa's hand.

"Was that a bad lady, Papa?" she asked eagerly.

"No."

"But she *looked* bad."

"There are very few bad people. There are just a lot of people that are unlucky."

"But she was all painted and. . . ."

"She was one who had seen better days." He like the phrase. "Yes, she may have seen better days." He fell into a thoughtful mood. Francie kept skipping ahead and collecting leaves.

They came upon the school and Francie proudly showed it to papa. The late afternoon sun warmed its softly-colored bricks and the small-paned windows seemed to dance in the sunshine. Johnny looked at it a long time, then he said,

"Yes, this is the school. This is it."

Then, as whenever he was moved or stirred, he had to put it into a song. He held his worn derby over his heart, stood up straight looking up at the school house and sang:

> *School days, school days,*
> *Dear old golden rule days.*
> *Readin' 'n writin' 'n 'rithmetic. . . .*

To a passing stranger, it might have looked silly—Johnny standing there in his greenish tuxedo and fresh linen holding the hand of a thin ragged child and singing the banal song so un-self-consciously on the street. But to Francie it seemed right and beautiful.

They crossed the street and wandered in the meadow that folks called "lots." Francie picked a bunch of goldenrod and wild asters to take home. Johnny explained that the place had once been an Indian burying ground and how as a boy, he had often come there to hunt arrowheads. Francie suggested they hunt for some. They searched for half an hour and found none. Johnny recalled that as a boy, he hadn't found any either. This struck Francie as funny and she laughed. Papa confessed that maybe it hadn't been an Indian cemetery after all; maybe someone had made up that story. Johnny was more than right because he had made up the whole story himself.

Soon it was time to go home and tears came into Francie's eyes because papa hadn't said anything about getting her into the new school. He saw the tears and figured out a scheme immediately.

"Tell you what we'll do, Baby. We'll walk around and pick out a nice house and take down the number. I'll write a letter to your principal saying you're moving there and want to be transferred to this school."

They found a house—a one-story white one with a slanting roof and late chrysanthemums growing in the yard. He copied the address carefully.

"You know that what we are going to do is wrong?"

"Is it, Papa?"

"But it's a wrong to gain a bigger good."

"Like a white lie?"

"Like a lie that helps someone out. So you must make up for the wrong by being twice as good. You must never be bad or absent or late. You must never do anything to make them send a letter home through the mails."

"I'll always be good, Papa, if I can go to that school."

"Yes. Now I'll show you a way to go to school through a little park. I know right where it is. Yes sir, I know right where it is."

He showed her the park and how she could walk through it diagonally to go to school.

"That should make you happy. You can see the seasons change as you come and go. What do you say to that?"

Francie, recalling something her mother had once read to her answered, "My cup runneth over." And she meant it.

When Katie heard of the plan, she said: "Suit yourself. But I'll have nothing to do with it. If the police come and arrest you for giving a false address, I'll say honestly that I had nothing to do with it. One school's as good or as bad as another. I don't know why she wants to change. There's homework no matter what school you go to."

"It's settled then," Johnny said. "Francie, here's a penny. Run down to the candy store and get a sheet of writing paper and an envelope."

Francie ran down and ran back. Johnny wrote a note saying Francie was going to live with relatives at such and such an address and wanted a transfer. He added that Neeley would continue living at home and wouldn't require a transfer. He signed his name and underlined it authoritatively.

Tremblingly, Francie handed the note to her principal next morning. That lady read it, grunted, made out the transfer, handed her her report card and told her to go; that the school was too crowded anyhow.

Francie presented herself and documents to the principal of the new school. He shook hands with her and said he hoped she'd be happy in the new school. A monitor took her to the classroom. The teacher stopped the work and introduced Francie to the class. Francie looked out over the rows of little girls. All were shabby but most were clean. She was given a seat to herself and happily fell into the routine of the new school.

The teachers and children here were not as brutalized as in the old school. Yes, some of the children were mean but it seemed a natural child-meanness and not a campaign. Often the teachers were impatient and cross but never naggingly cruel. There was no corporal punishment either. The parents were too American, too aware of the rights granted them by their Constitution to accept injustices meekly. They could not be bulldozed and exploited as could the immigrants and the second generation Americans.

THAT ELUSIVE IDENTITY

"Girl on sofa." By permission of M. E. Clayton, the artist.

Who am I?
What do I want?
Where am I going?
Why?

NISEI, NISEI!

Ferris Takahashi

I have no face—
This is a face,
(Nisei, Nisei!)
My face of astigmatic eyes,
5   Other eyes.

A composite of sneer and word,
The cherry blossom and the sword,
Where I hang as on gallows wood;
(Nisei, Nisei!)

10   Set in the island centuries
Of the mixed stock Yamato breeds.
(And this is censored:
No one reads
Of our dissimilarities,
15   Nisei, Nisei!)

Is this so yellow?
Brown and plain
White are the skins of old Japan.

I have no face.

20   My sallow cheek
Is greenish in the subway light,
My parents' mild and patient eyes
Mocked in these narrow apertures;
Look, glasses make this low-built nose
25   The shadow of a caricature.
(Nisei, Nisei!)

Give me the eyes that form my face!
All outside eyes, all looking down,
The eyes of every day that frown,
30   The starry world, the street, the job, the eating place—
All eyes I envy for their anonymity.
(Nisei, Nisei!)

Ferris Takahashi (Mary H. Constable), "Nisei, Nisei!" from *Common Ground,* 6 (Spring 1946). Reprinted by permission of the American Council for Nationalities Service.

This is mirage.
These are my twenty years of youth—
35   To look the thing I hate and what I am:
(Nisei, Nisei!)

Where is the heart to scour this enemy mask
Nailed on my flesh and artifact of my veins?
Where is the judge of the infernal poll
40   Where they vote round eyes honest and mine knave?

This is a dream.
These eyes, this face
(Nisei, Nisei!)
Clutched on my twitching plasm like a monstrous growth,
45   A twinning cyst of hair, of pulp, of teeth. . . .

Tell me this is no face,
This face of mine—
It is a face of Angloid eyes who hate.

NO DOGS AND CHINESE ALLOWED

Kumi Kilburn

On the front page of the newspaper, the headlines announced KUMI IS SITTING IN GRACE'S CHAIR. The article explained that Grace Kilburn, the School Board President, had changed back to her original Korean name. For an American suburban newspaper, it was news! It even included a picture.

As a School Board member, I had been invited to participate in workshops designed to help the school staff become sensitized to the problems of the visible minorities. As a visible minority in a position of influence, I was to lend support and approval by my presence. Instead, I had been caught in a maelstrom of memories swirling frighteningly with feelings of rage and anger. I thought the carefully hidden wounds had healed. I had been able, finally, to face this unique and wonderful Korean-American heritage by reclaiming my Korean name, Kumi.

That night I woke up sobbing. In the nightmare I had been at a fancy ball. A glittering mirrored globe suspended on the ceiling was flickering little lights on our masked faces. We were dancing gaily. The clock chimed and it was my turn to remove my hand held mask. A group of already unmasked people surrounded me, waiting. When they saw me unmasked, some of my friends turned their backs and walked away.

Tears and memories carefully locked away rush out. The image of an immaculately kept park in Shanghai came to mind with wide walkways with nurses in uniform, sitting or pushing

Reprinted by permission of the author.

the perambulators along tree shaded lanes. I had excitedly asked by Grandfather to take me in for a walk. He told me he couldn't. He explained that the sign at the gate said, "NO DOGS AND CHINESE ALLOWED." My nine year old mind knew the sign meant me too.

The park had been on the way to the exclusive part of town where all the Americans and the Europeans lived, separated by a river from the rest of the city. We had been walking to the one remaining grade school which was still operating, an American Catholic Mission School. In the aftermath of the end of the Second World War, no Japanese controlled institutions were in operation. In the office of the Mother Superior, Grandfather explained that now my name would be Grace. The Mother Superior had said that her Sisters could not cope with all the native names.

Upon returning home, Grandfather told me stories of wonderful things he had learned in America. He told me about President Wilson's belief in each country's right to self-determination and about the founding of a wonderful country far away based upon principles of equality and freedom, supporter of nations fighting for independence. He loved America and he said that someday, if I were good and studied hard, I could go to there.

In the late 1930's. Grandfather returned from Princeton Divinity School to Pyong Yang, Korea, a privileged full-fledged member of the American Presbyterian Mission. The American missionaries lived in two story brick houses within the American Mission Compound. He was assigned the gardner's cottage. He remained a native.

As a result of having seen America, the Japanese officials who governed Korea interrogated him more frequently. They were interested in his connections with the Underground working to liberate Korea. In retaliation, he packed all his wordly goods, and moved his family to Shanghai—his wife, six sons, two daughters, four daughters-in-law and seven grandchildren—to an independent Korean church and further away from Japan. I was three years old.

By elementary school age, the Second World War was raging in and around Shanghai. Koreans had to attend Japanese schools. It was the official policy of the Japanese government to obliterate any trace of Korean culture by eliminating our language. In school I learned to become part of an obedient group. We would rise quietly when the teacher entered the classroom and bow down with a greeting. At the end of the day's lessons we would dust and wet mop every corner of our classroom including our share of the hallway. With out identical uniforms and haircuts, clean and quiet indoor shoes, there was perfect order all day. We were taught that it was for the good of the country and for the honor of our family that we all did as were told.

Now the War was over. Shanghai was liberated by the Americans. I could attend an American school and was enrolled by my Grandfather. No matter that I lost my name, I would work hard, be a good girl and my family would be proud. Sitting with six year old first graders, I felt like an over-grown dunce. Trying to learn a new language English and to decipher its writing was hard. Face flaming and contorting to hold back the tears, I was forced to periodically parade through all the classrooms. Pinned to my back would be a particularly mistake-filled paper. If the Sister thought I had tried to slink through the room too quickly, I would have to weave in and out of each row of desks. I feared the ridicule of a teaching technique that was new and horrifying to me.

When the Korean community started a school of its own, I began again. Everyone spoke my language! There was no uniform. The classrooms were bright and cheerful. The woodwork was varnished in clear, natural color. The ceilings were not so tall and there were wall to wall windows. The dismal period was over. I was Kumi again.

This happy interlude lasted only two years. After the economy became precarious, my mother went grocery shopping with a strawbag full of paper money and we received daily reports that the Chinese Communists were close to Shanghai. One day we heard the distant booming of artillery.

Grandfather now allowed his children the option of leaving Shanghai for any part of the world. He returned to Korea. He had tried his best to keep our world stable. In keeping with the old Korean tradition, Grandfather, as the head of the family, had exercised his absolute authority. But the world was changing. His children had seen the new world and old ways were no longer acceptable. My father chose to move to Hong Kong. He left his parents for the first time at forty. He believed that the best legacy he could provide his children was an opportunity to become citizens of the world. He thought the English language would be the universal key. But it wasn't enough.

Are terrible daytime experiences "daymares?" I was now twenty years old and attending the University of Washington. Finally I was in America! My name was Grace. I had experienced no problem being part of any bantering group of classmates on campus. I spoke English fluently. But I never was dated. A Pre-Med student asked me to his fraternity dance, but several "brothers" visited him with the message that my presence would upset the sorority sisters. He was forbidden to bring me. Angrily he moved out of his fraternity house. My best friend, a sorority member, had been advised by a "sister" that the reputation of her house would suffer by her constant association with "that Oriental gal."

Then, one morning, I saw an "Oriental" face staring back at me in the mirror. Until then I hadn't known my face was Yellow! Had everyone seen that? I was shocked. My Yellowness was so plainly visible. I had never seen it.

Had I been aware during these years that I was a Korean? That I was different? Of course. In the schools I attended in Hong Kong as well as the American School in Japan, a point of pride had been the atmosphere of a children's United Nations. At one time there were over fifty nationalities represented in the school. I had acquired five languages. With equal ease and enjoyment, I knew how to eat with a fork in my right or left hand, or with chopsticks. Saddle shoes, bobby socks, skinny skirt and blazer felt as natural to me as to an American born student. Yet, I hadn't known that I was Yellow—that the *color* had mattered. The yellow pigment seemed to be an opaque barrier through which White America could not or did not want to see me.

Finally I removed my mask. My dream had shown me that "Grace" had been the mask. I discarded the "Grace" who tried so hard to eat, dress and talk like an "American." Would my neighbors and friends of twelve years become angry and reject me because I was Kumi, the proud *Korean*-American?

Now I am forty years old: mother of four boys; married to a Caucasian, the Pre-Med student, who is now a Pediatrician.

My sons' experiences show me how right I am to be Kumi. Through them I recognize that I have not been "too sensitive." One son, a first grader comes home and says that his classmates thought he and Doug were not Americans. Doug is a Japanese-American. Both boys were born in this country. They know little about their other identities. Another son, a ninth grader said, "Mom, the guys on this basketball team we were playing called me 'Chink' and 'Jap.' It's weird, isn't it? I think I look normal."

One day, the school Superintendent and his Deputy, both men, and I were walking into the office to interview two attorneys. The Superintendent introduced himself and as he was shaking their hands, said, "Gentlemen, I would like you to meet our Board President. . . ." Both well-dressed young men, with friendly smiles, turned to the Deputy with outstretched hands.

. . . "Kuni Kilburn." Their faces froze, but without breaking stride, they turned half circle to me. My three years in Japan had taught me something about form, about "face." The more grievous an insult, the more shameful an act committed, the more one must save "face" for them. I must save their "face. . . ." And I shook their hands.

My dark thoughts screamed, "someday I may not save their face. I may let them see their face—twisted with their fear of the unknown, fear of the different. The ugliness is in their eyes and not the pigment of my skin. I will cry for them, because I know how much it will hurt."

The night sobbing subsides. I am longer a girl at a ball or otherwise. But other dreams and nightmares haunt me. These too must be faced.

What's in a name? A cliche? No! The origins of awareness, the reality of language and culture. KUMI IS SITTING IN GRACE'S CHAIR.

Georgia Southwestern Anthropologist Don Chang Lee has written two works analyzing the adjustments of Korean-American women entitled (1) *Problems of Asian Wives of U.S. Citizens and Questions of the Governmental Role Regarding Counseling Asian Wives and Their Spouses* and (2) *Korean Wife-American Husband Families in America.*

AN APPEARANCE OF BEING CHINESE

Diana Chang

She was
I am

She is
I was

Still is
Always was, in fact

not quite
    equipped
        to . . .

Camels on my street
Acacias in palaces
    lies
        lies

Half-believing I'm not—
quite myself

(Yet who is
more me?)

I try to remember
    something
Strain to be what I started
    to be

Did I begin there,
    in her sleep?
Has Peking forgotten me?

A womb pulled through itself
like a sleeve

From *The New York Quarterly,* 1975, No. 17. Reprinted by permission of the author.

I am a tall tale
   sincerely
not quite equipped
    to
     be
       Chinese

My cat demands.
Through thick and thin,
You'll get fed, I promise.
I am his rock.

In China heaven is square,
but we feel shapeless

She rode a rickshaw in a typhoon,
pretending to be a native

I look more Chinese here
and pretend too

I inhabit my cat's thoughts,
living where I am

A Chinese seashore
made me small.
The gunfire comes back huge

My grandparents are dead
And I never properly introduced
I've always been
in search of a body
not quite Chinese
to call their own

Would a Chinese moon help?
Does memory want me?

A college friend was discovered at the
   Metropolitan looking up her family tree.
Something to do with a founding father and
   a lost cameo, though she'd been adopted.

Bodies in bed are real.
I'm Europe, I like to think, not quite here,
My cat Madagascar, south of my knee

I am thinking of me.
Imagine

A small thing frowning
The sea cutting me in two
To make do that way

My mother's mother blond,
flax woven into silk

Rice paddies
a suburb of matinees—
I do remember, then

But I don't believe . . .
Tibet is *not* off Fifth Avenue.
Ask anyone but me.

I followed a woman in a mink coat with one
   shoe on,
pursued her bare foot fifteen blocks
until I had to go home and start dinner.
Incomplete. Everything is incomplete.

I dreamt twice I woke up for good,
and they say dreams are sincere

The Hindus achieve a Self which is not a self.
There's no earthly call
for being real

Better no one
than anyone.
No. No.

My Chinese body
out of its American head,

Yet,
I have no talent for insanity

Instead,
we speak
English
reasonably

Anywhere's somewhere,
we're nowhere else

Just before words come,
me at my throat,
I most seem to be

I seem, therefore I
  seem.
It's as far as we go

And you are
so let us meet

as if she always were,

in the event
  I
    am

Two Poems

SAYING YES

Diana Chang

"Are you Chinese?"
"Yes."

"American?"
"Yes."

"*Really* Chinese?"
"No . . . not quite."

"*Really* American?"
"Well, actually, you see . . ."

But I would rather say
yes

Not neither-nor,
not maybe,
but both, and not only

The homes I've had,
the ways I am

I'd rather say it
twice,
yes

OTHERNESS

Diana Chang

"Are you Chinese?"
"Are you American?"

I am fascinated
but other

anywhere

so it follows
(laconically)

I
must
be

    Jewish

Leading to an eye-opener:
real Chinese in China,
not feeling other,
   not international,
   not cosmopolitan

are gentiles, no less

no wonder
I felt the way I did
in the crowd

my Israel
not there

not here

From ASIAN-AMERICAN HERITAGE, edited by David Hsin-Fu Wand, Simon & Schuster, Inc., Pocket Books, Washington Square Press. © 1974. Reprinted by permission of the author.

THE BARRIERS ARE NOT REAL

Katie Funk Wiebe

A few years ago I found an old notebook full of clippings and letters in the bottom of the trunk my parents had given me when I finished high school. On a loose sheet I had written:

> I'm afraid to be a writer. . . . I'm afraid to put things down on paper, things I might regret later on, as if these things really applied to me. But then they do; these things that I want to write are my thoughts, the things that keep me going, the things that slow me up and make me wish I was anywhere but where I am. I shouldn't be afraid. I know I shouldn't. No one will ever see these things I write. No one will ever know they belonged to a girl who once had hopes and dreams, but who never saw them realized.

Were those my words? Had this pressure to write started when I was still absorbed in boyfriends and suntans? I thought it had been the product of my middle years. But there it was, "I want to write. . . ."

Now, several decades later, I am writing. Did anyone in my family have the same longing? Most of my Mennonite ancestors had been farmers for centuries, poking the ground, making green things grow. I never knew my grandfather, the one who was a miller in South Russia. But my father? Did he ever want to describe with words how it felt to clomp around his father's mill in the village of Rosenthal on wooden *Schlorren*? Or to spend Christmas in a train boxcar as a homesick medic in the Russian army? Or to begin life anew in Canada with a red-haired wife, two toddlers, and twenty-five cents in his Russian-style trousers? Why do I know these stories as if I had seen pictures of them?

My paternal grandmother kept a genealogy. My forefathers were members of the group of Mennonites who settled, in peaceful villages in the Ukraine in Russia about 1786 upon the invitation of Empress Catherine the Great. They came from Prussia. And before that from Germany and Holland. Always they were wandering, wandering, in search of freedom to worship God according to the way they knew Him in the Bible.

Catherine the Great had promised the Mennonites religious privileges in exchange for becoming colonists in her country. She needed them. They had the reputation of being honest, hard-working thrifty farmers. They settled and developed the rich steppes of the Ukraine. At various periods when this precious freedom seemed threatened, they left Russia for other lands, many going to America about 1874. My German-speaking parents, who could also speak the language of their adopted country, left with hundreds of others for Canada in 1923 after the Russian revolution. It seemed certain Catherine's *Privilegium* would no longer be honored by the new regime: pacifist Mennonite young men would have to take up arms against their convictions.

So I was born in Canada. I was a New Canadian, my parents told me. I lived in a community that worked hard at the melting pot theory, yet I emerged as a member of an ethnic minority dominated by strong religious beliefs and barnacled by the cultural accredions of four hundred years of wandering from country to country.

Reprinted by permission of the author. (I am grateful to Georgia State University Emeritus Professor, George G. Thielman, for suggesting that I use Ms. Wiebe's work, and also for his hours of devoted research and interest in my anthology.)

But why, if I had received all my education in this new land of promise, did writing remain a silent wish, an undreamt dream, an unarticulated hope—something I could not personally envision happening to me?

Mennonites have always been an agrarian people. Only in the last decades have they moved in large numbers into business and the professions. On the traditional farm work was divided between husband and wife out of necessity. The men worked outside on the land. They were leaders in church and community, especially in Russia, where the government allowed them to regulate life in their own villages. Mennonites were a strongly patriarchal society, like many other Protestant groups developing out of the Reformation.

During the Mennonite interlude in Russia, women worked inside the home baking the *Zwiebach* and *Roggebrot* in the wall oven fired with straw. Sometimes a woman worked in the fields beside her men. The framework for the picture of the ideal Mennonite woman in Russia and in the early years in America was one most Mennonites found comfortable: silence, modesty, and obedience.

I can still see my father walking to church, about three steps ahead of Mother, and Mother calling to him to wait. She wanted the American way, but he had no patience with it. Men moved ahead, took the risks, and women followed. Men walked into church in one door and women in the other. They sat in separate pews. The *Bruderschaft* (council) was represented only by men. This was the way it had always been done, and it seemed right and normal.

Women's place was not with the men. Not with thinking. Not with dreaming, declaring, determining sin, disciplining, deciding to stay or leave Russia. Her place was at home kneading the soft dough with strong hands; stripping milk from soft, warm udders; serving *Prips* and *Schinkefleisch* to tired men when they came home from the fields; cradling children into quietness; loving deeply without open words; praying silently with head covered. The poetry of living had no real attachment to the poetry of words, as Mennonites in their search for a pure God-life isolated themselves from society through language, customs, and geography.

But I knew very little of this when I left high school. I had inherited a strong mixture of values—the freedom entrusted to one of the top students in a school where sex was never considered a deterrent to any vocational goal. Yet, at the same time, I had unconsciously absorbed the values of my Mennonite home in other areas. Mother, while she ladled sour cream gravy and fried Russian pancakes drew the family together through her open acceptance of her role as keeper of the home. Father, who had attended school for about three years, knew the hardships of earning a living without an education. He encouraged economic survival for me and my sisters. He had eaten gophers and crows during the famine in Russia of 1921-22. This new land would provide better for his family. But his limited understanding of what lay ahead in the New World for his daughters could not push me over the hurdles into writing.

I left our heterogenous community for the outside world and plummeted into the Mennonite world instead. I became an active member of the Mennonite Brethren youth group in the city where I began work after high school. In school I had been accustomed to speaking out and arguing with the boys, so I aired my ideas freely in the youth group. As a result I was elected president. Within a matter of weeks though, some of my "young brethren" asked me to resign at the request of pastor and church council. Something about my shape and bodily functions made it impossible for them to allow me to be president. I agreed. Perhaps my interest in leadership had only been a passing fancy.

About 1956 I typed myself a little note again:

> Today I have been doing a lot of thinking about writing. Is it worthwhile considering seriously or shall I just forget the thing altogether? The whole problem seems to resolve itself around the matter of having something to write about. If I have nothing to say, there is no use in writing that bit of nothing down on paper.

By this time I was married, had three children, and a preacher-husband who was studying religious journalism, and I had penetrated the Mennonite world even more deeply. But I did set up a desk in the corner and began to write. My first writing attempts led to helping my husband in his work of editing a small periodical for youth workers in the church. I enjoyed the creative activity, and, as my husband became busy in other activities, the editing became mostly my effort. When he suggested to the administrative committee that because I was doing most of the work and apparently quite successfully, I be appointed editor, their reaction was negative. In the Mennonite world, women did not teach nor usurp authority over the men, even in writing. I was crushed.

For a time I fought a battle against two enemies, both of whom should have been my best friends—God and myself. I felt guilty questioning what seemed right and pure: that a woman should find complete fulfillment in her role as wife and mother and never expect God to require anything more of her. She had her sphere of service. Was I trying to wiggle out from under the authority of God's Word by considering a sideline venture? My Mennonite conscience told me I should find sufficient meaning in life as the wife of Rev. Walter Wiebe, without making any specific contribution of my own. Most Mennonite women had done so. My mother had never had any other aspirations. Or had she? The thought dumbfounded me. Had she buried her longings for creative expression deep inside her as she baked pan after pan of *Zwiebach* and *Platz*?

If I fought what seemed to be the voice of God, I fought myself also. The craving inside me to write was part of me, yet I couldn't acknowledge it as mine. The men in the black suits and open Bible said it shouldn't be in me, and I did want to please them.

My perplexity is true for many women, ethnic and non-ethnic, in Protestant groups. It stems from the subtle leeching of her belief in her own power to think, to create, to choose, and to contribute as a person in her own right, especially in the arts, for this is part of the public sphere, which belongs to men by tradition. Women lack the psychic strength to give utterance to areas of life about which they have been trained to be silent. In social groups, I recall my husband drifted to the men's corner and the interesting talk about church and world politics. We women had to content ourselves with hemline lengths, new knitting patterns, canning successes and failures, and how to potty-train a child.

I wanted to write. I wanted to discover through writing the meaning of my life and to let others know how I felt. I needed a mentor, someone to encourage me, to stroke, to guide, to support my dreams and help put them into effect. My role models were loving, generous women who made excellent *Vereniki* and sewed fine stitches in quilts, but understood little of my longing to give myself away on paper. Writing was a frill, a luxury—not important for frugal, practical people. Further, it was unseemly for women to move into any field which might put them into competition with men or where they might judge masculine fields of endeavor.

As I began to write, both fear of success and fear of failure haunted me. Fear sat close to me every time I opened my typewriter. *How do you think you can write with authority? Mennonite women aren't an authority in any matter except familial concerns.* Desperately I wanted the opportunity for insight and comprehension which would make me an authority, but instead I was offered another coffeemaker to attend to.

Any woman wanting to write, coming from a culture which values family life highly, will battle her conscience in other areas. If fear sat on one side, guilt moved in close on the other. *Shouldn't you be baking another batch of cookies for the children? What will the family say if they get casserole again tonight?* Writing can seldom be a first for women, if they are wives and mothers. Mothers don't have a secretary. They don't have a wife. They can be interupted by children, husband, plumber and paperboy. So they are eased out of writing early, unless they make peace between family concerns and writing.

In "The Red Line," a short story of Rudy Wiebe[1], a young Mennonite girl on the ship crossing the ocean to her new home, becomes bored with life behind the barrier (a red line on the floor) which separates the immigrants from the first-class passengers. Boldly she crosses the red line into their life.

In a critical review of the story I wrote, "In defiance of her Mennonite-trained conscience she sets out to explore this new world and finds that the barriers are not real—only man-made. She can easily pass each one."

Though for a while every time I sat down to write, a jury of six solemn men in dark suits with large black thumb-indexed Bibles open to I Timothy watched me work, I slowly realized the barriers before me were not divine interdicts. The barriers were man-made, but they were also in me. I had to be persistent with my own creativity. With the help of editors, friends, and children, I moved toward the barrier once again. Bumping, blundering, blustering, battering, bluffing and blessing, I crossed over.

[1]No relative.

The story "The Red Line" appeared first as a short story in several Mennonite publications, and then later became Chapter 5: Over the Red Line in *The Blue Mountains of China* published by McClelland and Stewart in 1970.

TO A BROWN SPIDER: en el cielo

Angela de Hoyos

Brave arachnid
spinning with star-lit dreams
your daring web
—how precarious is your perch!

I too h
     a
     n
     g by a thread.

From ARISE, CHICANO! AND OTHER POEMS, Bilingual Edition, Spanish translations by Mireya Rebles, Backstage Books, 1975. Reprinted by permission of the author.

SUCH, SUCH WERE THE JOYS . . .

—George Orwell

Teruko Ogata Daniel

I am not comfortable in my yellow skin. At one time, until I was twelve, I was able to make myself believe it was special. I even thought it was beautiful most of the time. But no longer. Therefore, each night I stand watch, vigilantly guarding my discomfort while my family sleeps.

Stars and sun float, drifting in open air. Caught between the silent hours of midnight and the terrible fatigue of dawn, my past and present relentlessly divide and re-divide; fill and re-fill; shape and re-shape. Unsaid utterances flutter like restless wings, straining to light on pages of a dictionary to be transformed into orderly, sequential words.

Exhausted I seek my doctor's help.

"Menopausal insomnia. Neurasthenic hysteria," Dr. Cambell jots in my file. I accept the outstretched prescription and jam it into the chaos of my shoulder bag and leave. I say nothing. But I am trembling with silent outrage.

That night, I prowl the shadows prying and unearthing echoes and images buried deeply beneath mounded hills of today. Children's voices reverberating in a cave! Truimphantly I discover the shivering joys of fearful anticipation as I lurk behind a sandy pillar. We Ogatas, Onos, and Minatoyas are playing hide and seek in the cool caves beneath the surface of the empty, hot, sandy lot across from our home. (We are unaware that the caves were dug long ago to hid illegal Chinese immigrants waiting to hop the passing freight just a block away.) Kyoko, my sister, is IT and within touching distance from me but is distracted by a flitting movement

Reprinted by permission of the author.

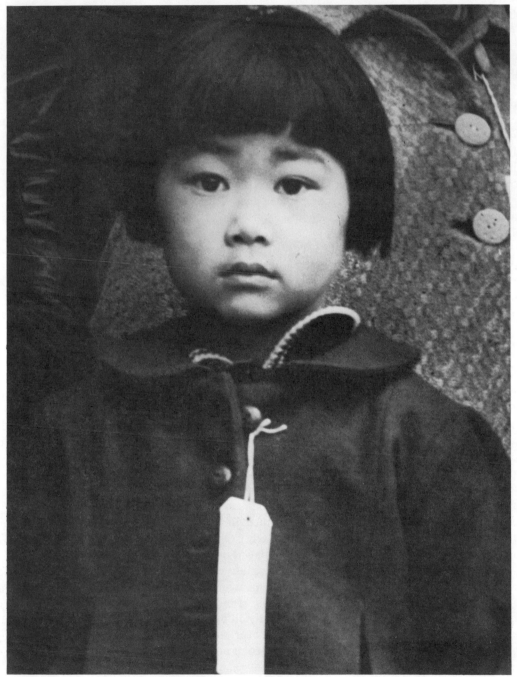

"Japanese-American girl." Dorothea Lange, War Relocation
Authority, Hayward, California, May 8, 1942. Reprinted by permission of the California Historical Society, San Francisco, California.

beyond the bend. That evening in the company of my seven sisters, I submerge myself into the drowsy, steamy warmth of the nightly bath knowing with full certainty that Oka-san will call us before we fall asleep in the deep, rectangular Japanese style tub. The next day, there is the cheery "Tadaiima, Oka-san!" as we troop home from school. This was being Japanese; this was the *real* world.

At age twelve, Pearl Harbor shattered the illusion of being totally Japanese. Either one was Japanese or American—without a hyphen. After hearing the news on the radio while visiting friends, we sped home. That night we children watched our parents frantically heaping letters, photographs, and family mementos onto the blazing bonfire in the front yard. The image of my pidgin English speaking parents trying to incinerate a lifetime of things Japanese struck me as ludicrous, unjust, and futile. Soon their frenzied panic ignited and swirled us into eager cooperation as we helped hurl anything and everything Japanese into the fire.

Early the next morning, two young F.B.I. agents dressed like respectable business men in brown suits arrived followed by smoky clouds of the cigar-biting, melon-bellied, Stetson-hatted Police Chief.

We all knew about him. Swollen with officious pomposity and patriotism he announced they were here to search our home for anything disloyal to the United States Government. As the search ensued he discovered a large green laundry bag in my bachelor uncle's bedroom crammed into a dresser drawer.

"Well . . ." he drawled triumphantly, "What have we got here, Charlie?"

"You wantee?" my uncle replied. And he reached into the bag and passed a handful of browned and cracked postcards of white ladies all posing in the nude. Mother gasped but we giggled. (We had spent many hot summer days feverishly enjoying his secret collection.)

The police chief's teeth snapped his cigar in two. Slowly, deliberately, he ground the gray tipped butt into the linoleum, and dumped the contents of the bag onto the floor. Then he walked over them as he moved toward the closet.

As the search continued, receipts written in Japanese to my father were discovered. The receipts, overlooked in the frenetic burning of the night before were receipts for tuition fees for my two older sisters living with relatives in Japan. An endless interrogation then followed. We were all shepherded to the laundry adjoining our living quarters where the three law men accused my father of sending cash in support of the Japanese Army. It was endless. Charges, allegations, threats; the lawmen would not be denied. The ordeal continued all day. Finally in late afternoon, my father, unable to convince them in his broken English of his innocence, consumed with frustration and fear, *cried*—IN FRONT OF US—his wife, his children, his brother. This show of weakness, this loss of filial strength was unbelievable.

At that moment, I hated being Japanese because I knew my mother had lied: We were not special—We were not better than the Whites. The white kids were right after all. My nose was too flat; my eyes were too slanted; my face was a moonface; and my short legs were radish shaped, not wiry. We were poor, too. That's why all our new dresses were the same except for color; Mother had had to use the same pattern over and over again and color coded us by age for expediency, just as our yellow skin color coded us at school.

I knew then it was not possible to be Japanese and survive in a White system. Survival meant acting, looking, achieving, and surpassing the whites.

So I cultivated, studied, aped, and perfected the art of ingratiating invisibility to atone for my guilt of being Japanese. We all did. Japanese living on the east side of the Columbia River in southeastern Washington were not evacuated to the concentration camps. As one of the three families Japanese living among so many whites during the War we struggled unceasingly to become members of a model minority who wanted to be good Americans! We became living examples of the poor, social outcasts who made good. My older sister set the tone. She received the Daughter's of the American Revolution Award during her high school graduation as Valedictorian of her class. I excelled in debate, the school paper, and like her, earned a scholarship to college. My favorite teacher advised me to reject it and attend business college so that I "could be with my own kind." Eventually we all graduated from various colleges as teachers. Later, we sought advanced degrees. We married and raised our children as whites.

In the subsequent loss of qualities and knowledge of traditions Japanese and the involuntary acceptance of elements "American" the nagging anger, the discomfort never withdraws. Nightly, I stand my watch, wakefully clinging to hopes and a notion that a hyphen, an identity, a sense of completion, a resurrection, a peace will creep silently in moonshine and dash away forever the hardball burst of anger.

ALL THE PRETTY LITTLE HORSES

Hushaby, don't you cry,
Go to sleepy, little baby.
When you wake, you shall have
   cake,
And all the pretty little horses.
Blacks and bays, dapples and grays,
Coach and six-a little horses.

Way down yonder in the meadow,
There's a poor little lambie;
The bees and the butterflies
   pickin' out his eyes,
The poor little thing cries,
   "Mammy."

Hushaby, don't you cry,
Go to sleepy, little baby.

"Raffle: Dark Bay Horse, "Star," Mulatto Girl, "Sarah," signed by Joseph Jennings." Bella C. Landerer Collection. Courtesy of The York Historical Society, New York City.

"All the Pretty Little Horses" is an authentic slave lullaby. I am grateful to Lucius Sanford for bringing this poem to my attention.

CHANUKAH, CAMP HILL, ALABAMA

Janet Rechtman

The Jewish kids played in the pasture, a sister and brother in an Alabama town. Soon the sun would set and Chanukah begin. The dry field grass scratched her legs when, Indian wrestling the girl rolled on the ground to break a fall. The incredible blue sky, sunless, chilled the sweat that sank salt into new wounds.

The wrestling became a spat and he left victorious. The girl played on alone, a new game. She pretended the holiday was not her own. She was neuter, no, a Christian, a Gulliver pinned by Jew hammers, Jew strings, and Jew nails, changed for a night to a Jew.

Her parents explained that it wasn't so bad. She had eight days of Christmas, not a sickly one. Eight times the joy! Eight times the gifts! Except she was ten, and she would only have one gift this year. And eight times the void on the other nights.

"Why is this night different from all others?" She didn't know what to say to the boy who came through the field with a cow. Bovine both, she was terrified. What if he asked another unaswerable question? Like "How come you're not saved?" She lacked the gifts to make herself understood and ran away mutely, leaving him laughing at the manure on her shoes.

Better stay near the house now. The sky was red.

Her little sisters played store in the back yard. They still had eight days—she'd seen the tiny oven that was the first of this year's potlatch. On the back stoop she watched them imitate a mother and friend: they did not ask her to join in. Impatient she found a stick and cleaned her shoes.

Sundown was close. Where should she be when they called?

She ran to the front yard, to the pecan tree with the rounded crotch that was her favorite perch when she was little. Tonight she was grown up, though. A more dignified spot was required. In the orchard down by the wild plums, perhaps—but she'd eaten the fruit already and she'd only get dirty on the red clay bank.

She was running to the grape arbor when she heard the call.

Eldest, she lit first, a pink shamas and a green spiraled taper, and read prayers from the paper that came with the candles. The two lights flickered in the silver menorah. She wanted to touch the flame but was afraid. "Boruch atoy adonay." She wondered at the ancient violence and longed for the prince of peace, for the easy tunes of Christmas instead of the tortured cadence she now sang. "Rock of ages let our song, vast thy saving power. Thou amidst the raging foe wast our sheltering tower."

They brought out the gifts, unwrapped as always. The first of eight for the others, one alone for her. A doll. Her friends had dolls and she'd wanted one too—but not like this, a lady doll with embarassing breasts, red lips and bouffant hair. She hated it, but acted pleased so no one would say she was childish.

Seven nights she brought the doll woman out, the badge of her growing up. Seven days she hid it in her room. On the eighth morning her brother found it and drew nipples on its breasts and a moustache of pubic hair between its legs.

From *Southern Exposure*, Vol. 4, No. 3, 1976. Reprinted by permission of the editor and the author.

That afternoon she went out to see what her friends had under their Christmas trees: skates, baby dolls, chemistry sets, BB guns, footballs and bikes. They were all laughing as they played, joking about how hard it was to be good all year.

The girl ran home crying. She cried because of the doll. She cried because she was captive, imprisoned where she did not belong. She cried because her parents had lied when they said there was no Santa Claus.

LEAVES FROM THE MENTAL PORTFOLIO OF AN EURASIAN

Sui Sin Far (Edith Maud Eaton)

Edith Maud Eaton (Sui Sin Far) 1867-1914 was born in the Far East and died in Montreal, Canada, the daughter of an English entrepeneur whose mother was either "a Chinese lady educated in England" (by Eaton's account), or "a Japanese noblewoman, adopted . . . as a child and educated in England." (In Eaton's New York Times obituary notice, April 9, 1914). She was a freelance journalist, secretary and author of stories about Chinese Americans and China.

Ms. Eaton was sensitive about being Eurasian, was more comfortable within the Chinese American community; yet, as a "lady journalist" she was proud of maintaining herself as "a very serious and sober-minded spinster indeed."

*In an 1896 review of one of her works, **Land of Sunshine,** the California reviewer said that the Chinese characters in her stories ". . . have an insight and sympathy which are probably unique. To others the alien . . . is at best mere 'literary material': in these stories he [or she] is a human being."**

I meet a half Chinese, half white girl. Her face is plastered with a thick white coat of paint and her eyelids and eyebrows are blackened so that the shape of her eyes and the whole expression of her face is changed. She was born in the East, and at the age of eighteen came West in answer to an advertisement. Living for many years among the working class, she had heard little but abuse of the Chinese. It is not difficult, in a land like California, for a half Chinese, half white girl to pass as one of Spanish or Mexican origin. This the poor child does, tho she lives in nervous dread of being "discovered." She becomes engaged to a young man, but fears to tell him what she is, and only does so when, compelled by a fearless American girl friend. This girl, who knows her origin, realizing that the truth sooner or later must be told, and better soon than late, advises the Eurasian to confide in the young man, assuring her that he loves her well enough not to allow her nationality to stand, a bar sinister, between them. But the Eurasian perfers to keep her secret, and only reveals it to the man who is to be her husband when driven to bay by the American girl, who declares that if the half-breed will not tell the truth she will.

From *The Independent,* 66, #3138 (January 1909). (I am grateful to S.E. [Sam Solberg] for sending this work to me, and for his enthusiastic interest and assistance.)

*Aiiieeeee! *An Anthology of Asian-American Writers.* Edited by Frank Chin, Jeffery Paul Chan, Lawson Fusao Inada, Shawn Wong (Anchor Press, Doubleday, 1975), p. 3.

When the young man hears that the girl he is engaged to has Chinese blood in her veins, he exclaims: "Oh, what will my folks say?" But that is all. Love is stronger than prejudice with him, and neither he nor she deems it necessary to inform his "folks."

The Americans, having for many years manifested a much higher regard for the Japanese than for the Chinese, several half Chinese young men and women, thinking to advance themselves, both in a social and business sense, pass as Japanese. They continue to be known as Eurasians; but a Japanese. Eurasian does not appear in the same light as a Chinese Eurasian. The unfortunate Chinese Eurasians! Are not those who compel them to thus cringe more to be blamed than they?

People, however, are not all alike. I meet white men, and women, too, who are proud to mate with those who have Chinese blood in their veins, and think it a great honor to be distinguished by the friendship of such. There are also Eurasians and Eurasians. I know of one who allowed herself to become engaged to a white man after refusing him nine times. She had discouraged him in every way possible, had warned him that she was half Chinese; that her people were poor, that every week or month she sent home a certain amount of her earnings, and that the man she married would have to do as much, if not more; also, most uncompromising truth of all, that she did not love him and never would. But the resolute and undaunted lover swore that it was a matter of indifference to him whether she was a Chinese or a Hottentot, that it would be his pleasure and privilege to allow her relations double what it was in her power to bestow, and as to not loving him—that did not matter at all. He loved her. So, because the young woman had a married mother and married sisters, who were always picking at her and gossiping over her independent manner of living, she finally consented to marry him, recording the agreement in her diary thus:

"I have promised to become the wife of _____ _____ on _____ _____ , 189__, because the world is so cruel and sneering to a single woman—and for no other reason."

Everything went smoothly until one day. The young man was driving a pair of beautiful horses and she was seated by his side, trying very hard to imagine herself in love with him, when a Chinese vegetable gardener's cart came rumbling along. The Chinaman was a jolly-looking individual in blue cotton blouse and pantaloons, his rakish looking hat being kept in place by a long queue which was pulled upward from his neck and wound around it. The young woman was suddenly possest with the spirit of mischief. "Look!" she cried, indicating the Chinaman, "there's my brother. Why don't you salute him?"

The man's face fell a little. He sank into a pensive mood. The wicked one by his side read him like an open book.

"When we are married," said she, "I intend to give a Chinese party every month."

No answer.

"As there are very few aristocratic Chinese in this city, I shall fill up with the laundrymen and vegetable farmers. I don't believe in being exclusive in democratic America, do you?"

He hadn't a grain of humor in his composition, but a sickly smile contorted his features as he replied:

"You shall do just as you please, my darling. But—but—consider a moment. Wouldn't it be just a little pleasanter for us if, after we are married, we allowed it to be presumed that you were—er—Japanese? So many of my friends have inquired of me if that is not your nationality. They would be so charmed to meet a little Japanese lady."

"Hadn't you better oblige them by finding one?"

"Why—er—what do you mean?"

"Nothing much in particular. Only—I am getting a little tired of this," taking off his ring.

"You don't mean what you say! Oh, put it back, dearest! You know I would not hurt your feelings for the world!"

"You haven't. I'm more than pleased. But I do mean what I say."

That evening the "ungrateful" Chinese Eurasian diaried, among other things, the following:

"Joy, oh, joy! I'm free once more. Never again shall I be untrue to my own heart. Never again will I allow any one to 'hound' or 'sneer' me into matrimony."

I secure transportation to many California points. I meet some literary people, chief among whom is the editor of the magazine who took my first Chinese stories. He and his wife give me a warm welcome to their ranch. They are broad-minded people, whose interest in me is sincere and intelligent, not affected and vulgar. I also meet some funny people who advise me to "trade" upon my nationality. They tell me that if I wish to succeed in literature in America I should dress in Chinese costume, carry a fan in my hand, wear a pair of scarlet beaded slippers, live in New York, and come of high birth. Instead of making myself familiar with the Chinese-Americans around me, I should discourse on my spirit acquaintance with Chinese ancestors and quote in between the "Good mornings" and "How d'ye dos" of editors,

> "Confucius, Confucius, how great is Confucius,
> Before Confucius, there never was Confucius.
> After Confucius, there never came Confucius,"
> etc., etc., etc.,

or something like that, both illuminating and obscuring, don't you know. They forget, or perhaps they are not aware that the old Chinese sage taught "The way of sincerity is the way of heaven."

My experiences as an Eurasian never cease; but people are not now as prejudiced as they have been. In the West, too, my friends are more advanced in all lines of thought than those whom I know in Eastern Canada—more genuine, more sincere, with less of the form of religion, but more of its spirit.

So I roam backward and forward across the continent. When I am East, my heart is West. When I am West, my heart is East. Before long I hope to be in China. As my life began in my father's country it may end in my mother's.

After all I have no nationality and am not anxious to claim any. Individuality is more than nationality. "You are you and I am I," says Confucius. I give my right hand to the Occidentals and my left to the Orientals, hoping that between them they will not utterly destroy the insignificant "connecting link."

THE JEWISH FEMINIST: CONFLICT IN IDENTITIES

Judith Plaskow

This is the text of an address to the National Jewish Women's Conference in New York, February 1973.

What I would like to discuss is our identity as Jewish women. It seems to me that the identity of the Jewish woman—or rather of some of the Jewish women I know including, first of all, myself—lies somewhere in the conflict between being a woman and being a Jew and in the necessity of combining the two in as yet unknown ways. So I want to speak about this conflict in three of its aspects.

I can best begin to explain what I mean by a conflict between being a woman and being a Jew by saying that it is not a coincidence that we are discussing the questions we are now discussing. We are not doing so due to some unfolding of the Jewish tradition, due to the fact that this is a Jewishly appropriate moment. We are here because a secular movement of the liberation of women has made it imperative that we raise certain Jewish issues now, because we will not let ourselves be defined as Jewish women in ways in which we cannot allow ourselves to be defined as women. This creates a conflict not just and not primarily because the women's movement is a secular movement whose principles we are attempting to apply to an ancient religious tradition, but because the women's movement is a different community around which we might center our lives. The conflict between communities is the first level on which I experience the conflict between being a woman and being a Jew.

Now of course we can belong to many different communities, and in fact we do. We identify as Jews, as women, as Americans, as students, as human beings. But it seems to me that though we can belong to many communities, only one can be our organizing center. Only one community can be the "Rosetta Stone"[1] through which we view and interpret and give room to others.

Since we are raising questions about the Jewish community because of it, it is clear that the women's movement makes some claim on us to be that organizing center. But it makes that claim not only because it forces us to raise new questions. For some of us—certainly for me— being involved in the women's movement has been one of the most important and exciting experiences of our lives. It has indeed changed the eyes through which we see the world. And through it we have experienced sisterhood—a community far more vital than anything most of us have experienced through the traditional institutions of the Jewish "community."

Despite this, our relationship with our Jewishness would not need to be one of conflict were it not for a second problem—that the Jewish community will not let us, as feminists, feel at home in it. Every time I let myself be lulled into thinking that I as a whole person am a member of this community, some event lets me know in no uncertain terms that I am wrong.

This sense of exclusion arises partly from the fact that everything in our written tradition comes from the hands of men. The *halakhah,* most obviously, is the product of many genera-

From *Response* Magazine, No. 18, Summer 1973. Reprinted by permission of the editor. (I am grateful to Rabbi Marc Wilson and Meta Wilson for bringing this work to my attention.)

tions of men. The same is true of the *aggadah*. The bible was written by men. The myths from which the Bible borrowed and which it used and transformed were written by men. The liturgy was written by men. Jewish philosophy is the work of men. Modern Jewish theology is the work of men. It was men who wrote even the special books for women, and it was men who designated women's three *mitzvot* and wrote the blessings.

Now my point is not that therefore all these things are irrelevant to us. That is simply not true, of course. The Bible is very much our Bible. There are male-written Jewish stories that we love. There are prayers that express our feelings as well as the feelings of the men who wrote them.

My point is rather that all these things have a *question mark* over them. As Mary Daly has said, women have had our power of *naming* stolen from us. From the day that God brought the animals to Adam in the garden of Eden to see what *he* would call them, it has been through the words of men that we have known and addressed the world.[2] Although we do not know in advance that their words are not our words, neither do we know that they are. At a time when we are newly discovering and naming ourselves, we need to name anew the world around us.

If there are certain things which we will just call by their old names again, there are other words we will most definitely need to speak for the first time, for there are many times when the male power of naming has oppressed and excluded us. I needn't discuss this fact in relation to *halakhah* since it has been and will be a central topic of discussion here. I do want to say though that the exclusion of women intrudes itself into other, very different areas of Jewish life. I was recently reading Franz Rosenzweig's beautiful essay "The Builders," in which he talks about how the assimilated Jew can return to and reappropriate the tradition. One point he makes is that the demarcation line between what is forbidden by Jewish law and what is outside the realm of law and therefore permitted must be broken down in order both that the law take on a positive character and that the realm of what is permitted become a Jewish realm. There I was, reading this essay, moved by it, trying to understand it as it was addressed to me, when all of a sudden, I came to an example of what he means by endowing the law with positive meaning. "In this united sphere of the doable lies, for instance," he says, "the legal exclusion of the woman from the religious congregation; but also in it lies with equal force her ruling rank in the home. . . ." Thus what was one moment my essay the next moment was not. What I wanted to use as a gate back into the whole tradition became a door shut against me.

Let me give an example of another very different way in which our tradition excludes women. There is the fact that we address God as *he*. And it is not just that we use the masculine pronoun in the absence of a neuter one, we image *him* in male terms. Thus he is King, Lord, Shepherd, Father, etc. Now there are times when this imagery would seem to work in our favor, to make it easier for us to relate to God. In the central part of *The Star of Redemption*, Rosenzweig has a long discussion of revelation in which the relation of the beloved and lover in "Song of Songs" becomes the model for the relation between God and humankind. In this case, it is the woman who symbolizes humanity while God is the lover. This is a conception of the human/God relation which is by no means limited to Rosenzweig. And this image, while a limited one, since we relate to God in many ways, is fine. But aside from the fact that the exclusive use of male imagery is inaccurate—we know that God is not male—we are just beginning to explore the effects that this use has on the self-image and understanding of men and women. I recently read an article which quoted several church commission reports on the admission of women to the ministry.[3] Many of the arguments they came up with against the ordination of women were just incredible. One not atypical clergyman argues that the minister, whether he likes it or not, is a God figure, and that since in the Bible God is imaged in exclusively male terms, it is inappropriate for women to take this role. Just think what a statement like that says about its author's attitude toward women—and toward men! The Jewish community has not yet needed to resort to arguments like this to exclude women from the rabbinate,[4] but there is no reason to suppose that the psychological dynamic they evidence is foreign to Jews, or that we do not draw equally horrendous—if unexpressed—conclusions after calling God "he" all our lives.

The problems we as women face in relation to our tradition are deep and complex, involving almost every aspect of tradition. Where then are we going to find the new words, our words, which need to be spoken? How can we find the words which are our words and yet are Jewish words? Can we—how can we—assure ourselves in advance that if we are true to our own experiences we can remain in continuity with tradition?

This brings me to the third aspect of the conflict I want to discuss. It is this. The difficulties in my speaking both from my own experiences and from tradition are aggravated by the fact that I have no way to Jewishly express my experiences in the women's movement. Let me explain what I mean by this.

This past summer, I participated in a week-long conference of about sixty women who had gathered to discuss what women as women have to contribute to theology.[5] Each morning, we broke into small groups to deal with different aspects of the question. One of the things the group I joined tried to examine was the issue of in what way our experiences in the women's movement could be considered religious experiences. Not until I got home did I realize that the "religious" language we were using to describe our experiences was in fact Christian language. The words that kept cropping up again and again in our conversation were "conversion," "self-transformation," "grace." We were using Protestant language, a vocabulary of personal change, to express the fact that within the community of women something very important happens to each of us individually.

There are two things to be said about this. One is that, looking back on our meetings, I don't think we used these words just because they are only common vocabulary and familiar to us. I think we used them because they are accurate. In any event, they accurately described my experiences. And the other thing is that there are no—or, I should say, I do not know any— Jewish words that express the same things. This may well be a reflection of my own ignorance. It could be that there are aspects of the Jewish tradition—mysticism, for example—that would be sources of a language of personal experience. But so far as I know, whereas the Protestant woman might claim that she is in contact with the true working of the Holy Spirit and understands grace in its full reality for the first time, I cannot, as a Jew, say any of these things. As a Jew, I must remain silent.

So again we come back to the problem of finding new words. Where will they come from? How can we speak who we are?

I don't have a solution to this problem. The questions are really much clearer to me than the answers, but I would like to conclude by saying something about the direction in which I think we need to look for answers.

I know that when I pose the question to myself, "How can I find new words to express my experiences as a woman?" I have a tendency to mythologize the expression "women's experience." What I mean by this is that I unconsciously assume that there is something called "women's experience" which is separate from ths lives and histories of real women and which we can discover only now that we have begun to question our traditional roles. In a way, this makes the lives of women who lived before us irrelevant. Only now are we going to find out who we really are, who we really have been. When I think about this objectively, however, I realize that this mythologizing process is also a falsifying one. There is no such thing as "women's experience" apart from what have been the experiences of real women, and that means experiences always in relation to what men have said being a woman means. This is the first factor in where our answers might be found.

The second is that in belonging to many different communities that shape and feed our lives, and despite the conflicts between them and the division of our loyalties, there are points in time in which our histories as Jews and our histories as women intersect—in Sarah's laughter at the idea of bearing a child in her old age, for example, in Miriam's song at the Red Sea, in Hannah's prayer at the dedication of Samuel, in Deborah's battle hymn, in Beruriah's learning. I think that if we want to speak words as women that will also be Jewish words, we need to try to recover and reappropriate the histories of Jewish women who managed to be persons within the boundaries alloted to them. If "women's experience" and the experience of women are the same thing, we have to begin looking for "women's experience" in their experiences. Can we know how they viewed their experiences? What in them do we want to appropriate? Are there things in their experiences that implicitly or explicitly judge the boundaries assigned to those experiences? What in them do we want to reject or to modify and why? It is not that through them we can say everything we want to say. But without them we might not even be able to begin.

With apologies to those of you who have heard it already, I would like to read the result of one attempt to reappropriate, with modifications, two of the women in our tradition.[6]

APPLESOURCE

In the beginning, the Lord God formed Adam and Lilith from the dust of the ground and breathed into their nostrils the breath of life. Created from the same source, they were equal in all ways. Adam, being a man, didn't like this situation, and he looked for ways to change it. He said, "I'll have my figs now, Lilith," ordering her to wait on him, and he tried to leave to her the daily tasks of life in the garden. But Lilith wasn't one to take any nonsense; she picked herself up, uttered God's holy name, and flew away. "Well now, Lord," complained Adam, "that uppity woman you sent me has gone and deserted me." The Lord, inclined to be sympathetic, sent his messengers after Lilith, telling her to shape up and return to Adam or face dire punishment. She, however, preferring anything to living with Adam, decided to stay right where she was. And so God, after more careful consideration this time, caused a deep sleep to fall upon Adam and out of one of his ribs created for him a second companion, Eve.

For a time, Eve and Adam had quite a good thing going. Adam was happy now, and Eve, though she occasionally sensed capacities within herself which remained undeveloped, was basically satisfied with the role of Adam's wife and helper. The only thing that really disturbed her was the excluding closeness of the relationship between Adam and God. Adam and God just seemed to have more in common, both being men, and Adam came to identify with God more and more. After a while that made God a bit uncomfortable too, and he started going over in his mind whether he may not have made a mistake letting Adam talk him into banishing Lilith and creating Eve, seeing the power that gave Adam.

Meanwhile Lilith, all alone, attempted from time to time to rejoin the human community in the garden. After her first fruitless attempt to breach its walls, Adam worked hard to build them stronger, even getting Eve to help him. He told her fearsome stories of the demon Lilith who threatens women in childbirth and steal children from their cradles in the middle of the night. The second time Lilith came, she stormed the garden's main gate, and a great battle between her and Adam ensued in which she was finally defeated. This time, however, before Lilith got away, Eve got a glimpse of her and saw she was a woman like herself.

After this encounter, seeds of curiosity and doubt began to grow in Eve's mind. Was Lilith indeed just another woman? Adam has said she was a demon. Another woman! The very idea attracted Eve. She had never seen another creature like herself before. And how beautiful and strong Lilith had looked! How bravely she had fought! Slowly, slowly, Eve began to think about the limits of her own life within the garden.

One day, after many months of strange and disturbing thoughts, Eve, wandering around the edge of the garden, noticed a young apple tree she and Adam had planted and saw that one of its branches stretched over the garden wall. Spontaneously, she tried to climb it, and, struggling to the top, swung herself over the wall.

She did not wander long on the other side before she met the one she had come to find, for Lilith was waiting. At first sight of her, Eve remembered the tales of Adam and was frightened—but Lilith understood and greeted her kindly. "Who are you?" they asked each other. "What is your story?" And they sat and spoke together, of the past and then of the future. They talked for many hours, not once, but many times. They taught each other many things, and told each other stories, and laughed together, and cried, over and over, till the bond of sisterhood grew between them.

Meanwhile, back in the garden, Adam was puzzled by Eve's comings and goings and disturbed by what he sensed to be her new attitude toward him. He talked to God about it, and God, having his own problems with Adam and a somewhat broader perspective, was able to help him out a little—but he was confused too. Something had failed to go according to plan. As in the days of Abraham, he needed counsel from his children. "I am who I am," thought God, "but I must become who I will become."

And God and Adam were expectant and afraid the day Eve and Lilith returned to the garden, bursting with possibilities, ready to rebuild it together.

NOTES

1. H. Richard Niebuhr. *The Meaning of Revelation* (New York: Macmillan, 1941), p. 113.
2. Mary Daly, "After the Demise of God the Father: A Call for the Castration of Sexist Religion," *Women and Religion: 1972* (Missoula, Mont.: American Academy of Religion, 1973), pp. 7-23.
3. Elizabeth Farians, "Phallic Worship: The Ultimate Idolatry," *Women and Religion: 1972* (Missoula, Mont.: American Academy of Religion, 1973), pp. 63-74.

4. Interestingly, since this speech was delivered, some Jewish leaders have resorted to exactly this argument against ordaining women as rabbis. See Mortimer Ostow's comments in "Women and Change in Jewish Law," *Conservative Judaism* XXIX(1) (Fall 1974): pp. 5-12.
5. At Grailville, Loveland, Ohio, June 18-25, 1972.
6. The ideas for the myth emerged from a Biblical/Theological subgroup at the Grailville conference: Karen Bloomquist, Margaret Early, Elizabeth Farians, and myself.

THE LIBERATION OF A FIRST GENERATION SLOVAK-AMERICAN WOMAN

Sonya Jason

As a member of an ethnic group who is still discovering the pristine delights of examining my ethnic roots, one thing seems certain. As I compare notes with women of other ethnic origins, some one or some other group appears responsible for all our failings. As has been the history of the past, so it is the trend of today, a scapegoat must be found. And when the various ethnic groups stop arguing long enough to agree, the culprit they collectively point to is the WASP.

Speaking from my own experience, this is nonsense and I am trying to pry that beam from my own Slovak-American eye before I attack that splinter in the eye of the Wasp.

As a child reared in the community that was in the past popularly termed a melting pot (a misnomer because ethnic cliques segregated themselves as surely did the borders of Europe) it was silliness to me when Czechs, Italians, Germans or other indicated a superiority over us Slovaks or visa versa. Of course, some were and the reverse is also true, but already I was painfully aware of the shortcomings of my own family which was typically patriarchical to care about what my neighbors thought. To America, as in eastern Europe, my parents carried the seeds of their early conditioning and the lives of their children paralleled the lives of the children of their siblings there I have no doubt. Here in America, as in Europe, the male was the ruler in the home and marriage a slave relationship at worst, a benevolent despotic sovereignty at best. Love, that miraculous quality that nurtures and expands the child was a luxury because the struggle for survival was all consuming. However, there was also the plight of the English, French, Indian, Oriental, and so forth as well as the Wasp of lower middle class or poverty level.

Repressed by the Austro-Hungarian regime for centuries, compulsory education for my parents in the early 20th century was not known. My mother, basically very intelligent, was taken out of school early to help with the rearing of her four sisters after her mother was widowed at an early age.

My father fared little better. He was the last of a dozen children whose mother died when he was only two. He was left to the care of siblings and a father too occupied with eking out a subsistence to be able to offer anything else.

Reprinted by permission of the author. (I am grateful to Michael Novak for suggesting that Ms. Jason contribute this work to my anthology.)

M E CLAYTON

"Slavic lady with a bun." By permission of M. E. Clayton, the artist.

Since time immemorial, and even since Freud, the attempt to change our lives has most always been to the outward—a change of environment. And unless the inner change prepares one for the exterior, the environment never yields what one hopes and dreams for. My parents learned this full well, as I was to do later.

After being widowed at the age of twenty-eight with three children, one severely handicapped, my mother did what all women of her generation did when confronted with a nonexistent job market and no education and a language barrier. She married again, my father, and proceeded to have seven more children. Through a depression and war, when societies were in upheaval, one thing was fairly certain for poor women of those days: a baby arrived about every two years, most of them desperately unwanted.

But here, credit must be given. Although often drinking himself into a stupor at the arrival of yet another mouth to feed, I never knew a man of European ethnic origin to desert his family. Harsh they often were in dealing with the families, but stay with them they did.

But in Waspish America, opportunities did exist. Those who mastered the English language did better. And for my generation of the 1930's, education was the key that unlocked the escape hatch from poverty.

Wasp teachers admired my sisters' intellect and in the case of the eldest, offered to educate her at their expense. I often ponder, as does she, on what she could have given countless children as the teacher she longed to be. I am sure her gifts equaled that of the Wasp principal who gave hundreds of us bewildered ethnic children not only ideals and guidance, but practical help when needed.

But ignorance, the scourge of my parents generation, prevailed. Following ancient tradition, she was given in marriage at age sixteen, sanctioned by ethnic society and the church. This was mourned greatly by her Wasp teachers, who no doubt shared the bride's disappointment.

My fate was only a little kinder although I resisted the prearranged marriage. But at fifteen, too poor to attend the high school four miles away, I did as my three older sisters had done before me and went to the city to get a job to support myself and those younger siblings. But as my mother before us who transversed an ocean and was on her way to a new era, I was launched into more than a job.

In later years, I too ponder on what it would have meant in displaced bitterness if I had had the courage to appeal for help to that Wasp principal for the education so desired. But at fifteen, with the repression on individual desires and guidance buried, I had not developed sufficient self-assertiveness to act for myself. Outwardly passive, I accepted my fate while inwardly a revolution of rebellion fermented as it always does beneath that swampy, sickly passivity.

The revolution erupted at the age of twenty-nine. Motivated by a life surge of do or die, and driven by the promise of compensation for being a nice girl for so long who always did what the men in her life directed, I enrolled in college. It meant eighteen hour days of caring for two young sons and a husband and home as well as full time credits. But the joyous possibility of filling that educational void was so energizing that it carried me on a high for four years. It was much too much, of course, but it was done because it had to be done.

The first wave of liberation from any repression is always followed by rage, blind chaotic anger. And the liberation of an individual or segment of society such as women is no different than class liberation. In turmoil, I left the male oriented Roman Catholic Church that I had joined at marriage. And often, the displaced fury of being denied any autonomy over my own body and soul was displaced upon my husband and sons because they were males and symbolized much of that torment. The pain of my parents' rejection of my femaleness and that of the male dominated church whose clergy was termed "fathers" was visited upon the grandsons and son-in-law of the father originally responsible unto the third generation, as Ecclesiastes so aptly foretold so long ago.

But at the age of seventy-four, shortly before his death, my father at long last gave me my long awaited priceless heritage: that gift of womanhood so little understood for its beauty as yet. "In the Old Country . . ." he said in tired resignation and sad confession, "When girls are born, everyone is sorry. They are only glad when a son is born. How stupid. To parents and to the world, the girls are the givers, the lightness in the home and make life fun and return to the parents what is given to them. And lucky the parents of many daughters." The "aha aha" of bitterness washed over me like a tidal wave that day. Too late. And a rising spark of compassion was obliterated by self-pity of that blighted childhood and I did not discern that this stern parent of my early years was only a severely deprived person himself. I could only rock to and fro in my rocker, holding that pain inside as I had, for to unleash it would tear my inner composure to shreds. And I did not understand that at thirty-four, the door to true liberation, which is enlightened self-knowledge was flung open for me at last by a man, my father. And it wasn't too late. It never is to bestow an inheritance. And curiously, I began to perceive that as different in appearance as possible, my mother and I were not unlike and our fates not too dissimilar. And the male has been as oppressed and deprived in large part as we women.

I had been as compulsively channelled into my role as had been my mother, as we mostly all are into ours. I was as mistaken about the woman I should be as she was. She, that tiny, blue-eyed blonde who loved music and parties gradually turned old and disillusioned under the mounds of clothes to wash and kettles of food to cook and a marriage turned difficult under poverty and care, but read the Wasp writers of that day. This was also the world of the pioneer woman, the "white trash" of Appalachia, and the South, the Scandanavians of the Midwest and all ethnic women everywhere. But, as with my mother, her salvation came through her religiosity. Not the churchianity that men have made of that primal-life resurgence that was hers, but a beam of light that accompanied her and guided her through loneliness, fear, harsh maltreatment at the hands of males, and a life that turned meaningless, if one did not follow that urge to turn inward and explore more deeply. My father, who professed agnosticism until near the end of his life, often questioned her. Why? Couldn't she see that there was no God? Denied development of her intellect too soon, she had to rely on that ancient boom of women, Instinct and Intuition. And it was sure. What measure of love and kindliness and mercy her children, friends and neighbors knew; it was from that fount of mystic wisdom she resorted to and was replenished from, and she gave in as full a measure as she had. Everything and everyone else let my mother down, but that was true and dependable.

At her funeral, carloads of people came to pay their respects and speak of her courage and love. "She was so kind. Always time to help." Or, "She was so sweet . . . so good . . ." and remembered this or that instance where she had met that need for love that is always present in all times.

As a near last measure, I decided at one point to emulate her discoveries for myself, my own. And true liberation began with that decision as myths, fears and passivity eroded and the courage to be a woman with all that it implies began. It is a journey that is totally unmarked for it is new and thereby lies its greatest danger. For in opening the door to greater freedoms, for individual or group, that seeking of liberation of the spirit that leads to vitality and life is not without its perils. One of them is the possibility of fragmentation. So long as a woman or society is torn with unresolved conflicts, rages, and energies, she is consumed in the effort to reconcile them. And so with groups. If we remain torn with strife concerning our mutual goals and how to achieve them, we will be rendered asunder by those inner "devils" that will lead us to chaotic struggles until we expire in exhaustion, nothing resolved.

I hope that ethnic women will join in that co-operation and that ethnic men, too, will be a part of this reach into greater life participation that began with women's determination to be liberated. For it is that part of the male psyche that contains the feeling aspect that has been repressed and is now crying out for release from chains of bondage in the macho cultures of the past as the comparable part of self-assertiveness spirit and intellect in women that are emerging from the cages of long centuries of repression.

As with individuals and in my own life experience, the victim is never totally blameless and this is true of ethnic women. Here is where ethnicity is falling into those ancient traps of dissent. Exploits of other groups are factual, as the Wasps, but it is here that those beams and splinters must be most minutely sifted out with caution.

The many efforts of the Wasps to encourage us to be freer must be acknowledged by ethnic women and groups. We must stand back now and take a careful view of where we have been, where we are and where we want to be for correction and change. Beyond that is prevention and we can declare all and every exploitive system as tyrannical and not to be so easily slipped on again: waspism, sexism, racism, Fascism, Marxism, or any and all "isms" and "isps." We are striving to become whole and healthy and we must reject anything that retards this effort.

Together in mutual co-operation, ethnic women and groups can succeed in bringing the richness and strengths of spirit that are the inheritance of women to the world. Anything less will be a backward dip into time and development and just another yoke-or joke-and it is always upon us women that it falls the heaviest.

THE LEGEND OF MISS SASAGAWARA

Hisaye Yamamoto

Even in that unlikely place of wind, sand, and heat, it was easy to imagine Miss Sasagawara a decorative ingredient of some ballet. Her daily costume, brief and fitting closely to her trifling waist, generously billowing below, and bringing together arrestingly rich colors like mustard yellow and forest green, appeared to have been cut from a coarse-textured homespun; her shining hair was so long it wound twice about her head to form a coronet; her face was delicate and pale, with a fine nose, pouting bright mouth, and glittering eyes; and her measured walk said, "Look, I'm *walking!*" as though walking were not a common but a rather special thing to be doing. I first saw her so one evening after mess, as she was coming out of the women's latrine, going towards her barracks, and after I thought she was out of hearing, I imitated the young men of the Block (No. 33), and gasped, "Wow! How much does *she* weigh?"

"Oh, haven't you heard?" said my friend Elsie Kubo, knowing very well I had not. "That's Miss Sasagawara."

It turned out Elsie knew all about Miss Sasagawara, who with her father was new to Block 33. Where had she accumulated all her items? Probably a morsel here and a morsel there, and, anyway, I forgot to ask her sources, because the picture she painted was so distracting: Miss Sasagawara's father was a Buddhist minister, and the two had gotten permission to come to this Japanese evacuation camp in Arizona from one farther north, after the death there of Mrs. Sasagawara. They had come here to join the Rev. Sasagawara's brother's family, who lived in a neighboring Block, but there had been some trouble between them, and just this week the immigrant pair had gotten leave to move over to Block 33. They were occupying one end of the Block's lone empty barracks, which had not been chopped up yet into the customary four apartments. The other end had been taken over by a young couple, also newcomers to the Block, who had moved in the same day.

"And do you know what, Kiku?" Elsie continued. "Oooh, that gal is really temperamental. I guess it's because she was a ballet dancer before she got stuck in camp, I hear people like that are temperamental. Anyway, the Sasakis, the new couple at the other end of the barracks, think she's crazy. The day they all moved in, the barracks was really dirty, all covered with dust from the dust storms and everything, so Mr. Sasaki was going to wash the whole barracks down with a hose, and he thought he'd be nice and do the Sasagawaras' side first. You know, do them a favor. But do you know what? Mr. Sasaki got the hose attached to the faucet outside and started to go in the door, and he said all the Sasagawaras' suitcases and things were on top of

From *The Kenyon Review,* Winter 1950. Copyright © 1977 by Hisaye Yamamoto DeSoto. Reprinted by permission of the author.

the Army cots and Miss Sasagawara was trying to clean the place out with a pail of water and a broom. He said, 'Here, let me flush the place out with a hose for you; it'll be faster''.' And she turned right around and screamed at him, 'What are you trying to do? Spy on me? Get out of here or I'll throw this water on you!' He said he was so surprised he couldn't move for a minute, and before he knew it, Miss Sasagawara just up and threw that water at him, pail and all. Oh, he said he got out of that place fast, but fast. Madwoman, he called her.''

But Elsie had already met Miss Sasagawara, too, over at the apartment of the Murakamis, where Miss Sasagawara was borrowing Mrs. Murakami's Singer, and had found her quite amiable. "She said she was thirty-nine years old—imagine, thirty-nine, she looks so young, more like twenty-five; but she said she wasn't sorry she never got married, because she's had her fun. She said she got to go all over the country a couple of times, dancing in the ballet.''

And after we emerged from the latrine, Elsie and I, slapping mosquitoes in the warm, gathering dusk, sat on the stoop of her apartment and talked awhile, jealously of the scintillating life Miss Sasagawara had led until now and nostalgically of the few ballets we had seen in the world outside (how faraway Los Angeles seemed!), but we ended up as we always did, agreeing that our mission in life, pushing twenty as we were, was first to finish college somewhere when and if the war ever ended and we were free again, and then to find good jobs and two nice, clean young men, preferably handsome, preferably rich, who would cherish us forever and a day.

My introduction, less spectacular, to the Rev. Sasagawara came later, as I noticed him, a slight and fragile-looking old man, in the Block mess hall (where I worked as a waitress, and Elsie, too) or laundry room or going to and from the latrine. Sometimes he would be farther out, perhaps going to the post-office or canteen or to visit friends in another Block or on some business to the Administration buildings, but wherever he was headed, however doubtless his destination, he always seemed to be wandering lostly. This may have been because he walked so slowly, with such negligible steps, or because he wore perpetually an air of bemusement, never talking directly to a person, as though, being what he was, he could not stop for an instant his meditation on the higher life.

I noticed, too, that Miss Sasagawara never came to the mess hall herself. Her father ate at the tables reserved for the occupants, mostly elderly, of the end barracks known as the bachelors' dormitory. After each meal, he came up to the counter and carried away a plate of food, protected with one of the pinkish apple wrappers we waitresses made as wrinkleless as possible and put out for napkins, and a mug of tea or coffee. Sometimes Miss Sasagawara could be seen rinsing out her empties at the one double-tub in the laundry that was reserved for private dishwashing.

If any one in the Block or in the entire camp of 15,000 or so people had talked at any length with Miss Sasagawara (everyone happening to speak of her called her that, although her first name, Mari, was simple enough and rather pretty) after her first and only visit to use Mrs. Murakami's sewing machine, I never heard of it. Nor did she ever willingly use the shower room, just off the latrine, when anyone else was there. Once, when I was up past midnight writing letters and went for my shower, I came upon her under the full needling force of a steamy spray, but she turned her back to me and did not answer my surprised hello. I hoped my body would be as smooth and spare and well-turned when I was thirty-nine. Another time, Elsie and I passed in front of the Sasagawara apartment, which was really only a cubicle because the once-empty barracks had soon been partitioned off into six units for families of two, and we saw her there on the wooden steps, sitting with her wide, wide skirt spread splendidly about her. She was intent on peeling a grapefruit, which her father had probably brought to her from the mess hall that morning, and Elsie called out, "Hello there!" Miss Sasagawara looked up and stared, without recognition. We were almost out of earshot when I heard her call, "Do I know you?" and I could have almost sworn that she sounded hopeful, if not downright wistful, but Elsie, already miffed at having expended friendliness so unprofitably, seemed not to have heard, and that was that.

Well, if Miss Sasagawara was not one to speak to, she was certainly one to speak of, and she came up quite often as topic for the endless conversations which helped along the monotonous days. My mother said she had met the late Mrs. Sasagawara once, many years before the war, and to hear her tell it, a sweeter, kindlier woman there never was. "I suppose," said my mother, "that I'll never meet anyone like her again; she was a lady in every sense of the word." Then she reminded me that I had seen the Rev. Sasagawara before. Didn't I remember him as one of the three bhikshus who had read the sutras at Grandfather's funeral?

I could not say that I did. I barely remembered Grandfather, my mother's father. The only thing that came back with clarity was my nausea at the wake and the funeral, the first and only ones I had ever had occasion to attend, because it had been reproduced several times since— each time, in fact, that I had crossed again the actual scent or a suspicion of burning incense. Dimly I recalled the inside of the Buddhist temple in Los Angeles, an immense, murky auditorium whose high and huge platform had held, centered in the background, a great golden shrine touched with black and white. Below this platform, Grandfather, veiled by gauze, had slept in a long, grey box which just fitted him. There had been flowers, oh, such flowers, everywhere. And right in front of Grandfather's box had been the incense stand, upon which squatted two small bowls, one with a cluster of straw-thin sticks sending up white tendrils of smoke, the other containing a heap of coarse, grey powder. Each mourner in turn had gone up to the stand, bowing once, his palms touching in prayer, before he reached it; had bent in prayer over the stand; had taken then a pinch of incense from the bowl of crumbs and, bowing over it reverently, cast it into the other, the active bowl; had bowed, the hands praying again; had retreated a few steps and bowed one last time, the hands still joined, before returning to his seat. (I knew the ceremony well for having been severely coached in it on the evening of hhe wake.) There had been tears and tears and here and there a sudden sob.

And all this while, three men in black robes had been on the platform, one standing in front of the shining altar, the others sitting on either side, and the entire trio incessantly chanting a strange, mellifluous language in unison. From time to time there had reverberated through the enormous room, above the singsong, above the weeping, above the fragrance, the sharp, startling whang of the gong.

So, one of those men had been Miss Sasagawara's father. . . . This information brought him closer to me, and I listened with interest later when it was told that he kept here in his apartment a small shrine, much more intricately constructed than that kept by the usual Buddhist household, before which, at regular hours of the day, he offered incense and chanted, tinkling (in lieu of the gong) a small bell. What did Miss Sasagawara do at these prayer periods, I wondered; did she participate, did she let it go in one ear and out the other, or did she abruptly go out on the steps, perhaps to eat a grapefruit?

Elsie and I tired one day of working in the mess hall. And this desire for greener fields came almost together with the Administration announcement that henceforth the wages of residents doing truly vital labor, such as in the hospital or on the garbage trucks that went from mess hall to mess hall, would be upped to nineteen dollars a month instead of the common sixteen.

"Oh, I've always wanted to be a nurse!" Elsie confided, as the Block manager sat down to his breakfast after reading out the day's bulletin in English and Japanese.

"What's stopped you?" I asked.

"Mom," Elsie said. "She thinks it's dirty work. And she's afraid I'll catch something. But I'll remind her of the extra three dollars."

"It's never appealed to me much, either," I confessed. "Why don't we go over to garbage? It's the same pay."

Elsie would not even consider it. "Very funny. Well, you don't have to be a nurse's aide, Kiku. The hospital's short all kinds of help. Dental assistants, receptionists. . . . Let's go apply after we finish this here."

So, willy-nilly, while Elsie plunged gleefully into the pleasure of wearing a trim blue-and-white striped seersucker, into the duties of taking temperatures and carrying bed-pans, and into the fringe of medical jargon (she spoke very casually now of catheters, enemas, primiparas, multiparas), I became a relief receptionist at the hospital's front desk, taking my hours as they were assigned. And it was on one of my midnight-to-morning shifts that I spoke to Miss Sasagawara for the first time.

The cooler in the corridor window was still whirring away (for that desert heat in Summer had a way of lingering intact through the night to merge with the warmth of the morning sun), but she entered bundled in an extraordinarily long black coat, her face made petulant, not unprettily, by lines of pain.

"I think I've got appendicitis," she said breathlessly, without preliminary.

"May I have your name and address?" I asked, unscrewing my pen.

Annoyance seemed to outbalance agony for a moment, but she answered soon enough, in a cold rush, "Mari Sasagawara. Thirty-three-seven C."

It was necessary also to learn her symptoms, and I wrote down that she had chills and a dull aching at the back of her head, as well as these excruciating flashes in her lower right abdomen.

"I'll have to go wake up the doctor. Here's a blanket, why don't you lie down over there on the bench until he comes?" I suggested.

She did not answer, so I tossed the Army blanket on the bench, and when I returned from the doctors' dormitory, after having tapped and tapped on the door of young Dr. Moritomo, who was on night duty, she was still standing where I had left her, immobile and holding onto the wooden railing shielding the desk.

"Dr. Moritomo's coming right away," I said. "Why don't you sit down at least?"

Miss Sasagawara said, "Yes," but did not move.

"Did you walk all the way?" I asked incredulously, for Block 33 was a good mile off, across the canal.

She nodded, as if that were not important, also as if to thank me kindly to mind my own business.

Dr. Moritomo (technically, the title was premature; evacuation had caught him with a few months to go on his degree), wearing a maroon bathrobe, shuffled in sleepily and asked her to come into the emergency room for an examination. A short while later, he guided her past my desk into the laboratory, saying he was going to take her blood count.

When they came out, she went over to the electric fountain for a drink of water, and Dr. Moritomo said reflectively, "Her count's all right. Not appendicitis. We should keep her for observation, but the general ward is pretty full, isn't it? Hm, well, I'll give her something to take. Will you tell one of the boys to take her home?"

This I did, but when I came back from arousing George, one of the ambulance boys, Miss Sasagawara was gone, and Dr. Moritomo was coming out of the laboratory where he had gone to push out the lights. "Here's George, but that girl must have walked home," I reported helplessly.

"She's in no condition to do that. George, better catch up with her and take her home," Dr. Moritomo ordered.

Shrugging, George strode down the hall; the doctor shuffled back to bed; and soom there was the shattering sound of one of the old Army ambulances backing out of the hospital drive.

George returned in no time at all to say that Miss Sasagawara had refused to get on the ambulance. "She wouldn't even listen to me. She just kept walking and I drove alongside and told her it was Dr. Moritomo's orders, but she wouldn't even listen to me."

"She wouldn't?"

"I hope Doc didn't expect me to drag her into the ambulance."

"Oh, well," I said. "I guess she'll get home all right. She walked all the way up here."

"Cripes, what a dame!" George complained, shaking his head as he started back to the ambulance room. "I never heard of such a thing. She wouldn't even listen to me."

Miss Sasagawara came back to the hospital about a month later. Elsie was the one who rushed up to the desk where I was on day duty to whisper, "Miss Sasagawara just tried to escape from the hospital!"

"Escape? What do you mean, escape?" I said.

"Well, she came in last night, and they didn't know what was wrong with her, so they kept her for observation. And this morning, just now, she ran out of the ward in just a hospital nightgown and the orderlies chased after her and caught her and brought her back. Oh, she was just fighting them. But once they got her back to bed, she calmed down right away, and Miss Morris asked her what was the big idea, you know, and do you know what she said? She said she didn't want any more of those doctors pawing her. *Pawing* her, imagine!"

After an instant's struggle with self-mockery, my curiosity led me down the entrance corridor after Elsie, into the longer, wider corridor admitting to the general ward. The whole hospital staff appeared to have gathered in the room to get a look at Miss Sasagawara, and the other patients, or those of them that could, were sitting up attentively in their high, white, and narrow beds. Miss Sasagawara had the corner bed to the left as we entered and, covered only by a brief hospital apron, she was sitting on the edge with her legs dangling over the side. With her head slightly bent, she was staring at a certain place on the floor, and I knew she must be aware of that concentrated gaze, of trembling old Dr. Kawamoto (he had retired several years before the war, but he had been drafted here), of Miss Morris, the head nurse, of Miss Bowman, the nurse in charge of the general ward during the day, of the other patients, of the nurse's aides, of the orderlies, and of everyone else who tripped in and out abashedly on some pretext or other in order to pass by her bed. I knew this by her smile, for as she continued to look at that same piece of the floor, she continued, unexpectedly, to seem wryly amused with the entire proceedings. I peered at her wonderingly through the triangular peep-hole created by someone's hand on hip, while Dr. Kawamoto, Miss Morris, and Miss Bowman tried to persuade her to lie down and relax. She was as smilingly immune to tactful suggestions as she was to tactless gawking.

There was no future to watching such a war of nerves as this, and besides, I was supposed to be at the front desk, so I hurried back in time to greet a frantic young mother and father, the latter carrying their small son who had had a hemorrhage this morning after a tonsillectomy yesterday in the out-patient clinic.

A couple of weeks later, on the late shift, I found George, the ambulance driver, in high spirits. This time he had been the one selected to drive a patient to Phoenix, where special cases were occasionally sent under escort, and he was looking forward to the moment when, for a few hours, the escort would permit him to go shopping around the city and perhaps take in a new movie. He showed me the list of things his friends had asked him to bring back for them, and we laughed together over the request of one plumpish nurse's aide for the biggest, richest chocolate cake he could find.

"You ought to have seen Mabel's eyes while she was describing the kind of cake she wanted," he said. "Man, she looked like she was eating it already!"

Just then one of the other drivers, Bobo Kunitomi, came up and nudged George, and they withdrew a few steps from my desk.

"Oh, I ain't particularly interested in that," I heard George saying.

There was some murmuring from Bobo, of which I caught the words, "Well, hell, you might as well, just as long as you're getting to go out there."

George shrugged, then nodded, and Bobo came over to the desk and asked for pencil and paper. "This is a good place . . ." he said, handing George what he had written.

Was it my imagination, or did George emerge from his chat with Bobo a little ruddier than usual? "Well, I guess I better go get ready," he said, taking leave. "Oh, anything you want, Kiku? Just say the word."

"Thanks, not this time," I said. "Well, enjoy yourself."

"Don't worry," he said. "I will!"

He had started down the hall when I remembered to ask, "Who are you taking, anyway?"

George turned around. "Miss Sa-sa-ga-wa-ra," he said, accenting every syllable. "Remember that dame? The one who wouldn't let me take her home?"

"Yes," I said. "What's the matter with her?"

George, saying not a word, pointed at his head and made several circles in the air with his first finger.

"Really?" I said.

Still mum, George nodded in emphasis and pity before he turned to go.

How long was she away? It must have been several months, and when, towards late Autumn, she returned at last from the sanitarium in Phoenix, everyone in Block 33 was amazed at the change. She said hello and how are you as often and easily as the next person, although many of those she greeted were surprised and suspicious, remembering the earlier rebuffs. There were some who never did get used to Miss Sasagawara as a friendly being.

One evening when I was going toward the latrine for my shower, my youngest sister, ten-year-old Michi, almost collided with me and said excitedly, "You going for your shower now, Kiku?"

"You want to fight about it?" I said, making fists.

"Don't go now, don't go now! Miss Sasagawara's in there," she whispered wickedly.

"Well," I demanded. "What's wrong with that, honey?"

"She's scary. Us kids were in there and she came in and we finished, so we got out, and she said, 'Don't be afraid of me. I won't hurt you'. Gee, we weren't even afraid of her, but when she said that, gee!"

"Oh, go on home and go to bed," I said.

Miss Sasagawara was indeed in the shower and she welcomed me with a smile. "Aren't you the girl who plays the violin?"

I giggled and explained. Elsie and I, after hearing Menuhin on the radio, had, in a fit of madness, sent to Sears and Roebuck for beginners' violins that cost five dollars each. We had received free instruction booklets, too, but, unable to make heads or tails from them, we contented ourselves with occasionally taking the violins out of their paper bags and sawing every whichway away.

Miss Sasagawara laughed aloud—a lovely sound. "Well, you're just about as good as I am. I sent for a Spanish guitar. I studied it about a year once, but that was so long ago I don't remember the first thing and I'm having to start all over again. We'd make a fine orchestra."

That was the only time we really exchanged words, and some weeks later, I understood she had organized a dancing class from among the younger girls in the Block. My sister Michi, becoming one of her pupils, got very attached to her and spoke of her frequently at home. So I knew that Miss Sasagawara and her father had decorated their apartment to look oh, so pretty, that Miss Sasagawara had a whole big suitcase full of dancing costumes, and that Miss Sasagawara had just lots and lots of books to read.

The fruits of Miss Sasagawara's patient labor were put on show at the Block Christmas party, the second such observance in camp. Again, it was a gay, if odd, celebration. The mess hall was hung with red and green crepe-paper streamers and the greyish mistletoe that grew abundantly on the ancient mesquite surrounding the camp. There were even electric decorations on the token Christmas tree. The oldest occupant of the bachelors' dormitory gave a tremulous monologue in an exaggerated Hiroshima dialect, one of the young boys wore a bow-tie and whispered a popular song while the girls shrieked and pretended to be growing faint, my mother sang an old Japanese song, four of the girls wore similar blue dresses and harmonized on a sweet tune, a little girl in a grass skirt and superfluous brassiere did a hula, and the chief cook came out with an ample saucepan and, assisted by the waitresses, performed the familiar *dojo-sukui,* the comic dance about a man who is merely trying to scoop up a few loaches from an un-cooperative lake. Then Miss Sasagawara shooed her eight little girls, including Michi, in front, and while they formed a stiff pattern and waited, self-conscious in the rustly crepe-paper dresses they had made themselves, she set up a portable phonograph on the floor and vigorously turned the crank.

Something was past its prime, either the machine or the record or the needle, for what came out was a feeble rasp but distantly related to the Mozart minuet it was supposed to be. After a bit I recognized the melody; I had learned it as a child to the words,

> When dames wore hoops and powdered hair,
> And very strict was e-ti-quette,
> When men were brave and ladies fair,
> They danced the min-u-et. . . .

And the little girls, who might have curtsied and stepped gracefully about under Miss Sasagawara's eyes alone, were all elbows and knees as they felt the Block's one-hundred-and-fifty or more pairs of eyes on them. Although there was sustained applause after their number, what we were benevolently approving was the great effort, for the achievement had been undeniably small. Then Santa came with a pillow for a stomach, his hands each dragging a bulging burlap bag. Church people outside had kindly sent these gifts, Santa announced, and every recipient must write and thank the person whose name he would find on an enclosed slip. So saying, he called by name each Block child under twelve and ceremoniously presented each eleemosynary package, and a couple of the youngest children screamed in fright at this new experience of a red and white man with a booming voice.

At the last, Santa called, "Miss Mari Sasagawara!" and when she came forward in surprise, he explained to the gathering that she was being rewarded for her help with the Block's younger generation. Everyone clapped and Miss Sasagawara, smiling graciously, opened her package then and there. She held up her gift, a peach-colored bath towel, so that it could be fully seen, and everyone clapped again.

Suddenly, I put this desert scene behind me. The notice I had long awaited, of permission to relocate to Philadelphia to attend college, finally came, and there was a prodigious amount of packing to do, leave papers to sign, and goodbyes to say. And once the wearying, sooty train trip was over, I found myself in an intoxicating new world of daily classes, afternoon teas, and evening concerts, from which I dutifully emerged now and then to answer the letters from home. When the beautiful semester was over, I returned to Arizona, to the glowing heat, to the camp, to the family, for although the war was still on, it had been decided to close down the camps, and I had been asked to go back and spread the good word about higher education among the young people who might be dispersed in this way.

Elsie was still working in the hospital, although she had applied for entrance into the cadet nurse corps and was expecting acceptance any day, and the long conversations we held were mostly about the good old days, the good old days when we had worked in the mess hall together, the good old days when we had worked in the hospital together.

"What ever became of Miss Sasagawara?" I asked one day, seeing the Rev. Sasagawara go abstractly by. "Did she relocate somewhere?"

"I didn't write you about her, did I?" Elsie said meaningfully. "Yes, she's relocated all right. Haven't seen her around, have you?"

"Where did she go?"

Elsie answered offhandedly. "California."

"California?" I exclaimed. "We can't go back to California. What's she doing in California?"

So Elsie told me: Miss Sasagawara had been sent back there to a state institution, oh, not so very long after I had left for school. She had begun slipping back into her aloof ways almost immediately after Christmas, giving up the dancing class and not speaking to people. Then Elsie had heard a couple of very strange, yes, very strange things about her. One thing had been told by young Mrs. Sasaki, that next-door neighbor of the Sasagawaras.

Mrs. Sasaki said she had once come upon Miss Sasagawara sitting, as was her habit, on the porch. Mrs. Sasaki had been shocked to the core to see that the face of this thirty-nine-year-old woman (or was she forty now?) wore a beatific expression as she watched the activity going on in the doorway of her neighbors across the way, the Yoshinagas. This activity had been the joking and loud laughter of Joe and Frank, the young Yoshinaga boys, and three or four of their friends. Mrs. Sasaki would have let the matter go, were it not for the fact that Miss Sasagawara was so absorbed a spectator of this horseplay that her head was bent to one side and she actually had one finger in her mouth as she gazed, in the manner of a shy child confronted with a marvel. "What's the matter with you, watching the boys like that?" Mrs. Sasaki had cried. "You're old enough to be their mother!" Startled, Miss Sasagawara had jumped up and dashed back into her apartment. And when Mrs. Sasaki had gone into hers, adjoining the Sasagawaras', she had been terrified to hear Miss Sasagawara begin to bang on the wooden walls with something heavy like a hammer. The banging, which sounded as though Miss Sasagawara were using all her strength on each blow, and continued wildly for at least five minutes. Then all had been still.

The other thing had been told by Joe Yoshinaga, who lived across the way from Miss Sasagawara. Joe and his brother slept on two Army cots pushed together on one side of the room, while their parents had a similar arrangement on the other side. Joe had standing by his bed an apple crate for a shelf, and he was in the habit of reading his sports and western magazines in bed and throwing them on top of the crate before he went to sleep. But one morning he had noticed his magazines all neatly stacked inside the crate, when he was sure he had carelessly thrown some on top the night before, as usual. This happened several times, and he finally asked his family whether one of them had been putting his magazines away after he fell asleep. They had said no and laughed, telling him he must be getting absent-minded. But the mystery had been solved late one night, when Joe gradually awoke in his cot with the feeling that he was being watched. Warily, he had opened one eye slightly and had been thoroughly awakened and chilled, in the bargain, by what he saw. For what he saw was Miss Sasagawara sitting there on his apple crate, her long hair all undone and flowing about her. She was dressed in a white nightgown and her hands were clasped on her lap. And all she was doing was sitting there watching him, Joe Yoshinaga. He could not help it, he had sat up and screamed. His mother, a light sleeper, came running to see what had happened, just as Miss Sasagawara was running out the door, the door they had always left unlatched, or even wide open in Summer. In the morning, Mrs. Yoshinaga had gone straight to the Rev. Sasagawara and asked him to do something about his daughter. The Rev. Sasagawara, sympathizing with her indignation in his benign but vague manner, had said he would have a talk with Mari.

And, concluded Elsie, Miss Sasagawara had gone away not long after. I was impressed, although Elsie's sources were not what I would ordinarily pay much attention to, Mrs. Sasaki, that plump and giggling young woman who always felt called upon to explain that she was childless by choice, and Joe Yoshinaga, who had a knack of blowing up, in his drawling voice, any incident in which he personally played even a small part (I could imagine the field day he had had with this one). Elsie puzzled aloud over the cause of Miss Sasagawara's derangement, and I, who had so newly had some contact with the recorded explorations into the virgin territory of the human mind, sagely explained that Miss Sasagawara had no doubt looked upon Joe Yoshinaga as the image of either the lost lover or the lost son. But my words made me uneasy by their glibness, and I began to wonder seriously about Miss Sasagawara for the first time.

Then there was this last word from Miss Sasagawara herself, making her strange legend as complete as I, at any rate, would probably ever know it. This came some time after I had gone back to Philadelphia and the family had joined me there, when I was neck deep in research for my final paper. I happened one day to be looking through the last issue of a small poetry magazine that had suspended publication midway through the war. I felt a thrill of recognition at the name, Mari Sasagawara, signed to a long poem, introduced as ". . . the first published poem of a Japanese-American woman who is, at present, an evacuee from the West Coast making her home in a War Relocation center in Arizona."

It was a *tour de force,* erratically brilliant and, through the first readings, tantalizingly obscure. It appeared to be about a man whose lifelong aim had been to achieve Nirvana, that saintly state of moral purity and universal wisdom. This man had in his way certain handicaps, all stemming from his having acquired, when young and unaware, a family for which he must provide. The day came at last, however, when his wife died and other circumstances made it unnecessary for him to earn a competitive living. These circumstances were considered by those about him as sheer imprisonment, but he had felt free for the first time in his long life. It became possible for him to extinguish within himself all unworthy desire and consequently all evil, to concentrate on that serene, eight-fold path of highest understanding, highest mindedness, highest speech, highest action, highest livelihood, highest recollectedness, highest endeavor, and highest meditation.

This man was certainly noble, the poet wrote, this man was beyond censure. The world was doubtless enriched by his presence. But say that someone else, someone sensitive, someone admiring, someone who had not achieved this sublime condition and who did not wish to, were somehow called to companion such a man. Was it not likely that the saint, blissfully bent on cleansing from his already radiant soul the last imperceptible blemishes (for, being perfect, would he not humbly suspect his own flawlessness?) would be deaf and blind to the human passions rising, subsiding, and again rising, perhaps in anguished silence, within the selfsame room? The poet could not speak for others, of course; she could only speak for herself. But she would describe this man's devotion as a sort of madness, the monstrous sort which, pure of itself and so with immunity, might possibly bring troublous, scented scenes to recur in the other's sleep.

ETHNICITY TO HUMANITY

Sharon Renée Twombly

A task I have taken upon myself is to try to place the subtle yet sublime importance of my heritage. This piercing quest must surely engage every human's attention at one point or another, if only evident in the conscious pride one takes in one's hometown. But in the larger world of the hometown, the roots emerge directly from the family. One feels one is the actual manifestation of the home. The goal then first seems to be to explore these narrow surroundings, in order to place one's Self solidly in the world.

Being perhaps no different in spirit from any other human, I have always jockeyed within and with my family for an identity. In these confines, I have found a position, a role to play and there to stay. The story is well known, yet individual. But it is as a child in reaction to the larger world that another identity develops. Like the circular growth rings in a tree's trunk, the family is the core. Subsequent growths and reactions to the larger world form an expanding concentricity.

Yet it seems to me that I am unique in that I surely have blossomed within, as it were, two of these patterned growths, each being seperate yet elementarily tied to the other. One can put commonplace labels to such intangible essences, that is, that I am, one and apart, American and German. I have within myself two identities and this consititutes the area of ethnicity—where the two conceptions overlap and merge, and block the described roots that the tree needs to freely breathe.

My mother is German born and bred. My father is American.

My mother is integrally cosmopolitan, my father's myth is of the hunter, the soul free to wander. It has taken me years to realize that both parents unconsciously live and are their roots. Whereas their roots are nationally pure in an immediate sense, mine are mixed. It is an awareness that has no name, besides my own.

I know, through this appraisal, that in many things I am not like others, but I do not know what I am really like. In some ways, I am my mother's daughter in that I have learned to cook her foods, decorate in a European manner; she has taught me the knicks and knacks that were her mother's. Yet I am without a doubt, a proclaimed American. The result of this mixture has been that both sides have been overshadowed. On the one hand, I have lived in a German culture always longing to actually experience that land, to seek and place the mother in me in her roots, and at the same time I have felt, irrationally to be sure, that I have not lived as a typical American, despite the melting pot. I have missed the American view, the purity, the unquestioning allegiance to America, as my birthright.

But the lack of an unquestioning allegiance is exactly the emotional point. It is the first circle, closest to, and containing the family core. I have felt both parents' rooted sides, although they never consciously chose to use their heritage as a point of contention. Yet sometimes when an inevitable disagreement arose, the matter would be transformed into a theme of European sophistication vs. American looseness, or conversely, European snobbery vs. American forthrightedness. Each parent was then basically asserting his individuality, which through identification, took on cultural form and significance. All in all, therein being an intangible element of Truth, it was the easy and obvious explanation to grasp for individual differences. Thus, when one realizes that a supposed nationality disharmony was not an inherently political question, but one too of opposing personalities, then it can be seen how emotional polarities may develop in their children. And these same children may not realize the placebo behind the "Different Backgrounds" remedy.

It then seems that a further ring to enclose this growth must be added: that of an intellectual understanding. The cultural aura must be seperated from the Self. It is to try to seek the experience of the personality as a whole out of the unconscious conditions it evolved in. These conditions necessarily refer to my parents. To absolutely see their elemental influences, it is necessary first, in this analysis, to differentiate them from myself. This search brought me to Europe, to my mother's home. Through the medium of a scholarship, I have had time to actively appraise the American culture from a distance and the German one at first hand. These flipped modes have afforded me, to be sure, abundant superficial differences. But in my visions, I have seen my mother walking on German streets; my Father however, cannot fit within these narrow cobblestone havens. I have placed my parents' backgrounds, around and within me.

But to acknowledge dissimilar roots has not been enough. It becomes groundless to consider my parents and myself within a closed circle. One must recognize the historical character inherent in our own individual psyches. No body is "new"—we are products of the generation of mankind. In the same way, the tree stands only as an element in cyclical nature. Components have endlessly recombined to form, so to speak, variations in the forest. Variations, then, resting within the realms of an inclusive nature. To grow within this third ring is, for me, to study the subjective history of mankind, through philosophy, psychology or mythology.

Only through a further and final growth and blossoming can I feel that all will come together. Only through an appreciation of the wholeness of nature can a tree become meaningful and cherished in its own right.

Roots serve no function alone for they require the supporting structure. And so it is that a woman is meaningless outside the world that has formed and fashioned her. She finds her myth rather through a Waldeinsamkeit, those spiritual feelings that arise from a walk in a deep forest. So it has been that through a narrow awareness of my heritage, I have endeavored to build a tree. The fourth ring then defines the whole and I have come to understand that each in his own way is one with all.

EXPLOITATION IN HUMAN RELATIONSHIPS

"Bitter girl." By permission of Maria de Noronha (Gallman), the artist.

I offered you love and this is what you gave me in return.

BALLAD OF PEARL MAY LEE

Gwendolyn Brooks

Then off they took you, off to the jail,
A hundred hooting after.
And you should have heard me at my house.
I cut my lungs with my laughter,
  Laughter,
  Laughter.
I cut my lungs with my laughter.

They dragged you into a dusty cell.
And a rat was in the corner.
And what was I doing? Laughing still.
Though never was a poor gal lorner,
  Lorner,
  Lorner.
Though never was a poor gal lorner.

The sheriff, he peeped in through the bars,
And (the red old thing) he told you,
"You son of a bitch, you're going to hell!"
'Cause you wanted white arms to enfold
you,
  Enfold you,
  Enfold you.
'Cause you wanted white arms to enfold
you.

But you paid for your white arms, Sammy
boy,
And you didn't pay with money.
You paid with your hide and my heart,
Sammy boy,
For your taste of pink and white honey,
  Honey,
  Honey.
For your taste of pink and white honey.

Oh, dig me out of my don't-despair.
Pull me out of my poor-me.
Get me a garment of red to wear.
You had it coming surely,
  Surely,
  Surely,
You had it coming surely.

At school, your girls were the bright little
girls.
You couldn't abide dark meat.
Yellow was for to look at,
Black for the famished to eat.
Yellow was for to look at,
Black for the famished to eat.

You grew up with bright skins on the brain,
And me in your black folks bed.
Often and often you cut me cold,
And often I wished you dead.
Often and often you cut me cold.
Often I wished you dead.

Then a white girl passed you by one day,
And, the vixen, she gave you the wink.
And your stomach got sick and your legs li-
quefied.
And you thought till you couldn't think.
  You thought,
  You thought,
You thought till you couldn't think.

I fancy you out on the fringe of town,
The moon an owl's eye minding;
The sweet and thick of the cricket-belled
dark,

The fire within you winding. . . .
　Winding,
　Winding. . . .
The fire within you winding.

Say, she was white like milk, though, wasn't she?
And her breasts were cups of cream.
In the back of her Buick you drank your fill.
Then she roused you out of your dream.
In the back of her Buick you drank your fill.
Then she roused you out of your dream.

"You raped me, nigger," she softly said.
(The shame was threading through.)
"You raped me, nigger, and what the hell
Do you think I'm going to do?
　What the hell,
　What the hell
Do you think I'm going to do?

"I'll tell every white man in this town.
I'll tell them all of my sorrow.
You got my body tonight, nigger boy.
I'll get your body tomorrow.
　Tomorrow.
　Tomorrow.
I'll get your body tomorrow."

And my glory but Sammy she did! She did!
And they stole you out of the jail.
They wrapped you around a cottonwood tree.

And they laughed when they heard you wail.
　Laughed,
　Laughed.
They laughed when they heard you wail.

And I was laughing, down at my house.
Laughing fit to kill.
You got what you wanted for dinner,
But brother you paid the bill.
　Brother,
　Brother,
Brother you paid the bill.

You paid for your dinner, Sammy boy,
And you didn't pay with money.
You paid with your hide and my heart, Sammy boy,
For your taste of pink and white honey,
　Honey,
　Honey.
For your taste of pink and white honey.

Oh, dig me out of my don't-despair.
Oh, pull me out of my poor-me.
Oh, get me a garment of red to wear.
You had it coming surely.
　Surely.
　Surely.
You had it coming surely.

BORN TO SUICIDE

LaVerne González

"And now, mi vida," Tony said, nodding toward the car, "We are going to make a stop to see a very ancient friend. You will cry." En route to Aguas Buenas we talked of many things, everything except the one thing I wanted to hear. What was the purpose of this impulsive, determined plunge through the hills and down these wretched roads on this very hot day?

The tiny dwelling before which we stopped did not surprise me; I knew Puerto Rican farm houses were often built of any available material and on stilts to keep the floor dry. Yet I felt a poignancy reach out to me, a tear began just behind the lid, and I had no idea why. At Tony's insistence, I walked with him to the hut, but slowly as in the presence of a mighty mystery I had no ability to penetrate. He knocked and waited patiently for the door to be opened. Then silently she stood there, the little, wrinkled memory of a woman. Actually I saw only her eyes; and if indeed through the eyes we see into the very soul of the person, her soul possessed magnificence. Those eyes glowed with a kind of translucency; the only memory I had of such another spectacle had occurred on a very dark night on Phosphorescent Bay when I had seen that ethereal glow suspended in the dark above the water. Then, as now, I felt translated to some high mount of transfiguration, completely enveloped by the supernatural.

She stood simply, silently removed from time into some realm of timelessness where haste would be the greatest offense. Tony, too, had lost his briskness; he stood, arms hanging limply, waiting. She recognized him with a little gasp, "Hijo, dios le bendiga."

"Tia, mi tia preciosa," he enfolded her tiny figure in his arms, forming a world complete, shutting me out tenderly. Very slowly he released her, yet still supporting her, he turned to me, "This is my angel aunt, María—the only saint our family claims." and turning again to her he entreated reverently in Spanish, "Otra bendición, Tia."

We went with her into the house. Never have I been in a place so barren and felt so full. Commanding one corner stood a life-sized statue of the Christ in simple blue garb, hands extended in blessing; candles burned on a shelf nearby and on the floor among bouquets of faded waxen flowers. Sharing the shelf with the candles sat a tarnished gold frame containing the picture of a gently handsome young man. We sat on boxes at a little table while she made the coffee over a small wood-burning stove. The only other furniture was a narrow metal cot. I listened to the conversation; and while they recounted the past, my mind slowly constructed the story of love and death, joy and sorrow, tenderness and rape that lay enshrined here. The curtain lifted on a fearful tableau. I saw her.

She sat, a small, black-clad, softly wailing figure, remote, completely withdrawn from those around her. Her eyes were intent on the stiff, immobile shell lying unseeing and uncaring on the bed before her. Automatically her fingers moved incessantly over the beads in her hand and the moaning never stopped; but it was as though she, herself, stood apart and viewed the narrow room with its straight wooden walls and noisy plank floor. The room was so familiar it was almost a part of her; and yet now it was only real as it brought memories of her son who lay dead and defeated in his bed.

Of course, she well knew each part of the coming event-the funeral-for death came frequently to these poor. Soon, kind friends, now mourning loudly beside her, would lift the lifeless form from the bed into the waiting coffin. The room already was full of the "death smell" the sickening blend of too many flowers and the burning wax of the candles. In this hot climate, one could not long hold her dead; in twenty-four hours the stench would be too great to endure; the body must be buried. After the body was lovingly covered in the coffin, strong brown hands would clasp each of the ten wooden prongs and the funeral procession would move slowly and wailingly to the cemetery. She had not been even faintly perturbed when the gravedigger, choosing the spot where her son would lie, had removed other bones to make for these—life and death, the inevitable partners, must go endlessly on. Of course, there was no money to hire some elder of the town to say a few words in eulogy; no, the funeral would be quite unobtrusive. For her, however, there would be no more light, no longer any reason for living.

Outside the neighbors gathered around in silent, patient-as-time-itself, groups. Here, too, one stood alone and withdrawn not by choice but ostracized as it were. Death had had a very sobering effect on this naturally carefree and careless young girl, Luisa—beautiful with the dusky, sensuous beauty often found in the mestizo. The traces of merriment in face and figure appeared as desolate as the remnants of last night's brawl. Grief and guilt struggled to possess her, or was it grief because of guilt that had brought her here to witness the grief of the black-clad María? Except for the mourners, within the house, all would honor the dead by keeping their mouths shut. Occasionally, however, someone dared to break the silence to risk disrespect to the dead with, "Mira, see how María mourns for him and no husband to comfort her!" Even had she heard these sympathetic whispers, she would not have moved or stirred from her huddled position. The nine days of mourning following the burial when Catholic and Protestant gathered side by side to count beads, burn endless candles and pray for the "fallecido" would not revive or relieve her. Steeped in her sorrow, she was oblivious to the present: time had receded and she saw in retrospect the beginning of her tragedy, stretched now inert and lifeless before her.

The past twenty-three years were blotted out and she was a young girl again. Don Antonio was justly proud of his lovely daughter with her black hair and blacker eyes, her oval, madonnalike face and the smooth, brown skin, a pleasant blending of her Indian and Spanish bloods. Any beauty found here was of the natural variety for no creams, lipsticks, or mascara were permitted in this household, nor were they needed. Hers was the freshness of youth and vitality. Yes, all of Lares boasted, "Ella es la más bella de todas las puertorriqueñas. She is the most beautiful Puerto Rican." Sometimes when don Antonio played cards and drank cerveza with the men in the local cantina, they spoke of María, of her face and form; her father grew warm with pleasure. Possessing little of material goods, they considered physical perfection, whether male or female, a gift of God, meant to be enjoyed. Unfortunately, what she possessed in beauty her father lacked in money; each child must find a way to bring money into the house. Early one learned to work and work hard at whatever task was at hand; María was no exception. There must be arroz y habichuelas—rice and beans in the house, a little milk for the biannual baby and always coffee. The one holiday, exceptional luxury was a bar of "maja" soap, made in Spain and smelling of lovely ladies in high mantillas and swirling skirts, their faces half-hidden behind provocative fans.

Because María was the eldest of eight, her duties seemed multiplied, but she had learned from her long suffering mother a calm acceptance of life, gleaned no doubt from some distant Indian in her ancestry; she had found the ability to look for the bright spot in a maze of black. Her father, Antonio Soto Belez, was a little man—little in stature, but he had the domineering and forceful mannerism of the Spanish male; he was absolute and unchallenged master of his household. If one looked only at the eyes, soft brown, almost hazel, a little slanted at the corners, one got the image of kindly good humor. However, the curious hoof-shaped scar on the forehead and thin, straight line of the mouth, gave quite another impression. There was perhaps a time in early childhood when revolt against discipline had arisen in María, but such demonstrations were quickly and violently squelched. By the time she was sixteen, there had developed a shy little smile, a strong, if superstitiously religious Catholic faith, and an un-complaining cognizance of her servile role in life. She had gone several different semesters to school; but the work demand at home was too great for any sustained attendance and eventu-ally, she no longer even tried to go. The pattern of her life coupled with her religious fears had made her completely acquiesent to circumstances.

The cycle of her life would have been set in a constant, unchanging rut if the depression years had not intervened. The already poor and child-laden families of Lares felt strongly the bitter, unrelenting whip of the depression, felt it as keenly as actual lashes across one's bare back. Farmer families managed somehow to make a meager living from the soil; at least there were orange and avocado trees which did not cease to yield their fruit if one could only manage to slip past the watchful eye of the overseer or "mayordomo," as he was disdainfully called. The almond tree was not at all particular and shed its welcome nuts in any spot; the banana trees, which grew wild, served the Sotos many a meal. Her mother stored carefully and zeal-ously as a squirrel, the pumpkin and other squash seeds to be planted which would in their turn feed her always hungry youngsters. Because her father was not only a stern, but also a shrewd man, he managed a method of field-flooding which enabled him to raise rice, the mainstay of the Puerto Rican family.

It was during these dull times when mere existence was a problem, and one asked only for today's needs that her father had returned late in the afternoon. Occasionally it was necessary to go to Aguadilla for provisions and, if one was lucky, a "bit of" added rations from the government, usually canned meat or cod fish. This time her father had been very fortunate and returned in excellent humor. Such was not always the case and often his children moved like shadows in order not to irritate him. Her father brought not only food but wonderful news. La Senora of the "casa grande" had called to him to inquire if María might come each Thursday to iron for her. "They were," as her father had explained, "favored of God, gracias a Dios, to have in the big house of their barrio a lady so gracious and helpful." If they watched carefully and she talked to La Señora, perhaps they could also find a place for several of her brothers. Tomorrow she would go at seven. And so it was arranged; never did it enter her mind to object; and if in her innermost being, there was a vague warning, a siren being sounded, an ominous portending of future evil, it was stifled so soon as not even to have existed. She was glad for an opportunity to help her family; the loveliness of her face was enhanced by the thought of ser-vice. Tomorrow she would rise very early that she might attend "misa" before undertaking her work.

Instantly she loved La Señora and the mistress was equally impressed with this fair child who ironed well and eagerly. The bond between them was even stronger because La Señora had had only sons, which pleased her husband and kept him home nights but left a void in her life. Into this vacant place in her heart, María crept. At first, La Señora found her shy; but after a time, María opened wide the door of her dream world and allowed her mistress to enter. Such times they had! Thursday of every week was a holiday indeed; forgotten for that brief time was her own small house, the struggle for survival, the anger or pleasure of her father. She loved to iron and she would make believe she was the owner of this grand house, of its fine fields and magnificent horses. It was another world. Under the warmth of La Señora's friendship, she flourished, budded, and blossomed as a wilted hydrangea to whose roots water is suddenly and mercifully released. She was encouraged to sing, and she sang in a small, lyric soprano which was a delight to any open ear. She learned bits of cultured living and absorbed each crumb gratefully.

It was almost time to return home one day, when she turned from her work to find her every move being watched by Enrique, the youngest son of La Señora. She had heard often of him and his escapades; indeed the whole town talked of this spoiled one who had grown to manhood unbridled; his mother catered to his every weakness hoping to gain a semblance of authority over him, rather she had lost him completely to his passions and his selfishness. He was tall for a Puerto Rican and very handsome with the straight, strong features of the aristocratic Spaniard without any of the tempering of the Indian strain. The skin was very white, almost marble-like; the eyes were a cold, bold, piercing black; the hair was smooth and black with only a slight inclination to wave. She shuddered involuntarily; the warning siren sounded again deep within her, but this time she heard it and knew there was no escape. He had on his face, in his cool, quiet appraisal of her, the set look of the "Conquistadores," the Spanish conquerors of South America who had conquered not so much by strength as by sheer arrogance and rigid, cruel determination. The villagers claimed that by virtue of his wickedness a distraught mother whose daughter he had wantonly destroyed had placed a curse upon him—and any future progeny. After that first encounter, he came often to watch her with his haughty, aloof stare, and she knew, as surely as the mouse knows when there is a cat in the house that sooner or later the game will end and it will be swallowed, her fate.

It was May; the gardenias, roses, and daisies blossomed in tangled beauty, wild and unrestrained in the fields; the rains came now only at noon and were so quickly dried up as to leave no trace. Birds sang, dizzy with the joy of life and living. María, in spite of her newly acquired cautious, everwatchful air had completely abandoned herself to the pleasure of the morning as she walked leisurely from the Mass to la casa grande. She still wore on her head the lacy, white mantilla which La Señora had given her. After marriage she must wear a black veil to pray, but now she wore happily the white mantilla, sign and seal of her virginity and purity of innocence. In the path before her she saw a figure emerge, as if awaiting an appointed rendezvous. She recognized Enrique; if only there was a way of retreat; but she knew it was useless, so she moved like a remote-controlled robot forward. "Perhaps she was wrong. It was mere chance that he was in the way," her mind insisted; but her heart said, "This is the day!"

He watched her approach with abstract and calculating manner. When she came near, he took her arm firmly and led her into a neighboring field. For her there was no resistance; no, it was an impossibility to resist for she was victim not of a man but of a way of life. She had been preconditioned to submission, "Si Dios quiere—If God wills;" moreover her blind devotion to La Señora rendered her completely docile. Just as her will was forever subject to others, so Enrique's will would prevail. His ego was in constant need of reassurance and each pretty face a new world to be conquered and laid waste. He took seriously only one old testament instruction, "It is not meet for a man's seed to be spilled on the ground." She did not struggle, nor when the act was finally consumated and he had gone his way, did she move. A strange emotion filled her—HATE.

For the next nine months an ever-smoldering all-consuming hate was her constant companion. Often her thoughts dwelt on the bliss of death. If she had been shy before, she had now become mute. Her song was stilled. She knew her secret could not long remain secret. La Señora tried to penetrate the wall between them, but María would only turn her eyes in tortured silence to gaze steadily and sadly at her, "Qué lástima! How sad that she could not have tamed her colt!" Perhaps though, her thoughts were not completely hidden from this kindly matron who knew so well the weakness of her son; she somehow sensed instinctively the truth. Soon, however, the thickened waist and full bosom advertised clearly her condition.

Her father ranted, stormed, cursed, "Maldita, it was impossible to feed another." Her weary mother sighed and moved more slowly through her limitless tasks; she had dared to hope for a time that life could be different for María. When her time came and her shrieks tolled the midnight hour, it was her father who hurried to bring the midwife that mother and child might be saved. The birth was long and labored and as María walked through dim shadows to give life to a son, any attendant shame was somehow swallowed within the closely knit walls of the family. A pebble cast on the water had caused a fleeting ripple and was soon forgotten. There only remained a child and a woman's hate.

Wanting not to see or touch her new-born child, María hovered between life and death. But the boy was strong, perfectly formed and had excellent lungs. Finally when the wet nurse's pale milk was inadequate and his insistent cries became louder, her mother brought the child and laid him beside his own mother. Then as the child, sucking hungrily and greedily from her full-to-over-flowing breast, nestled in her arms, there surged from some hidden spring the healing flood of motherhood and she was fulfilled. From that time she was reborn. Her hate was changed to love and this "nene" became her reason for living, her whole world. She had gone to her night of labor a child who too soon was forced out of childhood; she arose a woman. La Señora came once to see the child; and if she recognized the features of Enrique, she gave no indication of it. Still, weekly there were delivered food and other supplies from the big house "para el nene"—for the child.

Now María treasured each hour, each day. There was no time for convalescing in this house, and besides María had a driving force within her. She was a dynamo of energy and ambition. Always adapt at manual labor, she turned to sewing for her livelihood. Since there was no "maquina de coser"—sewing machine here, each stitch was done by hand. Of course, the very first project was the baptismal "ropa" for the "nene." Strange, that soft white material should arrive so soon from La Señora; María lovingly and painstakingly sewed small fine stitches, fashioning the pattern as she went. The child was baptized José Antonio Soto; for him there could never be two last names to denote the legitimacy of his birth. But she vowed as the magic words were said which would forever save her son from Hell, that he would have his chance in life, he would not be bound by the accident of his birth to endless poverty and degradation and death.

She was not a shy girl, but a determined woman with a purpose. José must be a doctor so she worked all day and far into the night. Another room had been added for them in her parent's house. For a time as she sewed, the child stayed close to her and played in the open doorway. It was a joy to watch him grow; he was strong and healthy for somehow with the birth of José poverty began to recede in the household. Perhaps it was the gifts from the big house, or perhaps it was the industry of María or a combination of the two. At any rate, salvation had come to this house. Now there was always milk for the child, a cow had been found mysteriously tied in the field; moreover, meat had been added to the daily rice and bean ration. Soon he was able to take his place with the others in the field.

Yet, somehow, from the beginning he was different, for one thing he was beautiful—boys are not supposed to be beautiful, but he was. His hair instead of being black was a rich chestnut; his eyes were very large and soft brown; the skin was smooth and white; the features were chiseled and classic. Different as was his appearance, his manner was even more so. In these poor people, the constant struggle to live had produced a necessary harshness, a callous indifference to suffering; but José was gentle, considerate, with such a sensitivity to others' pain and suffering. Often neighbors remarked, "Qué hijo tan sensitivo—such a sensitive child!" He worked as hard as the rest, yet he never seemed quite a part of either the work or the group. He often brought his mother a flower from the field, an avocado, a "china" the most succulent and sweetest of all the Puerto Rican oranges. The song that had died on her lips lived again. Her clear voice could be heard "Ay, ay, ay, canta y no llores—sing and don't cry," or more softly, "Ave María, madre de Dios—Holy Mary Mother of God." The love between these two warmed the house and caused even the grumbling father to mellow somewhat.

"Mamá, ven acá, el diablo—Mother, come here, the devil!," she heard the horrified call of José. Quickly she ran from the house to catch her son who, terrified, clung to her, muttering between sobs, "El diablo, el diablo—the devil is chasing me."

"Cállate, hijo—quiet, son," she stroked his forehead and soothed him with her calm voice, "Qué pasó?—what happened? All is well now. There, there, don't cry anymore. See, there is no one." So she soothed his fears and gave him back his security. When his sobs subsided, he returned to his play. Odd that he should fear so, for she had never resorted to the strange, wild, ghost-ridden tales many mothers used to subdue their children. She had never needed to. This incident filled her thoughts, leaving her shaken and frightened; there was no sleep for her that night. What did the future hold for him?

Delighted she watched him as he grew, slim, apparently fragile but actually agile and sinewy. It would take many years of school before he became a doctor so she sewed; and because each article was so lovingly wrought, her fame as a seamstress had spread and many came to her. Now there were shoes to cover the feet which had hitherto trod bare over the roughest places. Shoes in themselves were a luxury; as soon as he returned from school, they must be hung carefully on the two nails in the wall beside his bed. Once she heard the children as they returned from school. Evidently some of the boys had been shooting birds with the crude, but effective, slingshots they had fashioned from bits of wood and rubber. José had rebuked them, "Don't hurt the birds. You'll make the virgin cry!"

"El Cristo, El Cristo," one of the boys taunted. Soon others took it up and so he was nicknamed "the Christ." The name remained during the rest of his life. This, too, was food for thought. María fretted a bit, worried a bit, and then had stored it with the rest of her memories.

The days were crowding over each other now in their eagerness to hurry along. José was doing excellently in school. So well in fact that he was named valedictorian of his class. She was smug in her pride as she watched "el Maestro" pin the medal to the lapel of his suit she herself had made. It seemed her eyes could not see enough; so hard she watched that she might always keep the picture of this moment bright and untarnished in her memory book. Even La Señora came to the graduation exercises. After the girls, dressed in their frothy white dresses, had sung the school song, José Antonio Soto was called to deliver the valedictory address. He stepped forward with his serene, gentle movement completely master of the situation. What did it matter that his first glance went to the flirtatious, Luisa, lovely indeed in white? La Señora was seen to wipe a tear or two from her eye. Now certainly life was beginning for José, and María had already laid the ground work for his further education.

She had learned of a group of conscientious objectors from the mainland who had established a service camp at Castaner. She had heard of young people whom they had sent to study in the States. Ability, not religious faith, was the criterion they used in choosing the few to send. José would study medicine! She had gone several times to the camp to talk and to work that she might be sure she could trust these folks. Convinced of their sincerity and ability to help, she had sent Jose to work at odd jobs in the camp, to talk of his aspirations to the leader and if possible, exact a promise of their assistance. Intuition had told her that once they saw her handsome, gentle son, help would be forthcoming. And indeed she had been correct.

He returned one evening from Castañer and laid the boat ticket in her lap. All had been arranged; he was to leave within the week for the States to begin the long educational road to medicine. María was beside herself with joy; there was indeed a twinge of sorrow at the thought of the long separation. She quickly hid this beneath the hustle-bustle of preparation for the trip. There was even a bit of relief that he would soon be gone, several nights in the past she had been awakened by his restless movements and his tortured murmurings, "Luisa, Luisa." Only a week and so many things to be done! Thus she was totally unprepared for his ghastly appearance, "Ayúdame, Mamacita! Estoy muriendo—Help me Mother, I am dying."

"A Dios Mío," she shrieked and sprang to help him, "Call the priest, mi hijito, mi hijito." He leaned on her heavily as she led him to the bed. Frantically she tore back his clothes; she could find no wound nor pulse. "A Dios Mío!," her piercing cry rose even unto Heaven.

They told her then of his deed. He had gone to Luisa for the last goodbyes. His sensitive, oft-wounded spirit did not allow him to love lightly. The cross of only one last name and no father had not been easy for him to bear; and when he fell in love, he was completely possessed and possessive. He had vowed his undying love and begged Luisa's promise to wait for him. She had tossed her soft black hair over bare, brown shoulders and had laughed tauntingly, "Me, wait for you? Mira, how foolish you are! Ja! Ja! Ja! Life is short and I want to live all of it. Goodbye, 'Bobo'—fool dreamer." With a twist of her hand she flicked him away.

He had turned slowly, full of disbelief and wounded pride. It was not much of a problem to secure a little rat poison which he had mixed in a small glass of wine. When he returned to Luisa with a sad, calm smile on his pale face, he was already dying. "It is truly farewell, Mi Vida; there is no more torture for me. I have taken poison." Yes, they had told her all; but she was deaf, drowned in the murky abyss of her grief. "María, María," voices called to her, hands chook her gently and she was lifted to her feet, "Es la hora—it is time." Her son was already in his casket and María moved with the others slowly, sobbing.

"This nightmare must soon pass," she thought. It did not pass, and the procession moved along the mournful road to the cemetery. Inside the cold, impersonal cement cemetery walls which held the dead in their mute embrace, the mourners moved to the great, yawning jaws of the waiting grave. The men lowered the coffin into its place. Mechanically, María lifted a handful of dirt, kissed it and threw it onto the casket. She turned quickly away as they piled on the remaining dirt.

The wise said, "There could be no other end for this sensitive spirit encased in a house of clay. The very nature of his birth and being had predestined his death."

María knew only that the one whom the children had long ago called "El Cristo" in derision was dead. But for her he was truly named, for he had been her "Christ," her life.

The curtain dropped into place. The María of the tableau merged with the slight, shadow-woman speaking in hushed and reverent voice, "Truly el Cristo, born again to be slain by human carelessness."

"We must go, mi querida tia."

I followed him, stumblingly. "In a hut in Puerto Rico? A bastard son? El Cristo?"

CHON

Marina Rivera

Running through the house, out the gate
you chased me, tortilla in hand, you a
long-legged wolf, me the moppet but fleet.
How would you have done it, Uncle?
5   How open my mouth of sharp, strong teeth
how stuff it down, since my nails were long
and my soles could have struck you in a fine spot.

We'd feast on ice cream but you'd wait longer,
knew how to sit, pretending to grey, to wizen
10   with the sun's setting that you might frighten
me with stories till the long, low dragging began.
The Indians going home, street dusty, pot-holed,
darkening, figures morose, hunchbacked
in the wagons. You saying how they'd come
15   for me soon, stuff me in their gunny sacks,
the roar of the wagons growing. I could not
see the mules' ribs but sensed them,
the wagons dragging, not rolling.
Later you would marry, have children,
20   come to axe our two pet ducks that you
might feast, careful to persuade in my absence,
cautious to gobble yours at home, the ducks
I loved to feed, hear, watch bathe
glistening at us in segments no one ate,
25   parts too unlike friends to bury.

From MESTIZA by Marina Rivera, © 1977, published by Grilled Flowers. Reprinted by permission of the author. (See Ms. Rivera's poem "For Rita Kohn" in Unit Three, THE CLASSROOM AND BEYOND.

Returning the tent, you hid the gash.
I can see you shivering,
determined to chop wood in the tent at night,
your strokes fiercer till you brought in
30   darkness through the wet smile in the canvas.

It was always your flaw:
That you would warm yourself through force.
And always the darkness falling on your head.
35   Immensely tired, going grey, the nose longer,
face thinner—I know I ought to forgive you.
The hatred of the small, brown child
is the hardest kind to change, Chon.

See Ms. Rivera's poem "For Rita Kohn" in *The Classroom and Beyond* Unit 3.

LISTEN TO MY STORY

Eve Silver

Like all living things I suffered the shock and pain of uprooting but the opportunity to thrive in a benign environment healed some of the wounds of the holocaust upheaval.

At first rootlessness was a serious impediment to growth, but adjustments were made and there was a blossoming of the spirit and a glorious renewal of life.

Most of my family perished in the Holocaust of World War II and never knew life in a free country among civilized people. My own benign fate which guided me through the war years in Europe and on to the United States defies all rational explanation. Why it happened the way it happened I have never been able to explain.

During the years of war, hate and defiance, I began to look back on my Hassidic[1] childhood which took on a glow never anticipated. Away from the life I once knew, every Friday night I remembered the moment when after a day of polishing and cooking, with the appearance of the first star in the skies, the candles were lit in glowing candelabras and a period of lofty thoughts, melodius chanting and family closeness began.

The outside world howling and raging in bitter contests was effectively shut out and the security of togetherness was perfect in the stern elegance of a worthy tradition. Problems were discussed at the white satin-covered table but the holiday spirit overtook the depravity of living in the stetl.[2]

A warren[3] of poverty, hate and prejudice, the stetl in Poland was also the home of my happy childhood and glorious early youth. Mellow nostalgia adorns my thoughts now and permits me to look back with pleasure to those days in my Hassidic home and Polish schools.

Reprinted by permission of the author.

"Star of David." Sanctuary of Congregation Shearith Israel, Atlanta, Georgia. Editor's photograph.

Strong ideals of Polish patriotism and Jewish separatism intertwined and sometimes collided in an abrasive manner in that culture. There was no room for youthful whimsy or inconsequential behaviour. Everything was centered on achieving a certain station in life primarily through education.

Saturday afternoon strolls on the main street of the stetl would for me be a triumph fostering a deep belief in my worthiness. Blessed with a good complexion and rosy cheeks, hair glistening golden in the sun, I came to believe that like my neighbours even my enemies would love me. I always knew there were enemies and even those pleasure-strolls were a test of handling adversity.

My father in his black garbadine wrap-a-round coat, ritual garments clearly visible, with the fur "strimmel"[4] adding giant proportions to his slight statue bravely parading his daughter attired in a gentile uniform of the school heretofore run by Jesuits, clearly defied the codes of his fellow Hassidim. But he was always willing to enter into a discussion of the matter. The forefinger and thumb of one hand stroking his beard or twisting an earlock, he passionately explained to his interlocutionist the necessity of a secular education for this youngest of his five children. There would surely be nothing left for a dowry for the fifth child after the four older children were helped along to start their life. And so tradition must be sacrificed for the sake of a secular education.

Later on I would be able to appraise the advantages of life in this closed community where everyone knew each other's business and cared very much for each other. The knowledge of the outside world was limited and the danger of venturing out accentuated. The closeness of the community offered security and brotherhood. The leadership of charismatic patriarchs accepted. The rules were strictly proscribed and approval assured if the rules were observed. The homogenous society of the stetl lived by customs and symbols reflecting a strong sense of belonging to each other. Changes were seldom allowed and stability of known conditions preferred.

I remember the feeling of security on winter days when the omnipotent stillness and finality of snow cloacked the stetl. Smoke coming out of chimneys or a dim light peering through ice and frost-covered windows, provided hope and assurance.

The challenge I envisioned at my encounter with the outside world in no way corresponded to what I was pitted against during the Holocaust in my early youth. Coming out alive made the challenge of Judaism and Jewishness a lifelong apocalyptic substance. I would never again be able to consider being born a Jew a minor matter. It would remain a predominant element of my thinking and feeling.

I remember the day of my escape from the stetl. It was a day when women, men and children were told to get ready for death. The condemned didn't seem to comprehend what was happening. It was doomsday but feverish activity continued all day. The peasants were streaming into the stetl with their products as if it were country fair day. The samovars were set up and ears of corn freshly steamed were sold at exhorbitant prices. Like vultures the peasants looked on at the bounty they would arrogate upon the destruction of their neighbours.

Seeking explanation and consolation from older and wiser members of the community, a time honored custom in the stetl, I blithely knocked on many doors and entered many houses, but everyone was strangely absorbed, unresponsive and inhospitable. As dusk fell and curfew cleared the streets and alleys, deathly silence fell upon the wooden houses leaning as if under an unbearable strain. Soon the sound of marching boots hitting the cobblestone streets was heard. The troops were taking up their stations to surround the stetl. As I ran to my house where my mother and sister lived after the male members of the family escaped at the beginning of the war to the Russian side, I was startled by darkness and silence. They had found and gone to a hiding place.

Soon I realized that a bizzare misunderstanding left me out of the two hiding places I could have used. My family thought I would hide with my fiancé and he thought I would be hidden with my family.

Fright, anger and despair propelled me to run toward the railroad station, always in my fantasies the gate to the big open world. From that moment on every hour of every day and night for two and a half years hiding my identity in order to live was the main challenge.

Day in and day out my enemy was everybody. There was no tomorrow, but fear was not part of my life. Totally unfamiliar with the expression of that thought by either Montaigne, Thoreau or Roosevelt, I knew instinctively that fear could destroy me. My life-bearing roots having been brutally bulldozed, I hovered between life and death for two and a half years. Spiritually devastated by pains of lost young love, without an understandable future and nothing to live for, I spent each day defying everybody and everything. A half of a kilo of bread and a bottle of milk would see me through the day as long as I was able to pay for my room.

A combination of supercillious attitudes and a desperado disdain for safety made every day a deadly contest. Alone in the world and having to avoid people in order to stay alive, I turned to the pleasures of nature.

Off-limit parks and courtyards of the priviledged, with gardens and birds kept in cages, became a fair sport to me. There I could touch a leaf, walk on grass, listen to a chirping bird and enjoy the rain and snow in my desolate loneliness. If I were caught and shot on the spot it would certainly be a lot better than to be transported for no understandable reason to a concentration camp. Undertaking occasionally small, dangerous errands for some of the underground groups was a spiritual uplift.

My arrival in the South of the U.S. on an April morning was talismanic. The luxury of the trees and gardens within everybody's view and reach was unbelievable. In the stetl, the prickly thistle and the howling dog, protecting some privileged landowner's orchard, were the only contact with nature I knew. There I was surrounded by dead and abrasive objects and deprived people. Nature was a hostile quantity in my youth. Privacy was an unknown quality.

The majestic magnificence of a university's natural setting and the behaviour of civilized people almost defied my comprehension. Why is everybody smiling all the time? And without a particular reason! Servants and college presidents greet and smile at each other as if they are equals.

In the world I had known one needed to establish his superiority at first encounter. Only idiots smiled without reason. Laughter was also in an entirely different category in the Eastern European millieu. Satire and sarcasm meshed into one and laughter was sinister.

Here the smiles were effusive, the talk polite and charming, but most of it terminated as soon as pleasantries were exchanged and the discussion of the weather done. Religion, I learned, is a private matter, political convictions a private matter and, of course, private matters are private matters. Never reveal your feelings and innermost thoughts? What is the purpose of talking to friends then?

Never again will I be able to wave to someone sitting on the balcony, ask them to join me for a walk and immediately pour my heart out—talk about anything and everything. Privacy I learned is more valued than fraternization.

Never will I learn to substitute shopping for Chopin as a means for relaxation and hours spent in stores for hours spent in parks. And yet people, I noticed, centered more attention here on animals and nature than I imagined possible. Holidays, I now note, have lost their Biblical spirit and have become just sumptous affairs.

Something was lost then, but a lot was gained. To live among civilized people who consider it their obligation to hide their hostilities would make life so much more pleasant! And not having to live in Poland always striving for nationhood and almost never achieving it but instead to live in a nation founded on humanitarian principles would be the greatest gift.

NOTES

1. Hassidic—describes religious customs observed by Hassidim a religion sect originating in the 18th century in Eastern Europe.
2. The stetl—a small hamlet in Eastern Poland. A Yiddish word which is a version of the German word "Stadt."
3. A warren-enclosure, a preserve of land inhabited by a certain species.
4. Strimmel—a fur hat worn by the most orthodox religious Jews.

"Old Japanese-American woman on relocation day, May 1942." By
permission of Maria de Noronha (Gallman), the artist.

"LULLABYE"*

Janice Mirikitani

My mother merely shakes
her head
when we talk about the war,
the camps,
5   the bombs.

She won't discuss
the dying/her own
as she left her self
with the stored belongings.

10   She wrapped her shell
in kimono sleeves
and stamped it third class
delivery to Tule Lake.

       Futokoro no ko
15   child at my breast
       oya no nai
           parentless.

What does it mean to be citizen?

       It is privilege
20   to pack only what you can carry.

       It is dignity
       to be interned for your own good.

       It is peace of mind
       constituted by inalienable right.

25   She x'd the box marked "other"
pledging allegiance
to those who would have turned
on the gas mercifully.

From ASIAN-AMERICAN HERITAGE, edited by David Hsin-Fu Wand, Simon & Schuster, Inc., Pocket Books, Washington Square Press. © 1974. Reprinted by permission of the author.

*Notice that "lullaby" with the added "e" as selected for the poem's title, combines the word "lullaby" (meaning a song for lulling a baby to sleep) with "goodbye" (farewell or a contraction of God be with ye), perhaps implying the Japanese-American mother's farewell glance at a secure and peaceful lifestyle, as she embarked with babe in arms, upon an insecure, fearful one, seeking God's divine guidance to help both of them cope with and endure the relocation camp experience.

Her song:

30   shikata ga nai
     it can't be helped

She rode on the train
destined for omission
with an older cousin

35   who died next to her
gagging when her stomach burned out.

Who says you only die once?

My song:

Watashi wa machi no ko
40   I am a child waiting,
       waiting
watashi no hahaga umareta.
     for the birth of my mother.

THE WORKING WOMAN

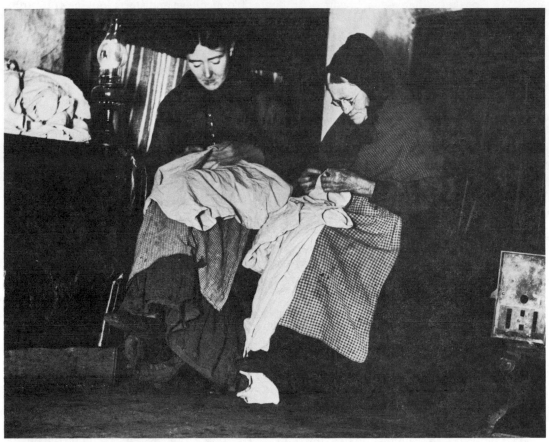

"Two Sewing Women in Elizabeth Street Attic" (from "How the Other Half Lives.") The Jacob A. Riis Collection. Reprinted by permission of the Photo Library Department of the Museum of the City of New York.

A BLACK CONGRESSWOMAN SPEAKS OUT FOR WOMEN'S RIGHTS

Shirley Chisholm

"Mr. Speaker, when a young woman graduates from college and starts looking for a job, she is likely to have a frustrating and even demeaning experience ahead of her. If she walks into an office for an interview, the first question she will be asked is, "Do you type?"

There is a calculated system of prejudice that lies unspoken behind that question. Why is it acceptable for women to be secretaries, librarians, and teachers, but totally unacceptable for them to be managers, administrators, doctors, lawyers, and members of Congress?

The unspoken assumption is that women are different. They do not have executive ability, orderly minds, stability, leadership skills and they are too emotional.

It has been observed before, that society for a long time discriminated against another minority, the blacks, on the same basis—that they were different and inferior. The happy little homemaker and the contended "old darky" on the plantation were both stereotypes produced by prejudice.

As a black person, I am no stranger to race prejudice. But the truth is that in the political world I have been far oftener discriminated against because I am a woman than because I am black.

As in the field of equal rights for blacks, Spanish-Americans, the American Indians, and other groups, laws will not change such deep-seated problems overnight. But they can be used to provide protection for those who are most abused, and to begin the process of evolutionary change by compelling the insensitive majority to reexamine its unconscious attitudes. . . .

From the *Congressional Record,* 21 May 1969, 115, No. 83. Reprinted by permission of Congresswoman Chisholm.

EVA JESSYE: EARTH MOTHER INCARNATE

Helen C. Smith

Her name is Eva, "mother of all living things." Her face is timeless. She could be the Earth Mother incarnate and even thinks of herself in those terms.

She holds the whole world in her arms.

It is all there—the humanity, the compassion, the love—in the very presence of Dr. Eva Jessye, she who was hand-picked by George Gershwin to conduct the chorus for the first version of his opera "Porgy and Bess." She has been a keeper of that flame ever since for many subsequent productions.

That sense of being nurtured and cared for and guided is evident, . . . and like any mother, she wants to pass on the accumulated wisdom of her years.

Excerpts from *The Atlantic Constitution,* February 6, 1978. Reprinted by permission of the author.

Those years are many now, 82 of them behind her. But she knows the weight of them only in her arthritic bones. Otherwise, her energy surpasses that of all others around her.

Dr. Jessye settles her ample body onto a piano bench, spreads her hands out on the desk in front of her and talks of the "directives" that have steered her life.

First there was her Aunt May. Dr. Jessye was a very young little Eva who thought she had found religion. As was the custom, she picked her star in the sky with the certain conviction that it would move across in recognition of her getting religion. The star remained immobile.

"You don't fight for religion," her Aunt May told her. "You live it."

Next, two cousins of hers gave her another guideline for life.

One of them was sitting on a swing. She asked her cousin to push her.

"I can't always be pushing you," the other cousin responded. "Put your foot on the ground and start yourself."

Dr. Jessye has been starting herself ever since.

She got another directive from Booker T. Washington whom she heard speak when she was only a teen-ager. "I hope the time will never come when we neglect and scorn the songs of our fathers," he had said in a speech.

Music, especially spirituals, became the very essence of Dr. Jessye. The Eva Jessye choir has concertized throughout America and abroad, as well as for a while on the NBC Artist Series with the late Leopold Stokowski conducting for over 40 years. Her folk oratorio, "Paradise Lost and Regained," based on the epic poem by John Milton, had its premiere at the Washington Cathedral and was hailed by press and public alike.

Dr. Jessye has been a breaker of barriers, a light on the horizon showing the way for many years. She was the first musical director of a motion picture starring black actors, MGM's "Hallelujah." She and her choir were the first to interpret the Virgil Thomson-Gertrude Stein opera, "Four Saints in Three Acts." Hers was the official choir for the historic march on Washington in 1963. Her ever-growing collection of Afro-American music, housed both at the University of Michigan and Clark College, is one of the largest treasure troves of authentic spirituals, including some of her own, in existence.

"I came from a singing family," says Dr. Jessye. "We had no radio, no television. We had to learn how to express ourselves. And then I could always see the drama in songs."

There were other things she assimilated from Booker T. Washington that helped her along the road. She counts them off, one-two-three, on her strong fingers.

"If your job doesn't honor you, you honor it. Education doesn't mean anything unless you use it."

Dr. Jessye has finished cataloging the list of directives by which she has lived her life. She has few regrets, save only that she hasn't had time to become a conductor of a symphony orchestra.

"I would love to do that," she says, with a faraway look in her eyes as if another life might grant her that wish.

In the meantime her mission is to do what she can to compensate for what she calls the "great neglect of folk music, both black and white."

That's where the soul of a people lives, and soul is what Dr. Jessye is all about.

DR. EVANGELINE PAPAGEORGE: A GREEK WHO BORE WARM GIFTS

Loral Graham

Most Americans associate the Greek spirit with Zorba the Greek or Ilya, the irrepressible prostitute in *Never On Sunday*. An eloquent definition of the quintessence of Greekness appears in the unlikely pages of a restaurant guide: R. B. Read's *The San Francisco Underground Gourmet*. The Greek ideal, Read writes, is "that intuitive recognition of what is fundamentally important, and the faculty of embracing it without any holding back or counting of the cost. It is the sure sense of when to exult and when to weep, when to move in or to get out, to love or to loathe, to rage or walk away, to gather the windfall or greet the inexorable. . . . This ideal expresses itself in a faculty of spontaneity that is at once intensely ethical and wholly converted into physical statement, and this I call the Greek spirit."

Evangeline Papageorge came to America in 1910 when she was only three years old. She is an American citizen; she grew up speaking English, and her lifestyle in most ways is indistinguishable from other Americans. But "she still has that Greek personality," as Emory University's medical school dean, Arthur Richardson, fondly remarks, and that is what makes her special.

"When people ask about Emory, they ask about Dr. Papageorge," Dr. Bruce Logue, one of Dr. Papageorge's biochemistry students at Emory in the Thirties, comments. "She's one of the things about Emory that hasn't changed." But last month it did change because Evangeline Papageorge retired, after 46 years on the staff of the Emory University School of Medicine.

She began at Emory in 1928 by preparing laboratory solutions to pay the tuition fees for her M.S. degree in biochemistry. A year later she was the only female faculty member in an all-male medical school. Over the next 20 years, she earned a Ph.D. degree at the University of Michigan and a post-doctorate fellowship at Yale, and climbed the rungs of academe at Emory. Last month when she retired, her title was executive associate dean.

TRADITION AND AMBITION

She was an anomaly in her time simply because she was a woman. But Dr. Papageorge dismisses that observation with an impatient: "In every generation in every country there have been ambitious women." She concedes, however, that she was different from the average Atlanta girl growing up in the Twenties. A tradition of academic achievement went back generations on both sides of her family. Her father was a Greek Orthodox priest and her father's father was a priest, too. Her mother, because she was a woman who grew up in a small Greek village, hadn't finished high school, though all her brothers had university degrees. She

Excerpts from Loral Graham, "Emory's Dr. Papageorge: A Greek Who Bore Warm Gifts," from *Atlanta*, September 1975, Vol. 15, No. 5. Copyright 1975 Atlanta Magazine. Excerpted by permission of Editor/Publisher Norman Shavin, Excerpts from John Keay Davidson, "Emory's Evangeline" from *Medicine at Emory* 1975, pp. 14–19. Evangeline Papageorge, "My Father, My Mother and My Greek Heritage." Reprinted by permission of the author.

was steeped in Greek mythology and history, however, and friends were always amazed to discover how limited her formal education had been.

Evangeline's parents never questioned her right to attend college and, in her words, "to *do* something if I wanted to." (Some members of her father's parish, however, raised their eyebrows at the uppity Evangeline.) And she was touched with the drive to excel, the sense of new beginnings and of building for future generations that immigrant families so often have. "Many Greek immigrants had very limited educations but they dreamed of their children getting one," recalls Dr. Papageorge. Her father died when she was in her junior year at Agnes Scott College, and she and her older brother felt it was their responsibility to put five younger children through college.

Evangeline remembers with affection that my father and mother taught us all to speak Greek and made it possible for me to learn to read and even to write a bit in Greek. They inbred us all with knowledge and pride in our ethnic background, but did not permit us to be chauvinistic about it. My mother taught us Greek Mythology and this in place of other fairy tales, since she knew well the Greek myths. From my father I got the love of history and geography. Also, he influenced me in seeking precision in quoting facts and in reporting events.

The two important Greek maxims drilled into us from our parents were:

1. Nothing too much (that is, the golden measure; or moderation)
2. Know thyself.

They loved beauty in art, music and dance and passed this on to us so that we learned to appreciate great works which they had not had the opportunity themselves to learn about.

The ambition of our parents was to see us all educated. They were kind but most unsympathetic if we blamed our teachers. They were loving but we knew discipline. They taught us ideals but let us know that one could not expect to attain them and that life had joys but also disappointments. They stressed the same virtues that America stands for (or did): courtesy, and above all freedom. They were not perfect but they did quite well in bringing us up to be honest and good citizens.

Great achievements were the products of their labors," historian Oscar Handlin wrote of the foreigners who settled in America during the 19th and early 20th centuries. "Without their contributions the country could not have taken the form it did. But they paid a heavy price, not only in the painful process of crossing and resettlement but also in the continuing ache of uprootedness. The ocean separated them forever from the old home, from the church, the village, and above all, the kinfolk—the whole circle of people and places on which they depended."

Thomas Papageorge was a hard-working Greek Orthodox priest in Constantinople (now Istanbul), Turkey, when in 1905 his superiors authorized him to go to America, where Greek orthodox churches were being organized. He moved his family to the island of Samos for the time that they would be apart. Then in 1907 he followed his wife's brother—also a priest—to the new land.

"They were very, very close; they were very much like brothers," recalls Papageorge's daughter, Evangeline. "And you must remember that they were young, they were adventurous, America was the country of adventure. And here were these young priests, who wanted to help establish churches here and moreover, help the Greek immigrants, and see America." She recalls this with a distant look in her eye, as though she can see her father stepping onto American soil.

The family wasn't sure about whether it should follow father Papageorge. His letters home indicated he was no longer so certain he would stay in the loud, bustling U.S. Mrs. Papageorge's mother didn't want her only daughter to leave; and Evangeline, not yet four, seemed too young for the rugged sea voyage.

But they left. They landed in Boston, and after some moving about with father Papageorge they settled in Atlanta. World War I had just ended.

Dr. Papageorge remembers herself as having been "a bossy little girl who wanted to teach." To imitate her teachers, she would wrap herself in her mother's tablecloth and write on the door with chalk. "And did I catch it!"

By the time she was attending Girls' High School in Atlanta, American women had won the right to vote. Though she has never been an "out-and-out feminist," she recalls that she believed early in equality of rights.

A friend of Evangeline's father once called her "the little suffragette."

She learned about teaching by tutoring in high school. But at Agnes Scott College, where she was elected to Phi Beta Kappa, she struggled to choose a subject to teach for the rest of her life. "French and history came very easy to me," she remembers. But she chose chemistry because she could "go into" it. "That decision really set the pattern for my life," she adds.

In the fall of 1928, Emory accepted her to do graduate work in biochemistry, and at 21 she had found the institution that would be her life-long professional home.

There were only three professors in the biochemistry department at that time. When one left, she was offered his position on condition that she take summer courses at the University of Chicago. These courses laid the groundwork for her Ph.D. in biological chemistry, which she eventually received from the University of Michigan. Later, she was awarded a Sterling fellowship for postdoctoral work in physiological chemistry at Yale.

Dr. Papageorge was the Emory medical school's first full-time woman faculty member, but she recalls no prejudicial treatment by her colleagues. "They were rather amused at me because I was about the same age as the medical students," she laughs.

She recalled during that momentous day in August, 1975; as I prepare to leave my cluttered office in the Woodruff Memorial Building, my thoughts and memories turn to a September day 47 years ago when a young Agnes Scott graduate came to Emory to begin her master's program in biochemistry in the old Chemistry Building (now being renovated to house such departments as languages and music). And there comes to mind the paraphrased aphorism, composed perhaps by a remote Greek ancestor, inscribed on the base of a marble head of Hippocrates discovered near Rome about 25 years ago:

> *"Short is the life, but long is the age we mortals spend below the ground; it is the lot of all of us to bear the fate, whatever it be, that God apportions."*

My nearly half-century at Emory seems short, in retrospect, but on reflecting that my career is drawing to an end, there is no regret for the lot apportioned to me. My life has been crowded with rich experiences, and the problem is to select a few in which my life's thread is woven into the pattern of the institution that has been my only professional home.

Evangeline Papageorge has all the qualities that employers prize: boundless energy, utter dedication and unquestioned ability to do the job. But what sets her apart from—and so far above—legions of faithful servants is her human warmth, a quality that has played a crucial role in her job performance. "She was a great, stimulating teacher," recalls Dr. Charles Stone, an Emory medical school graduate of 1937, "but if you were characterizing her you would have to say that she had heart." Almost half a century of Emory medical school graduates echo Dr. Stone's words: "She was a person who *cared*. . . . You could *feel* the empathy she had for you. . . . Everybody was crazy about her."

TENDER AND TOUGH

She knew when to be tender and when to be tough. As Dean Richardson phrased it: "She has the unusual knack of knowing when to be sympathetic and when to put the pressure on. She knows whether to pat them on the back or kick them in the fanny." Both characteristics are borne out in every person. She is a tiny 4 feet 11-and-a-quarter inches but her voice booms with vitality. She moves quickly and with a proverbial air of efficiency, but you never feel she is rushing you or doubt for a minute that her smile is anything but genuine.

The ideal mentor must be solid and sensitive—and Dr. Papageorge is both. There is a savvy air about her that makes you feel that you could tell her *anything* and she wouldn't be shocked. She is the rare person who both enjoys life to the fullest and adheres to ramrod principles as well. And that is what the Greek ideal is all about.

THE CHILDHOOD OF AN IMMIGRANT WORKING GIRL

Rose Schneiderman (1882-1972)

Rose Schneiderman, women's trade union organizer, describes her poor girlhood in New York's Lower East side. Although the burden of housekeeping and caring for younger siblings was traditionally the duty of the mother, in this family, Rose's mother sent her boys to an orphanage while one girl went to an aunt, and the oldest girl remained with the mother who was forced to work. Even under hardship conditions, girls were "sheltered" and "protected."

It was traditional that a girl deferred her education in favor of brothers and the one child to receive an education even at free City College would be a boy. The sisters' earnings usually supported the education of their brothers in the Jewish immigrant home. However, in Rose's case, she participated in domestic drudgery at home and as an underpaid factory worker while attempting to snatch bits of schooling whenever the family permitted her to fulfill her ambitions.

Rose Schneiderman helped organize the International Ladies Garment Workers Union, becoming the organization's vice-president in 1907. She later was appointed secretary of the New York State Department of Labor in 1937.

A CAP MAKER'S STORY

My name is Rose Schneiderman, and I was born in some small city of Russian Poland. I don't know the name of the city, and have no memory of that part of my childhood. When I was about five years of age my parents brought me to this country and we settled in New York.

So my earliest recollections are of living in a crowded street among the East Side Jews, for we also are Jews.

My father got work as a tailor, and we lived in two rooms on Eldridge Street, and did very well, though not so well as in Russia, because mother and father both earned money, and here father alone earned the money, while mother attended to the house. There were then two other children besides me, a boy of three and one of five.

I went to school until I was nine years old, enjoying it thoroughly and making great progress, but then my father died of brain fever and mother was left with three children and another one coming. So I had to stay at home to help her and she went out to look for work.

A month later the baby was born, and mother got work in a fur house, earning about $6 a week and afterward $8 a week, for she was clever and steady.

I was the house worker, preparing the meals and looking after the other children—the baby, a little girl of six years, and a boy of nine. I managed very well, tho the meals were not very elaborate. I could cook simple things like porridge, coffee and eggs, and mother used to prepare the meat before she went away in the morning, so that all I had to do was to put it in the pan at night. . . .

. . . I was a serious child, and cared little for children's play, and I knew nothing about the country, so it was not so bad for me as it might have been for another. . . .

Mother was absent from half-past seven o'clock in the morning till half-past six o'clock in the evening.

I was finally released by my little sister being taken by an aunt, and the two boys going to the Hebrew Orphan Asylum, which is a splendid institution, and turns out good men. One of these brothers is now a student in the City College, and the other is a page in the Stock Exchange.

When the other children were sent away mother was able to send me back to school, and I stayed in this school (Houston Street Grammar) till I had reached the Sixth Grammar Grade.

Then I had to leave in order to help support the family. I got a place in Hearn's as cash girl, and after working there three weeks changed to Ridley's, where I remained for two and a half years. I finally left because the pay was so very poor and there did not seem to be any chance of advancement, and a friend told me that I could do better making caps.

So I got a place in the factory of Hein & Fox. The hours were from 8 a.m. to 6 p.m., and we made all sorts of linings—or, rather, we stitched in the linings—golf caps, yachting caps, etc. It was piece work, and we received from 3 1/2 cents to 10 cents a dozen, according to the different grades. By working hard we could make an average of about $5 a week. We would have made more but had to provide our own machines, which cost us $45, we paying for them on the installment plan. We paid $5 down and $1 a month after that.

I learned the business in about two months, and then made as much as the others, and was consequently doing quite well when the factory burned down, destroying all our machines—150

From Rose Schneiderman, A CAP MAKER'S STORY, *The Independent,* LVIII, No. 2943 (April 27, 1905), pp. 935–936.

"Hester Street" (63) 1898. The Byron Collection. Reprinted by permission of the Photo Library Department of the Museum of the City of New York.

of them. This was very hard on the girls who had paid for their machines. It was not so bad for me, as I had only paid a little of what I owed.

The bosses got $500,000 insurance, so I heard, but they never gave the girls a cent to help them bear their losses. I think they might have given them $10, anyway.

Soon work went on again in four lofts, and a little later I became assistant sample maker. This is a position which, tho coveted by many, pays better in glory than in cash. It was still piece work, and tho the pay per dozen was better the work demanded was of a higher quality, and one could not rush through samples as through the other caps. So I still could average only about $5 per week. . . .

Unit Seven

RELIGION AND RITUAL

"Old woman by stained glass window." By permission of Harriett Warshaw, the artist.

> And God spoke all these words, saying:
> I am the Lord thy God, who brought thee out of the
>   land of Egypt, out of the house of bondage.
> Thou shalt have no other gods before Me.
>
> Exodus 20:1-3

WHAT MUST I SAY TO YOU?

Norma Rosen

When I open the door for Mrs. Cooper at two in the afternoon, three days a week, that is the one time her voice fails us both. She smiles over my left shoulder and hurries out the words "Just fine," to get past me. She is looking for the baby, either in the bassinet in the living room or in the crib in the baby's room. When she finds her, she can talk more easily to me—through the baby. But at the doorway again, in the early evening, taking leave, Mrs. Cooper speaks up in her rightful voice, strong and slow: "I am saying good night." It seems to me that the "I am saying" form, once removed from herself, frees her of her shyness. As if she had already left and were standing in the hall, away from strangers, and were sending back the message "I am saying good night."

Maybe. I know little about Mrs. Cooper, and so read much into her ways. Despite the differences between us, each of us seems to read the other the same—tender creature, prone to suffer. Mrs. Cooper says to me, many times a day, "That is all right, that is all right," in a soothing tone. I say to her, "That's such a help, thank you, such a help." What can I guess, except what reflects myself, about someone so different from me?

Mrs. Cooper is from Jamaica. She is round-faced and round-figured. She is my age, thirty, and about my height, five-five. But because she is twice my girth (not fat; if there is any unfavorable comparison to be drawn, it may as well be that I am, by her standard, meager) and because she has four children to my one, she seems older. She is very black; I am—as I remember the campus doctor at the women's college I attended saying— "surprisingly fair." Though, of course, not Anglo-Saxon. If you are not Anglo-Saxon, being fair counts only up to a point. I learned that at the women's college. I remember a conversation with a girl at college who had an ambiguous name—Green or Black or Brown. She said in the long run life was simpler if your name was Finkelstein. And I said it was better to be dark and done with it.

Mrs. Cooper had been coming to us, with her serious black bulk and her beautiful voice, for some months now, so that I can get on with my work, which is free-lance editorial. The name is lighthearted enough, but the lance is heavy and keeps me pinned to my desk. Mrs. Cooper's work, in her hands, seems delightful. Though she comes to relieve me of that same work, it is a little like watching Tom Sawyer paint a fence—so attractive one would gladly pay an apple to be allowed to lend a hand. Even the slippery bath, the howls as my daughter's sparse hairs are shampooed, become amusing mites on the giant surface of Mrs. Cooper's calm. They raise Mrs. Cooper's laugh. "Ooh, my! You can certainly sing!"

I sneak from my desk several times an afternoon to watch the work and to hear Mrs. Cooper speak. Her speech, with its trotty Jamaican rhythm, brings every syllable to life and pays exquisite attention to the final sounds of words. When she telephones home to instruct the oldest of her children in the care of the youngest, it is true that her syntax relaxes. I hear "Give she supper and put she to bed." Or "When I'm coming home I am going to wash the children them hair." But the tone of her voice is the same as when she speaks to me. It is warm, melodious. Always the diction is glorious—ready, with only a bit of memorizing, for Shakespeare. Or, if one could connect a woman's voice with the Old Testament, for that.

"God is not a God of confusion." Mrs. Cooper says that to me one day while the baby naps and she washes baby clothes in the double tub in the kitchen. I have come in to get an apple from the refrigerator. She refuses any fruit, and I stand and eat and watch the best work in the world: rhythmic rubbing-a-dubbing in a sudsy tub. With sturdy arms.

She says it again. "God is not a God of confusion, that is what my husband cousin say." A pause. "And that is what I see."

She washes; I suspend my apple.

"It is very noisy in these churches you have here." She has been in this country for three years—her husband came before, and later sent for her and the children, mildly surprising her mother, who had other daughters and daughters' kids similarly left but not reclaimed—and still she is bothered by noisy churches. Her family in Jamaica is Baptist. But when she goes to the Baptist church in Harlem, she is offended by the stamping and handclapping, by the shouted confessions and the tearful salvations. "They say wherever you go you are at home in your church. But we would never do that way at home."

She lifts her arms from the tub and pushes the suds down over her wrists and hands. "But I will find a church." The purity of her diction gives the words great strength. The tone and timbre would be fitting if she had said, "I will build a church."

Again she plunges her arms in suds. "Do you ever go," she asks me, "to that church? To that Baptist church?"

Now is the time for me to tell her that my husband and I are Jewish—and so, it occurs to me suddenly and absurdly, is our three-month-old daughter, Susan.

It is coming to Christmas. I have already mentioned to my husband that Mrs. Cooper, who has said how her children look forward to the tree, will wonder at our not having one for our child. "I don't feel like making any announcements," I tell my husband, "but I suppose I should. She'll wonder."

"You don't owe her an explanation." My husband doesn't know how close, on winter afternoons, a woman is drawn to another woman who works in her house. It would surprise him to hear that I have already mentioned to Mrs. Cooper certain intimate details of my life, and that she has revealed to me a heartache about her husband.

"But I think I'll tell her," I say. "Not even a spray of balsam. I'd rather have her think us Godless than heartless."

My husband suggests, "Tell her about Chanukah"—which with us is humor, because he knows I wouldn't know what to tell.

Mrs. Cooper stands before my tub in the lighted kitchen. I lean in the doorway, watching her. The kitchen window is black. Outside, it is a freezing four o'clock. Inside, time is suspended, always when the baby sleeps. I smell the hot, soaped flannel, wrung out and heaped on the drainboard, waiting to be rinsed in three pure waters. "We don't attend church," I say. "We go—at least, my husband goes—to a synagogue. My husband and I are Jewish, Mrs. Cooper."

Mrs. Cooper looks into the tub. After a moment, she says, "That is all right." She fishes below a cream of suds, pulls up a garment, and unrolls a mitten sleeve. She wrings it and rubs it and plunges it down to soak. Loving work, as she performs it—mother's work. As I watch, my body seems to pass into her body.

I am glad that my reluctance to speak of synagogues at all has led me to speak while Mrs. Cooper is working. That is the right way. We never, I realize while she scrubs, still seeming to be listening, talk face to face. She is always looking somewhere else—at the washing or the baby's toy she is going to pick up. Being a shy person, I have drilled myself to stare people in the eyes when I speak. But Mrs. Cooper convinces me this is wrong. The face-to-face stare is for selling something, or for saying, "Look here, I don't like you and I never have liked you," or for answering, "Oh, no, Madam, we never accept for refund after eight days."

The time Mrs. Cooper told me her husband had stopped going to church altogether, she was holding Susan, and she uttered those exquisite and grieved tones—"He will not go with me, or alone, or at all any more"—straight into the baby's face, not mine.

Mrs. Cooper now pulls the stopper from the tub and the suds choke down. While she is waiting, she casts a sidelong look at me, which I sense rather than see, as I am examining my apple core. She likes to see the expression on my face after I have spoken, though not while I speak. She looks back at the sucking tub.

When Mrs. Cooper comes again on Friday, she tells me, as she measures formula into bottles, "My husband says we do not believe Christmas is Christ's birthday."

I, of course, do not look at her, except to snatch a glance out of the corner of my eye, while I fold diapers unnecessarily. Her expression is calm and bland, high round cheekbones shining, slightly slanted eyes narrowed to the measuring. "He was born, we believe, sometime in April." After a bit, she adds, "We believe there is one God for everyone."

Though my husband has told me over and over again that this is what Jews say, Mrs. Cooper's words move me as though I have never heard them before. I murmur something about my work, and escape to my desk and my lance again.

Mrs. Cooper has quoted her husband to me several times. I am curious about him, as I am sure she is about my husband. She and my husband have at least met once or twice in the doorway, but I have only seen a snapshot of her husband: a stocky man with a mustache, who is as black as she, with no smiles for photographers. Mrs. Cooper has added, in the winter afternoons, certain details important to my picture.

Her husband plays cricket on Staten Island on Sundays and goes on vacations in the summer without her or the children, sometimes with the cricketers. But to balance that, he brings her shrimp and rice when he returns at 1:00 A.M. from cricket-club meetings on Friday nights. His opinion of the bus strike in the city was that wages should go up but it was unfair to make bus riders suffer. About Elizabeth Taylor he thought it was all just nonsense; she was not even what he called pretty—more like skinny and ugly.

In most other respects, it seems to me, he is taking on the coloration of a zestful America-adopter. There are two kinds of immigrants, I observe. One kind loves everything about America, is happy to throw off the ways of the old country, and thereafter looks back largely with contempt. The other kind dislikes, compares, regrets, awakens to *Welt-* and *Ichschmerz* and feels the new life mainly as a loss of the old. Often, the two marry each other.

Mr. Cooper, though he still plays cricket, now enjoys baseball, the fights on television, his factory job and union card, and the bustle and opportunity of New York. I mention this last with irony. Mr. Cooper's job opportunities here are infinitely better than in Jamaica, where there aren't employers even to turn him down. He goes to school two nights a week for technical training. He became a citizen three years ago, destroying his wife's hopes of returning to Jamaica in their young years. But she dreams of going back when they are old. She would have servants there, she told me. "Because there aren't enough jobs, servants are cheap." Her husband, in her dream, would have a job, and so they would also have a car. And a quiet, gossipy life. She lives to move slowly, and this, as she herself points out, is very nice for my baby.

Christmas Week comes, and we give Mrs. Cooper presents for her children. And since Christmas Day falls on the last of her regular three days a week, we pay her for her holiday at the end of the second day. "Merry Christmas, Mrs. Cooper," I say. "Have a happy holiday."

Mrs. Cooper looks with interest at the baby in my arms, whom she had a moment before handed over to me. Suddenly she laughs and ducks her knees. Her fingers fly with unaccustomed haste to her cheek and she asks, "What must I say to you?"

"You can wish me the same," I say. "We have a holiday. My husband gets the day off, too."

I am glad that Mrs. Cooper has not grown reticent, since her embarrassment at Christmas, in speaking to me of holidays. Soon she is telling me how the children are looking forward to Easter. The oldest girl is preparing already for her part in a church play.

I fuss with the can of Enfamil, helping Mrs. Cooper this way when what I want is to help her another way. "Will your husband come to the play?" I ask casually.

"I am not sure," she says. After a while, "We haven't told him yet." Another little while. "Because it seems also he is against these plays." Then, with just enough of a pause to send those tones to my heart, she says, "I think he will not come."

Because the Judaeo-Christian tradition will have its little joke, Passover Week sometimes coincides with Easter Week, overlaying it like a reproach. It does the year Mrs. Cooper is with us. First, Good Friday, then in a few days is the first day of Passover.

"This year," my husband says, "because of Susie, to celebrate her first year with us, I want us to put a mezuzah outside our door before Passover."

"I'm not in favor." I manage to say it quietly.

"You don't understand enough about it," my husband says.

"I understand that much."

"Do you know what a mezuzah is? Do you know what's in it?" Taking my silence as an admission of ignorance, my husband produces a Bible. "Deuteronomy," he says. He reads:

Hear, O Israel: The Lord our God, the Lord is one Lord:
And thou shalt love the Lord thy God with all thine heart, and with all thy soul, and with all thy
   might.
And these words, which I command thee this day, shall be in thine heart:
And thou shalt teach them diligently unto thy children, and shalt talk of them when thou sittest
   in thine house, and when thou walkest by the way, and when thou liest down, and when thou
   risest up. . . .

All this and more is written on a parchment that is rolled up tight and fitted into the metal or wooden mezuzah, which is no more than two inches high and less than half an inch across and is mounted on a base for fastening to the doorframe. My husband finishes his reading:

And thou shalt write them upon the door-posts of thine house, and upon they gates:
That your days may be multiplied, and the days of your children, in the land which the Lord
   sware unto your fathers to give them, as the days of heaven upon the earth.

The words might move me if I allowed them to, but I will not allow them to.

My husband closes the Bible and asks, "What did your family observe? What was Passover like?

"My grandfather sat on a pillow, and I was the youngest, so I found the matzos and he gave me money."

"No questions? No answers?"

"Just one. I would ask my grandfather, 'Where is my prize?' And he would laugh and give me money."

"Is that all?" my husband asks.

"That was a very nice ceremony in itself," I say. "And I remember it with pleasure, and my grandfather with love!"

"But besides the food, besides the children's game. Didn't your grandparents observe anything?"

"I don't remember."

"You sat at their table for eighteen years!"

"Well, my grandmother lit Friday-night candles, and that was something I think she did all her life. But she did it by herself, in the breakfast room."

"Didn't they go to a synagogue?"

"My grandmother did. My grandfather did, too, but then I remember he stopped. He'd be home on holidays, not at the services."

"Your parents didn't tell you anything?"

"My parents were the next generation," I say. "And I'm the generation after that. We evolved," I say—and luckily that is also humor between my husband and me.

But my husband rubs his head. It's different now, and not so funny, because this year we have Susan.

My husband was born in Europe, of an Orthodox family. He is neither Orthodox nor Reform. He is his own council of rabbis, selecting as he goes. He has plenty to say about the influence of American on Jewishness, Orthodox or not. "The European Jew," my husband says, "didn't necessarily feel that if he rose in the social or economic scale he had to stop observing his Jewishness. There were even a number of wealthy and prominent German Jews who were strictly observant."

"I'm sure that helped them a lot!" This is as close as I come to speaking of the unspeakable. Somewhere in the monstrous testimony I have read about concentration camps and killings are buried the small, intense lives of my husband's family. But why is it I am more bitter than my husband about his own experiences? And why should my bitterness cut the wrong way? It is the word "German" that does it to me. My soul knots in hate. "German!" Even the softening, pathetic sound of "Jew" that follows it now doesn't help. All words fail. If I could grasp words, I would come on words that would jump so to life they would jump into my heart and kill me. All I can do is make a fantasy. Somewhere in New York I will meet a smiling German. In his pocket smile the best export accounts in the city—he is from the land of scissors and knives and ground glass. Because I am surprisingly fair, he will be oh, so surprised when I strike at him with all my might. "For the children! For the children!" My words come out shrieks. He protests it was his duty and, besides, he didn't know. I am all leaking, dissolving. How can a mist break stone? Once we exchange words it is hopeless; the words of the eyewitness consume everything, as in a fire:

> The children were covered with sores. . . . They screamed and wept all night in the empty rooms where they had been put. . . . Then the police would go up and the children, screaming with terror, would be carried kicking and struggling to the courtyard.

How is it my husband doesn't know that after this there can be no mezuzahs?

"It's too painful to quarrel," my husband says. He puts his hands on my shoulders, his forehead against mine. "This is something I want very much. And you feel for me. I know you feel for me in this."

"Yes, I do, of course I do." I use Mrs. Cooper's trick, and even at that close range twist my head elsewhere. "Only that particular symbol—"

"No, with you it's all the symbols." My husband drops his hands from my shoulders. "You don't know enough about them to discard them."

I don't have the right to judge them—that is what I feel he means. Since I was not even scorched by the flames of their futility. As he was, and came out cursing less than I.

"But besides everything else"—I take hasty shelter in practicalness— "a mezuzah is ugly. I remember that ugly tin thing nailed to the door of my grandmother's room. If I spend three weeks picking out a light fixture for my foyer, why should I have something so ugly on my door?"

Then, as my husband answers, I see that this shabby attack has fixed my defeat, because he is immediately reasonable. "Now, that's something else. I won't argue aesthetics with you. The outer covering is of no importance. I'll find something attractive."

The next night my husband brings home a mezuzah made in the East. It is a narrow green rectangle, twice the normal size, inlaid with mosaic and outlined in brass. It does not look Jewish to me at all. It looks foreign—a strange bit of green enamel and brass.

"I don't like it," I say. "I'm sorry."

"But it's only the idea you don't like?" My husband smiles teasingly. "In looks, you at least relent?"

"It doesn't look bad," I admit.

"Well, that is the first step." I am happy to see the mezuzah disappear in his dresser drawer before we go in to our dinner.

When Mrs. Cooper comes next day, she asks, "What have you on your door?"

I step out to look, and at first have the impression that a praying mantis has somehow hatched out of season high on our doorway. Then I recognize it. "Oh, that's . . ." I say. "That's . . ." I find I cannot explain a mezuzah to someone who has never heard of one.

While Mrs. Cooper changes her clothes, I touch the mezuzah to see if it will fall off. But my husband has glued it firmly to the metal doorframe.

My husband's office works a three-quarter day on Good Friday. I ask Mrs. Cooper if she would like time off, but she says no, her husband will be home ahead of her to look after things. I have the impression she would rather be here.

My husband comes home early, bestowing strangeness on the rhythm of the house in lieu of celebration. I kiss him and put away his hat. "Well, that was a nasty thing to do." I say it lazily and with a smirk. The lazy tone is to show that I am not really involved, and the smirk that I intend to swallow it down like bad medicine. He will have his way, but I will have my say—that's all I mean. My say will be humorous, with just a little cut to it, as is proper between husband and wife. He will cut back a little, with a grin, and after Mrs. Cooper goes we will have our peaceful dinner. The conversation will meander, never actually picking sore points, but winding words about them, making pads and cushions, so that should they ever bleed, there, already softly wrapped around them, will be the bandages our words wove. Weave enough of these bandages and nothing will ever smash, I say. I always prepare in advance a last line, too, so that I will know where to stop. ''When mezuzahs last in the doorway bloomed,'' I will say tonight. And then I expect us both to laugh.

But where has he been all day? The same office, the same thirty-minute subway ride to and from each way, the same lunch with the same cronies. . . . But he has traveled somewhere else in his head. ''Doesn't anything mean anything to you?'' he says, and walks by me to the bedroom.

I follow with a bandage, but it slips from my hand. ''I know a lot of women who would have taken that right down!'' It is something of a shout, to my surprise.

He says nothing.

''I left it up. All I wanted was my say.''

He says nothing.

''I live here, too. That's my door also.''

He says nothing.

''And I don't like it!''

I hear a loud smashing of glass. It brings both our heads up. My husband is the first to understand. ''Mrs. Cooper broke a bottle.'' He puts his arms around me and says, ''Let's not quarrel about a doorway. Let's not quarrel at all, but especially not about the entrance to our home.''

I lower my face into his tie. What's a mezuzah? Let's have ten, I think, so long as nothing will smash.

Later, I reproach myself. I am in the living room, straightening piles of magazines, avoiding both kitchen and bedroom. A woman, I think, is the one creature who builds satisfaction of the pleasure she gets from giving in. What might the world be if women would continue the dialogue? But no, they must give in and be satisfied. Nevertheless, I don't intend to take back what I've given in on and thereby give up what I've gained.

I am aware of Mrs. Cooper, boiling formula in the kitchen, and of my baby, registering in sleep her parents' first quarrel since her birth. ''What must I say to you?'' I think of saying to my daughter—Mrs. Cooper's words come naturally to my mind.

I go to the kitchen doorway and look at Mrs. Cooper. Her face indicates deaf and dumb. She is finishing the bottles.

When Mrs. Cooper is dressed and ready to leave, she looks into the living room. ''I am saying good night.''

''I hope you and your family will have a happy Easter,'' I say, smiling for her.

I know in advance that Mrs. Cooper will ask, ''What must I say to you?''

This time she asks it soberly, and this time my husband, who has heard, comes in to tell Mrs. Cooper the story of Passover. As always in the traditional version, there is little mention of Moses, the Jews having set down from the beginning not the tragedy of one but their intuition for the tragedy of many.

When my husband leaves us, Mrs. Cooper takes four wrapped candies from the candy bowl on the desk, holds them up to be sure I see her taking them, and puts them in her purse. "I do hope everything will be all right," she says.

"Oh, yes," I say, looking at the magazines. "It was such a help today. I got so much work done. Thank you."

I hear that she is motionless.

"I will not be like this all the days of my life." It is a cry from the heart, stunningly articulated. I lift my head from the magazines, and this time I do stare. Not be like what? A Jamaican without a servant? A wife who never vacations? An exile? A baby nurse? A woman who gives in? What Mrs. Cooper might not want to be flashes up in a lighting jumble. "I am going to find a church," she says, and strains her face away from mine.

I think of all the descriptions of God I have ever heard—that He is jealous, loving, vengeful, waiting, teaching, forgetful, permissive, broken-hearted, dead, asleep.

Mrs. Cooper and I wish each other a pleasant weekend.

"GOD AND ETHNICITY"

Borghild Dahl

The Norwegian-American family at supper. Lyng has been given words of wisdom from Grandmother Skoglund about continuing her education and now she will be given some additional information.

Father has just had a drink.

"What about you?" Grandmother Skoglund suggested. "Don't you want to try it now, *Vesla-mi?*"

Lyng held up the third cup. Grandmother Skoglund put soda into it and stirred it and gave it back to Lyng. The drink had a sour-sweet taste and a pleasantly sharp tang that made the inside of her mouth tingle. She emptied the cup as quickly as the boys had done.

"There you see!" Grandmother Skoglund exclaimed triumphantly.

"Can we have more?" Kristian begged.

"One cup more for each of you," Grandmother Skoglund said, measuring out vinegar and sugar.

Haakon and Kristian gulped down their second cups.

"I'm thirsty," Kristian said.

"Enough is enough," Grandmother Skoglund said emphatically. "Now it's time to thank God for the food."

"I'll bet they don't say their prayers down by Minnehaha Falls," Lyng said.

Excerpt from HOMECOMING by Borghild Dahl, E.P. Dutton & Company, © 1953 by Borghild Dahl. Reprinted by permission of the author.

"We always thank God for the food, no matter where we eat it," Grandmother Skoglund said. "And it is correct to talk to Him in any language. He understands many of them, I'm sure, even though He may like Norwegian best."

"BLACK BAPTISM"

Laurraine Goreau

Orphaned at six (her father did not acknowledge her), Mahalia Jackson lived with her Aunt Duke in "Pinching Town," a New Orleans community clustered around the bend of the Mississippi River levee where black and white lived in common poverty. At fourteen, she dreamed of somehow "making something of herself," but found her greatest joy in church, where she could always "sing it out," surrounded by the multitude of cousins and aunts which included gentle Aunt Bell and Bell's daughter Celie.

* * *

Candidates for the sinner's bench, in Mt. Moriah eyes, were entirely too numerous: the whole youth choir was being eyed askance. Here was almost a grown set ready for the senior choir and not a one converted. Had the play-acting and worldly music made them light? Of course, all the choir had been duly christened and taken communion regularly. Couldn't miss that. ("Communion was a great day," said Mahalia, eyes alight. "If you weren't right with the Lord, you sat back on the mourner's bench and you meditated, and you got the spirit; then they'd give you communion.") So important was Communion Sunday that there was a "communicating church"—Broadway Missionary, Halie's daddy's church—the service of one shortened on the other's communion day each month so the sister congregation could walk over. Mt. Moriah, in fact, had two communicating churches, Pleasant Green being a split-off close by.

But communion wasn't rebirth. "You have to decide what side you going to be on—the Lord's side or the Devil. If it's not the Lord's, you can't stay in this building. And you know in your hearts, you all possessed by demons."

Abruptly facing their state, the youth choir agreed they all were possessed by demons. They started a revival to pray for conversion. It was one to remember . . . seeking and praying; singing and shouting in the spirit. *Hand me down my silver trumpet, Gabriel.* Jubilees! Happy in the service! Halie in the forefront of the number. But was true conversion on the way? How would you know when it came? At home, Halie got a private chance to ask Cousin Baby Rosa Williams—a churchgoer all her life, but religion in the full sense of the day and of the church had just come; her baptism was this coming-up Communion Sunday. Halie turned on her the glistening, well-deep look the world would learn to know: "How does it feel, Cousin Baby? When a person gets converted?"

"I can't say, child; I can't tell you how it feels but I know it's a good feeling but it's a terrible feeling, when you get real happy . . . you don't know yourself, you don't know what you're doing."

Duke's holler from up front was a trumpet: "Don't you be back there trying to convert Halie! Wait 'til she finds it for herself. She ain't going to go in that water no dry devil, come out a wet one. When she come out, she going have something will carry her everywhere she go—she going carry something she can lay down on and see Jesus with!"

Cousin Baby nodded. "Some people don't have no real conversion; they just think they do, tell theyself they do." Duke loomed. "Halie's not going to *think* it, she's going *know* she has it!"

Halie prayed. ("That was the old way," says Celie. "Today so many just go up and give their hand and say they believe. But in our day, you had to *seek* to *find* the Lord.") Deep within herself, hour by hour, Halie reached with all the ardor of her being, all the compacted intensity used and unused in her seeming long years of being. . . . And Mahala had her first vision. She was traveling through a valley, a green pasture, and she came upon Aunt Bell. "I am seeking for the Lord, Aunt Bell." Bell smiled with all her sweetness. "You just keep searching," she said softly. "Just search among the flowers."

"If I find Him, how will I know Him from any other man?" Halie heard herself ask.

"You'll know Him, because He wears salvation on His brow and He carries a wounded hand."

When Duke found her, she was rapt. "The Lord touched me, Aunt Duke. I have been reborn."

"We'll see."

Halie raced to Bell. "I was not asleep; and I was not awake; I was—"

"—in the spirit."

"You are my gospel mother, Aunt Bell, and you showed me my hymn."

It was a long meter—an old Dr. Watts, one of the scores known to Halie and the choir . . .

> *Jesus, my God, I know His name,*
> *I wonder where is He—*
> *Go down and search among the flowers,*
> *Perhaps you'll find Him there. . . .*

Halie was ready for the water. So were 19 others who eagerly spread the word, each with a hymn given him in prayer just as the revival had adjured they must ask God for—a hymn their own for all time (music so central to true religion at Mt. Moriah). All candidates to speak on Friday, final night of revival.

Pinching Town fairly throbbed. Not Duke. Nor Earlene Garrison's mother. Nor two others who felt the children "didn't have nothing, better put it off and pray." (One boy on the very Friday *played baseball*—so Albert was not reborn; he could just pray some more.)

What had the Lord meant? Without Duke's yes, Halie couldn't go down. Yet her own still waters were full to the brim. She would testify.

Not only the 16's families and Halie's crammed the little wooden church that night. Halie's voice was known from Greenville to Carrollton . . . listened for: when the rest were still ranged below the pulpit, Halie had been called to the loft above—her voice, her power, her motion bursting irresistibly through the formality of the senior choir like fireworks. So all around Mt. Moriah's grounds and every space in the street was crammed this night of the 16—windows and doors opened for the air and the candidates' witness. "We all talked," says Annise, "but Mahala talked the longest, and the loudest. That voice *carry!* She told the story of how she prayed and got converted . . . told her vision, and the moment when the Lord spoke to her . . . how she *knew* she had religion; there was not a doubt. Then she came through with that long meter and she set that church on *fire.*"

And Aunt Bell. "My mother weighed 225 pounds and she was tall," says Celie. "That night it took I don't know *how* many to hold her. People couldn't find words to explain it. The spirit of God is too high to explain."

Still Duke withheld. All about, sewing machines were whirring; hearts were thumping over new white shoes and stockings; gangling arms and legs held patient for fittings; mothers' and sisters' fingers were pricked without complaint for the all-important baptismal clothes: all clothing must be new. Pinching Town ached for Halie—collectively, their child. "Don't stand in her way," pleaded the bravest stewards, and some of the deacons too. "She's old enough to *know.*"

Duke was not swayed. Finally a group of her fellow stewards paid a formal visitation, Annise's mother among them: *They* were convinced. They had *felt* her. If Mrs. Duke would consent to Mahalie's baptism, they would get her ready. Please, Mrs. Duke, it was *real.*

If they were that sure, sighed Duke, go ahead.

Too late to join the 16, but no matter. Voile or organdy, accepted fabrics for the baptismal dress, were priced about equal, 25¢ a yard. They decided on voile. That was needed too for the white dress-up cap, trimmed in white lace and circled with little voile roses. Cotton batiste, at 15¢ a yard, was needed for the slip, for the long white gown to actually go down in, for the "Baptist tie" (the long white strip to wrap around your head for the water) and for the white piece tied around your waist—the Biblical girdle. The family got her white shoes and stockings.

Halie had never been so splendid. Straight and tall, her brown skin shone with more than the morning's scrubbing as she circled for them to see, all new from tip to toe. Only she and Amelia, Uncle Bos's wife (he finally in from Legonier) were going down this morning. A Sunday never looked so new. And something else—Broadway Missionary was communicating; her daddy would see her.

The block and a half to Mt. Moriah seemed short as they all trooped for service, a guest preacher taking the pulpit so Pastor E. D. Lawrence wouldn't go into the cold water too hot, too wrought up and exhausted. For Halie, seven stewards on that bench—seven who'd got her ready.

Now the long file issues from the church, singing . . . stewards all in white, so white it glitters, deacons in black or as close to black as they can come; the baptizing deacons and Rev. Lawrence marked by close-fitting black cotton caps; and the candidates, the candidates glowing white . . .

> *Let us go down to Jordan,*
> *Let us go down to Jordan,*
> *Let us go down to Jordan,*
> *Religion is so sweet.*

Singing, marching, gleaming, strung out blocks long, rounding the levee to the foot of Magazine where the Mississippi was safe to enter. Down in the water the pastor and one deacon, black robes billowing, the two congregations and more crowding the levee as Halie hands her shoes to a steward. Another steward ties a white string to the tail of her long gown so it won't float up in the water . . . *Let us go down to Jordan.* . . . Blessed, the Mississippi *is* the Jordan now. The two waiting deacons take Halie's arms; they wade in the water. "I baptize you, Mahala Jackson, according to the faith, in the name of the Father and of the Son and of the Holy Ghost, amen!" Eyes shut, a quick plunge . . . time only for a blink . . . not muddy, but clear! clear! . . . red! Halie was clapping her hands as she came up out of the water, reborn, a new creature in Jesus Christ. "Oh, she was a happy soul!" exults Cousin Baby.

Hustled up to a waiting blanket, the hobbling string cut, the march back . . . into the real dress-up clothes to parade the neighborhood, receiving congratulations and sharing the glow. Home to a baptismal banquet from Duke which matched in every degree the one Aunt Alice had given Celie that spring. ("That Duke was a cake-baking thing," says Cousin Baby.) Then the afternoon of callers, congratulations, refreshments, and back to church to receive the right hand of fellowship.

Next day the world was the same but it was not. Not one to air her private feelings, she yet answered a questioning Celie. "I have a new look. I have a desire to serve the Lord in spirit and in truth—"

"You always had *that,*" injected Celie.

"He told me to open my mouth in His name."

That message itself had spread—clear over to Mt. Triumph Baptist uptown where Rev. Curtis pastored. "My daddy said they all felt she had the gift," says Celestine Curtis Graves; "and when they wanted somebody to keep the church where it should *be,* they sent for *her.* Yes, while she was just 14." She couldn't guess that Rev. Curtis would one day watch Halie in far-off wonder, nor that Celestine would see her change a life with a vow.

Ms. Goreau adds this tribute to Mahalia:

Mahalia Jackson's is one of the most unlikely crowning-success stories of any American. From obscure, sometimes bizarre beginnings, she would become one of the World's Most Admired People (Gallup Poll); intimate of Presidents, politicians, statesmen, janitors, religious leaders, housemaids, newsmen, educators, entertainment stars—sought out by the Empress of Japan, the Prime Minister of India, royalty of Britain, Belgium, Monaco, each finding a strange magnetism in this black woman who never forgot her origins, never compromised with the faith of which, exclusively, she sang.

"Statue of The Virgin Mary outside of the rectory of The Immaculate Heart of Mary Church," Atlanta, Georgia. Editor's photograph.

GROWING UP AS A POLISH AMERICAN

(My tribute to the Polish Star on its 75th Anniversary)

Sister M. Florence Tumasz

To the Poles, faith and fatherland, religion and ethnicity have almost always been identical: like two strong threads they were so intertwined they could hardly be separated. This was, of course, true of Poland. It was also true, in a great measure, of the United States where the Polish immigrants transferred so many of their traditions.

In this respect, as in so many others, my dear Mom was a typical Pole. Her faith, for instance, was never anything to be put on, like a special dress worn only on Sundays or holidays. It was part of her everyday life. To be Polish and not to be Roman Catholic seemed inconceivable to her. There was a time when everything, well, almost everything, non-Polish was Protestant!

On this score, one of my sisters can relate a sad experience. As a senior at West Catholic High School here in Philadelphia, she received as an award for some achievement, an English Missal from her favorite nun and showed it to her mother with deep pride and joy. When the next Sunday came, however, she found the Missal gone. A frantic search for it proved to no avail. After a few days, Mom owned up to the "crime" she had burned it! "Well," she said, "it was Protestant! It just had to be! It wasn't Polish!" Of course, that was a good number of years ago and before she died in 1967, we succeeded in educating her along more ecumenical lines.

Sister M. Florence Tumasz, CSFN, "Growing Up as a Polish American" from *Gwiazda (Polish Star)*, Philadelphia, Pa., August 12, 1976. Reprinted by permission of the author. (I am grateful to Katharine D. Newman, Editor of the Newsletter/Journal of The Society for the Study of the Multi-ethnic Literature of the United States (MELUS) for advising me of this work.)

Almost innate in Mom and in the Poles was a great respect for the clergy. The very word for priest in Polish is "ksiadz," coined from the word "ksiaze," meaning "prince." Priests were truly princes among the people.

Even today in Communist Poland, one can overhear, "Go to the priest for advice! He, at least, will tell you the truth!"

Still on another occasion when, after Mom had seen something of the TV presentation of Graham Green's *Labyrinthine Ways* which one of her daughters was watching—it is the story, you will remember of a wayward priest—Mom expressed her indigation aloud: "That's terrible! How could they show such a story on TV? I only hope very few people are watching it!" When this was reported to me, I recalled how we as children were sent upstairs to bed very early one night because a neighbor's gossip about the doings of a certain parish priest made Mom's charitable Polish heart uncomfortable, especially in the presence of her children.

Among my childhood memories of "Growing Up in America," (in Philadelphia, the Bicentennial City, to be exact), was our family's attending July 4th ceremonies at Independence Hall; visiting the great Philadelphia Zoo and Fairmount Park; taking my first ride on the then new Frankford Elevated; and looking on with wonder at the Benjamin Franklin Bridge (it was called the Delaware River Bridge then) shortly after it was opened for traffic. I still recall how thrilled I was to learn that it was a Polish-American, Ralph Modjeski, who had designed it. I was already an adult—actually it was only last year—that I learned that he designed the Tacony-Palmyra Bridge also.

But even more vividly, I remember going as a family group for different services to our parish Church (St. Adalbert's on Allegheny Avenue in Port Richmond). In addition to Sunday Mass, we would go in the afternoon to sing Vespers, in Polish, of course. When Lent came, we would go not only Friday nights for the Way of the Cross but also Wednesday nights to sing *Gorskie Zale,* the traditional "Complaints or Lamentations of the Passion." If sometimes we would not make it, Mom would make sure that we children gathered about her, Polish hymn books in hand, to sing along with her while she sewed or ironed. She did not need to look at the words: she knew them from memory!

Palm Sunday meant getting the blessed palms from church. Generally, Dad would bring them home after High Mass. Mother took in an earlier Mass to give her time to prepare Sunday dinner while we children went to the Children's Mass under the supervision of our religious teachers. Returning with those palms, Dad would strike us gently reciting an old Polish verse which ended with, "And in seven nights Easter will be here."

The week before Easter there was the long Holy Week Services at our church and the visiting of other neighboring churches. At home there was much preparation; baking and cooking and the coloring of *pisanki,* the specially colored eggs. When Easter itself arrived, in more American than Polish fashion, there would be egg-hunting throughout the house and the game of the breaking of the egg in which Dad loved to join us. The accompanying cries of "Upper! Upper!" and the shouts of the children filled the rooms.

All food eaten at Easter was blessed by a priest who came especially to the home, blessing the food elaborately set out on the table. Later, to make it easier on the priests, the families would bring baskets of food to the parish hall to be blessed. But before we sat down to eat our solemn meal with the family or when relatives or other guests dropped by to pay us a visit during Eastertide, we shared with them the blessed egg, the "swieconka," to show the love and the solidarity with the one with whom we shared the food.

With May there came May devotions, the rosary said in common, and the singing of the *Godzinki,* the "Little Hours" honoring Our Lady. Dad knew them by heart and we would all join in. We would kneel, I recall, in front of a large picture of Our Lady of Ostrobrama, my father's favorite, which he brought over on the ship carrying him across the Atlantic.

June ushered in Sacred Heart devotions and participation in the beautiful Corpus Christi procession. This was the all-parish outdoors manifestation of faith with adults carrying candles and banners. The children crying "Swiety, Swiety, Pan Bog zastepow" ("Holy, Holy, Lord God of hosts") strewed flowers on the street before the Blessed Sacrament carried solemnly in a monstrance by the pastor.

June also brought June weddings, three-day-long affairs, mind you! In fact *Life* magazine some years before it went out of circulation had a very lengthy feature on a Polish wedding in Detroit, I believe. And, of course, there were the June feastday celebrations of St. Anthony and St. John. Namesday, not birthdays were, and in some cases, still are, celebrated among Polish-Americans. With fall came the Harvest Festival, the "Dozynki" and with it singing and dancing and parading by all, the first couple carrying garlands and sheaves of wheat.

Noteworthy is the fact that a "Dozynki Festival" is one of the cultural events planned by the Poles of Philadelphia for the week of the International Eucharistic Congress. Traces of this can still be found also in Philadelphia in a *Biesiada,* a harvest dinner, typical of those given in manors in medieval Poland. The Polish Heritage Society, a society of professional Polish-Americans established for preserving Polish cultural traditions, gives such a dinner here annually.

Christmas was a whole world of beautiful diversified traditions. These Christmas traditions far surpassed all the others and have etched themselves incredibly on my heart and mind.

The most beautiful part of the Polish Christmas was the *Wigilia,* the Christmas Eve supper, with its breaking of the *oplatek, the* Christmas wafer. Let me imaginatively at this point be an artist and paint for you some Christmas scenes as I remember them in my family circle.

The first picture shows a little girl, about ten years old called "Genny" and her smaller brother "Henry" pulling a wagon down the street towards a stable, yes, a Philadelphia stable with real horses in it, to get some real straw and hay. This was destined to go under the tablecloth for the Christmas Eve supper as a reminder to everyone that it was in a stable that the Christ Child was born.

Another picture shows two little girls, one dark-haired and solemn called "Helen," the other, a smiling blonde little girl, "Wanda," all bundled up against the December cold, standing outside the door and looking up into the darkening sky for the first sign of "the first star I see tonight." And when they saw it, the same Christmas star which once looked down upon Bethlehem, they read its twinkling message: "Hurry, children! Tell your Mom it's time to start the Christmas *Wigilia!*" and then ran into the house shouting "We saw the star, Mom! We can start right now!"

Still another picture shows the whole family already at the table—and I mean the whole family, not only Mom and Dad and the four children but all of our cousins, all our uncles, all our aunts, and sometimes, I think, all our neighbors too. A good number of those who lived in the same "wioski" (villages) back in Poland from which Dad and Mom came turned up during the holidays. The house must have had rubber walls which just stretched and stretched. Certainly the dining room table often had to be extended with extra leaves.

The picture of a Christmas tree comes next! It was always beautiful and big, its highest branch tipped with a star reaching up to the ceiling. I do remember, however, going out late at night one Christmas Eve with Dad and small Henry tagging along to buy a little straggling one which, because others did not want it, Dad obtained for a cheaper price. We had no electric lights on our tree in those days but the pink, green, and yellow candles when lit up were beautiful. Of course, Mom and Dad had some anxious moments watching carefully lest fire break out. The Christmas Manger which we never tired of looking at was placed under the tree!

The Christmas food! I'm still painting pictures but I know that I cannot describe the appearance of that banquet-like table with its fruits, its nuts, its special breads, *rogale,* I think Mom called them, with raisin—dotted *babka* and sugar-coated *chrusciki.* Then there was a variety of fishes, a large one baked whole, and small minnows, and *sledzie* (herrings) pickled as only Mom knew how; and *pierogi* (dumplings) filled with sour-kraut, with prunes, or with cottage cheese; macaroni with *mak* (poppy seeds) and a special kind of soup with mushrooms, or was it *zupa nic* (the nothing soup) with bits of almonds floating in it? There was meat, too, *szynka* and *kielbasa swojej roboty* (home made), but these could only be eaten after midnight because of the Church regulations on fast and abstinence. Stryja Maciej, our Dad's oldest brother, would always make a big show of waiting. When the clock struck twelve he would enjoy his *szynka,* an unforgettable picture, that! I remember one particular Christmas a small roasted pig was made to stand proudly in the center of the table with a shiny red apple in its mouth.

And then there were carols. We must have been the ''singingest'' family in the world and the Trapp Family singers had nothing on us. We would sing if we knew the words and sing if we did not know them, for somehow we always managed to come in on the choruses. Our favorite was *Dzisiaj w Betleem* and we would tease Stryja Joe, Dad's younger brother, with the verse ''I Jozef stary'' (''and Joseph the old man''). Our *Gloria in Excelsis* rang out through the house and out of the house far into the street. We sang *Adeste Fideles* and *Jingle Bells* too and always *Silent Night,* which we alternated with its Polish version of *Cicha Noc.*

But nothing of this could take place, no gift unwrapped, no morsel of food eaten, no carol sung before the *lamanie sie opatkiem* (the breaking of the Christmas wafer), as the head of the house took the ''oplatek'' in his hand and stood by his chair. It was almost a religious ceremony and Dad in his best Sunday clothes and all the dignity he could muster was its high priest. When everyone else rose, he said a prayer and broke off a bit of the wafer sharing it first with our Mom and then with everyone present from the oldest to the youngest child. Those were solemn moments as we came up to him one by one. Sometimes words of apology and of forgiveness would be murmured and usually tears of joy or gratitude would be seen stealing down some cheeks. But always wishes would be expressed.

This beautiful Christmas tradition of the ''breaking of the 'oplatek' '' is very dear to the hearts of the Poles no matter how far from Poland fate may have led them. There is a legend which Ignacy Kraszewski, the nineteenth century Polish novelist, gives us in his work *The Exiles.* In it he tells us how during the American Revolution, on Christmas Eve of 1777, Casimir Pulaski played host to another great Polish patriot, Thaddeus Kosciuszko. Pulaski's aide, Maciej by name, made preparations for the ''Wigilia'' but he could not procure the ''oplatek.'' Upon learning that a French priest was living nearby, he went to him, explained his plight, and obtained a wafer from him. When the call for supper came, you can imagine the look of surprise on the face of the two great Polish generals and the gratitude and joy that was in their hearts.

The tradition is symbolic, too, since the wafer is really bread made of unleavened flour which, in turn, is made of many grains of wheat. Thus, bread stands for unity, for togetherness, for harmony, and for love. To break bread with someone always meant sharing all you had with someone; the very word "companion" has that meaning: "one who shares bread." To break bread then is to show hospitality, generosity of heart, universal brotherhood, and love.

And so when we kept that beautiful tradition of breaking our "oplatek" with each other those Christmas Eves of long ago, perhaps we did not say all that was in our hearts but it was all implied like a good piece of music with a simple obligato underlaying its changing melody.

Long ago I expressed the meaning of the "oplatek" in verse form. In conclusion, I repeat the lines here as a prayerful wish, a "consummation devoutly to be wished," a God-blessed hope, not for Polish-Americans only, nor for Italian-Americans, nor for other ethnic groups, but for all America:

> Breaking this wafer
> On Christmas Day,
> Into brief words we put
> What hearts would say:
> "Peace be on earth
> As it is in heaven!
> Peace be and love
> Life's potent leaven.
> Love be and peace to stay!

SEDER

Lyn Lifshin

my grandfather like
a shrivelled monkey
a prune at the end
of the table as far
away from his wife
as she could arrange
My sister and i are
watching the uncles
thru sweet red wine
They curve and get
smaller the tumors
unwinding like some
bulb that will push

up thru the snow the
fire getting ready
slowly on Main St
as still as the "h"
should be in herbs
my uncle is sharp
to remind me my
face burns as red
as the wine i am
crying under the
table where no one
can see the night
breaking like matzoh

Reprinted by permission of the author. (See Ms. Lifshin's other poems, "Beryl" and "Never the City's Name" in Unit Two, TANGLED VINES, THORNS, AND FLOWERS, and Unit Ten, THE IMMIGRANT EXPERIENCE.)

from
LETTER TO THE FRONT

Muriel Rukeyser

To be a Jew in the twentieth century
Is to be offered a gift. If you refuse,
Wishing to be invisible, you choose
Death of the spirit, the stone insanity.
5   Accepting, take full life. Full agonies:
Your evening deep in labyrinthine blood
Of those who resist, fail, and resist; and God
Reduced to a hostage among hostages.

The gift is torment. Not alone the still
10   Torture, isolation; or torture of the flesh.
That may come also. But the accepting wish,
The whole and fertile spirit as guarantee
For every human freedom, suffering to be free,
Daring to live for the impossible.

REACHING OUT: MEMORIES, DREAMS, HOPES

"Pensive girl." By permission of M. C. Clayton, the artist.

"Fool, to flap your wings and fuss like an idiot/Searching for a leafy branch that exists no more/Did you suppose you'd find a home exactly as you found it a year gone by/Because you're a bluebird and skilled to fly?

"Fool, to wander in a warmer clime without a care/Thinking that the tree you loved would stand forever/While you explored some sea-kissed beach that flashed in the heat of sun/Freely soaring as you pleased with the soft, the fair, the gentle breeze.

"Sad bird, because your tree you loved so well stands no longer brave and tall/Be glad you were away when the proud one fell and moaned to be brought down.

"Sad bird, go your way in peace and hush your song of woe and hurt surprise/Sing again of merry cheer, forget your stalwart home and find another, aged and true/No longer be aghast. Fool, friend, sad bird. Nothing on earth lasts."

Author and origins unknown

THINGS IN COMMON

May Swenson

We have a good relationship, the elevator boy and I.
I can always be cheerful with him.
We make jokes. We both belong to the TGIF Club.
No matter how artificial and stiff I've had to be in the office,
5   seems like I can be natural with *him*.
We have basic things in common—
the weather, baseball, hangovers,
the superiority of Friday over Monday.

It's true I make it a point to be pleasant to him. Why?
10   Honest, its because I really like him.
Individually, I mean.
There's something about him—relaxed and balanced
like a dancer or a cat—
as if he knows who he is and where he's at.
15   At least he knows how to act like that.
Wish I could say the same for myself.

I like his looks, his manner, his red shirt,
the smooth panther shape to his head and neck.

I like it that he knows I don't mean to flirt—
20   even though I really like him.
I feel he knows I know the score.
It's all in the gleam of his eyes,
the white of his teeth, when he slides back the door
and says, "TGIF, Ma'am, have a nice weekend."

25   He's strong muscled, good looking—could be 35—
though with his cap off he's 50, I suppose.
So am I. Hope he thinks I look younger too.
I want him to like it that my eyes are blue—
I want him to really like me.
30   We look straight at each other when we say goodnight.
Is he thinking it's only an accident I'm white?
"TGIF," we say. "Have a nice weekend."

That's the way it's been so far.
We have a good relationship, just the two of us
35   and the little stool on which he never sits, in the car.
Fridays I work late. I'm the last one down.
Been, let's see, 11 years now . . .
These days I hug the newspaper to me so the headlines won't show.
Why he never has a paper I don't know.
40   Probably not supposed to read in the elevator.

Lately I've asked myself why don't I say:
"What do you think of the mess down South, Willie?
Or for that matter, right here in D.C.?"
Wish I dared ask him. Or that he'd find a way to put it to me.
45   I'd like to say bluntly, "Willie, will there be war?"
Neither of us has been able to say it so far.
Will I dare, someday? I doubt it . . . Not *me*, to *him*. . . .
"Thank God It's Friday," we say. "Have a nice weekend."

```
                M
                A
                Y

                S
                W
                E        *ICONOGRAPHS
                N                 O
                S                 E
                O                 M
        I  C  O  N  O  G  R  A  P  H  S
```

BLACKTUESDAYBLACKTUESDAYBLACKTUESDAYBLACKTUESDAYBLACKTUESDAYBLACKTUESDAY

Blесséd is the man of color
for his blood is rich with
the nuclear sap of the sun.
Blесséd is his spirit which
a savage history has
refined to intercept
whitest lightnings of
vision. Blесséd the neck
of the black man made
muscular by the weight of
the yoke made proud
bursting the lynch rope.
Blесséd his body meek on
the slave block thunderous
on the porch of revolt.
Blесséd his head hewn with
animal beauty for he has
grappled as the lion bled
as the lamb and extracted
the excellence of each for
his character. Blесséd the
black and the white of his
eye.

For Martin Luther King
April 4, 1968

*See Ms. Swenson's note about iconographs on the next page.

A NOTE ABOUT *ICONOGRAPHS*

May Swenson

To have material and mold evolve together and become a symbiotic whole. To cause an instant object-to-eye encounter with each poem even before it is read word-after-word. To have simultaneity as well as sequence. To make an existence in space, as well as in time, for the poem. These have been, I suppose, the impulses behind the typed shapes and frames invented for this collection.

I call the poems *Iconographs* with such dictionary derivations in mind as these:

icon	"a symbol hardly distinguished from the object symbolized"
icono-	from the Greek *eikonos* meaning "image" or "likeness"
graph	"diagram" or "system of connections or interrelations"
-graph	from the Greek *graphe* meaning "carve" . . . "indicating the instrument as well as the written product of the instrument"

Also, this comment on "The Art of the Middle Ages" (Columbia Encyclopedia, 3rd Edition) helped me choose the title:

". . . (It) was governed by a kind of sacred mathematics, in which position, grouping, symmetry, and number were of extraordinary importance and were themselves an integral part of the inconography. From earliest times it has likewise been a symbolic code, showing men one thing and inviting them to see in it the figure of another . . ."

I suppose that these were my aims. But I come to definition and direction only *afterwards*. It has always been my tendency to let each poem "make itself"—to develop, in process of becoming, its own individual physique. Maybe this is why, once the texts were fixed, I have wanted to give for each an individual arrangement in the space of the page.

I have not meant the poems to depend upon, or depend from, their shapes or their frames; these were thought of only after the whole language structure and behavior was complete in each instance. What the poems say or show, their way of doing it with *language,* is the main thing.

Poetry is made with words of a language. And we say, "But, of course." It is just this "matter of course" that poetry holds to the nostrils, sticks into the ears, puts on the tongue, flashes into the eyes of anyone who comes to meet it. It is done with words; with their combination—sometimes with their unstringing. If so, it is in order to make the mind remember (by dismemberment) the elements, the smallest particles, ventricles, radicals, down to, or into, the Grain—the buried grain of language on which depends the transfer and expansion of consciousness—of Sense. And no grain, of sense, without sensation. To *sense* then becomes to *make sense.*

With the physical senses we meet the world and each other—a world of objects, human and otherwise, where words on a page are objects, too. The first instrument to make contact, it seems to me, and the quickest to report it, is the eye. The poems in *Iconographs,* with their profiles, or space patterns, or other graphic emphases, signal that they are to be seen, as well as read and heard, I suppose.

DOWNTOWN SAN ANTONIO IN FRONT OF THE MAJESTIC THEATRE

Evangelina Vigil

I saw a young, sprightly Black girl
Drop a coin
Into one wrinkled blue veined palm
Held by another palid withered palm
Of an old white blind man

A TRACE OF GOLD

Phyllis J. Scherle

INTRODUCTION

A woman reflecting on childhood visits to the home of her German-American grandparents may have no recollection of the harsh realities of that time, i.e., the incessant struggle for the necessities of life, the near-slavery of the wife, the unquestioned dominance of the husband; for memory, like the refining of gold, may burn away the dross, leaving only the pure metal, ready to be fashioned into an object of beauty to be treasured forever. Such a reminiscence may even serve as a touchstone for the contemplation of the very nature of life itself.

• • •

Time has a way of erasing all physical signs of men or places. Fields once breathing life-sustaining wheat or corn become barren, arid stretches of land dusted with fierce wind; deep forests of oak, hickory, and popular evolve into mazes of jerry-built houses jabbed into patches of blotchy lawn; even sumac-covered hills fall away at the whim of the highway builder's pen. Immortality . . . infinity . . . are they qualities of the "inward eye"[1] only?

It is certain that I can no longer view that weather-beaten three-room house hidden in the hills of Southern Illinois, even though its imprint shows in my life and those of my children: coal stripping has left only rutted, rocky scars, sparsely concealed with scrub trees, blackberry briars, and foxgrass. The people, too, are gone, "tot,"[2] lying within the limestone-walled yard beside the unpretentious Lutheran church. But, in my fancy, as swift as the flutter of the hummingbird's wing, I can travel the wood-bordered, dirt road to a rough, grey gate. I lift the latch, rush down the sandy, red hill, past the shallow, trickling brook guarded by a twisted willow, through the "Weide"[3] straight to the picket fence that shuts out only the open fields and the gentle cows. Past the four-o'clocks and hollyhocks and the flowerpots' moss, tumbled red, yellow, and orange by the touch of the noon sun straight to Grossmutter Reisinger, to feel her soft warm arms reach me and hear, "Ich liebe dich, Kleine."[4]

Tall and large, over two hundred pounds, she daily forced her feet into shoes a size too small (genteel ladies had small feet). Her dress of bright, dainty, red-flowered, navy calico wore a stiffly starched, white floursack apron; her heavy, grey-black hair was primly parted in the center and softly pulled into a bun at the neck. She seemed interminably in the kitchen, stirring, mixing, peeling, baking, washing. It was she who stirred into flame the pine kindling slumbering in the huge black range, sending flickering light throughout the room, rousing the fire to a ready fury to bake the "Brot."[5] It was she who lifted the cloth cover from boxes near the fire, awakening the goslings placed near it for warmth from the chilly night: creatures of soft, yellow fluff, all action and sound, seemingly, in their awkward clamor for food and life. She fried the potato pancakes, mixed the dumplings, and canned the watermelon preserves. She seemed invulnerable, "unsterblich,"[6] a spirit of the dim, kerosene-lighted kitchen, full of warmth and the singing teakettle, aroma of mingled "Sauerbraten," "Kohl,"[7] and "Kuchen."[8] Making patchwork quilts by the evening firelight: Jerusalem Star, Nine Patch, Flower Garden; picking the down from ducks and geese for pillows; stuffing the pillow-ticking mattresses with freshly-mown hay. In her tow I gathered the eggs from nest boxes and secret caches in the hayloft. Sometimes, I suffered from a stern rebuke for my carelessness in breaking an egg or spilling cream that I'd skimmed from the blue crock of cooled, jersey milk: "Kindlein, sei vorsichtig!."[9]

But she was not all work, sensibility, and practicality. She had a hunger, an innate yearning for beauty that nothing could check: She knew where the wood ran amuck with wild violets of blue, lavender, and white; she sought the sweet williams, Dutchmen's breeches, and jack-in-the-pulpit. Together, we rousted the fallen leaves from the ground to gather gunny sacks full of hickory nuts, stripped the hazelnuts from their clustered security, and gathered autumn bouquets of bittersweet, red sumac, and spikey brown cattail. We found pawpaws and wild grapes. At times, we plunged deep into the woods and spent hours quietly waiting, just on the chance that we might hear the song of the Wood Thrush. Each night the whippoorwill called through the soft dark.

And there was an acute awareness of death: A bird lying silenced on the ground, a flower broken by a storm, a snake humped by the frog swallowed whole. An omnipresent disturbing presence yes, but no cause for lasting dismay: "Das Böse und das Gute bestehen zusammen. Kind, das musst du Wissen!"[10]

On a still, snowy night, with only the hoot owl to keep the time outside, we'd boil the sorghum for taffy, pouring the brown mixture into narrow strips on a dishpan full of snow, taking the maleable ribbons in our hands, pulling them until they were light and chewy. We'd take the ears of yellow popcorn, shell-out the kernels, blow the chaff away, placing the bounty into the screenwire popper over the open flames from the kitchen grate, watching it fill white. Sometimes we'd grab our coats, rush to the earth-mounded pit in the garden to reach for crisp, red apples from the strawed depths, their skin splitting with the first bit of the frigid, juicy spheres.

As darkness closed in, the front room stirred with the sounds of the fiddle or the mandolin. There was a strumming, a listening, a refining, a plucking; finally the pitch rang clear. Sitting together around the woodstove, we lost ourselves in the spell cast by the mastered movements of Grossvater's rough, coal-blackened hands as he coaxed the box to sing his heart's dreams of fields and rivers of childhood, vicarious runes of the heart. His thick, dark hair falling, his foot rhythmically tapping. Soul and music poured into the room, melting into an aura of visionary lamplight, driving all else far away, alien, forgotten and unwanted. Senses lulled, tantalized, intoxicated by the extrapolations—motifs repeated, of life—and death—pulsating within, transposed into scenes "Of what is past, or passing, or to come."[11] Even Time lost his power—until Grossvater would conclude, "That's all. Lights out. Morning will come too soon."

Does Time function as a microscope, magnifying those moments that we catalogue and hoard within the brief span that encompasses our lives? Does Time gild each of these treasured moments with nostalgia as we call them to remembrance, or were those moments truly idyllic? Those hours I spent, naive, innocent, confident that life was an endless, limitless possibility, unaware of death in any form except its most trivial and common—that of nature, not of man nor his vision, nor of his hope—those hours slipped from my reach without even a sigh. The wind, the fog, the snow, Nature's unchanging gait, leveled the grey-boarded house even before the gargantuan bites of the coal shovels gouged out the farm's green life and drove away the deep-wood birds, leaving only a rough wilderness of rock, scrub, and waste coal. A few miles away, dark ivy climbs the stones marking the graves of those who lived there: scenes and beings alike have merged into the mocking mileau of what has passed, to live only in the minds of those who remain.

NOTES

1. William Wordsworth, "I Wandered Lonely As A Cloud."
2. dead.
3. meadow.
4. I love you, little one.
5. bread.
6. immortal.
7. cabbage.
8. and cake.
9. "Take care, granddaughter."
10. The good and the bad always exist together, child. That you must know!
11. William Butler Yeats, "Sailing to Byzantium."

EVERYDAY USE

for your grandmama

Alice Walker

I will wait for her in the yard that Maggie and I made so clean and wavy yesterday afternoon. A yard like this is more comfortable than most people know. It is not just a yard. It is like an extended living room. When the hard clay is swept clean as a floor and the fine sand around the edges lined with tiny, irregular grooves, anyone can come and sit and look up into the elm tree and wait for the breezes that never come inside the house.

Maggie will be nervous until after her sister goes: she will stand hopelessly in corners, homely and ashamed of the burn scars down her arms and legs, eying her sister with a mixture of envy and awe. She thinks her sister has held life always in the palm of one hand, that "no" is a word the world never learned to say to her.

You've no doubt seen those TV shows where the child who has "made it" is confronted, as a surprise, by her own mother and father, tottering in weakly from backstage. (A pleasant surprise, of course: What would they do if parent and child came on the show only to curse out and insult each other?) On TV mother and child embrace and smile into each other's faces. Sometimes the mother and father weep, the child wraps them in her arms and leans across the table to tell how she would not have made it without their help. I have seen these programs.

Sometimes I dream a dream in which Dee and I are suddenly brought together on a TV program of this sort. Out of a dark and soft-seated limousine I am ushered into a bright room filled with many people. There I meet a smiling, gray, sporty man like Johnny Carson who shakes my hand and tells me what a fine girl I have. Then we are on the stage and Dee is embracing me with tears in her eyes. She pins on my dress a large orchid, even though she has told me once that she thinks orchids are tacky flowers.

In real life I am a large, big-boned woman with rough, man-working hands. In the winter I wear flannel nightgowns to bed and overalls during the day. I can kill and clean a hog as mercilessly as a man. My fat keeps me hot in zero weather. I can work outside all day, breaking ice to get water for washing; I can eat pork liver cooked over the open fire minutes after it comes steaming from the hog. One winter I knocked a bull calf straight in the brain between the eyes with a sledge hammer and had the meat hung up to chill before nightfall. But of course all this does not show on television. I am the way my daughter would want me to be: a hundred pounds lighter, my skin like an uncooked barley pancake. My hair glistens in the hot bright lights. Johnny Carson has much to do to keep up with my quick and witty tongue.

But that is a mistake. I know even before I wake up. Who ever knew a Johnson with a quick tongue? Who can even imagine me looking a strange white man in the eye? It seems to me I have talked to them always with one foot raised in flight, with my head turned in whichever way is farthest from them. Dee, though. She would always look anyone in the eye. Hesitation was no part of her nature.

"How do I look, Mama?" Maggie says, showing just enough of her thin body enveloped in pink skirt and red blouse for me to know she's there, almost hidden by the door.

"Come out into the yard," I say.

Have you ever seen a lame animal, perhaps a dog run over by some careless person rich enough to own a car, sidle up to someone who is ignorant enough to be kind to him? That is the way my Maggie walks. She has been like this, chin on chest, eyes on ground, feet in shuffle, ever since the fire that burned the other house to the ground.

Dee is lighter than Maggie, with nicer hair and a fuller figure. She's a woman now, though sometimes I forget. How long ago was it that the other house burned? Ten, twelve years? Sometimes I can still hear the flames and feel Maggie's arms sticking to me, her hair smoking and her dress falling off her in little black papery flakes. Her eyes seemed stretched open, blazed open by the flames reflected in them. And Dee. I see her standing off under the sweet gum tree she used to dig gum out of; a look of concentration on her face as she watched the last dingy gray board of the house fall in toward the red-hot brick chimney. Why don't you do a dance around the ashes? I'd wanted to ask her. She had hated the house that much.

I used to think she hated Maggie, too. But that was before we raised the money, the church and me, to send her to Augusta to school. She used to read to us without pity; forcing words, lies, other folks' habits, whole lives upon us two, sitting trapped and ignorant underneath her voice. She washed us in a river of make-believe, burned us with a lot of knowledge we didn't necessarily need to know. Pressed us to her with the serious way she read, to shove us away at just the moment, like dimwits, we seemed about to understand.

Dee wanted nice things. A yellow organdy dress to wear to her graduation from high school; black pumps to match a green suit she'd made from an old suit somebody gave me. She was determined to stare down any disaster in her efforts. Her eyelids would not flicker for minutes at a time. Often I fought off the temptation to shake her. At sixteen she had a style of her own: and knew what style was.

I never had an education myself. After second grade the school was closed down. Don't ask me why: in 1927 colored asked fewer questions than they do now. Sometimes Maggie reads to me. She stumbles along good-naturedly but can't see well. She knows she is not bright. Like good looks and money, quickness passed her by. She will marry John Thomas (who has mossy teeth in an earnest face) and then I'll be free to sit here and I guess just sing church songs to myself. Although I never was a good singer. Never could carry a tune. I was always better at a man's job. I used to love to milk till I was hooked in the side in '49. Cows are soothing and slow and don't bother you, unless you try to milk them the wrong way.

I have deliberately turned my back on the house. It is three rooms, just like the one that burned, except the roof is tin; they don't make shingle roofs any more. There are no real windows, just some holes cut in the sides, like the portholes in a ship, but not round and not square, with rawhide holding the shutters up on the outside. This house is in a pasture, too, like the other one. No doubt when Dee sees it she will want to tear it down. She wrote me once that no matter where we "choose" to live, she will manage to come see us. But she will never bring her friends. Maggie and I thought about this and Maggie asked me, "Mama, when did Dee ever *have* any friends?"

She had a few. Furtive boys in pink shirts hanging about on washday after school. Nervous girls who never laughed. Impressed with her they worshiped the well-turned phrase, the cute shape, the scalding humor that erupted like bubbles in lye. She read to them.

When she was courting Jimmy T she didn't have much time to pay to us, but turned all her faultfinding power on him. He *flew* to marry a cheap city girl from a family of ignorant flashy people. She hardly had time to recompose herself.

When she comes I will meet—but there they are!

Maggie attempts to make a dash for the house, in her shuffling way, but I stay her with my hand. "Come back here," I say. And she stops and tries to dig a well in the sand with her toe.

It is hard to see them clearly through the strong sun. But even the first glimpse of leg out of the car tells me it is Dee. Her feet were always neat-looking, as if God himself had shaped them with a certain style. From the other side of the car comes a short, stocky man. Hair is all over his head a foot long and hanging from his chin like a kinky mule tail. I hear Maggie suck in her breath. "Uhnnnh," is what it sounds like. Like when you see the wriggling end of a snake just in front of your foot on the road. "Uhnnnh."

Dee next. A dress down to the ground, in this hot weather. A dress so loud it hurts my eyes. There are yellows and oranges enough to throw back the light of the sun. I feel my whole face warming from the heat waves it throws out. Earrings gold, too, and hanging down to her shoulders. Bracelets dangling and making noises when she moves her arm up to shake the folds of the dress out of her armpits. The dress is loose and flows, and as she walks closer, I like it. I hear Maggie go "Uhnnnh" again. It is her sister's hair. It stands straight up like the wool on a sheep. It is black as night and around the edges are two long pigtails that rope about like small lizards disappearing behind her ears.

"Wa-su-zo-Tean-o!" she says, coming on in that gliding way the dress makes her move. The short stocky fellow with the hair to his navel is all grinning and he follows up with "Asalamalakim, my mother and sister!" He moves to hug Maggie but she falls back, right up against the back of my chair. I feel her trembling there and when I look up I see the perspiration falling off her chin.

"Don't get up," says Dee. Since I am stout it takes something of a push. You can see me trying to move a second or two before I make it. She turns, showing white heels through her sandals, and goes back to the car. Out she peeks next with a Polaroid. She stoops down quickly and lines up picture after picture of me sitting there in front of the house with Maggie cowering behind me. She never takes a shot without making sure the house is included. When a cow comes nibbling around the edge of the yard she snaps it and me and Maggie *and* the house. Then she puts the Polaroid in the back seat of the car, and comes up and kisses me on the forehead.

Meanwhile Asalmalakim is going through motions with Maggie's hand. Maggie's hand is as limp as a fish, and probably as cold, despite the sweat, and she keeps trying to pull it back. It looks like Asalamalakim wants to shake hands but wants to do it fancy. Or maybe he don't know how people shake hands. Anyhow, he soon gives up on Maggie.

"Well," I say. "Dee."

"No, Mama," she says. "Not 'Dee,' Wangero Leewanika Kemanjo!"

"What happened to 'Dee'?" I wanted to know.

"She's dead," Wangero said. "I couldn't bear it any longer, being named after the people who oppress me."

"You know as well as me you was named after your aunt Dicie," I said. Dicie is my sister. She named Dee. We called her "Big Dee" after Dee was born.

"But who was *she* named after?" asked Wangero.

"I guess after Grandma Dee," I said.

"And who was she named after?" asked Wangero.

"Her mother," I said, and saw Wangero was getting tired. "That's about as far back as I can trace it," I said. Though, in fact, I probably could have carried it back beyond the Civil War through the branches.

"Well," said Asalamalakim, "there you are."

"Uhnnnh," I heard Maggie say.

"There I was not," I said, "before 'Dicie' cropped up in our family, so why should I try to trace it that far back?"

He just stood there grinning, looking down on me like somebody inspecting a Model A car. Every once in a while he and Wangero sent eye signals over my head.

"How do you pronounce this name?" I asked.

"You don't have to call me by it if you don't want to," said Wangero.

"Why shouldn't I?" I asked. "If that's what you want us to call you, we'll call you."

"I know it might sound awkward at first," said Wangero.

"I'll get used to it," I said. "Ream it out again."

Well, soon we got the name out of the way. Asalamalakim had a name twice as long and three times as hard. After I tripped over it two or three times he told me to just call him Hakim-a-barber. I wanted to ask him was he a barber, but I didn't really think he was, so I didn't ask.

"You must belong to those beef-cattle peoples down the road," I said. They said "Asalamalakim" when they met you, too, but they didn't shake hands. Always too busy: feeding the cattle, fixing the fences, putting up salt-lick shelters, throwing down hay. When the white folks poisoned some of the herd the men stayed up all night with rifles in their hands. I walked a mile and a half just to see the sight.

Hakim-a-barber said, "I accept some of their doctrines, but farming and raising cattle is not my style." (They didn't tell me, and I didn't ask, whether Wangero (Dee) had really gone and married him.)

We sat down to eat and right away he said he didn't eat collards and pork was unclean. Wangero, though, went on through the chitlins and corn bread, the greens and everything else. She talked a blue streak over the sweet potatoes. Everything delighted her. Even the fact that we still used the benches her daddy made for the table when we couldn't afford to buy chairs.

"Oh, Mama!" she cried. Then turned to Hakim-a-barber. "I never knew how lovely these benches are. You can feel the rump prints," she said, running her hands underneath her and along the bench. Then she gave a sigh and her hand closed over Grandma Dee's butter dish. "That's it!" she said. "I knew there was something I wanted to ask you if I could have." She jumped up from the table and went over in the corner where the churn stood, the milk in it clabber by now. She looked at the churn and looked at it.

"This churn top is what I need," she said. "Didn't Uncle Buddy whittle it out of a tree you all used to have?"

"Yes," I said.

"Uh huh," she said happily. "And I want the dasher, too."

"Uncle Buddy whittle that, too?" asked the barber.

Dee (Wangero) looked up at me.

"Aunt Dee's first husband whittled the dash," said Maggie so low you almost couldn't hear her. "His name was Henry, but they called him Stash."

"Maggie's brain is like an elephant's," Wangero said, laughing. "I can use the churn top as a centerpiece for the alcove table," she said, sliding a plate over the churn, "and I'll think of something artistic to do with the dasher."

When she finished wrapping the dasher the handle stuck out. I took it for a moment in my hands. You didn't even have to look close to see where hands pushing the dasher up and down to make butter had left a kind of sink in the wood. In fact, there were a lot of small sinks; you could see where thumbs and fingers had sunk into the wood. It was beautiful light yellow wood, from a tree that grew in the yard where Big Dee and Stash had lived.

After dinner Dee (Wangero) went to the trunk at the foot of my bed and started rifling through it. Maggie hung back in the kitchen over the dishpan. Out came Wangero with two quilts. They had been pieced by Grandma Dee and then Big Dee and me had hung them on the quilt frames on the front porch and quilted them. One was in the Lone Star pattern. The other was Walk Around the Mountain. In both of them were scraps of dresses Grandma Dee had worn fifty and more years ago. Bits and pieces of Grandpa Jarrell's Paisley shirts. And one teeny faded blue piece, about the size of a penny matchbox, that was from Great Grandpa Ezra's uniform that he worn in the Civil War.

"Mama," Wangero said sweet as a bird. "Can I have these old quilts."

I heard something fall in the kitchen, and a minute later the kitchen door slammed.

"Why don't you take one or two of the others?" I asked. "These old things was just done by me and Big Dee from some tops your grandma pieced before she died."

"No," said Wangero. "I don't want those. They are stitched around the borders by machine."

"That'll make them last better," I said.

"That's not the point," said Wangero. "These are all pieces of dresses Grandma used to wear. She did all this stitching by hand. Imagine!" She held the quilts securely in her arms, stroking them.

"Some of the pieces, like those lavender ones, come from old clothes her mother handed down to her," I said, moving up to touch the quilts. Dee (Wangero) moved back just enough so that I couln't reach the quilts. They already belonged to her.

"Imagine!" she breathed again, clutching them closely to her bosom.

"The truth is," I said, "I promised to give them quilts to Maggie, for when she marries John Thomas."

She gasped like a bee had stung her.

"Maggie can't appreciate these quilts!" she said. "She'd probably be backward enough to put them to everyday use."

"I reckon she would," I said, "God knows I been saving 'em for long enough with nobody using 'em. I hope she will!" I didn't want to bring up how I had offered Dee (Wangero) a quilt when she went away to college. Then she had told me they were old-fashioned, out of style.

"But they're *priceless*!" she was saying now, furiously; for she has a temper. "Maggie would put them on the bed and in five years they'd be in rags. Less than that!"

"She can always make some more," I said. "Maggie knows how to quilt."

Dee (Wangero) looked at me with hatred. "You just will not understand. The point is these quilts, *these* quilts!"

"Well," I said, stumped. "What would *you* do with them?"

"Hang them," she said. As if that was the only thing you *could* do with quilts.

Maggie by now was standing in the door. I could almost hear the sound her feet made as they scraped over each other.

"She can have them Mama," she said, like somebody used to never winning anything, or having anything reserved for her. "I can 'member Grandma Dee without the quilts."

I looked at her hard. She had filled her bottom lip with checkerberry snuff and it gave her face a kind of dopey, hangdog look. It was Grandma Dee and Big Dee who taught her how to quilt herself. She stood there with her scarred hands hidden in the folds of her skirt. She looked at her sister with something like fear but she wasn't mad at her. This was Maggie's portion. This was the way she knew God to work.

When I looked at her like that something hit me in the top of my head and ran down to the soles of my feet. Just like when I'm in church and the spirit of God touches me and I get happy and shout. I did something I never had done before: hugged Maggie to me, then dragged her on into the room, snatched the quilts out of Miss Wangero's hands and dumped them into Maggie's lap. Maggie just sat there on my bed with her mouth open.

"Take one or two of the others," I said to Dee.

But she turned without a word and went out to Hakim-a-barber.

"You just don't understand," she said, as Maggie and I came out to the car.

"What don't I understand?" I wanted to know.

"Your heritage," she said. And then she turned to Maggie, kissed her, and said, "You ought to try to make something of yourself, too, Maggie. It's really a new day for us. But from the way you and Mama still live you'd never know it."

She put on some sunglasses that hid everything above the tip of her nose and her chin.

Maggie smiled; maybe at the sunglasses. But a real smile, not scared. After we watched the car dust settle I asked Maggie to bring me a dip of snuff. And then the two of us sat there just enjoying, until it was time to go in the house and go to bed.

FOR MY PEOPLE

Margaret Walker

> For my people everywhere singing their slave songs repeat-
>   edly: their dirges and their ditties and their blues and
>   jubilees, praying their prayers nightly to an unknown
>   god, bending their knees humbly to an unseen power;

From FOR MY PEOPLE by Margaret Walker, Yale University Press, 1942. Copyright © 1974 by Margaret Walker. Reprinted by permission of the author. (See Ms. Walker's poem "Now" in the INTRODUCTION.)

5   For my people lending their strength to the years, to the gone
        years and the now years and the maybe years, washing
        ironing cooking scrubbing sewing mending hoeing
        plowing digging planting pruning patching dragging
        along never gaining never reaping never knowing and
10   never understanding;

        For my playmates in the clay and dust and sand of Alabama
        backyards playing baptizing and preaching and doc-
        tor and jail and soldier and school and mama and
        cooking and playhouse and concert and store and hair
15   and Miss Choomby and company;

        For the cramped bewildered years we went to school to learn
        to know the reasons why and the answers to and the
        people who and the places where and the days when,
        in memory of the bitter hours when we discovered we
20   were black and poor and small and different and
        nobody cared and nobody wondered and nobody
        understood;

        For the boys and girls who grew in spite of these things to be
        man and woman, to laugh and dance and sing and
25   play and drink their wine and religion and success, to
        marry their playmates and bear children and then die
        of consumption and anemia and lynching;

        For my people thronging 47th Street in Chicago and Lenox
        Avenue in New York and Rampart Street in New
30   Orleans, lost disinherited dispossessed and happy
        people filling the cabarets and taverns and other
        people's pockets needing bread and shoes and milk
        and land and money and something—something all
        our own;

35   For my people walking blindly spreading joy, losing time
        being lazy, sleeping when hungry, shouting when
        burdened, drinking when hopeless, tied and shackled
        and tangled among ourselves by the unseen creatures
        who tower over us omnisciently and laugh;

40   For my people blundering and groping and floundering in
        the dark of churches and schools and clubs and
        societies, associations and councils and committees
        and conventions, distressed and disturbed and de-
        ceived and devoured by money-hungry glory-craving
45   leeches, preyed on by facile force of state and fad and
        novelty, by false prophet and holy believer;

50   For my people standing staring trying to fashion a better
way from confusion, from hypocrisy and misunderstanding, trying to fashion a world that will hold all
the people, all the faces, all the adams and eves and
their countless generations;

55   Let a new earth rise. Let another world be born. Let a bloody
peace by written in the sky. Let a second generation
full of courage issue forth; let a people loving freedom come to growth. Let a beauty full of healing
and a strength of final clenching be the pulsing in
our spirits and our blood. Let the marital songs be
written, let the dirges disappear. Let a race of men
now rise and take control.

THE PARADE
Liz Sohappy

The light glows bright
as the parade begins.
Not everyone has come,
only the old ones.
5   The Eastern tribes came far,
dressed in cloth, wearing silver.
From the southeast trailed teared travelers
of the Five Civilized Tribes.
From the plains came buffalo hunters
10   dressed in beaded, fringed buckskin.
The light glows brighter
as each tribe passes.

It was such a long time ago
when he was first sighted,
15   running through the forest
like a frightened, swift lean deer.
When he danced in bird feathers,
dancing frenzied around blue ashes.
In the twilight of dawn, again he dances.
20   Drums thunder over creeks
to the swishing grasses on the plains.
Chants echo across the land of yellow maize,
along the paths of the sacred buffalo.

"The Parade," by Liz Sohappy from THE WHISPERING WIND by Terry Allen. Copyright © 1972 by The Institute of American Indian Arts. Used by permission of Doubleday & Company, Inc. (Ms. Sohappy's "The Indian
Market" and "Once Again" are included in Unit Nine, ETHNIC PRIDE.)

the years flow like running water.
25   Grasses grow yellow, rocks crumble to crust
as old ones come, they pass.

"Blackfeet Chief Wades-In Water and wife, Julia." He was the son
of Chief Running Crane and served as Chief of Police on the
Blackfeet Reservation for twenty-five years. Julia was the only Indian Policewoman in the country at the same time and also retired
after twenty-five years of service. Their beautiful costumes combine
the finest of beadwork and porcupine quill decoration with the
handsome long fringing no longer seen in Plains' costumes. By permission of the Bureau of Indian Affairs.

"Eastern European-American Lady," By permission of Maria de
Noronha, (Gallman), the artist.

KEROSENE LAMP

Valentina Sinkevich

A kerosene lamp
displayed in the window
of an antique store.
People walk by without
stopping or looking.
A kerosene lamp in the window . . .
I stop, open the door
and walk into the past . . .

My mother—a widow
when I was ten.
Then came the war—
she heard no more
or her children.
There was war,
there was winter—
and the burning kerosene lamp.

A kerosene lamp of my childhood—
an old family heirloom,
tenacious like a small monkey;
it forces to go topsy-turvy
all that was . . .
I watch the smoldering wick;
see the filly that kicked
snowdust while it ambled.
And behind the filly,
under kerosene
flickering starlight—
a man's solitary stride.

A kerosene lamp in the window.
People walk by without
stopping or looking . . .

A kerosene lamp of my childhood,—
its age is less than a hundred,
the wick still continues to burn.

Reprinted by permission of the author.

Again, memory searches
for meanings, thoughts, thousands
of words to explain fates
I saw under the kerosene
lamp . . . And a store
displays in its window
on a day—clear and windless,
on some other planet,
in summary daylight
a lamp that can never explain.

"Polish-American peasant lady preparing a meal." By permission
of Maria de Noronha (Gallman), the artist.

MEMORIES OF OUR OLD WOOD STOVE

Marie Prisland

Our children, much less our grandchildren, barely remember the old wood stove; but when fall brings its chilly winds, I often am warmed by the memory of our sturdy old wood range.

When I moved into our new home as a bride, the huge stove occupied the longest wall of our old-fashioned kitchen. The stove needed a lot of space because of its size and because of the hot water reservoir attached to it.

When I wanted a roaring fire, I would pull a metal bar in front of the stove and open the damper in the pipe. The stove crackled with glowing warmth. No modern stove could accomplish what the wood fire did.

In 1910 the iron range was a model of efficiency. With her polished black surface and nickel-plated trim, she was a beauty! Once a week she was given a dazzling shine with "Black Joe" stove polish. The nickel was washed with soap and water and then dried and polished.

We always had homemade bread, potica, pies, cookies, and coffee cake. There was no stove thermometer, but I knew by putting my hand into the oven whether it was exactly the right temperature for baking.

The range burned mostly wood but when winter came with near zero weather, we banked the fire with coal. The ashes were shaken carefully from the grates so that they fell into a narrow ash pan below. If the shakings were too vigorous, the grates dumped all their coals and then a new fire had to be started.

There were times when the warmth of the old stove was a great comfort. My son remembers having a bath as a child in the washtub in front of the open warm oven, and my daughters still recall the aroma of the red apples they placed on top of the hot stove to warm a little before they were eaten.

Snuggled around the warm stove the children were doing their homework and I was telling or reading them stories.

The children especially were fond of the old stove in winter. It warmed their cold and numb feet and dried their wet shoes and their soggy mittens which were hung behind the stove. One cold spring we brought our newly-hatched chickens into the kitchen. The mother hen watched over her brood, which was housed in a neat box beside the warm stove.

Yes, the old stove is gone, and gone with it is the tightly-knit family which gathered around the stove warming hands and hearts. . . .

Marie Prisland, "Memories of Our Old Wood Stove," from ANTHOLOGY OF SLOVENIAN AMERICAN LITERATURE, edited by Giles Edward Gobetz and Adele Donchenko, 1977, Slovenian Research Center of America, Inc. Reprinted by permission of the publisher.

ETHNIC PRIDE

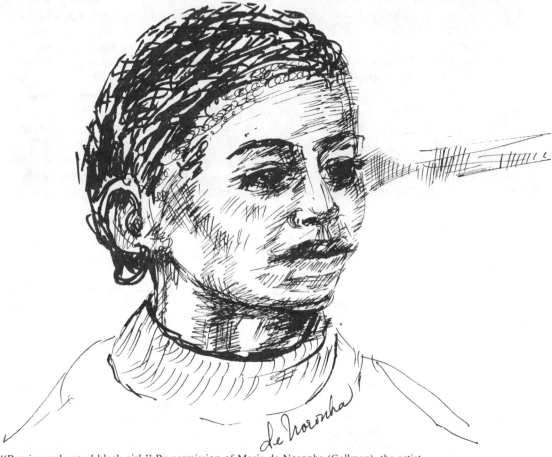

"Pensive and proud black girl." By permission of Maria de Noronha (Gallman), the artist.

"The juice from tomatoes is not called merely juice. It is always called tomato juice. If you go into a restaurant desiring tomato juice you do not order the waiter to bring you "juice"; you request, distinctly, TOMATO juice. The juice from cranberries is called cranberry juice. The juice from oranges is called orange juice. The [writing] from Black [writers] is called Black [writing]."

Gwendolyn Brooks

281

"BLACK MARDI GRAS AND THE FLYING WHITE HORSES"

Laurraine Goreau

A driving energy, a restless yearning to know and to be, propelled thirteen year old Mahalia Jackson into innocent but daring exploits which sent shivers through her young black world in the obscure pocket of 1936 New Orleans in which they lived, worked, and played. For their staunch churchgoing families, though, Mardi Gras—its black portion, all they knew—was no "play." Mahalia was ready to pay the price for finding out. She did. And she never forgot.

"The flying horses are strictly for white!" . . . "I don't care. You watch. *I'll* show you how! . . . Halie was at it again. Some nerve! It wasn't enough she passed herself as a boy—pushed that nappy hair under Peter's cap and pulled on his pants so she could go caddy. Unheard of for a girl, but they understood. How else she going get the money for her costumes for the church programs? ("I'll get the money, Mrs. Jackson, if you buy the tarlatan! I'll pay you back!" Then Annise's big sister Lily would make Halie's costume too. After all, the child had neither mother nor sister to do it.) But ride the flying horses? Boy *or* girl, if you were black, that was strictly *out*. The group was vague about the consequence, but it stretched infinitely dire.

"I said I would and I will! You wait, I'll be back."

Halie hurried into an old white uniform of Aunt Duke's. She'd wash and press it clean again and Duke never know. Get her a basket. Now find that light-skin child lives on Adam. . . .

The slim, prim nursemaid sauntered through Audubon Park, her fair-haired, light-skinned charge in hand, basket over her arm to amuse the child by pulling moss or pepper grass. Alongside the flying horses—the most alluring attraction of Audubon Park, its horses and chariots and mythical beasts circling endlessly to a calliope—the two stopped. A safe distance in back, behind trees like shadows, a dark scattering stopped too. Breathlessly, they saw Halie bend to her charge, gesture, get a nod and a grin, and the pair mount the best of all, an up-and-down horse, solicitous maid holding the child on her lap. Round and round . . . Halie didn't dare grab for the brass ring that might have won them another ride: just one fare; nursemaid didn't count. But the air had never seemed so sweet as they rounded the circle, on and on, 'til the calliope died; the motion with it.

Off the maid, off the child, to walk primly into the trees, and whoop. "I told you I'd do it. Some day you *all* going do it; but you remember now, I'm the *first colored person* rode the flying horses!"

She had never heard of civil rights.

Now, her fame flared for weeks—almost until Carnival: Beside *that* glittering peak, all else paled. But not everybody clapped. "I'm not going out there. Mama said no. It's dangerous! And I know what Aunt Duke going do to you!"

"That's for you to know and me to find out. I'm going, first thing." At her cousin Celie's gasp of alarm, "Oh, ain' nothing going happen to me!"

Excerpts from JUST MAHALIA, BABY by Laurraine Goreau, © 1975, Word Books, Waco, Texas. Reprinted by permission of the author. (Another excerpt from this book appears in Unit Seven, RELIGION AND RITUAL.)

Carnival had originated with 19th century whites, led by secret groups, as a glorious letting-loose before the ashes of Lent stilled the Catholic city. Black had created their own secret parallel (secrecy the very bone marrow of Carnival's being and social status) with its panoply of signs, symbols, and traditions—if fewer strictures. Mardi Gras, the "Fat Tuesday" climax, was the one day when whites came to make obeisance to blacks: The tribes of Indian Chiefs and the Baby Dolls (top-echelon whores) were widely sought as the most splendid in the city, bar none—the costumes usually scrimped for, penny by penny, year-round. The black Zulu parade was topped only by Rex, to white eyes; by none, to black, who on this one day couldn't care less what any white thought. It was Mardi Gras! Masks were encouraged, not to come off 'til sundown. The law looked the other way (it couldn't have coped anyway).

As the city blinked awake, its children knew they were unloved if they weren't hurried into costume and painted and put in position early to watch the parades and all the big "Mardi Graws"—strange beings today, mystifying friends, encircling strangers . . . the air electric, miming made easy as beer and liquor coursed their channels.

Nothing like this in Legonier. Gentle Bell forbid Celie ever to put her head outside. And although Bell had a picture of a soft-eyed Charity in a cowboy hat—so Halie knew her mother used to take her out to see the sights—a scandalized Aunt Duke brooked no such.

Halie ducked out, of course, out before good light. She could take her licks. She wasn't going miss anything. Especially the Indians! Heading out on a long, erratic course from 6th and Willow—at Charlie Brannon's Corner, the barroom where they began to make up at 5 A.M., more or less—some tribes might begin getting here to their streets by six, stomping out a war dance, crying way for the Chief, starting on the chants. One chant Halie could sing along with them—just in her head: wouldn't dare no other way.

> *Boom boom bah hoo*
> *He he he nah*
> *Me me hah nah*
> *Boom bah—*

Tribe on the move! And you never knew. The costumes were new each year, all bright feathers and beads on leather stitched by the Indian himself—no woman to touch the sacred garment. Splendid Spy Boys scouted the streets, a piercing "Aeeeeeeeaaaaaaah! Aeeeeeeeaaaaaaah!" warning Indians on the warpath.

> *If you don't bow,*
> *When my chief come by,*
> *Chah tah wa tah*
> *Poo nah nay. . . .*

A feathered spear is hurled into the dirt street; it sticks there, quivering; the dense crowd backs off, leaving a clear path: Chief coming through, let him have his way. Rival scouts in the block? They must bow-wow. One tribe give and take low? If not, it was spear and knife to first blood.

The chief who struck real terror was Brother Tilman. You knew his tribe by the special glory of their garb, the fierce paint, the special chant. No disgrace for another tribe to take low to Brother Tilman, else first blood could be last.

The sun was so bright nobody wore a coat. The street swirled with masked clowns, cowboys, cowgirls, Indians, bears, bushmen, rabbits, tramps, a man with pop caps head to foot, some ladies like playing cards. . . . And Indian Chiefs. Halie rocked. Brother Tilman!

> *All out the way!*
> *Pah co nah na,*
> *Get out the way!*
> *Ah no mah na. . . .*

Another chant grew. To Halie it sounded like *Two way pack a way, Pock a way.* But she didn't dare voice this one even in her head. Shutter doors were slamming shut; people snatched their children indoors. The street emptied in a flash. But this wasn't Esther St. Halie could only shrink against the closest siding. *"Two way pack a way. . . ."* Stomping and circling. Rivals visible now, standing their ground. *"Two way. . . ."* The moment of wah-wah, a knife flashed in the sun, an agonized scream—war erupted. Halie dove into the grocery bar against which she'd backed. People were packed in, falling all over each other, the smell of whiskey and beer and wine thick even where she was, on hands and knees. Suddenly, fighting here too—not Indians, some private vengeance—Halie trapped, scuttling this way and that until she scrambled through fists and feet and stood outside torn, panting, revolted. What she saw made it worse: bloodied bodies on the ground as the Tilman tribe receded, drunker now with their own glory. Halie raced for home, paced by panic and something more.

A frightened, furious Duke put her out.

She circled the block. "Aunt Alice," the voice small, "can I stay by you?"

By the time Alice walked her home next day, the storm was over; Duke's furies were short-lived as they were sudden. But Halie never faced another Mardi Gras or spoke of it without a shudder. Aunt Duke was right. There was more on her mind, anyway, than murder and vengeance. A window had slipped open in Heaven.

THE LAST SONG

Joy Harjo

how can you stand it
he said
the hot oklahoma summers
where you were born
this humid thick air
is choking me
and i want to go back
to new mexico

it is the only way
i know how to breathe
an ancient chant
that my mother knew
came out of a history
woven from wet tall grass
in her womb
and i know no other way
than to surround my voice
with the summer songs of crickets
in this moist south night air

oklahoma will be the last song
i'll ever sing

From THE FACE OF POETRY edited by LaVerne Harrell Clark and Mary MacArthur (Gallimaufry, Arlington, Virginia, © 1976). Reprinted by permission of the author. (I am grateful to LaVerne H. Clark for suggesting this poem.)

SING WITH YOUR BODY

Janice Mirikitani

To my daughter, Tianne Tsukiko

We love with great difficulty
spinning in one place
afraid to create
      spaces
         new/rhythm

the beat of a child
dangled by her own inner ear
takes Aretha with her
        upstairs, somewhere.

go quickly, Tsukiko,
        into your circled dance
go quickly
      before your steps are
      halted by who you are not

go quickly
      to learn the mixed
      rhythm of your tongue,

go quickly
      to who you are

      before

        your mother swallows
        what she has lost.

5

10

15

20

From ASIAN-AMERICAN HERITAGE, edited by David Hsin-Fu Wand, Simon & Schuster, Inc., Pocket Books, Washington Square Press. © 1974. Reprinted by permission of the author.

THE INDIAN MARKET

Liz Sohappy

Come! What shall it be?
Bitterroot noodles,
sweetroot carrots,
and baby potatoes
5   for our supper tonight?

Quick! Look about! No one is near.
That tree, that leafy branch,
it blackens my hair, makes it grow.
That other tree, with red buds hanging,
10   we will drink it for our sweating bodies.

Look! Up there, it is yellow.
Grasp it gently, now pull it slow,
here, into my beaded pouch—
Rouge for our faces,
15   war paint for our men.

Come! There is work to be done.
There are salmon to be cleaned,
venison to be dried,
eels to be roasted,
20   and berries to be picked.

Come! Our moccasin prints lead us home.
We will return tomorrow.

"Native Americans." Last Rider and his wife, Blackfeet Indians, stand beside their tipi on the Montana reservation. The magnificent quilled and beaded costumes with the long fringes they are wearing are seldom seen these days outside of museums fortunate enough to possess them. By permission of the Bureau of Indian Affairs.

ONCE AGAIN

Liz Sohappy

Let go of the present and death.
Go to the place nearest the stars,
gather twigs, logs;
build a small fire,
5   a huge angry fire.

Gather nature's skin,
wet it, stretch it,
make a hard drum,
fill it with water
10   to muffle the sound.

Gather dry leaves, herbs,
feed into the fire.
Let the smoke rise
up to the dark sky,
15   to the roundness of the sun.

Moisten your lips,
loosen your tongue,
let the chant echo
from desert, to valley, to peak—
20   wherever your home may be.

Remember the smoke,
the chants, the drums,
the stick grandfather held
as he spoke in the dark
25   of the power of his fathers?

Gather your memories
into a basket, into a pot,
into your cornhusk bag, and
grandfather is alive
30   for us to see once again.

AS RED AS IT WAS

Aviva Barzel

In memory of all who fell in Israel's wars

In every blood covenant
Renewed between us
The blood has been our blood.

You prefaced every miracle
With a blow that outlasted it,
Then saved us from all your blows.

And the sins have been cleansed
by the travails
And are as white as snow
And only the pain is as red as it was.

PASS OVER THE BLOOD

Aviva Barzel

Translated from Hebrew by Ida Cohen Selavan

When God desired
To free us from Egypt
In order that his angel recognize us
He commanded us to stain
The doorposts of our house with blood.

From that time until this day
We have not yet freed ourselves
And every one of our homes drips blood.

Make it so, O Lord, that on this Passover
The angel will recognize us
By the fragrance of spring flowers
That we shall join to our doorposts
And desire our freedom fully
Without first being stained with blood.

WHO WAS REALLY THE SAVAGE?

Rose Mary (Shingobe) Barstow

Ms. Barstow, formerly a member of Minnesota's Indian Affairs Commission, is now an Ojibwe Teaching Specialist at the University of Minnesota preparing school curriculum material. She has thirty-six grandchildren.

In her autobiographical sketch, Rose Mary (Shingobe) Bartow writes that she was born in 1915, but that her mother had converted to the Catholic faith, so she was not given an Indian name or the traditional ceremony for a new member of the tribe until some old ladies felt sorry for her and did so when she was about two or three.

When she was seven, her mother died and she was sent a year later to a mission boarding school where "the sisters cut my braids off." In addition, she goes on to say that they "made me wear a gingham dress with a big bow. I looked like everybody else. I felt . . . lost."

Willing to learn English, she studied hard in school, but when she returned home to her grandparents, she had almost forgotten her native tribal tongue, Ojibwe and was embarrassed. Her aunt did not understand and accused her of having foolish pride—bishigwadis—which Rose Mary says is "a terrible insult to our people because we're taught that you're never an entity by yourself. You're always a part of something." So the young girl relearned her tribal language and became fluent in two languages.

A year later, as she tells her story;

I went back to school in the fall. Now that I could speak English, I never kept my mouth shut. We read a history book about "the savages." The pictures were in color. There was one of a group of warriors attacking white people—a woman held a baby in her arms. I saw hatchets, blood dripping, feathers flying. I showed the picture to the Sister. She said, "Rose Mary, don't you know you're Indian?" I said, "No, I'm not." She said, "Yes, you are." I said, "No!" And I ran behind a clump of juniper trees, and cried and cried. I spent a week in the infirmary. I didn't eat. I was really sick.

When I went home I told Grandfather. He said, "I've heard about those books. They call us savages. Some of our old people wonder who was really the savage. Whites came here with a man nailed to a cross and used it to subdue us. They took everything from us. They said that we scalped our enemies. But you know, they bought Indian scalps for a dollar a head. That's not in those history books. You must return to school, Rose Mary. The Great Spirit gave you a mind of your own. Someday, my girl, you will write the truth in our language. You will write of the goodness of our people, and the tranquility."

Excerpts from I AM THE FIRE OF TIME, edited by Jane B. Katz. (New York: E.P. Dutton & Company, 1977) pp. 117-118.

"RUBY'S DISCOVERY"

Ruby Reyes Flowers

Betty laughed as she handed the snapshot to me, "My goodness, Ruby, you look just like a foreigner in this one."

I looked at the picture again, more closely this time. There I sat—all five feet of me— perched on Betty's desk (surrounded by medical books, patients' records, and Betty's private arsenal of secretarial aids): dark brown hair, smooth and shiney, curling up just as it touched my shoulders; brown eyes fringed with short straight lashes; white teeth even whiter against my olive skin; high cheek bones set in a slender face; and a high-bridged, long straight nose (the one part of my face that had refused to be influenced by my father. His is a typical Filipino nose: short, broad, and flattened across the bridge.) My white uniform, which my job as an x-ray technician demanded, gleamed in contrast to my dark skin.

"I am a foreigner, Betty," I answered to her mortification, "I'm a Filipina."

How could Betty, my friend and co-worker of three years, have known? Except for my dark hair and eyes and year-round suntan ("Where did you get that beautiful tan?" "From my father!").

I am a typical small-town Southern woman. Grits and ham and gumbo and Southern fried chicken are my favorite foods; the strains of "Dixie" cause my heart to pound and the hair on my neck to prickle; the fragrance of gardenias and honeysuckle and magnolia frescatas bring back sweet memories of childhood; Jeff Davis and Robert E. Lee are high on my list of heroes; and my Southern drawl is indescribable—the result of being brought up in a mill town near Mobile, Alabama, and spending many hours in conversation with the black woman who helped care for me.

Yet, I still cling to my Filipino heritage—a heritage I cherish and am grateful for.

Taal, a small town on the southwestern coast of the island of Luzon, is famous in the Philippines for her industrious citizens. My father, Felipe, is no exception to this rule. Indeed, he is the personification of industry, honesty, ambition, and service—a true son of Taal. Filipinos are, by nature, fun-loving and out-going and, again, Felipe is true to his colors. Prestige, earned through service to neighbors and community, is cherished; and the love and respect of his family and friends is necessary to the Filipino's happiness.

Yes, it's to my father I owe my sense of pride in family name and appreciation for the values he stands for.

Taal, the birthplace of my father and grandfather, lies just across the Pansipit River from the town of Lemery and Batangas Bay. In fact, you can see Bantangas Bay from the window of my father's childhood home. And, from the same window, you can also see the Basilica de Sainte Martine, originally built in 1575, a visual symbol of the influence the Catholic Church has exerted in the Philippines since Spanish colonial times. The Church is an important part of a Filipino's life and some of my father's fondest memories are of his family's religious observances; particularly, the family altar where his grandmother listened nightly to the children's prayers. This was followed by each child in the family sniffing the back of her hand in respect, a custom in the Philippines where sniffing is a show of affection comparable to a kiss. (Sometimes, we children would sniff Daddy's hand just to delight him.) The wide-planked native hardwood floors still gleam from years of polishing with banana oil in that beautiful upstairs room where he prayed. The windows of capiz shell admit only the softest of light. And, when thrown open to the cool tropical breezes, they treat you to the sights and sounds of that busy town. (Across the street is the Taal Volcano Restaurant, proudly bearing the Rotary Club Wheel; the members of this prestigious organization meet there every Sunday afternoon.) The high ceilings, with large boxed-in columns in each corner of the room which are connected to each other by arches of similar shape and size, give the room a cathedral-like feeling. This room served as a main parlor as well as a sleeping area for the children. A large bedroom where his parents slept and the kitchen complete the upstairs. The recreation room downstairs where his father's pool table could be found was also the residence of his highly-prized game cocks.

My father left this beautiful home sixty years ago when, as a twelve-year-old orphan, he walked to Manila (some 75 miles north) in search of an orphanage. His relief upon arriving was short-lived when he was refused admittance for not having the proper papers. He had no one to sponsor him in the orphanage; and, being a minor, he couldn't sponsor himself. This unfortunate situation was soon remedied when he found a job in a brick factory. He even managed to attend night-school. It is no wonder that an American business executive from Hawaii, was impressed with this enterprising young man—impressed enough to take Felipe home with him to Honolulu and to educate him. It was there, some years later, that Felipe became a seaman; and it was on an American ship that, at the age of twenty-seven he came to Mobile, where he met Shirley, a lovely blue-eyed blonde of the South.

She was fifteen years old, and even though her father and mother were separated, she had the security of her mother's large family. Their ancestors had come to the Mobile area some 100 years before, and their roots were firmly established—politically, socially, and financially. Her grandfather was a leading citizen in the town and a great-uncle was a past mayor. No citizen of the town—black or white—could be found who did not recognize that family name.

It was love at first sight. They met at a local park; she was with a group of girl-friends and he, some local Filipino friends. Shirley had no idea that this handsome, well-dressed, black-haired man was a foreigner. She insists that she had no problems understanding his accented English, and she still remembers her first words upon seeing him— "Hands off, girls, this one belongs to me." And, he did. Three dates later, he proposed, and three months (a ship's voyage) later, they were married. Her mother and only brother stood staunchly by her. The rest of her family were aghast. "Your children will be monkeys," her favorite uncle and name-sake angrily assured her. (She took her first-born to this same uncle as soon as possible and defied him to find a monkey's tail on her Filipino baby.)

Felipe's determination to succeed as a merchant seaman was second only to his desire to become a first-rate American citizen. He succeeded in both instances. Slowly, he inched his way up the ladder of acceptance. A highlight of his life was being admitted to the local Masonic Order. He became the youngest steward to sail with Waterman Steamship Company—and a Filipino steward at that! His efforts were rewarded when he was hired by a shipping company to initiate a training school for teaching aspiring young men the fine art of planning, preparing and serving meals on shipboard. His program is still in use today by seafaring unions. He provided not only for his own wife and children, but for his mother-in-law and any other relatives who needed his assistance.

It's not surprising, then, that from earliest childhood, I can remember only love and respect from my mother's family toward my father. As a matter of fact, I was convinced that he was their very favorite in-law. And, time has not changed my opinion on that.

Mother, in the meantime, made every effort to insure her children's acceptance by the entire community. She spent hours attending and participating in the P.T.A.; she was a room mother without equal: cooking fudge, cakes, cookies, gumbo, and spaghetti dinners for any occasion; she was the football team's greatest fan, and the baseball team's most faithful chauffeur; our friends sought her out for advice and information. And her four children lived a most enviable life! When Daddy was gone to sea, she spent her days playing with us. Summer was just one long picnic. There were trips to the creek to swim. (Watermelons were taken along and put in the cold creek water until they were chilled just perfectly.) We were taught at a very early age the delicate art of gently pulling a crab from the bay while he was busily engrossed with the bait dangled from a string and, then, when he was within reach, swooping the net under him and lifting him out of the water. How many gallons of Kool-aid and how many dozens of sandwiches did we consume on those hot summer days? There were trips to the fishing camp, too, where we were free to paddle the boat around in the river, or fish, or just sit on the banks in the shade and enjoy the balmy, beautiful days.

But our pleasure wasn't confined to sunny days. In the fall, there were long drives across the bay to the woods where we examined the rocks and leaves and pine cones. Once, we found an unusually beautiful branch blown from an oak tree. Mother brought it home, sprayed it silver, draped it with colored lights and angel hair, and created our favorite Christmas tree—it was the talk of the neighborhood! On cold winter nights, we gathered around the kitchen table to sip hot chocolate and eat cheese toast, hot from the oven, while Mother told us tales of her childhood and ghost stories that made our hair stand on end. Yes, we lived an enviable life!

Joking with Betty about her "foot-in-mouth disease," my thoughts were carried back to that day long ago when I myself discovered that I was a foreigner. Betty was no more surprised than I was on that summer day. I was about nine years old.

The smell of fish frying woke me that morning. It reminded me that Daddy was home from his latest voyage. The house always smelled different when he was there, for he would cook the native dishes he loved so well and the whole house would be filled with the aroma of garlic and onions and vinegar, poultry seasoning and paprika. (Just as you remember a favorite aunt when the fragrance of roses is in the air, so will I always think of Daddy when I catch the scent of garlic.) Turning over in bed, I could see the bluest of skies, and I knew this would be a good day! The warm air, smelling of sunshine, floated in the open window, and I felt wonderfully wrapped in summer.

Slipping into my shorts and blouse, I quietly joined Daddy. We were usually the first ones up in the house—he from habit as a steward on the ship and I, perhaps from a desire to spend special hours with him, since he was rarely home. For most of my growing-up years, he was on a cargo ship that sailed from New York to New Orleans with two days in Mobile. Our lives revolved around a fixed schedule: three weeks without Daddy; drive to New Orleans for an extra day with him; and back to Mobile where we'd meet his ship again. Our trips to New Orleans were made even more special by the fact that Daddy had cousins there and we always stayed with them.

It was always fiesta time when we were with Aunt Mim and Uncle Maning—with joking and teasing and music and food and, always, much laughter. There was no doubt that Daddy was in his element there. And Mother was just as much at home. During the early years of their marriage, Mother and Daddy had lived with these same cousins, and the bond of love and respect woven then became only stronger as years passed.

Daddy offered me some fish, which, as usual, I turned down. I just couldn't learn to eat fried fish for breakfast! But I would eat a plate of the fried rice sprinkled with black pepper. It was one of my favorite Filipino dishes, even though it was also one of the simplest. (Daddy is a good cook and the whole family enjoys his spicey dishes. Adobo, chicken stewed with garlic and onions, is a specialty; as is his yellow rice, a meal in itself with bits of pork, chicken, shrimp and vegetables mingled with the tenderest of rice. Strangers to the family raise their eyebrows at our delight when we announce, "Daddy's cooking rice tonight!")

While Daddy watched, I cleaned my plate, always aware of how seriously it hurt him to see food wasted. (I know, now, that his feelings were based on a childhood that knew hunger and want. Even today in the Philippines, food is not wasted but revered and appreciated. One of the most humorous examples I can remember of his abhorrence of waste was the time Mother found the chicken's feet in the stew pot. "Adds flavor," he said calmly, as she tried to explain why you don't cook chicken feet.)

Over steaming cups of coffee laced generously with milk and sugar, we made our plans for the day. "Ruby, I have errands for you today," he spoke in his own peculiar accent. (I was in high school before I realized that he had an accent; it had always been familiar to me! None of us four children had his accent, though, as Mother had refused to allow him to teach us his language—the musical Tagalog, a mixture of the Malaysian and Polynesian languages. No foreign accent for her children!)

He brought out the bills, his checkbook, and the ledger. The routine was familiar. First, he would show me how much he earned, then he would list the bills and write the checks. I felt suddenly mature as he discussed with me, as to an adult, his financial situation. I didn't realize then that he was bestowing on me the same honor his own father had him, and in the same way—the honor of recognizing my sense of responsibility. I don't know why Daddy chose to share these matters with me rather than my two older brothers who were, also responsible and mature. It was said that I was his favorite child. I'm not sure about that, but I do know that I am special to him. Recently, a cousin visiting from Taal told Daddy that I look very much like his own mother had. Could this be the reason he felt so close to me? I do know that he appreciated my love of books and learning; and he impressed me, at a very early age, with the fact that I was not limited in my choices of a vocation simply because I was female. When he discovered I wanted to be a nurse, he encouraged me to go further and be a doctor or a dentist. "There are women dentists and doctors in the Philippines," he would point out, "it's not so unusual."

I dressed, putting on my favorite skirt and blouse. Mother had made it for me. She made many of our clothes in an effort to keep us well-dressed. As I slipped on the green printed skirt, I thought of how beautiful it was when I twirled around, faster and faster. It would stand straight out! And, if I slipped the white blouse off my shoulders, I looked just like a gypsy! Studying my image in the mirror, I was glad for my long, dark hair and my big, brown eyes. (Were they like the "flashing eyes" of a gypsy? I wondered.)

"Go to the bank and pay the house mortgage first," Daddy told me as he kissed me good-bye. And, even as I left the house, the sweet odor ("the Filipino smell," Mother called it) of Daddy followed me. Money in hand, I walked importantly down the street, past the Wilson house and Taylor's grocery store (I would stop in on my way home for a special treat from the candy jars). I could name each family as I passed their homes; many were old friends of my grandmother's family. And, so, on to the wide main street of our town, three blocks from home.

I slowed my pace as I passed the shoe store, trying to get a glimpse of the soft, black ballerina slippers. Though neither of us were dancers, my sister, Stella, and I would buy a pair as soon as we had each saved the $3.08 they cost. And we'd wear them until they were past recognition and had rubbed callouses on our heels. The callouses were worth it, though, because we were convinced that the slippers made us as graceful as dancers.

My thoughts were shattered by a loud screaming, "Nigger, nigger, nigger." Looking around, I saw a little cotton-headed girl leaning from the window of a parked car. She was such a little girl—only four or five years old. Her pale blonde hair curled about her head and gleamed in the sunlight, and long black lashes framed the deepest blue eyes. Beneath her tiny freckled nose, her rosebud mouth revealed rows of even, white teeth. She was beautiful; and, if not for the despising look on her face, could only be described as angelic. In the front seat of the dirty unkempt car, her unshaven father sat nodding in the sun; his rumpled work clothes were stained with grease. His big, boney hands slumped tiredly over the steering wheel. He seemed too tired to notice or care about his daughter' behaviour. I glanced around to see who she must be yelling at, and, much to my surprise, I found myself alone. Could she have been speaking to me? It must be, I decided, as she taunted me once more. Yes. She was speaking of me!

At last I knew what Mother had been trying to tell me all those times when she would say, "Don't worry about what people call you. You know what you are."

Throwing my chest out and my chin up in an effort to appear taller (and prouder, too, I suppose), I felt very superior to that little girl. Her father didn't care that she was yelling from a car window; mine would have—it wasn't ladylike. Her father didn't notice her hatred toward me, a stranger; my father would have noticed and been appalled—hatred wasn't in him. And, as for that word, "Nigger," I had been taught by my black friend, Marie, that ladies don't use that word—not even in jest; and hadn't she always taught me to be a lady? And wasn't I the very special daughter of two very special people: loved and cherished and respected?

Yes, I knew what I was. But, it was this incident that made me know once and for all that I was different, a foreigner. Something I'd never thought of before. I was not only the daughter of a foreigner—I was a foreigner.

Even now, people sometimes ask me, "Are you from South America?" Or "Mexico?" The more tactful might state, "There was a man who looked just like your father who ran our laundry" ("Are you Chinese?") or "I once knew a girl who looked just like you—she was from Brazil." I just smile and say, "I'm Filipina." I know what I am!

THE IMMIGRANT EXPERIENCE

"Steerage deck of the S.S. Pennland of the Red Star Line, 1893."
The Byron Collection. Reprinted by permission of the Photo
Library Department of the Museum of the City of New York.

Letter from M.M., North Dakota, Swedish-American Immigrant (no date).

". . . I set off with a light heart for the great land in the West. And I have never regretted that journey. Certainly I have had to work, but I was considered a human being even when I was poor."

H. Arnold Barton (excerpt) from *Letters from the Promised Land, Swedes in America,* 1840-1914.

THE BEST OF TWO WORLDS

Heidi Rockwood

Belonging to a particular ethnic group, being of German origin—what does it all mean? How does it influence anyone's life? To many these questions may have a ring of seriousness, of committment, of ties to a certain cultural and national heritage which certainly makes them "different" and sets them aside from others. To me personally, however, it has always meant that I could and did have the best of two possible worlds.

My childhood in Southern Germany, first Bavaria and then the Stuttgart area, evokes only happy memories. My parents loved the arts, and music especially became a dominant influence in our lives. Not only would we all sing folksongs together wherever we could—in the car on trips, under the Christmas tree or on our hikes through the forest—but at home radio and record player were tuned to classical music, above all opera. Mozart arias were the "pop songs" of my childhood, and when our first grade teacher in elementary school once asked whether anyone could sing a song they hadn't learned in school, I proudly got up and presented Sarastro's aria "In diesen Heil'gen Hallen" from Mozart's "Magic Flute" to the class. To this day I don't know how the lovely lady who taught us could—with a straight face—sit through the recital of a bass aria by a seven-year-old with a very high voice.

With the remains of several centuries of a varied and colorful history practically on our doorstep, I was early introduced to architectural styles. Our family explored the baroque splendor of Bavarian churches like Wies or Ottobeuren, or Gothic cathedrals like Ulm, and the late-medieval romanticism of 1,000 year old cities such as Rothenburg or Dinkelsbuhl. As soon as we could afford a car after the second World War, we went on regular weekend outings together, and my father would point out and explain the characteristics of the various architectural periods to us. If the weather was good enough we usually ended our exploration trips with a long picnic on some quiet forest path, working off all those calories afterwards by picking berries or mushrooms. In retrospect it all seems very idyllic, and for the most part it was. The sterner spirit of school life, with its fixed and rather arduous schedules the embodiment of the Germans' reputed love for authority and regimentation, represented security rather than a threat to our freedom. I was after all part of the 50's generation, and we were not yet a very rebellious group.

We all were rather shielded from the harsher realities of the German past. While I was growing up we rarely ever felt that Germany was just recovering from one of the worst periods in its history. Our home life was stable and secure, and my parents made almost a religion of being apolitical. They both disliked being herded into any organized party-activity and had largely avoided the clannishness of the Hitler era and mistrusted its emotional rallies. Their pride in Germany had nothing to do with the size and strength or the amount of "Lebensraum" it possessed. Obviously nobody had been able to stay completely aloof during the infamous Third Reich, but living in a small town in Silesia, at the eastern edge of the "Grossdeutsches Reich" kept my parents far enough removed from the mainstream of political activity to allow them to remain primarily private citizens. My father, as the manager of a factory which ordinarily made men's suits, had to switch the operation to uniforms. Since he fulfilled a vital function at home, he was spared from having to join the army. When we began asking questions about Germany's immediate past, we met with a certain amount of helplessness. My parents seemed as upset as we were about the atrocities that had been unearthed since the end of the war. If it seems inconceivable that they should not have known of some of the large-scale operations going on during Hitler's time, we must remember that the news media were heavily censored and that people tended to excuse isolated instances of racial discrimination as exceptions; and to regard the open instances thereof—such as the proof couples had to furnish before getting married that they were both of "Aryan blood"—as silly nuisances. My mother once mentioned a friend who, about to tell a political joke during the war, had looked around carefully to see whether they were not being overheard since she, as she said, "didn't want to end up in Dachau." Mother remembered wondering what on earth there was about Dachau that made it so fearsome.

My generation emerged from the confrontation with the past rather cynical and wary of the political process. We felt that we had to know our history if we were to prevent it from happening again, but also that we should be primarily allowed to concentrate on building the present. When I left Germany in 1964 to study in Great Britain for seven months, I was rather apprehensive about the prospect of having to defend my country against accusations, since we were told that the British were still quite unforgiving towards the Germans. Personally I never found this to be true. While many of the young people I came in contact with were curious about the past, they all stated that as far as they were concerned it lay behind us. A good friend of mine, however, once got drawn into a conversation with an elderly lady in Hyde Park in London, and on being spotted as German by her accent had to listen to quite a tirade about the lady's suffering during the London blitz. When I came to the United States in 1966, the time for remembering Germany's wrongdoings seemed to have largely passed. America was beginning to go through its own nightmare, Vietnam, and had more important questions to solve.

Coming to the United States was at first supposed to be merely a one-year adventure for me since as an English major, I had been given a scholarship which sent me to a small, private Southern college. Having been to other foreign countries before, I did not expect to experience "culture shock," but I did nevertheless. However, it was an amusing rather than a frightening experience. Americans were geographically much farther removed from Germany than any other nation I had ever come in contact with, and cultural awareness of what "being German" really meant was low among my new friends. I had little interest in being associated with the standard tourist image of the hefty lady in a Dirndl, or the massive young man in Lederhosen, guzzling enormous quantities of strong beer while listening to Bavarian oompah music. Therefore it seemed to be the wisest thing to shelve "being German" for the short time I planned to be in America and to try "being American" for a change. It was exciting to learn to live totally within a new language and culture. Much of it seemed shallow and commercialized in the small-college atmosphere of the mid-sixties, as yet hardly touched by the protests that were beginning to shake the rest of the nation, but coming from the reserved and impersonal atmosphere of a large German university, I also liked the openness and friendliness of the young people I met. I was immediately in the active social life on campus—something totally unknown at a German university, where students lived far apart from each other somewhere in town and where social contact among them was rare.

Somehow I was eased into living in America. When I met my husband and decided to settle here, the transition was no longer a major problem. Certainly there were anxious moments such as wondering how I was going to master the awesome moral responsibility of owning a credit card, but I was not forced into the kind of identity crisis which struck a young woman I knew casually. She had come to the United States to marry her boyfriend without ever having been here before, and the considerable difference in lifestyles she encountered must have thrown her into a panic. Afraid of losing herself, she tenaciously clung to everything German and went so far as to import her brooms, convinced that they were of superior quality.

Switching over to the American educational system was not easy. The universities I came in contact with had no idea what my German courses "meant" in terms of credits and grades, but once my initial difficulties had been settled, the more personal atmosphere and the better defined outlines of the American university system suited me and allowed me to remain in touch with German culture by taking first an MA in German literature and later a PhD in Linguistics.

Now, as a teacher, I keep up contact with my native country through newspapers and books—for example a small group made up of colleagues from different universities in the area regularly meets to discuss recent German literary works. While I can no longer go to the opera as often as I would like to, I can listen to records or the radio, and my husband and I manage to visit Germany occasionally. While the general outline of our life is American, we both love a German touch here or there—from our imported china and crystal, and the carefully preserved wrapping paper that comes with presents from overseas, to the obligatory advent wreath made of pine twigs and decorated with real candles that used to mark the beginning of the Christmas season when I was a child. My mother would bake Lebkuchen and other specialties, and on the first Sunday of Advent we would gather round the table, sing our familiar Christmas songs, munch on nuts and cookies and dream of December twenty-fourth, when the Christchild would bring our presents. Now I hope to keep these traditions alive for my own little girl. Maybe she too will grow up speaking two languages and loving two cultures.

It is in the area of language that I myself feel a sense of change and even loss most vividly. With the years it is inevitable that the native language suffers. Memories fade, words slip away, English phrases often intrude and translate themselves literally in inappropriate spots, new areas of knowledge are no longer covered by available German vocabulary. On rereading my Master's theses, which is written in German, one or two years after it had been put together, I was embarassed to find that I had at one point written "in 19 . . ," a literal rendering of the English phraseology, but incorrect German, since there no preposition is used with this kind of time expression. I find it nearly impossible to tell my mother what I am doing in Linguistics, since I do not have the necessary German vocabulary for that particular field, but on the other hand I still do all my mathematics in German, since I have never taken math or science courses in English.

I find that having grown up with German even now shapes the way I react to certain situations. The easy familiarity of being addressed and addressing everybody with "you" can be charming, but at times also annoying. There are times where I yearn for the more formal "polite form" of address that exists in German and the almost imperceptible distance it can create between you and another person. I still find the manner of being addressed by my first name in doctors' offices jarring. Since I am not able to reciprocate by calling the doctor by *his* first name I am—seen from the German vantage point—put into the position of a child who is addressed with "du" while having to call the other person "sie." I got particularly allergic to the gynecologist's office while I was expecting a baby—this particular practice always made me feel like an unwed teenage mother.

On the whole, however, coming to America has given me the freedom to build up an existence unobstructed by the expectations that people had in me since childhood. I doubt that even if I had stayed in Germany I would have become a typical "Hausfrau," concerned only with "Kinder, Kuche and Kirche." My mother had all her life envied women who had careers outside the home, even though she herself was the marvellous housewife par excellence, and she always stressed to me how important it was to be able to be on your own. Too many German women of her generation had seen their lives radically changed by losing their husbands in the war. Nevertheless, coming to the United States opened up possibilities that I would have hardly found in Germany. "The American university atmosphere with its smaller classes and closer contact with one's teachers was so completely different from the impersonal mass production spirit of the German system and the aloofness of its professors that it gave me impetus and courage to explore possibilities and develop talents I had hardly known to exist." Thus, I have been able to get the best of two worlds.

THE NORWEGIAN-AMERICAN IMMIGRANT GIRL AND MORALITY

In a Norwegian-American novel a newly arrived girl learned that the young women of immigrant families had to maintain higher moral codes than those of the same age in the old country. She also learned that when one of these girls had an illegitimate baby, the father was "never the son of a Norwegian immigrant, but someone of another nationality—or a Norwegian newcomer.* A wise old woman tried to teach her motherless granddaughter about the reticence, even hypocrisy about sex in Dakota several generations ago:

> There are good mothers in this town who are quick with their tongues about the young, but conceived themselves before their marriage vows . . . I do not mean to frighten you, but who will talk about such things when I am gone? Time runs through my fingers like sand in the sea. I am of the old country, where even the young saw birth and death, and knew the stuff of which our stormy lives are made."

*Waldemar Agar, *Paa veien til smeltepotten.* (Eau Claire, Wisc., 1917), p. 160. Found in Dorothy Burton Skärdal's well-detailed, thought-provoking study of the Scandinavian experience through literature entitled *The Divided Heart* (University of Nebraska Press, 1974), p. 237. (I am grateful to Professor H. Arnold Barton for suggesting Skärdal's work for this anthology.) Two letters from Barton's book, *Letters from the Promised Land, Swedes in America,* 1840–1914 (University of Minnesota Press, and Swedish Pioneer Historical Society, 1975) are in *The Immigrant Experience Unit.*

NO PROBLEMS OR PROTESTS: I LIKE THE LIFESTYLE

Avril Sutin

I left Dover aboard the Queen Mary on April 4, 1956, my twenty-seventh birthday, filled with excited anticipation; my American fiancé would, his telegram had assured me, be waiting "with open arms" when we docked in New York. I had not seen him for over a year but was confident and enthusiastic at the prospect of our future together in the United States. The Cunard Company hospitably provided an excellent dinner for the guests of departing passengers, and as we ate I repeatedly assured my anxious parents that if I had any doubts about my future happiness I would unhesitatingly, and with no feeling of failure, return home. The assurance was insincere as I inwardly rejected such a possibility. Nevertheless, I promised them that for this reason I would not arrange the wedding too quickly; my aunt, concerned but cynical, advising in counterpoint a speedy ceremony before my fiancé could change his mind. The strain of parting was diminished as soon as I knew that my parents would visit us when I was settled, and so, as soon as the great liner had pulled out to sea, and we had waved each other out of sight, I was filled with excitement and an unreserved optimism that, in retrospect, seems surprising, if not dim-witted.

Expectations seems too defined a word for the vague conceptions or misconceptions that floated in my mind about the United States. They were born of a miscellany of unrelated memories. During the war a large luxury hotel near where I was living had been requisitioned to provide "rest and relaxation" for American soldiers, white American soldiers. Our pleasant seaside town was off limits to the Negro troops at the request of the United States Army, reportedly to "avoid trouble." "Trouble" was illustrated by stories of fights resulting from racial tensions within the American army. As a teenage girl brought up in a racially homogenous society, I discounted the stories, regarding the restrictions more as a consequence of officious bureaucracy, than of an innate hostility which had no counterpart in my own experience.

My mother, who did volunteer work at the canteen, came home with stories of the odd eating habits of men who cut up their food immediately, as for a baby, then ate it with the fork in the right hand, having first covered everything with ketchup. The English hold the fork in the left hand, the knife in the right throughout, and cut each bite immediately before transferring it to the mouth. My friends and I constantly asked to be allowed to volunteer for work in the canteen, but the American troops were considered potential hazards for young girls because, in the phrase currently popular with jealous British males, they were "over-paid, over-sexed, and over here."

One night an American soldier joined us for dinner and brought me a present; a doll. My fourteen year old sophistication was insulted; surely American girls of my age were not still immature enough to play with dolls. I did not believe it, even though, of course, their experiences had been very different from my own.

The war had started when I was ten. My family were then living on the south coast and children were "evacuated" from such areas of potential risk to areas that were considered

Reprinted by permission of the author.

safer. Many were billeted with private families, where some were welcomed and some were not. For a short time I attended a boarding school in the country, and then my mother took me with her to my grandparents' house in Liverpool. The timing was bad and we were there throughout the Liverpool blitz, listening intently, when the wail of the sirens had announced another air raid, for the whistling of the V.1 pilotless planes to stop so that we could try to anticipate roughly where the explosion would occur. I remember standing in the doorway watching houses flaming streets away; I looked with more excitement than fear. It is extraordinary the extent to which a child's fear can be allayed by the presence of mother and grandparents who spell safety in spite of all the evidence of the senses to the contrary. I do not remember witnessing any panic, and the only times I recall feeling any was during air raids when the maid and I (regarded as prime responsibilities) were shut in the dark broom closet under the stairs. This was supposed to be the safest place to be if a bomb hit; it was claustrophobic and I hated it.

We left Liverpool to spend a few months in Wales, where we were joined by my aunt and my cousin, Janice, five years younger than I. Janice and I would leave for school in the mornings with our books and our gas masks. At school there was gas mask drill; the rubber of these masks fit tight around our faces and was fronted with a perforated snout through which we were supposed to breath purified air. I never could! Awareness of the unpleasant smell of the rubber as I put it on was superceded by heat and a feeling of strangulation until I inserted a finger between my chin and the rubber adhering to it to gasp in the outside air, hoping I would not be seen and receive the obvious and inevitable lecture. Although others seemed to have less trouble, I regarded gas masks as an exercise in futility, offering a choice between gasing and suffocation; it was, however, an unshakable rule that they accompany us everywhere. At this time a Nazi invasion was considered almost inevitable. Church bells were not rung and we knew if we heard them it was the signal that the Germans landed; at the sound of the bells I was to find Janice and run home with her immediately.

Even though the soldier's gift reminded me that my American contemporaries, further removed from the imminent threat of the Nazi horror, had known a greater continuity in their lives, I was still sceptical at the notion that they played with dolls. I would lie in bed at this time, listening to the American soldiers march on our street, straining to make sense of the command "Hup, hup!" convinced that it had to mean something if I could only hear it correctly.

Other isolated and disconnected experiences helped to form hazy impressions of life in America. At the end of the war a friend who had been "evacuated" to California returned with a stunning wardrobe of "playclothes," bright and colorful, flattering to her developing figure, the styling and fit a world removed from the dress of the British schoolgirl of the time. Until I was eighteen I wore a school uniform that consisted of a white blouse, a tie, a navy blue gym slip which was full and box-pleated below the yoke, cinched at what would have been the waist with a long band, or girdle, fastened in the same way as the tie, the colours and stripe of the tie and girdle identified the school, as did the band around the hat, which ugly headpiece was panama straw in summer, felt in winter. The uniform called for black woolen stockings and laced shoes; make-up was taboo. The effect of the assembled girls was neat and tidy; the appearance of the individual girl was guaranteed to avert at the least the sin of vanity. My school was a girls' boarding school which allowed a few locals such as myself to attend daily. In the evening the girls were allowed to change into "their own" clothes, which were little different in styling from those worn by their mothers. The propaganda slogan was "make do and mend";

that is, be satisfied with what you have, be innovative about incorporating minor changes into your current wardrobe, and, if possible, repair rather than replace. The propaganda must have been effective; my expectations were not high and I did not feel deprived.

The Andy Hardy movies acted out our fantasies, portraying a freer, less troubled environment, where the schools held dances instead of Latin exams, and the complications of dating ritual seemed to dominate life. We were not sure that it was an accurate portrayal, but felt that it probably contained a strong element of truth. A friend had acquired a waffle iron from America and I was treated to waffles with butter and syrup which, I was assured, Americans ate all the time. I thought they were scrumptious. We would spend the afternoon in a record shop, playing record after record, and might select on Frank Sinatra disk, quite different in style from the entertainment on the B.B.C. or at our local music hall. Later I saw copies of American magazines like "Seventeen!" Women's magazines in Britain were not geared to the youth market, were printed on dull paper and lacked all the glamour of the American glossies. The glamour of the magazines, like the glamour of the Hollywood movies, was projected upon American life generally.

When I was twenty-three I moved to London where I was employed by the Head Office of a chain store, Marks and Spencer, Ltd. The following year I met Jerry, an American student who was finishing up a P.h.D. program and had come to England to study. Through Jerry I became acquainted with a little enclave of American students; compared to the British business men I was dating, I found them naive and unsophisticated, but unusually open, friendly and relaxing to be with. Jerry's roommate was always getting involved with girls who treated him very badly and cheated him out of his money; the type of girl he involved himself with would make this reasonably forseeable but he had an unshakable credulity. When propositioned in a notorious neighbourhood by streetwalkers who claimed to be working their way through college, the boys regarded it as quite possibly true.

Fun was more plentiful than money and we would see more shows in cheaper seats, eat the whale-meat steaks still being served in a local restaurant or spend a Sunday afternoon in the British museum. Jerry bought some oil paints, and we sat at the big table in his attic apartment and experiments with still life and self-portraits. We played a lot of scrabble. It was a good year.

Jerry returned to America and when he was offered a position as Instructor in Connecticut for the following year we decided that, as we would be living in the United States, we would be married there. There were some formalities to be gone through at the American embassy; I remember being fingerprinted and being affronted by some of their quite reasonable questions—"Ever been married before?"—"No!"—"Any children?" Finally I was on the "Queen Mary," eating my trousseau tight with a congenial group of tablemates selected from single young people like myself.

Jerry was waiting as we disembarked and, after out long parting, it was good to be together again. As we drove to his parents' home upstate New York I was fascinated by the unfamiliar design of the houses and their frame construction; comparable homes in England would be of brick and two-story and probably semi-detached, the right half of the building being self-contained for one family and the left half self-contained for another. The welcome that I received could not have been warmer, and I was immediately and without reserve incorporated into the household. We stayed a few days; I met family unto the third and fourth generation and was welcomed by all with an immediate and encompassing acceptance. I have wondered how many of my countrymen in the same position, would without hesitation, have projected and sustained the wholehearted warmth and affection with which they welcomed a complete stranger into their family. While there would obviously be great variations between one family and another in each country, I suspect I might have met from an English family some barrier of reserve in the same situation, even if it were only in the mode of communication and not in the feeling behind it.

We left New York for professional meetings in Atlantic City, New Jersey, where it was striking to see substituting for the concrete "front" or "prom" (promenade) of an English seaside a "boardwalk," quite literaly a walk made of planks. In the hotel, following English custom, I left my shoes for cleaning outside the door of my room. Jerry saw them and insisted I take them in again; it seemed very odd that shoe cleaning was not a part of American hotel service. I had seen other examples: gas station attendants who would automatically wash the windshield of each car. I was introduced to the pleasures of steamed clams and corn-on-the-cob in a restaurant where waiters gave us huge bibs to put around our necks. After a few days we had to fly to Los Angeles where we would spend the final two months of Jerry's fellowship, and where I would live with a girl who was a friend of Carmine, Jerry's former roommate.

Carmine and his bride met us at the airport and took us to lunch at a Mexican restaurant. It was pointed out that my selection was very "hot" and to my innocent ear this sounded good. Stubbornly I insisted that it was delicious, as my eyes watered. Food was frequently a novelty in those days; a first pizza, a first avocado, a first barbecue, a first ice cream soda. I was used to a less varied and more predictable diet. Although today in England foreign, and in particular Indian restaurants abound, in those days English families invariably had their well-done "joint," of roast of beef, for mid-day, dinner every Sunday, with Yorkshire pudding, roast potatoes and a green vegetable. On Monday the left-over roast would be sliced cold and served with salad or made into Shepherd's pie, ground and mixed with sauteed onions and left-over gravy then baked, sandwiched between layers of mashed potatoes. Fish, particularly fried fish, and chips (french fries), were a popular part of the menu; in fact we liked, as a British play of a few years ago suggested, "Chips with Everything." As we were cholesterol-conscious, eggs with limp bacon were for many people a daily breakfast; the bacon would have been considered ruined if it were crisped in the American fashion. Tomatoes were very often broiled or fried, baked beans were served on toast, welsh rarebit (a creamed dish of melted cheese flavoured with mustard and served on toast) was a favourite lunch, and popular supper were big thick tasty pork sausages with mashed potatoes (colloquially bangers and mash). Meat pies were very popular; the hot steak and kidney pie or the cold pork pie that often contained hardboiled eggs. We sloshed custard sauce over most of our deserts (which we called "sweets"), and had a variety of cookies (which we called "biscuits"), and cakes to serve with the tea that British children started to drink, mixed with lots of milk, from the age of two or three. A properly made cup tea for each cupful; the water poured over this four or five times a day, was a deprivation from which I was suffering withdrawal symptoms. By a properly made cup of tea I mean that the pot should be rinsed with boiling water before putting in a spoon of tea for each cupful; the water poured over this should be at a full boil and it should be allowed to rest or "steep" long enough to extract the full strength and flavour. Today in England tea bags are fashionable, but they still use water that is at a full boil and that makes all the difference. Portions were always much smaller in England. In American portions were, to my eye, gigantic, especially portions of meat; to someone brought up to consider waste sinful, the monstrous servings offered the alternative of feeling uncomfortable physically or mentally. In spite of this, and my initial Mexican lunch, I thoroughly enjoyed the opportunity to sample a great variety of new foods in California.

From my stay in Los Angeles I retain a kalaeidescope of impressions. I was conscious of the lavishness of material possessions and appalled by how little they were appreciated; a record would be selected from an immense collection, played on superb stereophonic equipment, and then everyone would talk through it. The records, the equipment were commonplace and could be taken for granted, they were not a rarity to be prized. I was surprised by women the age of my mother who wore trousers to entertain guests. I realize now that even older American women felt free to dress and act in a youthful and informal manner, and perhaps this was especially true in California. After twenty-one years I thoroughly appreciate that I can take advantage of this more relaxed attitude. It took time, however, for my experience of what was "dignified" for a mature lady (somehow that seemed important in those days) and what was appropriate for a given occasion, to blend with the situation as I found it. At times terminology could be confusing. One of my more embarrassing memories is of a barbecue party; when I pressed Jerry to explain what this was, he ill-advisedly described it as a garden party. With an English garden party in mind I was the only embroidered silk dress slinking uncomfortably amongst the shorts.

After the English climate the bright sunny skies were a delight. In May, just hours from the sunshine of Los Angeles, we were in the huge redwood forests of Sequoia where snow lay on the ground and we stood pygmy sized against the massive trees. The evening we returned from Sequoia we were given a bridal shower. To say it was a surprise is an understatement. It was a large gathering. Showers (of the gift-giving variety) were unknown in England, and that all these people, most of whom I did not know, should be giving us beautiful and expensive gifts seemed incredible. A hand-mixer might have been a commonplace in an American kitchen, but for an English housewife it would be a real luxury.

The American reputation for generosity seemed richly deserved. I found that no-one took walks; legs were used for locomotion via brake and accelerator pedals. Jerry taught me to drive in a few death-defying trips on busy freeways, and my ineptitude was rewarded by the city of Los Angeles with a license to commit vehicular mayhem. For a long time, especially when distracted or tired, instinct drew me to the left side of the road, British-fashion, and often threatened me with sinister results. It was a novelty to eat hamburgers in the car and to see movies in the car too, but for many years I was quite seriously frustrated by the inevitability of the automobile and the impossibility of having easy access by bus or on foot to shops, libraries, places of entertainment, or to the homes of many of my friends. Before we left Los Angeles, we put a bar over the back seat to hold our clothing, loaded all our possessions, and with our closest friends set out for the city hall to be married.

At the city hall there was a short wait while the judge concluded some divorce proceedings. A civil ceremony in England would be conducted by the Registrar of Births, Marriages and Deaths; he is not a judge, and, as divorces would be carried out in a court of law, the couples a Registrar marries are not at that time brought face to face with the evidence of marital failure. The most memorable part of our contact with the judge was when he told us that marriage was a serious step not to be taken precipitously and we should think long hard before entering into it; before we had quite assimilated that profundity, we found that we were half way through the ceremony. After breakfast at a restaurant with the evocative name of "The Fox and Hounds" we started our trip back across the country to New York for a religious wedding at the home of Jerry's parents. Once united, both in the eyes of the State and the eyes of God, we were off to Connecticut to set up housekeeping and, in due course, to produce two new infant American citizens.

As must by now be clear, my experience as an immigrant was remarkably free of problems, I have nothing against which to protest and, while retaining a love for my native home, England, which I visit as often as I can, I would not willingly relinquish the lifestyle to which I have become accustomed in my adopted country, America.

THE NEW COLOSSUS

Emma Lazarus

Emma Lazarus (1849-1887) was born into a wealthy New York family of Sephardic ancestry, and lived there during her thirty-eight years. Before her early death, she wrote poems which brought her to the attention of Ralph Waldo Emerson and other gifted writers. This verse, "The New Colossus" expressed her devotion to America as a haven for the oppressed. Written in response to the waves of East European Jewish immigrants, she wrote this poem which was cast in bronze and placed at the base of the Statue of Liberty.

> Not like the brazen giant of Greek fame,
> With conquering limbs astride from land to land,
> Here at our sea-washed, sunset gates shall stand
> A mighty woman with a torch, whose flame
> Is the imprisoned lightning, and her name
> Mother of Exiles. From her beacon-hand
> Glows world-wide welcome; her mild eyes command
> The air-bridged harbor that twin-cities frame.
>
> "Keep, ancient lands, your storied pomp!" Cries she,
> With silent lips. "Give me your tired, your poor,
> Your huddled masses yearning to breathe free,
> The wretched refuse of your teeming shore.
> Send these, the homeless, tempest-tost to me.
> I lift my lamp beside the golden door!"

From Emma Lazarus, SONGS OF A SEMITE, 1882, in A HISTORY OF THE JEWS IN THE UNITED STATES, edited by Rabbi Lee J. Levinger, Union of American Hebrew Congregations, Cincinnati, 1952.

308 The Immigrant Experience

THE CROWING OF THE RED COCK

Emma Lazarus

Her concern for the Russian pogroms of 1881 is evident in this poem, since she worked as a philanthropist and organized relief for persecuted Jews immigrating to the United States from Czarist oppression.

Across the Eastern sky has glowed
　　The flicker of a blood-red dawn,
Once more the clarion cock has crowed,
　　Once more the sword of Christ is drawn.
5　　A million burning rooftrees light
　　The world-wide path of Israel's flight.

Where is the Hebrew's fatherland?
　　The folk of Christ is sore bestead;
The Son of Man is bruised and banned,
10　　Nor finds whereon to rest his head.
　　His cup is gall, his meat is tears,
　　His passion lasts a thousand years.

Each crime that wakes in man the beast
　　Is visited upon his kind,
15　　The lust of mobs, the greed of priest,
　　The tyranny of kings, combined
　　To root his seed from earth again;
　　His record is one cry of pain.

When the long roll of Christian guilt
20　　Against his sires and kin is known,
The flood of tears, the life-blood spilt,
　　The agony of ages shown,
　　What oceans can the stain remove,
　　From Christian law and Christian love?

25　　Nay, close the book; not now, not here,
　　The hideous tale of sin narrate,
Reechoing in the martyr's ear,
　　Even he might nurse revengeful hate,
　　Even he might turn in wrath sublime,
30　　With blood for blood and crime for crime.

Coward? Not he, who faces death,
Who singly against worlds has fought,
For what? A name he may not breathe,
For liberty of prayer and thought.
35   The angry sword he will not whet,
His noblest task is—to forget.

TWO LETTERS FROM SWEDISH-AMERICAN IMMIGRANT WOMEN*

Letter from M.M. North Dakota, No Date (Probably Between 1890-1908)

M. M., North Dakota. [Year of emigration not indicated.] From Varmlands lan.

I am a woman, born in Varmland and belonged to the poor class. I had to go out and earn my bread already at the age of eight. Most of what I did was to look after children. Had to get up at four o'clock in the morning with the others. Seldom got anything to eat or drink before eight o'clock, for the coffee mixed with rye was thought dangerous to the health. I got rotten herring and potatoes, served out in small amounts so that I would not have the chance to eat myself sick. That was my usual fare. In particular a corporal of the crown and his wife, who I was with for two summers, distinguished themselves by their stinginess and cruelty. From the military on land and sea protect us, dear Lord! Poor conscripts who have to serve as slaves under such wretches!

I did not have time to go to school very much. I had to learn the catechism, naturally, and that I had to do during the time I was watching the cows or some child. But I was not allowed to neglect Sunday school, for they wanted to drill into us poor people certain biblical passages, such as "Be godly and let us be contented," and so forth. Meanwhile the rich heard, "If your sins were red as blood, yet would they be white as snow," etc. So passed the days of my childhood and I got far enough along so that I was considered worthy of being admitted to holy communion, which is supposed to be a turning point in a person's life. But whichever way I turned things, the future looked just as dark. Still I had to struggle along five more years before I could be considered a proper hired girl and get any wage. And what a wage! And what work! No hope of saving anything in case of illness, but rather I could see the poorhouse waiting for me in the distance.

Then one day, I was then in my seventeenth year, the hour of freedom struck. I got a ticket from my two brothers, who had managed to get to America, after living through a childhood like mine. I was soon ready to travel, my few possessions were packed in a bundle: my New Testament, which I had gotten from the pastor, a bad report card from school, one *krona* in money which two kind women gave me. Thus prepared, I set off with a light heart for the great

From LETTERS FROM THE PROMISED LAND, SWEDES IN AMERICA, 1840-1914, by H. Arnold Barton, University of Minnesota Press, 1975.

land in the West. And I have never regretted that journey. Certainly I have had to work, but I was considered a human being even when I was poor. Have a good home here. Am not burdened with love for the fatherland so I have no wish ever to return to Sweden, and I do not believe many Swedish Americans can stay there for long either. Would be best to get the Chinese to emigrate to Sweden. I remember when I was at missionary meetings in Sweden, how they cried and complained over the poor Chinese and his poor soul, and gave substantial contributions to improve his condition. Best to chase out your poor countrymen and take in the dear Chinese instead. . . .

I am grateful to Professor Barton for his enthusiastic interest in my anthology and for his advice and suggestions.

In response to my letter requesting he could provide some background on "M.M.," he said he could not because "it was published in 1908 by the Swedish government Commission on Emigration in a volume of letters solicited from Swedes in North American to learn their reasons for having left Sweden and their experiences since emigrating. The Commission thus identified the letter writers only by fictional initials (not even their real ones), plus state of their present residence, year of emigration, and home province in Sweden."

"Under cover of anonymity they also felt free to criticize Sweden's shortcomings—and in some cases conditions in North America—with unusual condor." (p. 270, headnote introduction, Professor Barton's book).

From Minnesota, Emma Blom Writes Home to Jämtland

18 May 1915

It has been a hard winter for me as long as the children were going to school. I had five children to have ready, off to school, and two at home, all of them so young and difficult, all under nine years old. But I am glad that they had gotten a good start with reading, although it cannot be so much in one winter. The children began school on 8 September and they went every day until 30 April and will begin again in September. Three of our children will go then, this winter only Mikael and Jenny went, but we had three for other people. You want to know if they are reading English. Yes, I must say in all truth that English is just as usual for us as Swedish is in Frostviken. It comes just as easily for our children to read English as it does for Agda to read Swedish. But we are thinking of teaching them Swedish ourselves. Mikael can read a little Swedish. We are near to the school, only five minutes' walk, it is right beyond our pasture. Here in this country the children never receive any Christian instruction in the public schools. The Bible is strictly forbidden in school, because there are so many kinds of people and so many doctrines. The parents must take care of that themselves. Around here they are mostly Catholics. Our children have gone to Sunday school every Sunday for a long time now, to a pastor, and we are teaching them to read the Bible ourselves. We have books and newspapers of all kinds in both languages and when they have learned everything they are to learn in English, we are thinking of sending them to a Swedish-speaking Lutheran pastor for a winter for confirmation instruction. There are many people in this country who never let their children go to communion school but all our children will go. . . .

"RETURN TO ROMANIA"

Juliana Geran Pilon

The following is part of a diary-memoir written on the occasion of my return to my native Romania in June of 1975. My family (my parents, sister, grandmother, and her son Bandi who suffered from Parkinson's disease) left with me in 1961, penniless, after seventeen years of trying to emigrate. The reasons for leaving were many. Having miraculously survived the war as Jews (most of our relatives had perished in concentration camps), my parents soon realized that no one could be truly safe under the new communist regime: many an innocent found himself imprisoned with no explanation of the charges. Countless were killed. We were surrounded, moreover, by lies and bribery, by famine, by censorship. Ironically, being Jewish and also having family abroad (my mother's father and three of her siblings had come to the U.S. in the twenties) had its advantages: one was at least allowed to ask permission to leave. Romanian citizens were ordinarily denied that privilege, though many escaped illegally nevertheless, defying the many risks. Not that a person who asks to emigrate is assured an exist visa. Concerned that we might still never be let out, and realizing how painful it would be for me and my sister to live in a highly political atmosphere without full allegiance to the ruling ideology, my parents never told us of their intention to emigrate. While they listened to Radio Free Europe, we children saluted the bloody flag of the Revolution. It came to me as a complete surprise, therefore, that we had received permission to leave the country (were, in fact, ordered to "clear out" within three weeks). It soon became apparent that on that autumn day my childhood— and with it a whole galaxy of illusions—was to end, as abruptly as a summer shower. I was fourteen years old.

On my return to Romania with my parents, it all came back to me: our train ride to Paris, grandma's gentle, unanswered prayers, my toys, my school friends (many of whom have managed to escape by now to the West). For me these are, indeed, memories of another self. Yet one main reason for my concern to capture some of the feelings from that return has been to provide a kind of warning: for those who have never left their homeland, for those who have never really shed innocence, for those who cannot imagine the loss of freedom, my diary-memoir is a reminder that there is another side of night.

I

Floating above the clouds . . . we could land anywhere. The galaxies don't require passports: round, inscrutable celestial mythology. Each revolution a question: Where does the heart beat? What makes the comet smoke? The puffs of cloud tease the traveler, familiar as breath, they are the testimony of eternity. I try to take them seriously but can't just now; eternity is so irrelevant from this perspective. Going home, the archetypal attempt. The clouds are a pretext—my mind is infested with fragments of memory, swept together in bits and pieces, not even trying to make sense. A patchwork of impressions; will they fit any of what's left?

I sip my coffee to pretend this is an ordinary trip, from one corner of smug civilization to another. We passed through a dense night, much like the usual but for the proximity of clouds and the curtain of noise. Slowly, there was light, as if to reclaim us. It must be the same sun, the same night. We won't drop into timelessness, I know the signs of voyage. The stewardess smiles tired (no one worth flirting with—she longs for her hotel bed and a cigarette in peace). The trappings of reality.

But still a dream: to have returned, after adulthood, to that familiar language—the grammar of fear, the semantics of ideology. No, it's not the same sun, not the same night. How do we spell the new words? They mean what we want them to mean.

My coffee seems bitter. A bit like Expresso, a bit like that hellish potion we prepared on our trip to the West, our unlikely journey into exile.

*

The train was probing through the mountains, the wine-colored autumn trees, muttering its old song: clickety-clack, you'll come back, clickety clack-clack don't come back, come back, come back. . . . Our few pieces of luggage nestled on the racks were hopping to the rhythmic noise, as if acused. Most of our belongings had been packed away in a trunk, not to be opened till after we have crossed the mighty ocean. A government list had been issued to remind us of what we can expect to need, though in effect impressing upon us what we must do without. Lesson worthy of a pampered Lear.

The Romanian mountains were lavish with foliage, festive for autumn. They made it seem as if we were leaving before a holiday and all the fun was to start after we've gone. But we knew better.

We watched the scenery, paying no attention to the road-signs—there would be no need to remember. Soon we'd have to learn to spell other, more exotic geographical landmarks. Each foreign word is a lot like the name of a new town: mysterious at first, symbolic of a whole galaxy of relations, it intimidates, then becomes as familiar as the inhabitants themselves, friendly and so evident that no other group of sounds seems quite as appropriate.

While passing through the Transylvanian countryside, mother cried silently, thinking about home, unable still to accept the nomadic turn. No one said anything. Nor did we comfort her. Or blame her. Maybe we didn't have the courage to take her pain for real—each had his own terror to confront. Silence seemed better than confusion even if its price was loneliness— paid in emotional currency we could ill afford. Huddled together, we felt less sorry for one another than for ourselves. This was it: the road. And every one of us was convinced of being the least equipped to comprehend it, most vulnerable.

Once across the border into Austria, the mountains became less cluttered with leafy beauty, valleys were broader, homes cleaner. Small houses everywhere, with fresh laundry innocently, invitingly, drying in the yard. Why, to think that an individual family could have a little house like that all to itself! The serenity of these immaculate dwellings contrasted sharply with the lurking anxiety ticking like a persistent bomb inside each of us. Where were we headed? Why didn't we just stop right there, at the next small village? After all, Austria looked like a free enough country. And then we wouldn't have to go so far, so damn far!

The wooden benches were hard—we were riding in an old train, the same kind of train we always took to grandma's house except this time we spent a couple of nights in it. We discovered that it's very uncomfortable to lie (let alone fall asleep) on these ancient benches, even when you're tired. Grandma and uncle Bandi were in adjacent sleeping cars, where we visited them a few times during the trip. They didn't seem to be able to rest very much either. Actually, the benches didn't bother us for long, since the noise, the smell, the romance of transition, together conspired to create a vaguely picturesque atmosphere. And besides, sleeping little made us all feel a bit drunk or drugged or slightly mad so at times the trip kept floating inside the brain like an illusion, an uninvited hallucination.

My father was closest to reality, or in any case looked most lucid. He was preoccupied, or tried to be, and relieved too, after signing so many papers, bribing right and left, while making sure the bribe was appropriate, surreptitious enough, and undisclosed, to prevent a last selfish or envious political knife-wound. He must have been concerned about us, suspecting secret fear in our excitement, though sensing as well a healthy residue of courage not tested so rudely before. We could tell he was proud of his two little daughters, and that made things easier because it somehow gave us a sense of responsibility. But in fact we worried a bit too, not knowing if his pride was really justified. By way of reassurance, we pretended to be calm.

There was lots to eat; we had brought salami and chocolate from Romania. But it all tasted like plaster—perhaps because our stomachs had been so violently abused, or because the quality of this sustenance was below any sensible requirements of human consumption. The chocolate was made with a very unusual ingredient—we wondered about it being a cereal. As for the Expresso coffee—there was nothing quite like it. The bitterness is still with me. It's very hard to say why we ate at all, really; on that trip, we were not in the least hungry.

*

I sip my coffee again. It's cold. I notice the stewardess's polite impatience—she must clear the tables before landing. I hand her the cup with apologies for my distraction, and adjust my seat-belt. I don't look out the window, still pretending. It had been easier to come to believe, through the years, that home is where your toothbrush rests, a metaphor at best. And yet, as the plane confronts the ground with the familiar jolt, I awaken: this is my motherland, the Socialist Republic of Romania.

II

The tired Americans parade one by one before the stern customs officials. No one says anything to us, as if our very presence were an implicit insult. Passports are stamped without even a glance. I examine the man who will check my papers: fortyish, suntanned but very tired looking, he barely nods at the people passing by. A stern if not ferocious Cerberus jealously guarding the dwelling of a caste none of us intends to molest, he will not acknowledge those who enter. His thoughts are made of granit; no one dares to address him unless asked to confirm the trivial essentials in the passport. How little blood must run through the grooves of his spongy brain. . . . Have those circumvolutions of the imagination, thin channels of the mind, dried too soon? And where do they lead? The labyrinth might reveal another House of

Shadows, yet Cerberus cannot conceive; he stamps papers automatically. His fixed gaze seems to count corpses, not men. Not women. I watch his moist lips, tightened, clenched like a fist. Perhaps he will say something when he notices I was born in Bucharest. Do I hope for a greeting, a smile, a human sign? In vain. Unwise of me to try to forget that these men cannot smile. We are the "enemies," the capitalists whose money they need, whose women they worship, whose luxuries they envy, but whom they must shun. The sunburnt official's lips are cold with secret burning—were he bold enough to awaken, this tamed Cerberus would howl to the skies. But the skies are dark blue, empty of meteors; the price is high for howling. I pick up my bag and pass beyond the gates.

Those gates! How mighty and awful they seem when you happen to be on the wrong side! All the things, small and not so small, they don't allow through! Photographs: twenty per person. No unnecessary trinkets, jewels, or diaries. Not even toys.

No toys. I couldn't rescue my small collection of amusement tools. However few, they had served their purpose as well as any pampered American child's treasure, and even a trifle better.

*

The first toy I owned was a life-size dachsund with fur made of burgundy-colored velvet. He wasn't soft enough nor did he look friendly enough to be played with, at first; but he was held in high esteem and, as I grew older, he participated in my games. Dolls (my favorite) I had two: first Nina (whose natural-looking hair became inexplicably more unnatural as I desperately tried combing it to restore its original shine); then Karen (with eyes that closed when she laid on her back—a feature I had long wanted in a doll). The names themselves are of some significance—"Nina" reflecting my early Russophile brainwashing, "Karen" expressing a barely conscious protest.

Dolls were lots of fun: to make clothes for, to talk to, to put to sleep, to sleep with. I didn't even consider whether they were ugly or pretty, too small or too old. As companions, my dolls were fully satisfying. The idea of throwing them out in favor of more expensive, better attired ones, was out of the question. Until my real sister arrived, when I was six, they were my silent, gentle, understanding toy-sisters.

*Besides Daki and the dolls, I had two other toy items: my sand pail and Little Bear. The sand pail served for sand dunes we called "castles." Every day I would go to the park across the street to make my little mountains. The sand had to be slightly moist, but not too wet, for the mold to come out right. After eagerly stuffing the pail with the proper ingredient, I would rapidly turn it over then watch the "castle" emerge, very slowly: imperfect every time. Since the next one **had** to be flawless, the attempts were endless and invariably exciting.*

Yet it was Little Bear who became first and foremost among my toy-friends. When offered to me by close family friends, Little Bear had already spent twenty five years as companion to their daughters (now married, with children of their own). His most remarkable quality was that, when turned on his tummy, Little Bear growled. Actually, Little Bear was so named only out of affection, for he was truly monstrous—at the time he joined me his size was double my own. Understandably, for quite a while I didn't go near him, just in case he might forget himself and impetuously bite his new owner.

Once I started to trust him, we took dream-trips together: he would lead the way to the glass forests where red-hooded imps lived on raspberries and nectar. We were always welcome in their kingdom, though I never managed to meet their silent, long-bearded monarch residing at the bottom of the lake. I would have had to swim there myself, which would have meant running into frogs and various small monsters. Since Little Bear couldn't swim there would have been no one to growl at them and frighten the evil spirits.

With such trips, assured of his gentleness, Little Bear was allowed to share my world. We both knew that the two of us were very different from the way others, who judged from mere appearance, expected us to be. We thus fooled everyone, on purpose—for I was really much naughtier than grownups thought, and he very learned. With time, then, Little Bear became more of an equal than a toy—partly, I admit, because of his respectable size.

The authorities, of course, did not allow any objects that might have contained some kind of concealed literature or information to be brought out of Romania, so Nina, Karen, Daki, and Little Bear were left behind. Actually, the authorities had been right: my toys were indeed full of outrageous facts, full of secrets and laughter, and altogether enough joy to amaze any customs officer charged with the job of tearing apart their make-believe bodies, their make-believe souls, in search of treason, of forbidden worlds.

*

It's just as well these men don't smile, for I might smile back, implicitly acknowledging an official greeting, a welcome. And I am on no official visit; if no one greets me perhaps I will believe that I don't exist, only the memories of one who has died here. (A ghost haunting its home, the never-buried soul unacceptable to the Dark House. I never had my Antigone, ready to find my limbs and risk giving my grave a name. So when I sing, echoing prior harmonies, those I meet have neither eyes nor ears for me—and I, no rest.)

The custom men's faces look green: the sweat, the boredom, has changed the natural color of flesh. Perhaps they are the ghosts, not I. A silly thought. Just because they think of nothing, dream of nothing, wish nothing, their throats are none the less clogged.

It is very warm indeed. In the absence of air-conditioning, the heat will continue to haunt me throughout the trip, preventing sleep, creating that halo of sour smell around each person, melting the brain to a point of gentle torpor, more vulnerable to flights of reminiscence.

[The pilgrimage continued: we visited our old "house" (a two-room apartment which actually exceeded the allowed living-space for a family of four), the cemeteries, the parks, our old friends. It was hard to get in touch with people by telephone: to spare them a visit from the Secret Police we didn't call from the hotel which was completely bugged, and pay-phones that worked were a rarity. Yet we found everyone easily enough: our friends lived at their old addresses. Even children who had married by now were still with their parents—the new spouse had simply moved in. This practice was usually not a sign of excessive attachment to the original atomic family but an arrangement of mutual benefit. The parents could thereby avoid having to accommodate total strangers (who would be forced to move in to take the space of the child who had moved out), while the young ones would be spared the anxiety of being assigned to live in another city, the long waiting period preceding the assignment, the inconvenience of shabby new buildings carelessly constructed, and the rent which for most newlyweds was too high. But this is to speak only of the physical discomfort. Above all, what struck us was the disillusion. . . . I shall let my diary speak on:]

"It's late, after midnight, ordinary public transportation is no longer available—I must take a taxi. After a long wait, I spot one. The young driver warns me politely that he must get some gas—if I'm in a hurry, therefore, he suggests I wait for another car. Of course I'm in no rush, I'm delighted to find him—the first well-mannered stranger I've met all day.

He's very young, probably out of school—he wouldn't be working "on the side" while going to college (he would need all his time to study and get the best possible grades, in order that the state assign him to as good a job as possible). I ask if this is his profession. He tells me he cannot pass the university entrance exams, doesn't know why. I notice a plastic Madonna, and I ask if he is allowed to display it in a taxi. "Actually, they've given me a lot of trouble about it," he says. No, he isn't Catholic; Romanian Orthodox. Yes, a believer. He was given this Madonna by a foreigner. It occurs to me that there may be many like him who are having trouble passing the entrance exams.

He asks me no questions but I sense a kinship and would like to be friends; I decide to tell him I'm a visitor from America. The shy young man now becomes totally silent. Is he afraid? Does he imagine I don't know I must be discreet? Perhaps he thinks I have forgotten the taste of danger; and probably I have. Maybe I don't understand his Madonna either, my pretensions to the contrary notwithstanding. We talk no more and let the night engulf us both, separately. I feel rather ashamed for causing him any alarm. When we arrive at the hotel I gave him a big tip which he doesn't acknowledge—thanking me quite briefly.

The first thing I do the next day is visit the little church.

*

In front of our school was a beautiful little church, always empty it seemed. Strangely anachronistic, its Byzantine roof out of place among the ordinary apartment buildings, the church was almost too fancy, like an exotic ring on the hand of a milkmaid. I had often wondered what the church was like inside and why it was there, but for years I never set foot in it. Did the knowledge that I wasn't supposed to go inside a church hold me back? The apprehension that if I did go I would be found out and questioned by the Young Pioneers organization? Possibly. More likely, however, I simply didn't wish to visit a building which according to my textbooks symbolized oppression and superstition.

Yet one day I did go in. The smell of candles and incense struck me first: inebriating, romantic, almost too strong for a place of worship. Along the stone walls were many gilded icons, primitive, even clumsy, but strikingly simple. (The nobility of symbol.) The silence, solemn but reassuring, defined the sanctuary's calm beauty most appropriately: to avoid intrusion into the believer's mind. This is his place; mine.

What did I know of this? In truth, next to nothing. The subleties of the Romanian Orthodox faith were a mystery to me, as to my friends. "Religion is the opium of the people." On Christmas and Easter, the school would organize parties—without music or fun, just gatherings with attendance required, designed to keep children away from churches and even away from home should some unenlightened rebellious parent celebrate the barbaric holidays in some religious fashion. And this little church seemed so harmless, so peaceful, so sad. . . .

But who comes here anymore? Looking around, I saw that I wasn't alone: a woman knelt not far from me, motionless, her head buried in her hands. Never before having seen a stranger kneeling to pray, I felt slightly embarrassed. She didn't cry, showed no pain, didn't even seem to sense my presence. Did she take comfort in her prayer? Did she think the Virgin was listening? Perhaps the sainted Mother was answering back, saying something of peculiar importance to the quiet woman.

And to think that I was there as an ignorant visitor, on a "tour" like in a museum. . . . The icons seemed to scrutinize my intentions, tacitly inviting me to meditate. For an instant, I sensed a mute insistence—demanding that I make up my mind whether I would direct the scenery with cold, analytic disapproval or else would let myself contemplate. Abruptly, almost afraid, I left the church having decided I wouldn't allow it to reach me, wouldn't let the temptation of a peaceful infinite cause havoc among my well-ordered, properly indexed beliefs.

Only many years later did I begin to unleash my mind in the silence of the sanctuary. On the campus of the University of Chicago, in little Bond Chapel, I started teaching myself the rudiments of listening to that compelling silence, to hear the heartbeat of the Sun. With no religious vocabulary, I couldn't pray; kneeling seemed awkward and pointless. But the music of the organ could harness the furies in my crowded brain, and clear my skies to a familiar ether. If this be opium, the Harmonies work wondrous tricks to construct the most plausible of truths.

*

On my return to the old spot I find the little church gone. It has been torn down, I am told, and in its place will be a new apartment complex: the school children are helping to build it by working during their summer vacation "for free." I look at the bricks, the frames of these new buildings, the dust, and remember the old church with the gentle icons. Soon enough, all plastic Madonnas will have to be recycled.

[From Bucharest, where I grew up, my family went to visit Brasov—the place where my parents lived their youth, where they watched whole neighborhoods explode under aerial attack, where they saw friends and relatives depart peacefully, credulously, for what turned out to be the gas chambers. To me, however, Brasov was "grandma's town"—a mixture of poetry and delicacy, flowers and warm toast with honey. As we approached grandma's house, we stopped to reconsider: we were almost afraid to allow ourselves to remember.]

*

Someone has noticed us. From the balcony on the first floor of the adjacent building, she is looking straight at us, smiling. "Mariana," I say, "do you remember us?" "Juliana," she whispers.

Mariana is a retarded girl, about my age. People used to make fun of her because she spoke strangely and could make you feel uneasy: with a scrutinizing, almost piercing gaze, she smiled—not obsequiously, but as if to reassure you that she would accept your condescension. She forgave her ignorant critics without knowing why she repelled us. We would see her taking walks then stopping to look at some dog, or peeping through a fence, or staring at nothing any of us could identify. She was fond of grandma and used to do chores for her, and talk to Bandi, my paralyzed uncle who had been ill with Parkinson's disease for over thirty years, since the age of twelve. When Bandi was able to answer, Mariana was delighted but we weren't sure that she could make out what he said—her reaction was less to the words themselves than to his friendly acknowledgment of her person. The language they used was essentially physical: two creatures society had shunned for being unsightly and slower, they kept a reservoir of affection and need augmented by the constant rejections they had come to expect.

Mariana is looking at us with that same intrusive stare. She does remember. Her eyes are peaceful, touched by an otherworldly compassion, as if she understood.

A woman appears at the window. "Come in," she invites us, warmly. She too has recognized us. "We used to live next door, in the basement," she reminds us. "There is another family living here too. We built a wall to divide the house—well, you know, we don't really get along. Filthy people, very. Separate entrances, yes. We broke the back wall for a new door. Please come in." She takes us inside. We walk in, as if under a spell.

*

Grandma's bedroom—really everyone's bedroom after grandpa died and the state reduced grandma's allotted living space to one room plus kitchen—was full of treasures, each with its unique history, however small its monetary value. But of all her possessions, the wall behind her bed kept the most precious: a few dozen pictures her children had sent from America. She talked about each of them as if they came to visit her each Sunday for dinner: she often dreamt about them, and afterward recounted the unconsciously weaved stories as the literal truth.

But her children in fact wrote seldom and little, so we didn't really know what their lives were like. The censors added to our ignorance by confiscating letters containing "harmful" news. The most reliable information came through the occasional packages full of silky-soft, wild-printed fabrics, comfortable shoes with a lining that lasted for years, and tasty canned goods we ate slowly, wishing they could sustain us for a lifetime.

*We knew next to nothing about the United States of America—why "United"? By whom? What "States"? Wasn't "America" the same as "The United States"? How would one distinguish America from its continent? Was the U.S. master of the entire (American) continent, **de facto** if not **de jure**? All that our high school history book had said about the evolution of this big nation amounted to four small pages.*

First we learned that the Indians had been killed off; then little happened till the Civil War broke out over the issue of slavery. That issue, we were told, was never resolved and the blacks are still starving, jobless, deprived of all civil rights. Monopoly is the rule in the American economy, a few producers get together and fix prices, which are prohibitive. The "little guy" has no chance: the poor get poorer while the rich get richer. And in America money rules—there is no compassion. (I am told that even today the amount of information about the U.S. available to school children is essentially nil, and similarly simplified. Those with whom I spoke cannot understand, for example, the concept of "welfare" even after I tried repeatedly to explain it. Why, in Romania everyone is forced to have a job—even if it means laying bricks or cleaning toilets after having finished a degree in architecture—or else be jailed for "parasitism.") At the shocking news that our family was to leave for America, therefore, I couldn't help wondering how we would survive the greedy monopolists.

Once over the ocean it took a very short time to realize that we wouldn't starve. The New World proved eager to have us, to smile with us, to watch the new sun rise. But grandma's little treasures had been left behind, including the pictures of her children—the people who refused to help us come to America, afraid of financial burdens. Although they had grossly overstated the extent of the epidemic, my malicious textbooks had been right about the existence of the deadly virus of materialism.

You knew it, when you saw grandma delirious in Paris, Adolph; you knew you had forgiven her long ago. When you lay dying of cancer you told her once more in your dreams that you had been a good son who had written her long letters and had sent her packages of food during the war. You knew she always loved you, her firstborn; she still loves you and your family.

I hope she has forgiven you too, Bella, her cold nervous daughter, "our heart failed you in the end for lack of spiritual fuel, I'd say. But it had stopped so long ago of an overdose of bitterness and pain, it's a wonder you lived to middle age. Perhaps grandma had wronged you, perhaps she should have suckled you longer—who can say? You fought her to the end and then you both lost. She could have loved you still."

Grandma's children didn't wish to kill anyone. An innocence hangs in the American air. A dangerous, sometimes charming, but in the end very frightening innocence indeed. . . . We soon came to realize that some of our new countrymen had too many walls to fill, with no room left for dear photographs, for pictures of another world.

*

The woman probably expects us to give her something. But we don't have anything, we don't think of her, we didn't know she would be here. And even if we had, somehow we can't be generous, we can't help feeling that she has no right to be in grandma's house—an absurd thought. We must leave right away and avoid looking at those weeds, this disaster that used to be the loveliest, richest garden in the neighborhood. We must run out and never, never come back.

[Our journey to Romania brought back so many memories, it seemed that we were walking on dream-ground. But we also realized that we were looking at America as well, and wondering about its comfortable indifference. . . .]

We return to Bucharest for the journey back to America. The detour to Brasov, like a brief nightmare, is lingering on against our will.

In a few hours I will be in Chicago again, and all shall be quietly forgotten—back to my daily concerns, the phallic skyscrapers, and CBS News. Who will believe my journey? How many of my well-intentioned friends will allow themselves a lucid instant away from their psychodelic visions of socialist utopia? Growing up in the America of *The New York Times,* how easily we become the victims of the Idols of the Theatre. . . . The prism of fashion and commonplace will shape the eye, crossing the nerves; it short-circuits common sense and the blackout proceeds to conquer all. The fall within.

My dear U.S.A., World of the Best Possible Hamburger. . . . The politics of catsup and potato chips has ruined our palates. We don't believe in the finer distinctions; government by The-people for The-people. (What-people? Us-people—yous'n-me.) The best-looking silicone-filled bikinis under the sun, one-way ticket to paradise all expenses paid on Bankamericard, what this country needs is a good healthy piss in every pot. My dear U.S.A., you sleep so soundly your Sominex-dreamful sleep. . . .

Look in the Yellow Pages under P for Pursuit of Happiness—we cater to the Jeffersonian myth 24 hours a day, pursuing forever; we'll never go out of business! An Equal Opportunity Outfit catering to all shapes and sizes. (Have a glass of vodka, honey—no taste but it gets to you like dynamite: we toast to brotherhood and Wonder Bread!)

To think that only a few hours from Chicago people have given up on us and on each other, shouting slogans of unity while sharing bathrooms with "comrades" they despise. . . . My photographs are so few, and beginning to blurr. . . .

NEVER THE CITY'S NAME

Lyn Lifshin

Coming early spring
with winter buds still frozen,
seadreamt from Lithuania,

the nine brothers and sisters
and your ten thin years and cold
Boston early March, the weather

just turning. But no words for
telling then. What were the other
reasons later when I was coloring the

crossing—were you skimming the
water sleekly on a walrus or floating in
on a pink gull, puffing like a fat man

or on a dove's wing
flying over all the houses?
I used to wonder but you never said,

maybe remembering a place you left but
never telling except that there were
feather beds and ducks and chickens in the

distant house, tremendous pines.
But all the years we shared the same roof
as if together,

you never gave the city's name
or yourself.

From BLACK APPLES by Lyn Lifshin, The Crossing Press, Trumansburg, New York. Reprinted by permission of the author. (Other poems by Ms. Lifshin are included in Unit Two, TANGLED VINES, THORNS, AND FLOWERS, and Unit Seven, RELIGION AND RITUAL.)

FROM COUNTY CORK TO NEW YORK WITH THE JACKSONS

Enid Mescon

Sixty-seven years ago on February 11, 1911, when the Lusitania arrived at New York's Ellis island, my mother, her mother, and six of her brothers and sisters arrived in the United States from Ireland.

Almost immediately, the children saw their father on the dock. It had been 11 months ago since he had left County Cork with the oldest son Joe to go to America. Tevye Jackson actually had not wanted to leave the home and life he had established in County Cork. All his family, brothers and sisters were there. His wife, however, urged the move. Financially, things were not going too well in Ireland. They had a nice home, plenty of food, freedom of religion, but something was lacking. My grandmother insisted that Ireland did not offer any future for her daughters. Probably, the most important thing was her brother Sol and her mother were settled in America and wanted the Jackson family with them. They had a good family business in America and Tevye and his family would be all they needed to make things perfect. Tevye would be put into the factory as the manager and bookkeeper, so that Uncle Sol would be free to travel around and sell merchandise. Much, much discussion preceded this move. Finally, it was decided. My grandfather would go, and since it would be difficult to leave the oldest son without a father's guidance, Joe would accompany his father. My grandmother's brother, Sol, sent the two one way tickets to America and so set the stage for a new beginning.

How had the Jackson family come to County Cork? People have always questioned me about being an Irish Jew. It was simple enough. The young couple, my grandparents, left Russia with my grandfathers, brothers and sisters on their way to America. Shortly before the boat reached Queenstown, a crisis arose. The boat was out of kosher food. What would they do? Without hesitation, the Zacks family decided they would get off the boat. With no idea or fear of what they would find, the decision was made. The details are sketchy from that point on but a new life began in Ireland. The name "Zacks" was translated, as so often was done, to "Jackson" and so started my family tree.

The Jackson family lived in County Cork and my grandfather has his shop next door. He had started as a peddler and eventually had his own shop where he sold supplies such as clothing, piece goods and linens to other peddlers. He also had an interest in horses and had several stables where he bought and sold thoroughbreds. The Jacksons had nine children all born in County Cork. Two of the nine died young and are buried there.

County Cork was a good place to rear a family. The family house had a beautiful garden and a yard full of chickens and ducks. The children remembered collecting chicken eggs each morning and then standing in line to have their eyes wiped with the warm chicken eggs. Superstition had it that this kept their eyes healthy and bright. After dinner each evening, their father would take them out with a pony and traps, carriage. The whole family could not fit at one sitting, so they had to go in small groups.

Brigit was the name of the maid who helped run the family. She worked for the Jacksons for many years. She and my grandmother did all of the cooking. My grandfather, however, did

Reprinted by permission of the author.

all of the shopping for the family. Brigit looked after the children. She checked each child before and after school. If she found a spot or even worse a tear in a shirt or pinafore, they were in bad trouble. Sometimes, they would climb over the brickfence and hide to escape Brigit's eagle eye. Each night Brigit lined up and polished all the shoes for the next day.

Mrs. Sullivan was also a respected family helper. She came once a week from the next township to wash and iron all the family's clothes. The clothing was boiled outside in a huge pot.

Each season of the year the family had a seamstress come in from the country and make all the clothing for the family. Since my grandfather sold piece goods, the children had a wide variety to choose from. Their parents prided themselves on how handsomely the children were always dressed. The family was very religious at that time and the children all had special clothes for going to synagogue on the Sabbath. The girls remembered vividly how Brigit would tie their Irish lace handkerchiefs around their wrists because they were not allowed to carry any on the Sabbath. On Friday at noon, everything came to a standstill so that the Jewish families could prepare for the Sabbath. The Jews were well respected in Cork. Usually, on Friday afternoon, Father O'Brien would come to the house and my grandmother would give him fresh made Challah and traditional Jewish foods to take to his home. The children recalled the tradition of having to kneel when they passed either a priest or monk on the street.

The children went to Cheder (religious school) three times a week. My aunt recalled one day she tied a bag of pepper to the coat of the teacher. This was easy to do as the teacher always left his coat on the back of the chair when he left the room. He sneezed so much and so hard, that he finally dismissed the children for the day. After class, some of the children told the teacher that Bertha Jackson was the culprit. Aunt Bertha ran home and hid in her room. Her mother knocked on the door and told her to come out and tell her what had happened. Bertha said, "No." Then the teacher knocked on the front door and he told my grandmother the whole story. After he left, Bertha came out and said, "I was not the only one." My grandmother said "it costs money to go to Cheder; when your father comes home I will tell him what you did." This was a relief for Bertha because she knew her father never hit the children. Bertha offered a good many complaints that night. She did not want to go to Cheder anymore. Why was Jean, the oldest sister, allowed to take piano lessons? Why did Jean get to go to Dublin on a holiday? All this to no avail, but at least she was not hit physically.

When Brigit found out that the family was leaving for America she began to cry that she wanted to go with them. What would she do without them, how would she manage without the children? At first the family thought that maybe she could go with them. It would have been nice for all involved. But Uncle Sol put an end to this matter when he wrote that it would be impossible for Brigit to come to America with the family. The very next day Brigit left for her regular day off. My grandmother sat up all that night watching and waiting for her to return. It was so unlike dependable Brigit. Early the next morning a policeman came to the door to inquire if Brigit was employed by the family. He asked my grandmother to accompany him. The children were warned to stay in the house. It seems Brigit in her desperation had thrown herself off the Parnell Bridge and drowned. Oh, the sorrow that the family suffered. They had to send a telegram to Brigit's brother who lived in the country to notify him to come to Cork and claim the body. Sadness prevailed over the household. Yet, even in death Brigit brought both humor and pathos to the family. It seems that when Brigit's body was recovered from the river, in each pocket of her apron there was a live flounder thrashing around. The irony of life and death.

The next momentous family decision was what to do with "Pinky" the family's pet cat. The laundress, Mrs. Sullivan saved the day. She said she would take "Pinky" to her house and give him a good home. So on the following Monday, "Pinky," in a basket, left with Mrs. Sullivan. The next day there were peculiar, yet familiar sounds coming out of the coal bin. Out came "Pinky." All his white spots were black with coal dust.

The next Monday, Mrs. Sullivan was distressed when she came to work. She was relieved to see "Pinky" because she was sure he had been lost after he ran away.

Again, that afternoon, "Pinky" left with Mrs. Sullivan. That was the last the family saw or heard from him.

The next day, the family left Cork to go to Queenstown where they boarded the boat. Uncle Sol had purchased their tickets in America and they were traveling second class. They did not realize how fortunate they were not be crowded into steerage class with many other immigrants going to America. The crew on board the Lucitania were shocked to see Jews, going to America, who could speak English and what was more astonishing was the fact that they had an Irish brogue. This tells you something about the immigrants coming to America. The Jackson family was a rare occurrence. My grandmother sympathized with the many Jewish immigrants in steerage. Every morning she instructed her six children to wait on the deck for her while she went below and spoke Yiddish with the immigrants. She wanted to make sure they had enough food and that their traveling conditions were bearable. They had kosher food, but not the foods that they craved, black bread and herring. But they had to take what they got. Everyday my grandmother saved the extra food that was left over from her family's meals. She wrapped this up and each morning took this below with her to share with the others. She made known the wishes of the steerage class to the captain. I do not know if he was able to accommodate them, but it was good for all to have a go-between.

The landing at Ellis Island five days later was memorable! The children spotted their father, but where was brother Joe? Because they were second class, they did not have to go through the various examinations that the other immigrants were subjected to. Even in 1911, money made things a lot easier and more pleasant. They were detained shortly behind bars while their luggage went thru customs and then they were released to their father, Uncle Sol and their grandmother. Where was brother Joe? Joe was waiting for them at their new apartment. Their father thought the girls looked pale, but my grandmother assured him it was only the boat trip that tired them out. The boat arrived on Saturday. From the dock, they took a trolley car to their new home. Aunt Bertha said in her loudest voice, "we are riding on Shabaas." My grandfather shushed her up. They arrived in Brooklyn to a huge, eight family house on the second floor. My grandfather explained that in America you did not live by yourself in a house unless you were very rich. Bertha said, "All the people will hear us fight," and my grandfather in his gentle way said, "Then you won't fight!"

When they entered their new home everything had been completely furnished. Sol's wife had done a beautiful job. The children even remembered that there was a sewing box on the side table with needles and thread. The table was set in both the living room and dining room for their first meal in America. And there was Joe, already Americanized and very much at home. He told them all immediately that he was studying for his Bar Mitzvah in America. Every night the family all sat down and discussed the day's happenings. This was one custom that America did not change for the Jackson family. And so their new life began. The Jacksons had arrived in Brooklyn, U.S.A.

* * *

And so a whole lifetime, a whole generation passed on.

* * *

One of the highlights of my mother's later life was a return trip to Ireland. She knocked on a familiar door and told the present owner that she had been born in this very house. The lady invited her in for tea.

My mother said the house looked the very same, even the landing on the stairs where she served her brothers a tea party. There was only one thing different. The kitchen pantry had been removed and in its place was a television set. So goes progress. The other thing my dear mother could not figure out was how a family of nine could manage in that little house with only one bathroom. This, mother dear, was also progress.

THE PLEASURES AND PAINS OF THE INDIA-N-AMERICAN ETHNIC EXPERIENCE

Uma Majmudar

"They all say that one day
they'll all go back to India
but the day never comes."

My friend Meena's words haunt me as I flip through the pages of our family album. It tells the story of our life in "these United States" over the past decade. As I show the pictures to my young daughter, memories of friends, places, parties, scenes, flash back.

We first came to the Northeastern United States when my husband accepted the chief-residency at a hospital. We were as new here as a shiny minted coin and as naive as a green horn. How emphatically I told a friend: "We would and we must return to India after five years when our exchange visitors' visa expires."

Now we are American citizens. What happened during those first five years that changed our minds? Wasn't my pragmatic Indian friend right about what she said? "Most Indians continue making declarations about returning to the Motherland but stay on indefinitely."

Was our case any different or special at all? Since I do not feel guilty for having altered my decision, I plead "nolo contendere" here. Without trying to justify our reasons in favor of settling here, I'll just state the facts.

Just one year short of the date of our visa expiration, my physician-husband was offered an assistant professorship at a Southern Medical University. With a passion for teaching, he could not resist this "dream-come-true-offer."

Reprinted by permission of the author.

"Mother and child from India." By permission of Maria de Noronha (Gallman), the artist.

I had been working also as a community worker. Working helped me understand Americans, their lifestyle and customs, more clearly than reading or watching television in the seclusion of my home. Now, I knew from my colleagues about holidays like Easter, Christmas, and Thanksgiving. I began to feel like I was part of American traditions and I no longer felt like a "fish out of water." My mind absorbed every new impression like a sponge and it was here I learned first-hand how to cook hamburgers and make soups and steaks the American way. I learned how to build a fire and survive outdoors in the company of bloodsucking ticks and mosquitos at the camp. Many American expressions such as "going bananas," "chicken out," and "neat and cool" tickled me and added a touch of life to my living here.

Finally, an important decisive factor was a brilliant kindergarten performance by my four-year-old, when her teacher reported that she could read like a second grader and had a very high I.Q.

As we stayed, we realized how this country offers, to all without prejudice or discrimination, a chance to develop one's potential free from limitations, restrictions or taboos. With ample choice and freedom, one can pursue here the goal of a "total life experience." Where there is freedom, there is also a chance of going astray, but we thought we would rather take that chance and live in a world of wider horizons. Mixing with many races and people of different nationalities, we and our children would have an exposure to see, to learn, and to understand the heights and chasms of human achievements, the successes and the failures, the pluses and minuses of the American way. Being aliens, we would have a double advantage to look and compare from an outsider's point of view and select what best suits our background and beliefs.

Immigrants here are always able to have a big bite from the American apple pie. The initial years of adjustment for any ethnic person are the most crucial. In the first year or two, I felt like a bride whose father's home is 8,000 miles away in India and who is going to pieces inside, but who wants to adjust here because she has married the United States for love. With a nostalgic yearning for the past, all she wants to do is run away to those familiar corners and places of her old life: her alma mater, cinema houses and crowded Indian streets; to live where her family and friends live and where everyone looks, speaks, and acts like her.

Literally and metaphorically speaking, there is a difference of day and night between the two worlds. The climate, the language, the food, the dress, the religion, the history, the color, the ways of sitting, the ways of talking, the social standards—all are in striking contrast.

For example, the climates of the two countries are at extremes. Whereas America is a cold country, India can be as hot as a furnace in the summer months, with temperatures ranging from 100 degrees F to 120 degrees or more in the western and southern states. In my hometown, Ahmedabad, the capital of Gujarat State, over 100 degree temperatures are accepted as normally as below-zero temperatures are accepted in the Northern United States during the winter months. India, a tropical country, has a regular monsoon season from the end of July to late September. In mountainous regions, the rainfall is abundant. Schools and colleges close at the end of March to reopen in June.

Air conditioning is found only in cinema houses and big theatres or in formal government offices. Rich people have a room in their bungalows which is air conditioned. Doctors' offices, radio stations, big restaurants and hotels also take pride in owning them. Ceiling fans, pedestal fans, cool drinks and sleeping in terraces help in relieving the terrible heat. People swarm in public parks and open areas to get a fresh cool breeze.

Indians are accustomed to an open-door living. The cement-and-brick-built houses have a flat roof and a terrace on the top, without glass windows or screen doors. Mosquitos and bugs are kept out at night time by using mosquito nets. I remember how much I missed sleeping under the open sky in my terrace and how strongly I wished to fling open the windows of my house when I first came to America. In India, curtains are used only for formal decoration. You can see, talk, and communicate with your neighbors. Few telephones are needed.

Every Indian newcomer suffers acutely from loneliness in the beginning. It is not only the case of homesickness for one's family and friends, but it is that overpowering and smothering feeling of a person who is shut in. In the first week of my arrival, after my husband left for work, I looked out to see some sign of life, some people walking on the roads. I didn't care whether they were white or red or were dressed in a strange manner. All I saw was a parking lot filled with big and small cars. I asked myself, "Where is everybody? Doesn't anyone live here at all?" Back home, I would see hundreds of pedestrians walking on the streets, I would hear cars and buses honking harshly to make their way through the teeming people, rickshaws and scooters zigzagging and almost running over the crowds. I thought that America is a strange country with strange ways and wondered why people would give anything to come and settle here!!!

Even little things provide a contrast, such as the size of the newspapers in America and in India. Even the Sunday edition of the local Indian newspaper would be hardly twenty pages. I wondered why so much bulk and waste of paper existed, but I realized that almost everything in the United States is produced and meant to be disposable. In an Indian household, we would have metal (stainless steel or galvinized brass) plates and bowls for dinner, to be cleaned and reused. China dishes are for certain formal or special use only. Clothes are hand washed everyday mostly by our domestic helpers called "ghatis." In the first few days here, I used to wash clothes daily in my washing machine before I became more efficient as a housewife.

Indian food is full of seasonings, using fresh coriander leaves, coconut, mint leaves, black mustard seeds, cumin, coriander seeds, turmeric powder for yellow color and red hot pepper needed for cooking vegetables, lentils and soups. Garlic and onions are used with green hot chillies. Indian desserts would be a little sweet to most Americans and our pastries are not oven baked: they are cooked on the stove and grill.

Spicy-food-loving vegetarian Indians find it hard to adjust to a bland diet. Now they have Indianized the hamburgers, hot dogs, and chicken as much as natives here have Americanized Italian and Mexican recipes. A friend of ours said for most of us: "If I have to go home sometime, I'd miss the pizzas and pastas more than anything American." It's a secret wish of every Indian that fast food restaurants may start serving "samosas" (snack) and Idli-Dosas (South Indian food).

In an ancient land of thousands of years' history and culture, customs, traditions and holidays play a vital role. With the Hindu religion observed by the majority, other religions like Buddhism, Christianity, Parsi and Islam also exist, with some seasonal and religious holidays all year round. Holi is a spring festival based on mythology. Diwali is a national, annual holiday falling in either October or November, a festival of lights, manifesting the triumph of good over the evil forces and is followed by the New Year. Durga-puja is a nine-day festival in worship of the Goddess Durga. There are thousands of gods and goddesses symbolizing different aspects of Divinity. Our Mother Goddess stands as a protective, benevolent spirit who is harsh in punishing the wicked whereas she is tender and kind to her devotees. She is The Guiding Light, a source of energy and an inspiring force behind all human activities.

Respect for women, especially in those roles as mother and wife, is rooted in religion and mythology. In marriage and within the family, an Indian woman may appear to be playing a subservient role, but in most families no decision would be made without her consultation. An American woman may seem to have more social freedom, but mainly she is striving to prove herself as someone who is more than a sex-object or housewife. As professionals, doctors, lawyers, politicians, social workers, women are more easily accepted, respected and sought after by Indian society.

Because of India's extended family system, children and parents are not always on each other's nerves. I was raised amidst grandparents, aunts, cousins and visiting relatives. Privacy is not only a luxury which sometimes even the newly-wed couples cannot afford, but it is also a social stigma. Neighbors and relatives can drop in any time they want. Each member in the house would not have a separate room and except for the young marrieds, sleeping arrangements on the mattresses and cots are in a large common room. In modern India, however, families are becoming the nucleus-type and more individualistic.

Young boys and girls do not meet as freely and as openly as in America, with no socially accepted dating tradition. Most marriages take place with parental permission if not by parental arrangement. With higher education among women, the marriage date is extended to the mid-twenties. Children of any age are required to respect and obey parents. Now the wind of change is noticeable everywhere and more "love marriages" and separate living instances are occurring. However, divorces are far harder to get and fewer in numbers.

If Indian society has certain social stigmas and taboos, the American society seems to represent the other extreme of promoting interest in sex, resulting in children born out of wedlock and venereal diseases among the teens. Alcoholic drinks are prohibited in some Indian states and cigarette smoking is looked down upon among women and also men in some families.

I have mixed feelings about rearing my children in the United States. Trying to understand the weak points in both cultures and lifestyles, we try to incorporate the better in both, stressing close family relationships and faith.

* * * *

After the first color shock, culture shock and climate shock is over, the second stage for the immigrant begins. Convalescence sets in and your mind becomes clear, open and receptive. Time which heals the biggest wounds and helps the fruits to ripen, also teaches you to put your life and goals in perspective.

I remember how I cried in ecstasy at the sight of snow, torrential silver rain pouring from the Heavens. In no time it engulfed the trees, the rooftops, carhoods, the ground, the windowsills and the porch of my house. I rushed to call my husband home. Watching snow while eating our lunch together, we made our first sweet memories in this country.

The snow also made me cry bitterly and openly in public during that first Northeastern winter. Clad in a saree, walking down the streets in my Indian sandals (champals), I felt as if millions of ants were at my feet. Wiggling my toes and doing acrobatics didn't help except for providing amusement to people. The pain became so excrutiating that I sobbed all the way home: no car and no snowboots at that time. Ignorance did not prove to be bliss.

English, as it is spoken by our highly educated Indians, is quite a novelty for the American listener and also vice-versa. As bilinguals, most fellow Indians use English as a garment for the outside world which they shed the moment they reach home. Our children understand the following dialogue, a result of combining a phrase from this and a phrase from that language: " 'Are Beta, chalo, jaldi karo' (O.K. honey, hurry up), quickly eat 'karlo' (eat as quickly as you can)."

Differences in religion, national and other holidays do not create any maladjustments. Indian associations exist, which celebrate major Indian holidays, show movies from the Mother Country and arrange cultural programs with the Indian community's active participation.

Surmounting the problems of initial adjustment is only a first positive step toward a permanent, happy settlement. In a country where career and personal growth opportunities are plentiful, many professional women feel frustrated. Some women-physicians from India have been turned down by their prospective employers because they are women and because they are foreigners. I, for example, with a masters in education and many years of teaching experience could not obtain a job. A new career has opened up for me in journalism and as a free-lance writer because I was determined to start all over again, in spite of giving birth to a second child.

My career dream is still waiting for fulfillment. Between diaper changes, dish washing, cooking, and cleaning, I continue to write hoping that some day I'll be working for a newspaper or a magazine. My talents of acting and broadcasting are almost starved to death because of the language and accent differences. From time to time, I write and direct plays for the cultural programs of my Indian community.

Child rearing, from the moment of prenatal and postnatal care to the later stages of early childhood and adolescence, is the biggest predicament for Indian-American women. Without one's parents or relatives, a pregnant Indian woman finds herself helpless and nervous. My second child's birth was by Caesarian and I was bed-ridden for a few days after coming home from the hospital. My inexperienced husband had to be "all in all" for me and the baby. Friends did their share during the daytime, but that first night home was a nightmare. Not knowing how to put on or change a diaper, my half-awake doctor-husband flushed the whole plastic diaper down the toilet. Next I saw him frantically floating in a pool of water gushing out of the bathroom!

Raising a teenager is an ordeal no matter who or where you are. Our first daughter has her growing pains and as the first generation of alien parents here, we also feel as if we are on a ride on a "scream machine." In a permissive society with some promiscuous sexual behavior, it is very difficult blowing a different horn. Trying to be conscientious parents, we keep our communication lines open, but we cannot worry about the future because, que sera sera, it is not ours to see.

SEEKING A BETTER TOMORROW
HERMANO

Angela de Hoyos

"Remember the Alamo"
. . . and my Spanish ancestors
who had the sense to build it.

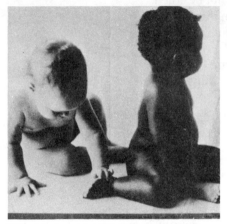

"Black baby and white baby." Art Kane
for *Look* Magazine.

I was born too late
in a land
that no longer belongs to me
(so it says, right here in this Texas History).

• • •

(The land belongs) to a pilgrim
arrived here only yesterday
whose racist tongue says to me: I hate
Meskins. You're a Meskin. Why don't you
go back to where you came from?
Yes, amigo . . . ! Why don't I? Why don't I
resurrect the Pinta, the Niña and the Santa María

and you can scare up your little 'Flor de Mayo'
so we can all sail back
to where we came from: the motherland womb.

I was born too late
or perhaps I was born too soon:
It is not yet my time;
this is not yet my home.

I must wait for the conquering barbarian
to learn the Spanish word for love:

HERMANO

From ARISE, CHICANO! AND OTHER POEMS, Bilingual Edition, Spanish translations by Mireya Rebles, Backstage Books, 1975. Reprinted by permission of the author. (See Ms. de Hoyos' poem "To A Brown Spider" in Unit Four, THAT ELUSIVE IDENTITY.)

THE LOVERS OF THE POOR

Gwendolyn Brooks

      arrive. The ladies from the Ladies' Betterment
  League
Arrive in the afternoon, the late light slanting
In diluted gold bars across the boulevard brag
Of proud, seamed faces with mercy and murder hinting
Here, there, interrupting, all deep and debonair,
The pink paint on the innocence of fear;
Walk in a gingerly manner up the hall.
Cutting with knives served by their softest care,
Served by their love, so barbarously fair.
Whose mothers taught: You'd better not be cruel!
You had better not throw stones upon the wrens!
Herein they kiss and coddle and assault
Anew and dearly in the innocence
With which they baffle nature. Who are full,
Sleek, tender-clad, fit, fiftyish, a-glow, all
Sweetly abortive, hinting at fat fruit,
Judge it high time that fiftyish fingers felt
Beneath the lovelier planes of enterprise.
To resurrect. To moisten with milky chill.
To be a random hitching post or plush.
To be, for wet eyes, random and handy hem.
      Their guild is giving money to the poor.
The worthy poor. The very very worthy
And beautiful poor. Perhaps just not too swarthy?
Perhaps just not too dirty nor too dim
Nor—passionate. In truth, what they could wish
Is—something less than derelict or dull.
Not staunch enough to stab, though, gaze for gaze!
God shield them sharply from the beggar-bold!
The noxious needy ones whose battle's bald
Nonetheless for being voiceless, hits one down.
      But it's all so bad! and entirely too much for them.
The stench; the urine, cabbage, and dead beans,
Dead porridges of assorted dusty grains,
The old smoke, *heavy* diapers, and, they're told,

Something called chitterlings. The darkness. Drawn
Darkness, or dirty light. The soil that stirs
The soil that looks the soil of centuries.
And for that matter the *general* oldness. Old
Wood. Old marble. Old tile. Old old old.
Not homekind Oldness! Not Lake Forest, Glencoe.
Nothing is sturdy, nothing is majestic,
There is no quiet drama, no rubbed glaze, no
Unkillable infirmity of such
A tasteful turn as lately they have left,
Glencoe, Lake Forest, and to which their cars
Must presently restore them. When they're done
Will dullards and distortions of this fistic
Patience of the poor and put-upon.
      They've never seen such a make-do-ness as
Newspaper rugs before! In this, this "flat,"
Their hostess is gathering up the oozed, the rich
Rugs of the morning (tattered! the bespattered . . .),
Readies to spread clean rugs for afternoon.
Here is a scene for you. The Ladies look,
In horror, behind a substantial citizeness
Whose trains clank out across her swollen heart.
Who, arms akimbo, almost fills a door.
All tumbling children, quilts dragged to the floor
And tortured thereover, potato peelings, soft-
Eyed kitten, hunched-up, haggard, to-be-hurt.
      Their League is allotting largesse to the Lost.
But to put their clean, their pretty money, to put
Their money collected from delicate rose-fingers
Tipped with their hundred flawless rose-nails seems . . .
      They own Spode, Lowestoft, candelabra,
Mantels, and hostess gowns, and sunburst clocks,
Turtle soup, Chippendale, red satin "hangings,"
Aubussons and Hattie Carnegie. They Winter
In Palm Beach; cross the Water in June; attend,
When suitable, the nice Art Institute;
Buy the right books in the best bindings; saunter
On Michigan, Easter mornings, in sun or wind.
Oh Squalor! This sick four-story hulk, this fibre
With fissures everywhere! Why, what are bringings
Of loathe-love largesse? What shall peril hungers
So old old, what shall flatter the desolate?
Tin can, blocked fire escape and chitterling
And swaggering seeking youth and the puzzled wreckage

Of the middle passage, and urine and stale shames
And, again, the porridges of the underslung
And children children children. Heavens! That
Was a rat, surely, off there, in the shadows? Long
And long-tailed? Gray? The Ladies from the Ladies'
Betterment League agree it will be better
To achieve the outer air that rights and steadies
To hie to a house that does not holler, to ring
Bells elsetime, better presently to cater
To no more Possibilities, to get
Away. Perhaps the money can be posted.
Perhaps they two may choose another Slum!
Some serious sooty half-unhappy home!—
Where loathe-love likelier may be invested.

      Keeping their scented bodies in the center
Of the hall as they walk down the hysterical hall,
They allow their lovely skirts to graze no wall,
Are off at what they manage of a canter,
And, resuming all the clues of what they were,
Try to avoid inhaling the laden air.

SPEECH OF WOMAN'S SUFFRAGE

Sojourner Truth (c. 1797-1883)

Sojourner Truth, born a slave in New York was a legend during her lifetime. She stands alone among black women in the nineteenth century in staunchly combining defense of her race with feminism and with the suffragettes.

When New York's laws abolished slavery in 1827, the young woman, named Isabella Baumfree by her master, took her own freedom and sued her master for the freedom of her child, who had been sold South, and rescued the boy. She was working as a domestic when, in 1843, a religious vision convinced her to become a preacher and change her name to Sojourner Truth "because I was to travel up and down the land showing the people their sins and bring a sign unto them. . . . I was to declare the truth to the people."

Never having learned to read or write, she spoke extemporaneously. Stenographic reporters or admiring friends from time to time recorded her words such as the following when she expressed her spirited sense of self-worth in this famous speech at the Akron, Ohio, women's rights convention in 1851, in which she created the refrain "and ar'nt I a woman?" into a poetic metaphor for the unique plight of black women.

From NARRATIVE OF SOJOURNER TRUTH: A BONDSWOMAN OF OLDEN TIME, WITH A HISTORY OF HER LABORS AND CORRESPONDENCE DRAWN FROM HER "BOOK OF LIFE," 1881, edited by Mary Derby. (I am grateful to Archivist Casper LeRoy Jordan at the Trevor Arnett Library of Atlanta University for suggesting I select this speech for use in this anthology.

" 'Well, children, whar dar is so much racket dar must be something out o' kilter. I tink dat 'twixt de niggers of de Souf and de women at de Norf all a talkin' 'bout rights, de white men will be in a fix pretty soon. But what's all dis here talkin' 'bout! Dat man ober dar say dat women needs to be helped into carriages, and lifted ober ditches, and to have de best places every whar. Nobody eber help me into carriages, or ober mud puddles, or gives me any best place [and raising herself to her full height and her voice to a pitch like rolling thunder, she asked], and ar'nt I a woman! Look at me! Look at my arm! [And she bared her right arm to the shoulder, showing her tremendous muscular power.] I have plowed, and planted, and gathered into barns, and no man could head me—and ar'nt I a woman! I could work as much and eat as much as a man (when I could get it), and bear de lash as well—and ar'nt I a woman! I have borne thirteen children and seen 'em mos' all sold off into slavery, and when I cried out with a mother's grief, none but Jesus heard—and ar'nt I a woman! Den dey talks 'bout dis ting in de head—what dis day call it?' 'Intellect', whispered some one near. 'Dat's it honey. What's dat got to do with women's rights or niggers' rights? If my cup won't hold but a pint and yourn holds a quart, wouldn't ye be mean not to let me have my little half-measure full?' And she pointed her significant finger and sent a keen glance at the minister who had made the argument. The cheering was long and loud.

" 'Den dat little man in black dar, he say women can't have as much rights as man, cause Christ want a woman. Whar did your Christ come from?' Rolling thunder could not have stilled the crowd as did those deep, wonderful tones, as she stood there with outstretched arms and eye of fire. Raising her voice still louder, she repeated, 'Whar did your Christ come from? From God and a woman. Man had nothing to do with him.' ''. . .

THE BURNING OF PAPER INSTEAD OF CHILDREN

Adrienne Rich

I was in danger of verbalizing my moral impulses out of existence.

—Fr. Daniel Berrigan, on trial in Baltimore.

"Girl's face with troubled expression." By permission of Maria de Noronha (Gallman), the artist.

1. My neighbor, a scientist and art-collector, telephones me in a state of violent emotion. He tells me that my son and his, aged eleven and twelve, have on the last day of school burned a mathematics text-book in the backyard. He has forbidden my son to come to his house for a

week, and has forbidden his own son to leave the house during that time. "The burning of a book," he says, "arouses terrible sensations in me, memories of Hitler; there are few things that upset me so much as the idea of burning a book."

Back there: the library, walled
with green Britannicas
Looking again
in Durer's *Complete Works*
the MELANCOLIA, the baffled woman

the crocodiles in Herodotus
the Book of the Dead
the *Trial of Jeanne d' Arc,* so blue
I think, It is her color

and they take the book away
because I dream of her too often

love and fear in a house
knowledge of the oppressor

I know it hurts to burn

2. To imagine a time of silence
or few words
a time of chemistry and music

the hollows above your buttocks
traced by my hand
or, *hair is like flesh,* you said

an age of long silence

relief

from this tongue   the slab of limestone
or reinforced concrete
fanatics and traders
dumped on this coast   wildgreen   clayred
that breathed once
in signals of smoke
sweep of the wind

knowledge of the oppressor
this is the oppressor's language

yet I need it to talk to you

3. "People suffer highly in poverty and it takes dignity and intelligence to overcome this suffering. Some of the suffering are: a child did not had dinner last night: a child steal because he did not have money to buy it: to hear a mother say she do not have money to buy food for her children and to see a child without cloth it will make tears in your eyes."

(the fracture of order
the repair of speech
to overcome this suffering)

4. We lie under the sheet
after making love, speaking
of loneliness
relieved in a book
relived in a book
so on that page
the clot and fissure
of it appears
words of a man
in pain
a naked word
entering the clot
a hand grasping
through bars:

deliverance

What happens between us
has happened for centuries
we know it from literature

still it happens

sexual jealousy
outflung hand
beating bed

dryness of mouth
after panting

there are books that describe all this
all they are useless

You walk into the woods behind a house
there in that country
you find a temple
built eighteen hundred years ago
you enter without knowing
what it is you enter

so it is with us

no one knows what may happen
though the books tell everything

burn the texts   said Artaud

5. I am composing on the typewriter late at night, thinking of today. How well we all spoke. A language is a map of our failures. Frederick Douglass wrote an English purer than Milton's. People suffer highly in poverty. There are methods but we do not use them. Joan, who could not read, spoke some peasant form of French. Some of the suffering are: it is hard to tell the truth; this is America; I cannot touch you now. In America we have only the present tense. I am in danger. You are in danger. The burning of a book arouses no sensation in me. I know it hurts to burn. There are flames of napalm in Catonsville, Maryland. I know it hurts to burn. The typewriter is overheated, my mouth is burning, I cannot touch you and this is the oppressor's language.

1968

"CHILDREN"

Rowena Wildin

The children of Hiroshima
Wrote angry poems.
If I have children,
I hope that they never see
Bombs in action,
Death and agony,
Or write angry poems
About the wars
They've lived through.
Even so, let me say
That I prefer angry poems
To silent death
Or twisted bodies.

"Japanese-American mother and child." By permission of Maria de Noronha (Gallman), the artist.

From *Asian American Women,* May 1976. Reprinted by permission of the editor of *Asian American Women,* Stanford University, Box 9546, Stanford, Calif.

REFUSE TO BE A VICTIM

Buffy Sainte-Marie

Buffy Sainte-Marie was born on the Cree Reservation in Saskatchewan, Canada. She was adopted and brought up by an Anglos family in the United States. She has been active in protest movements and she is a popular folk singer.

Truth for me has been a wandering path that's crisscrossed all the shades of ecstasy, all the shadows of bitterness.

My heart leaps when I look into the face of my beautiful Indian child, wrapped in the strength of his father's arms: together, we are the flag of North America. We're growing free and joyful.

But the same day, my teeth clench in horror at our history, what's been done to us, what's going on still today, what's in store for us by virtue of our Indianness.

I sing the songs of both our summer and our winter. I write throughout all the phases of the moon, because they're all true.

My country is dying, but my nation is healing up. . . .

My mother's father was a great and lovely family man, and a Cree chief. His name was Star Blanket. He knew Sitting Bull of the Sioux, and so did my father's grandfather, Piapot, also a Cree chief. We are Crees, and Sitting Bull was a Sioux. My husband is Sioux, a descendant of Little Crow, and our child is both Cree and Sioux, and I'm proud of us all—Star Blanket, Piapot, Sitting Bull, Little Crow, our parents, our relatives, and ourselves.

You can take an Indian child, hold him by the feet and dunk him in a bucket of whitewash, up and down, day after day, year after year, and it's still only a "maybe" whether or not you'll kill the Indian in him. You might, and you might not. In my case, a white-dipped childhood gave me enough suffocation to show me the difference between breath and death, between Indian sharing values and white gobbledy greed. Day after day, my white-dipped childhood stuck me with little needles, painful little needles piercing me in places where I should have known joy—my heart, my eyes, my woman place, my sleep—giving me little doses of hate regularly, frequently, silently.

So I became immune to the ravages of hate; immune to the disease of the *mooniyasuk,* the whiteman, the *keshagesuk,* the greedy-guts—though it terrified me.

Because I sleep in fear of the blue-eyed Nazi wrapped up in red-white-and-blue, I will never again be caught napping. Because I was attacked, I learned readiness, but what a cost, what a cost!

The whites carry the greed disease. It kills some of them, and most of us. They need to be cured, but they usually don't mind their disease, or even recognize it, because it's all they know and their leaders encourage them in it, and many of them are beyond help. We need strong,

From *Akwesasne Notes,* Early Winter, 1976, p. 29. Reprinted by permission of the editor of AN.

healthy medicine, and wise native doctors if we are to survive the plague of the *keshagesuk*—the greed-mad unholy gold-worshipers. . . . They've cut themselves off from nature. They dope their children with cornflakes and Chevrolets, and they think they can't live without money. . . .

But their ways are different from ours, Brothers and Sisters. In their eyes, it's all right for them to victimize Indian people, Indian culture, if we stand in the way of their holy quest for a railroad fortune, a gold fortune, an oil fortune, a uranium fortune, a pipline fortune, a cattle fortune, a water fortune, a political fortune, a fortune in the church, or some other kind of fortune, which they will inevitably call ''progress'' to dress it up.

But it still comes down to this: if an Indian stands between a *mooniyas* and his money, the Indian is expendable. The teachers, churches, and courts will suddenly effect a double standard, and the Indian will get lost in the shuffle.

Our advantage is that we are used to living skinny. Even if we're full of fry-bread and beans, fat and gas, carbohydrates and malnutrition, we are skinny on the inside. What is skinny? My uncle, Pius Kiasuatum sings me an old Cree song. It goes, ''Heyo-hey-ay-oh, my sister-in-law, we are so skinny.'' It's a strong, sad song that came in wartime.

Skinny can be malnourished, but it's still alive.

Skinny can be bitter, but light and wiry.

Skinny can be tough.

Skinny can be well practiced in the art of living on nothing, nothing to eat, nothing to dream.

Skinny can teach you who your friends are, which pays off in the long run, if you survive—if you don't get to drinking and doping and wasting away your medicine power.

Skinny can be like it used to be—for fasting as one of the steps to finding your vision, if you are a smart Indian and not a stupid victim. . . .

It's self-destructive to save bitterness. Bitterness is meant to be used. It's part of our long-term vision to understand how we've been victimized, but the trick is to break the cycle. . . .

Scream the bloody truth of how we've been raped in every possible way, and then *rise up and dig the beauty of our people*.

Rejoice in our survival and our ways.

"Adolescent girls." By permission of M. E. Clayton, the artist.

ADULTHOOD

Nikki Giovanni

(for claudia)

i usta wonder who i'd be

when i was a little girl in indianapolis
sitting on doctors porches with post-dawn pre-debs
(wondering would my aunt drag me to church sunday)
5   i was meaningless
and i wondered if life
would give me a chance to mean

i found a new life in the withdrawal from all things
not like my image

From BLACK FEELING, BLACK TALK, by Nikki Giovanni, Broadside/Crummell Press. Copyright © 1970 by Nikki Giovanni. Reprinted by permission of the author. (See Ms. Giovanni's poem "Nikki-Rosa" in Unit Two, TANGLED VINES, THORNS, AND FLOWERS.)

10   when i was a teen-ager i usta sit
        on front steps conversing
        the gym teachers son with embryonic eyes
        about the essential essence of the universe
        (and other bullshit stuff)
15   recognizing the basic powerlessness of me

        but then i went to college where i learned
        that just because everything i was was unreal
        i could be real and not just real through withdrawal
        into emotional crosshairs or colored bourgeoisie intellectual pretensions
20   but from involvement with things approaching reality
        i could possibly have a life

        so catatonic emotions and time wasting sex games
        were replaced with functioning commitments to logic and
        necessity and the gray area was slowly darkened into
25   a black thing
        for a while progress was being made along with a certain degree
        of happiness cause i wrote a book and found a love
        and organized a threatre and even gave some lectures on
        Black history
30   and began to believe all good people could get
        together and win without bloodshed
        then
        hammarskjold was killed
        and lumumba was killed
35   and diem was killed
        and kennedy was killed
        and malcolm was killed
        and evers was killed
        and schwerner, chaney and goodman were killed
40   and liuzzo was killed
        and stokely fled the country
        and le roi was arrested
        and rap was arrested
        and pollard, thompson and cooper were killed
45   and king was killed
        and kennedy was killed
        and i sometimes wonder why i didn't become a debutante
        sitting on porches, going to church all the time, wondering
        is my eye make-up on straight
50   or a withdrawn discoursing on the stars and moon
        instead of a for real Black person who must now feel
        and inflict
        pain

LITERARY CRITIQUES

"Ethnic women at bus stop." By permission of M. E. Clayton, the
artist.

THE ITALIAN IMMIGRANT WOMAN IN AMERICAN LITERATURE

Rose Basile Green

The Italian-American woman in American literature has been discussed previously in terms narrowed down by comparison and selection.[1] For our purposes there is an added illuminating value in analyzing in depth the Italian woman who came to this country with the hopeful projection of becoming an American. However, the difficulty in making this analysis lies in the fact that few Italian-American writers have depicted the immigrant Italian woman effectively, while non-Italian-American writers in American literature have noticed her almost not at all.

Among the Italian-American writers who characterize this immigrant, Eugene Mirabelli has prototyped wistfully the grandmother in *The Way In*,[2] a delicate version of the media-fixed stereotype—the little woman in black, inviting everyone to the table. She is the *Nonna* whom tradition urges the family to visit on Sunday to be approved by her warm, brown eyes. From her corner, she does not participate in the angry vocal reactions to the word "Wop," and she smiles quizzically at the daughter who has been educated by nuns and has become part of the society of symphonies and tea-dances.

Pietro DiDonato, on the other hand, has created a contrasting figure in Annunziata of *Christ in Concrete*,[3] the really prototypical Italian-American earth mother. While stroking away a boy's fears, she forces people, places, and things to form large identities. In *Three Circles of Light*[4] she is the resisting force against the superstition that La Smorfia excites in the neighborhood. With firm conviction, she seals the proclamation that the Italian-American woman remains loyal to her husband, despite the allusions to his mistress. Undaunted, she plays the visible role of the sacrificial moral leader; but her inner struggle is unknown.

Directly opposite to this type of role-character is the creation of the mother in Francis Pollini's *Night*.[5] The reader meets the woman only as she is recalled in the tormented memory of the Italian-American soldier whose Chinese oppressor is brain-washing. The inquisitor pushes Marty's mind back to Trent Street, the locale where the mother had felt enslaved and degraded while crying for the better life she had left in Italy where she had known love and respect. As this becomes a mind-experience for the reader, the narration of the woman's collapse and despair becomes a vivid demonstration of the psychological conflict that tore some Italian immigrant women in America.

In most instances, among other writers to whom one might refer this woman is portrayed in an accepted, fixed relationship in a violently man-oriented world reported factually from a male author's point of view. There are few exceptions like Marion Benasutti's grandmother in *No Steady Job For Papa*,[6] who is the beloved leader of family, home, and neighborhood. With her charming stories of Italian poets, tales she extends with artful flattery to the people of "Back Street," she radiates her surroundings with her spirit, illuminating the weighty rationalization of life and death around her. The delicate nuances of her portrayal are due ob-

Rose Basile Green, "The Italian Immigrant Woman in American Literature, delivered at the conference on THE ITALIAN IMMIGRANT WOMAN IN NORTH AMERICA, co-sponsored by the Canadian Italian Historical Association and the American Italian Historical Association, Toronto, Canada, October 29, 1977. Reprinted by permission of the author.

"Vegetable Stand on Mulberry Bend (Italian section of the Lower East Side)." The Jacob A. Riis Collection. Reprinted by permission of the Photo Library Department of the Museum of the City of New York.

viously to the perception of the writer, a woman who has known such a woman intimately. This sensitive dimension of portrayal, however, is not usual.

One extremely negative characterization is that of the mother, Filomena Faustino, in Rocco Fumento's *Tree of Dark Reflection*,[7] who is decidedly not the strong leader who keeps the family together. On the contrary, Filomena's corrosive subservience destroys, not only herself, but everyone around her. As she accepts her husband Domenico's invectives with a meek degradation of pride that is an insult to all womanhood, her misplaced sanctity disgusts the reader, and her admission of tolerance of her husband's infidelities strikes us as immoral (p. 135). Her husband, in turn, raves against her strangling pity and the choking tears that he cannot tolerate (p. 170). While she places her problems before the Blessed Virgin (p. 185), she never clears the air with decisive action. This Filomena is an exaggerated portrayal of the immigrant woman, who, deserted by her husband's betrayal and her children's independence, has no alternative but to withdraw into dreams of the past.

There is none of this self-obliteration in Lucia Santa Angeluzzi-Corbo, Mario Puzo's *The Fortunate Pilgrim*.[8] Puzo's Italian immigrant woman in America is a transplanted Roman heating goddess who guards the family, especially the children playing in the darkness of the streets (p. 6). Describing her as healthy, fearless, wary, and alert, Puzo says she has only one weakness—the lack of the natural cunning and shrewdness that are "more profitable than virtue.'' Despite this flaw that causes a lack of rapport with her son, Gino, she assumes her role as matriarch and holds the scales of power and justice in performing the duty of living. Informing her children that only the mother makes the decisions in the family, she rears proper Italian sons who are respectful to elders, helpful, industrious, sober, and law-abiding. More than as a self-projecting personality, Puzo creates her as the dramatis persona of a staged ethnic code: guidance of children, control of personal love, measure of honor, expedition of duty, and, above all, the perpetuation of the nuclear family in a dissolving structure of the larger society. However, despite the fact that she is a monolith in her own world, she is a tragic figure. Her children do not understand her when she speaks, and she does not understand them when they cry (p. 242). Hers is a deliberated victory through which the reader's convictions rather than the emotions triumph as, in the end, she rides in the limousine to her new home in Long Island.

Generally speaking, therefore, Italian-American writers have consigned the Italian immigrant woman to a framed role-character, the central position in the family, be it moral, heroic, strong, tragic, weak, or merely pathetic. None of these portrayals, however, has yet emerged as a breathing, life-struggling ethnic presentation. Even non-Italian writers who have created Italian immigrant women in America in their writing have done so from the confined filters of the place of origin of the subject and of the limitation of the writer's experience. A demonstration of this fact may be studied in a variety of works ranging, for example, from Marie Hall Ets' *Rosa, the Life of an Italian Immigrant*, and Tennessee Williams's *The Rose Tattoo*. For the sake of comprehensive treatment, this choice includes one that portrays an immigrant silk-maker from Lombardia, while the other dramatizes a Sicilian.

Marie Hall Ets has given the most nearly representative view of the Italian immigrant woman in America in her remarkably vibrant story of *Rosa, the Life of an Italian Immigrant*. This book has been described as ''the life story of an Italian woman who came to America in 1884, one of the peak years in the nineteenth-century wave of immigration. A vivid, personal account, the narrative is fascinating in its own right.''[9]

Referring to the universal quality in this ''more than an interesting story,'' Rudolph J. Vecoli, director of the Center for Immigration Studies at the University of Minnesota, writes in the ''Foreward'' of the book that *Rosa* has literary as well as historical value. It bears more resemblance to the fictional accounts of immigrant life than to immigrant autobiographies. It is important, furthermore, to note that Professor Vecoli finds that Rosa has more in common with Willa Cather's Antonia or Ole Rölvaag's Beret than with Mary Antin or Bella V. Dodd.

The literary value of *Rosa*, therefore, depends not only on its facts, but on the power of the style in which the story is told. While its historical documentation is authenticated by rich detail, the progressive creation of the character in action engages the reader. With neither self-pity nor self-justification, Rosa shares with us her intimate feelings and psychological experiences. In her own language, she recalls totally an event that she shares with candid honesty and cryptic nuance. Rosa, therefore, emerges, not only as the positive and exuberant Italian woman in America, but also as a dynamic human being able to encounter challenge anywhere.

The validity of Rosa as a literary protagonist with whom the reader becomes engaged is measured by the progressive action through which she is developed. From her girlhood in Bugiarno, where we are introduced to the social and economic structure of a ''silk-making village,'' we understand the various factors that are indigenous in her background: the employers and workers, the parents and children, the priests and the laity, the socially accepted and the ostracized. When Rosa's foster mother becomes aware of the child's seductive maturity, she arranges a marriage for her to an older man who is about to leave for work in the iron mines of Missouri. When her husband sends for her (1884), Rosa becomes one of the millions who emigrated to America from Italy between 1876 and 1926. Rosa, therefore, is as close as we have in American literature to a role-character of the Italian immigrant woman in America.

In this story, Rosa details with dramatic augmentation the events of the newly-arrived from the moment she is victimized by a confidence man in New York to the eventual resolution of being settled in a secure mode of living in Missouri. Her account of her years in Chicago bears apt comparison with Upton Sinclair's *The Jungle*. For example, graphically describing the sights, sounds, and smells of the slum, Rosa refers to a swill box, "It was stinking so. . . . Inside those boxes the wood was all rotten and juicy. One whole box of garbage was nothing but white worms. . . . I don't know why everybody in Chicago didn't die" (p. 222).

Perhaps the underlying factor that makes this account a good story is due to Rosa herself who has a natural genius for storytelling. Ets writes that "Rosa, Mrs. Cavalleri, or 'Mrs. C.' was famous as a story-teller in all the settlement houses in Chicago, as well as to various women's clubs downtown and to classes in story-telling at several universities in the area. . . . And she was never paid. She did it because she loved to" (p. 5). However, since Mrs. C. could read and write no English and very little Italian, Ets informs us, she had to tell her stories as she remembered them, speaking in a heavy dialect. For this reason, the author has simplified the text but has retained the style and character of the spoken words.

It was Rosa's own Zia Maria who gave her the proverbial pat of hope with "It is wonderful to go to America even if you don't want to go to Santino. You will get smart in America. And in America you will not be so poor" (p. 162). This is the hope that sustains her in the bottom of the ship with its rows of wooden shelves where they all must sleep,"—the Italians, the Germans, the Polish, the Swede, the French—every kind . . . like rats trapped in a hole" (p. 163). It is the tenacious hope that increases as they all enter the harbor of New York, the relentless hope that strengthens her at the Castle Garden reception that she shares with her Lombardi paesani.

With the progression of the brutal mistreatment she receives from her villainous husband, Rosa's history becomes a personal as well as a social drama. Santino may well be an excessive extension of a type of Italian-immigrant male arrogance, but his accentuated characterization serves to demonstrate the masculine exploitation of some Italian immigrant women in America. This is the husband who, according to Pep, "Every Saturday night he's pinching . . . bad women over Freddy's saloon. But he wouldn't squeeze the hand of a man—even to keep out of hell" (p. 173). Then, he would come looking for her, cursing at the crucifix over her bed. Rosa, however, was not the stereotyped submissive Filomena portrayed by Rocco Fumento. She emphasizes that "A wife doesn't have to do something against God or the Madonna." The reader admires her more positive concept of religious guidance in which her own strength bolsters her belief. Santino's eventually divorcing her to marry one of his "bad women" proves a blessing, freeing her for Gionin, the man who really loves her.

Rosa is, also, a living testament of the social problem of the acceptance of the immigrants by the established society. While it is true that some native Americans despised the newcomers, others became actively involved in helping them. Rosa informs us that her growing Americanism was fostered by the "friendliness of other Americans," particularly those like "old Mr. Miller and his daughter, Miss Mabel, in the store at Union" (p. 176). "They were the boss of the store and the post office, but they were treating me like I was as good as them. . . . And as it grew cold with the winter they made me come in to dry my feet and get warm. And they gave me coffee." This was welcome affection to a woman, who, on the day when she had given birth to her child, had looked to her husband who merely stared at her and, swearing at this new burden, told her "if I wanted something to eat to get up and get it myself" (p. 181).

Speaking of the compassionate treatment she had received from the teachers at the Commons, Rosa vowed she would never leave the place with which she had grown old after fifty years of domestic work and of telling stories. Furthermore, as the only Italian woman in the Club, she was invited to the English circle, in whose activities she participated, even in the games that included the others, "especially the Norwegians and Germans."

The uncomplicated strength with which she bore her vicissitudes had been ingrained in her as a young silk weaver in Bugiarno. In America, her forbearance fed her indomitable and infectious spirit. In telling her story, Rosa generates the ultimate appreciation of the settled life in America that she compares with heaven: "no man to scold me and make me do this and stop me to do that. . . . I have my house to live and Luie pays the food, so I don't have to worry about the living. I keep my little job in the settlement house, so I have that money extra and I can go to the picture show and see the good story. I have it like heaven. . . . I'm my own boss. The place I've got now it pays me for all the trouble I had in my life . . ." (p. 253).

She has only one more wish: "to go in *Italia* again before I die" where "I wouldn't be afraid now—not of anybody. I'd be proud I come from America and speak English. . . . They wouldn't dare hurt me now I come from America. Me, that's why I love America. That's what I learned in America: not to be afraid" (p. 254).

Thus, Rosa Cavalleri is the Italian immigrant woman in America who has helped to illuminate the path of her compatriots. While she encompasses a broader and more liberal view of the nineteenth century newcomer to this country, she opens the door to welcome others of narrower ethnic interpretation.

More and more, specific people are being treated with increasingly penetrating depth. One that has attracted much attention is Serafina delle Rose in *The Rose Tattoo* by Tennessee Williams. In his proclaimed timeless world of a play, Williams has sharpened the picture of the Italian immigrant woman who discovers herself via her American experience.

Williams has said that "*The Rosa Tattoo* was my love-play to the world" and that "Anna Magnani was magnificent as Serafina in the movie version."[10] We may conclude, therefore, that Serafina is creatively related to Magnani whom the playwright describes as being "as unconventional a woman as I have known in or out of my professional world" and that "she never exhibited any lack of self-assurance, any timidity in her relations with that society outside of whose conventions she quite publicly existed" (p. 162).

The brilliantly animated and expansive spirit that Williams found in Magnani, a Roman, he seems to have drawn into a more restrictive frame in Serafina, a Sicilian. In his own description of the character in the stage directions of Act I, Scene I, he describes Serafina as being "like a plump little Italian opera singer in the role of Madame Butterfly"[11] with her high pompadour, glittering jewelry, French-heeled slippers, rose-silk sheath, and the yellow paper fan on which is painted a highly visible rose. With this characterization, Williams drew from some critics the judgment that *The Rose Tattoo* is better suited as an opera than as a play. In any event, the lines of the drama project the conflict of the Italian immigrant woman posed against a hostile community. Serafina, a paradox of innocence of her own condition and her realistic scorn of mysticism, announces that "Now, them ain't the star-noises. They're termites, eating the house up . . ." (p. 3).

This perception does not protect Serafina from her personal problem as one particular immigrant woman against a larger environment. In a village populated mostly by Sicilians "somewhere along the Gulf Coast between New Orleans and Mobile," she is emotionally and socially detached in her own world as the loving and submissive wife of her adored husband. She proclaims her love for Rosario in a symbol that she declares a miracle—the tattoo on her body that she has absorbed from her husband at the moment of the fruition of his love in her. With such transcendental "wonder of some kind," she is emblematic of the obsessive loyalty most immigrant women have had for their husbands. Her faith is so inviolable that she refuses to believe the gossip around her of the Puritanic tongues that mock her as the unwary victim of the predatory Estelle Hohengarten, who, as Rosario's mistress, perpetrates the man's death. The prostitute's demands on him had led him to the illicit transporting of narcotics, the only choice he has had for added income. The ensuing connections are implied.

Williams enlarges the characterization of Serafin to the general type of the Italian immigrant woman by having her occupy the traditional position as the undisputed mistress of her home. When her husband dies, her position goes with him. Hence, the very faith that she had placed in her husband becomes the projection of her ensuing social degradation. It is only when she tries to impose the structures of her inherited standards upon her daughter's suitor that she generates the conflict of her personal drama. She forces young Jack Hunter to kneel before the Madonna and promise not to violate her daughter sexually. Thus, she approaches the crisis in the challenge of a new American life in action.

Like so many women caught between two cultures, Serafina is the victim both of her husband's behavior and then of her daughter's disdain. The pathos of her being trapped in a time capsule is dramatically symbolized by Williams in Serafina's attempt to give her daughter the graduation gift, a wrist-watch that she never succeeds to deliver. As her daughter goes off with "Lasciami stare!" (p. 28), Serafina embodies the tragic immigrant mother whose only cry is "Ho solo te, solo te-in questo mondo!"

This poignant situation is emphasized by the action of her having to sew all the graduation dresses for the daughters of the other women in the community. Serafina, however, harassed to work until the final hour before the exercises, has neither the time to make herself a dress, nor the strength to attend the program.

There is, nevertheless, an indomitable strain of power in her that sustains her, a carry-over of the first idealism that had wreathed her coming to America. She despises the women around her for "They make the life without glory. Instead of the heart they got the deep-freeze in the house" (Act II, Scene I). Furthermore, she has the courage to confront the priest who chose not to come to her when she needed him, because he had to baptize the grandson of the Mayor. Her subsequent argument with him does not weaken her faith, however, and the dramatic progression continues with her "Lady, give me a sign!"

Serafina's eventual submission to Alvaro demonstrates the adjustment of old-world mores to the necessities of a new experience. The dismissal of her excessive loyalty to her traditional standards as perpetrated by her shattered faith in the dead Rosario is a catharsis through which she rids herself of an irretrievable past. She is now able to welcome a new love and another way of life. Therefore, she accepts Alvaro, but she does so without any of his possible tricks. As Williams writes, she speaks to her suitor "with the great dignity of a widow whose respectability has stood the test" (Act III, Scene I) (p. 116). Verbally, she is American enough even to tell him to "Tell it to the marines!"

As Serafina thus rejects both death and ashes, she is, according to Gerald Weales,[12] Williams's most affirmative statement of sex as consolation and comfort. She has proved herself superior to the scoffing neighborhood women by declaring, "Give them my love; give everybody my love. . . ." (Act III, Scene I) (p. 124). Weales points out that, as Serafina shouts her love and goes off with Alvaro, this declaration of love and life is possible because the characters are Sicilian. However, in the *New York Post*, April 24, 1958, Williams was quoted as saying that he did not share the Anglo-Saxon myth that is so sure that Latin people are richly capable of uncomplicated sex-lives. It would seem that Serafina's affirmation is the logical result of a too-long-restrained complication—an inner struggle that she demonstrates as not too unusual with the Italian immigrant woman in America. This linear example may be applied to many areas of this immigrant's horizon.

In summary, we find some constants about the portrayal of the Italian immigrant woman in American literature, whether the characters have been created by Italian-Americans or by other Americans with sincere perceptions of Italianism. These constants have a few variables according to immigrants from the North or South of Italy; but, all in all, there surface the basic traits of overcoming fixed and imposed restrictions that dissolve before human experiences of a universal nature. A woman who looks to the future must adjust to change. Thus, whether she be Maria Corbo, Rosa Cavalleri, or Serafina delle Rose, she is accepting her challenge, encountering it, and overcoming it. As a result, she becomes a fuller, even a nobler person. This is the process that is, at last, penetrating to the depiction of the Italian immigrant woman as a constructive American.

The evolving image of this all-encompassing woman may eventually super-impose the once indelible but now fading portrait of the stereotype. The process may lead, finally, to the representative creation of a great character by some writer, a character that will contain completely and dynamically the Italian-American woman.

NOTES

1. *The Interaction of Italians and Jews in America*, edited by Jean A. Scarpaci, papers presented by the American Italian Historical Association, November 14-15, 1974.
2. Eugene Mirabelli, *The Way In* (New York: The Viking Press, 1968).
3. Pietro DiDonato, *Christ in Concrete* (Indianapolis: Bobbs-Merrill, 1939).
4. Ibid, *Three Circles of Light* (New York: Julian Messner, Inc., 1960).
5. Francis Pollini, *Night* (New York: G.P. Putnam's Sons, 1961).
6. Marion Benasutti, *No Steady Job For Papa* (New York: Vanguard Press, 1966).
7. Rocco Fumento, *Tree of Dark Reflection* (New York: Alfred A. Knopf, 1962).
8. Mario Puzo, *The Fortunate Pilgrim* (New York: Atheneum, 1965).
9. Marie Hall Ets, *Rosa, the Life of an Italian Immigrant* (University of Minnesota Press: Minneapolis, 1970) Front map.
10. Tennessee Williams, *Memoirs* (New York: Doubleday & Company, Inc., 1975), p. 162.
11. Tennessee Williams, *The Rose Tattoo* (New York: New Directions, 1951), p. 2.
12. Gerald Weales, *American Drama Since World War II* (New York: Harcourt Brace & World, Inc., 1962) p. 26.

ETHNIC GIRLS SPEAK OUT

Edith Blicksilver

There is a euphemistic tendency for sociologists to use words like "inner city" or disadvantaged geographical area," but the word "slum" to most of the people, especially the children living there, means poverty, violence, dirt and despair.

My intention in this analysis is to show that urban ethnic children, if given the chance and a sympathetic audience, have good insights into their condition, separate the illusions from the realities of their home and their environment, and, most important of all, are a neglected teaching source in a multiethnic course or a study on minority problems. Too frequently attention is directed toward the urban problems of ethnic *adults*, not enough concern is given to the need for ghetto children to have an audience in order for them to speak out, express their dreams and hopes for a better life than their parents have had and maybe vent their frustrations before these frustrations are expressed more tragically through violent acts or conversely through withdrawal, despair and loss of all hope in bettering their own lifestyles.

So the voices of children should be heard even if their ability to write is not always equal to their ideas. All children are special and it is important for teachers to encourage them to be freer in their writing and to describe what it is like to be a member of a distinct minority group.

In addition, these children should feel free to speak without fear of being evaluated or judged. They have to explore their ideas and not be concerned about teacher approval of their life style or of their literary work. The more rigid the teacher's requirements regarding neatness, micrometer margins or perfect spelling, the more rigid the writing. In other words, discipline in writing has to be imposed from within because these children have to feel free to express themselves on paper with attention to mastering the mechanics of writing *after* they have spoken from their hearts. Creative writing workshops encourage young people to honestly express their feelings and thereby discover a little bit of what they want out of life, why their family life is intolerable, how they can leave an unhappy urban environment, through self-fulfillment.

One approach in order to encourage children to express themselves is to write one word on the blackboard such as "Death" or "Love" or "Fear" or "Hope" and then say "write." Children can even be told to take their writings with them if it is too personal to show or to read aloud. Once they have written, perhaps just a paragraph at first and then a page or two as their confidence increases, they can either sign their names or not as they wish. A poem is an ideal way of self expression, too. Follow up personal conferences are valuable so that the teacher can encourage children to revise their papers stressing correct spelling and advising them to polish their style. Usually a sympathetic classroom will encourage environmental and honest expressions of internal feelings.

Gradually as they feel more self confident and trust the other members of the class, the creative writing workshop can serve as a vehicle whereby they can read their papers aloud, discuss their problems, accept the advice of others as the sympathy of those in similar situations

Excerpts from ETHNIC CHILDREN SPEAK OUT, Georgia English Counselor, Vol. XVI, No. 18, Spring 1977, pp. 4-5. Reprinted by permission of the editor, Linda Lycett.

and even polish each others writing style. Imagine the pride in becoming a literary critic and having someone actually accept your suggestions for a sentence revision.

If students trust the teacher and the other class members, the writing is intensely personal and fulfills the purpose of telling exactly what urban experiences are like after a certain stage in their lives.

Children can also be encouraged to keep a journal to describe their reactions in a spontaneous way. Gradually they will learn how to stress unity and discipline their writing focusing upon a specific subject. They have to be reminded that even professional writers struggle with the same problems of disunity and evasion. For example, F. Scott Fitzgerald kept a journal in which he recorded situations and observations. Students should be encouraged to write down anecdotes, unrelated flashes of thought or memory, with disconnected words and phrases. Thus, daily writing helps them loosen up and let the images follow each other loosely by association and, most important of all helps them understand themselves better. Indeed, there is an intimate relationship between use of language and understanding of ourselves and of others. Ethnic groups have different cultural and behavior patterns and are influenced by self-image and socio-economic status. In particular, language reflects cultural differences and ethnic patterns as well.

The four categories that can be explored through the writings of ethnic children are: (1) *Who Am I?* in which they write about their families, friends, and school but mostly what it's like to be specifically Black, Chicano, Puerto Rican, Asian American or Native American. The writing is sensitive, perceptive, sometimes bitterly resentful, occasionally heart-breaking but through this means, young people can creatively express their feelings and learn to know themselves better. (2) *How I see my neighborhood* in which they reveal the realities of urban life telling about poverty, drugs, and violence. Some children are filled with despair, others reveal their growing anger, bitterness or bewilderment. But ghetto children have happy experiences, too, and pride in being part of a close-knit ethnic community as some of the writings reveal. (3) *The world beyond* in which children have contact with life outside the urban community through radio, television and the movies. They are exposed to a world in which cat food commercials show people concerned about catering to their pets' fussy eating habits or the jet set vacationing on the French Riviera. Children have the opportunity through their writings to fantasize about money and what they would do and buy with it. (4) Finally, *The Cycle of Life, the world I can't see or touch* in which children analyze their feelings about love, growing up and have a chance to write down their perceptions about God, their fear of dying, hope and joy.*

A few children will write what they think a teacher wants to read, but most write honestly because they seek fulfillment or they want to speak for themselves instead of letting ethnic adults, psychiatrists or sociologists speak for them.

Hopefully, now ethnic children, girls as well as boys, are able to tell about their painful or joyful experiences as they search for their unique identity and as they explore the world beyond their classroom and community. We must give all children, espec ially those of ethnic origins who have unhappy memories associated with their cultural lifestyles, the opportunity to express

---

*Stephen M. Joseph's introduction to *the me nobody knows* contains innovative teaching techniques. (New York: Avon Books, 1972). I have elaborated upon his four topic development ideas.

themselves freely, to speak for themselves. Proud ethnic American children should never feel that their cultural past is imprisoned in Anglos history or that their only future is as invisible swimmers in the American mainstream.

"Young people embracing." By permission of Maria de Noronha (Gallman), the artist.

CONTENTS BY LITERARY FORM

Non-fiction and Scholarly Critiques

Joan Baez, "Thoughts on a Sunday Afternoon"
Rose Mary (Shingobe) Barstow (excerpts) from "Who Was Really the Savage?"
Doras Reed Benbow, "My Grandmother the Wasp"
Teruko Ogata Daniel, "Such, Such Were the Joys . . . George Orwell"
Edith Maud Eaton (Sui Sin Far), "Mental Portfolio of an Eurasian"
Ruby Reyes Flowers, "Ruby's Discovery"
Maria B. Frangis, "An Ancient Heritage in a New World"
Dorothy Friedman, "The Rent Money in the Garbage Pail and Other Tenement Memories"
Helen S. Garson, "Rich Is Better"
Loral Graham, "A Greek Who Bore Warm Gifts" and John Keay Davidson, "Emory's Evangeline"
Rose Basile Green, "The Italian Immigrant Woman in American Literature"
Ann C. Hooper, "The Proper Thing to Say, to Do and to Wear"
Sonya Jason, "The Liberation of a First Generation Slovak-American Woman"
Kumi Kilburn, "No Dogs and Chinese Allowed"
Uma Majmudar, "The Pleasures and Pains of the India-n-American Ethnic Experience"
Enid Mescon, "From County Cork to New York with the Jacksons"
Evangeline Papageorge, "My Father, My Mother and My Greek Heritage"
Arlene G. Peck, "The Southern Jewish American Princess (In the Fabulous Fifties)"
Juliana Geran Pilon, "Return to Romania"
Judith Plaskow, "The Jewish Feminist: Conflict in Identities"
Marie Prisland, "Memories of Our Old Wood Stove"
Rose Mary Prosen, "Looking Back"
Janet Rechtman, "Chanukah, Camp Hill, Alabama"
Heidi Rockwood, "The Best of Two Worlds"
Buffy Sainte-Marie, "Refuse to be a Victim"
Phyllis J. Scherle, "A Trace of Gold"
Rose Schneiderman, "The Childhood of an Immigrant Working Girl"
Eve Silver, "Listen to My Story"
Helen C. Smith, "Eva Jessye: Earth Mother Incarnate"
Virginia Driving Hawk Sneve, "Special Places"
Avril Sutin, "No Problems, or Protests: I Like the Lifestyle"
Sojourner Truth, "Speech on Woman's Suffrage"
Sister M. Florence Tumasz, CSFN, "Growing Up as a Polish American"
Sharon Renée Twombly, "Ethnicity to Humanity"

Two Letters from Swedish-American Women

Letter from M.M. North Dakota, no date
and
Letter from Minnesota, Emma Bloom, 18 of May, 1915
Katie Funk Wiebe, "The Barriers Are Not Real"

Short Stories

Toni Cade Bambara, "The Lesson"
Elizabeth Cullinan, "The Power of Prayer"
Teruko Ogata Daniel, "We Wise Children"
LaVerne González, "Born to Suicide"
Monica Krawczyk, "For Dimes and Quarters"
Grace Paley, "Goodbye and Good Luck"
Norma Rosen, "What Must I Say to You?"
Leslie Silko, "Lullaby"
Mary Elizabeth Vroman, "See How They Run"
Alice Walker, "Everyday Use"
Hisaye Yamamoto, "The Legend of Miss Sasagawara"

Poems

Anonymous, "All the Pretty Little Horses"
Aviva Barzel, "As Red as It Was" and "Pass Over the Blood"
Gwendolyn Brooks, "Ballad of Pearl May Lee" and "The Lovers of the Poor"
Diana Chang, "An Appearance of Being Chinese" and *Two Poems*: "Saying Yes" and "Otherness"
Angela De Hoyos, "To a Brown Spider: En El Cielo" and "HERMANO"
Nikki Giovanni, "Nikki-Rosa" and "Adulthood"
Joy Harjo, "The Last Song"
Emma Lazarus, "The New Colossus" and "The Crowing of the Red Cock"
Lyn Lifshin, "Beryl," "Seder" and "Never the City's Name"
Janice Mirikitani, "Sing with Your Body" and "Lullabye"
Lisel Mueller, "The Cremona Violin" and "More Light"
Nila Northsun, "The Ways/ The Way It Is" (nine poems)
Rose Mary Posen, "Polka, A Memorial Tribute for my Mother and Father," "Chronicle, 1931-1945"
    and "Olga"
Adrienne Rich, "The Burning of Paper Instead of Children"
Marina Rivera, "Chon" and "For Rita Kohn"
Muriel Rukeyser, from "Letter to the Front"
Esta Seaton, "Her Life" and "Explanation"
Valentina Sinkevich, "Kerosene Lamp"
Liz Sohappy, "The Indian Market," "Once Again" and "The Parade"
May Swenson, "Things in Common" and "Black Tuesday" for Martin Luther King, April 4, 1968
Ferris Takahashi, "Nisei, Nisei!"
Evangelina Vigil, "Downtown San Antonio in Front of the Majestic Theatre"
Margaret Walker, "Now" and "For My People"
Anne Webster, "My Father's War"
Rowena Wildin, "Children"
Marya Zaturenska, "A Russian Easter 1920"

A Chapter or Excerpt from a Larger Work

Chisholm, "A Black Congresswoman Speaks out for Women's Rights"
Borghild Dahl, excerpt from *Homecoming*
Laurraine Goreau, "Mardi Gras and the White Flying Horses" and "Black Baptism," from *Just Mahalia, Baby*
Jeanne Wakatsuki Houston and James D. Houston, "Whatever He Did Had Flourish" from *Farewell to Manzanar*
Thelma Jones, "My Norwegian-American Parents' Courtship" from *Skinny Angel*
Maxine Hong Kingston, "No Name Woman" from *The Woman Warrior*

Irina Kirk, page from *Born with the Dead*

Camille Lessard, "Vic's Revolt" from *Canuck*

Mary McCarthy, "To the Reader" from *Memories of a Catholic Girlhood*

Nicholasa Mohr, "A Very Special Pet" from *El Bronx Remembered*

Ntozake Shange, "Toussaint" from *for colored girls who have considered suicide/when the rainbow is enuf*

Betty Smith, "The Ethnic Child and the Classroom Experience" from *A Tree Grows in Brooklyn*

Jade Snow Wong, "Artistic Achievements," excerpt from "Puritans from the Orient"

CONTENTS BY ETHNIC GROUPS REPRESENTED BY AUTHOR'S NAME

(The categories refer to the subject matter of the work,
not the author's ethnicity, although they may be the same)

The Asian-American Woman

Chinese-American

Diana Chang
Edith Maud Eaton (Sui Sin Far)
Maxine Hong Kingston
Jade Snow Wong

Filipino-American

Ruby Reyes Flowers

Indian-American

Uma Majmudar

Japanese-American

Taruko Ogata Daniel
Jeanne Wakatsuki Houston
Janice Mirikitani
Ferris Takahashi
Rowena Wildin
Hisaye Yamamoto

Korean-American

Kumi Kilburn

The Black Woman

Anonymous
Toni Cade Bambara
Gwendolyn Brooks
Shirley Chisholm
Nikki Giovanni
Laurraine Goreau
Ann C. Hooper
Mahalia Jackson
Eva Jessye
Norma Rosen
Ntozake Shange
Helen C. Smith

Sojourner Truth
Mary Elizabeth Vroman
Alice Walker
Margaret Walker

The Hispanic American Woman

Chicano

Joan Baez
Angelo De Hoyos
Marina Rivera
Evangelina Vigil

Puerto Rican-American

La Verne González
Nicholasa Mohr

The Jewish American Woman

Aviva Barzel (translated by Ida Cohen Selavan) (*Israeli-American*)
Dorothy Friedman
Helen S. Garson
Emma Lazarus
Lyn Lifshin
Enid Mescon
Grace Paley
Arlene G. Peck
Judith Plaskow
Janet Rechtman
Adrienne Rich
Norma Rosen
Muriel Rukeyser
Rose Schneiderman
Esta Seaton
Eve Silver

The Native American Woman

Rose Mary (Shingobe) Barstow
Joy Harjo

Nila Northsun
Buffy Sainte-Marie
Leslie Silko
Virginia Driving Hawk Sneve
Liz Sohappy
Anne Webster

The White Ethnic-American Woman

English-American

Doras Reed Benbow (*Anglos-American*)
Avril Sutin
Anne Webster (*Anglos-American*)

Franco-American

Camille Lessard (translated by Armand B. Chartier)

German-American

Lisel Mueller
Heidi Rockwood
Phyllis J. Scherle
Sharon Renée Twombly

Greek-American

John Keay Davidson
Maria B. Frangis
Loral Graham
Evangeline Papageorge

Israeli-American

Aviva Barzel (translated by Ida Cohen Selavan)

Irish-American

Elizabeth Cullinan
Mary McCarthy
Enid Mescon
Betty Smith

Italian-American

Rose Basile Green

Mennonite-American

Katie Funk Wiebe

Norwegian-American

Thelma Jones

Polish-American

Monica Krawczyk
Rose Schneiderman
Sister M. Florence Tumasz

Rumanian-American

Juliana Geran Pilon

Russian-American

Irina Kirk
Emma Lazarus
Rose Schneiderman
Valentina Sinkevich
Marya Zaturenska

Slavic-American

Sonya Jason
Marie Prisland
Rose Mary Prosen

Swedish-American

H. Arnold Barton
Borghild Dahl
May Swenson

The Multi-Ethnic-American Woman

Edith Blicksilver

CLASS DISCUSSION, WRITTEN/ RESEARCH TOPICS

1. Using some of the selections from Unit One, *Growing Up Ethnic*, decide: (a) what problems are described and why they exist, (b) determine if they are due to ethnic origins or (c) if they would exist anyway, and (d) elaborate, using the evidence from the works chosen.

2. Do the same thing, except substitute the word "pleasures" for "problems" and develop this topic using the same or different selections from Unit One.

3. Analyze the connotative meaning of Virginia Driving Hawk Sneve's title, "Special Places" and also Arlene G. Peck's title, "The Southern Jewish American Princess (In The Fabulous Fifties)." Consider if the "Seventies Scene" has changed the role and values of young men and especially young women growing up during this decade. Elaborate.

4. Compare the role and lifestyle of the Dakota woman as described in the Sneve analysis (Unit One) with the Polish-American woman's values and life as a mother in Monica Krawczyk's "For Dimes and Quarters" (Unit Three).

5. Using several of the stories from Unit One, *Growing Up Ethnic*, decide how the process of assimilation, and/or alienation took place and how/why some ethnic groups had more difficulties in achieving happiness in America with reasons included.

6. Discuss the humorous aspects of the works by Peck and Friedman (Unit One) and how ethnicity is revealed in each case. You may wish to conclude that the humor is universal, regional, dated, rather than ethnic in origin. Feel free to do so, but be specific, using evidence.

7. Discuss the connotative meaning of the visual imagery and figurative language in the following works: (a) Rose Mary Prosen's poems in Unit Two, "Polka, A Memorial Tribute for my Mother and Father," "Chronicle, 1931-1945," and "Olga." Determine how and why these poems are so powerful in their emotional intensity. Do the same using the following: (b) Lyn Lifshin's, "Beryl" and consider its sensitivity too (c) Anne Webster's, "My Father's War." In this situation, consider if the point of view would have been different and, if so, how/why, if the other sister had written this poem about the father.

8. Read Anne Webster's "My Father's War," (Unit Two) and Ruby Reyes Flower's "Ruby's Discovery," (Unit Nine). Compare/contrast the role of the young woman in each work, as she has reacted to the ethnic differences of her mother and her father. (a) Which woman seems more content? Why? (b) Consider if parental ethnic differences are a source of conflict/pride. Elaborate.

9. How does the use of color help to create emotional/visual images in the following works: (a) Marya Zaturenska's poem "A Russian Easter 1920" (Introduction) (b) Esta Seaton's "Her Life" (Unit Two) (c) Rose Mary Prosen's "Polka, A Memorial Tribute for my Mother and Father," (and, if you wish, the other two Prosen poems as well, if pertinent) (Unit Two) (d) Phyllis J. Scherle's "A Trace of Gold" (Unit Eight).

10. Compare/contrast the way in which Seaton's "Explanation" and Bambara's "The Lesson" have approximated the cadences of Yiddish-American and Inner City New Yorkese. (a) What would have been lost/gained if the works had been written by an upper class aristocrat, or a woman such as Benbow's grandmother?

11. Compare/contrast how ethnic pride is evident in the works by Ntozake Shang, "Toussaint," (Unit Three) and Nikki Giovanni's "Nikki-Rosa," (Unit Two).

12. Compare the importance of the power of money as it is described in Bambara's "The Lesson" and Garson's "Rich is Better." (a) In what specific ways does each story call attention to the enormous inequality in the distribution of wealth in America? (b) How does each story combine humor with a serious intent?

13. Compare the values and attitudes toward understanding pride in craftsmanship as revealed by the attitudes of Dee and Maggie toward the quilts in Alice Walker's "Everyday Use" in Unit Eight. (a) Who has a better understanding of her heritage? Why?

14. If Walker's "Everyday Use" has been written by a white writer, what would have been gained/lost? (a) Is the work offensive to blacks? (b) Would it have been more offensive to blacks if a white writer had written it? Elaborate.

15. Compare the mother/daughter relationship in Kingston's "No Name Woman," (Unit One) with that in Seaton's "Explanation," (Unit Two) determining how an aunt, in each case, is an important symbol of ethnicity and family values. (a) Consider, too, the importance of the generation gap, the Americanization process as each daughter tries to come to terms with her mother's lifestyle.

16. In Seaton's "Explanation," what does the contrast between the words "neurotic" and "nervous" tell us about the differences of the mother and the daughter. (a) Notice, too, how the poet has approximated the cadences of Yiddish-American speech. Consider how these speech patterns affect the point of view of the poem. (Do they sharpen the sense of a generation gap that is basically cultural?) (b) Consider, finally, are people really different nowadays, especially women, or is the real difference a matter of the way one *perceives* the situation?

17. In Seaton's "Her Life," one should be aware that the life of an immigrant woman, in particular, was different in America in the early decades of the twentieth century from life today. This is the case, of course, of men too. Cite specific details in this poem that illustrate this difference. (a) What is the effect of the use of the word "grey"? (b) Consider, why is the doctor's inability to deal with the woman's problem the climax of her difficult life? (c) How would you explain his "advice?" (d) Is he unfeeling or merely equally helpless?

18. Using Zaturenska's poem "A Russian Easter 1920," consider the following: (a) Two references are made to the "great cathedral" in the opening stanza. How do the remaining stanzas describe the cathedral? Is this a central image within the poem? (b) How does the introduction of proper names and color help to create concrete emotional and visual images within the poem? (c) Does the use of the future tense give a clue to the state of mind of the narrator's loneliness, and, if so, how? (d) Is the poem dated? Elaborate. (e) Notice structure. For example, the three beginning stanzas describe what is occurring in another place and time. The last stanza describes what the narrator will be doing. How does the contrast between the first three stanzas and the last express the loneliness of the immigrant in a new country? (f) Is this a specifically religious poem? Elaborate. (g) Then, or at the same time, consider the importance of religion in the Tumasz' work "Growing Up as a Polish-American." (Unit Seven).

19. Grace Paley has recreated a wild, colorful and fanciful group of characters, especially Aunt Rose, in "Goodbye and Good Luck," (Unit Two). Develop this statement and discuss how the author makes her characters human as well as amusing. (b) To what extent is Aunt Tose to be admired? Pitied? Or what? Elaborate. (c) Finally, compare the lifestyles of Aunt Rose with Kingston's aunt in "No Name Woman," considering ethnicity, community and cultural influences, the condemnation of society and how each woman copes.

20. Discuss the ironies present in Daniel's "We Wise Children," (Unit Two), especially the ironic implications of the title and the point of view. (a) How would the story be different if it were told by the Japanese-American woman? Her husband? (b) Do a research project and discuss the historical patterns that brought Asian-American women, in this case, Japanese women, to the United States. Notice, in particular, the custom to select a husband through the use of a photograph and to marry by proxy. Consider the problems this procedure could create in the relationship.

21. Select some of the letters of elderly women in your family or in your neighborhood who migrated to America and then read some of the letters to the editor by immigrant women in Isaac Metzker's *A Bintl Brief* (Ballantine). Compare their adjustments to the new world with the letters of the two Swedish women in Unit Ten. (a) What characteristics do these women seem to have in common? (b) What differences are obvious and why do they exist? (c) Are the adjustment problems based upon ethnic differences, character differences, environmental differences, economic differences, economic differences, or what? (The "bintl brief" letters were those written to Abraham Cahan for the *Jewish Daily Forward* from 1906 to the present. The term means "bundle of letters" in Yiddish).

22. Discuss the lessons learned by both teacher and student in the following works: (a) Vroman's "See How They Run," (b) Bambara's "The Lesson," and (c) Marina Rivera's "For Rita Kohn." (Unit Three).

23. Compare the black school experience in Vroman's "See How They Run" with Hooper's in "The Proper Thing to Say, to Do and to Wear" and consider whether the differences are merely economic and/or regional. (a) Or are these differences of a more important nature in which specific values and lifestyles are emphasized? (b) Are the stories relevant to our own time or are they dated? Elaborate.

24. Discuss the important role of education as it is revealed in Monica Krawczyk's "For Dimes and Quarters" and in Rose Schneiderman's "The Childhood of an Immigrant Working Girl," (Units Three and Six, respectively). (a) Do these Eastern-European women have the same/different reasons for seeking an education as compared with the reasons given in Dahl's excerpt, "Grandmother Skoglund's Advice to Lyng and The University Experience"? (b) In other words, does a Norwegian-American have the same career goals, values, Americanization adjustments? Elaborate.

25. Compare the girlhoods of the three Irish-American young women discussed in this anthology: Mary McCarthy's "To the Reader" from *Memories of a Catholic Girlhood*, Elizabeth Cullinan's "The Power of Prayer," and Betty Smith's "The Ethnic Child and the Classroom Experience" from Chapter XXIII, *A Tree Grows in Brooklyn*. (a) Consider, how important was ethnicity, family life, religion and ritual in the girlhoods of each of the narrators? (b) Which author, in your opinion, was the most/least effective in sketching the lifestyles of the girls? Give reasons for your opinions, using evidence to strengthen your arguments.

26. Compare the ambitious career goals of Wiebe's narrator in "The Barriers Are Not Real," (Unit Four) with those of Rose Schneiderman's story, (Unit Six). (a) Then, or at the same time, what conclusions do you reach about these women, their characters, the differences they had and how they handled them? (b) Do similar difficulties exist for women who want careers now? Elaborate.

27. What purpose does the mice symbolism serve in the Vroman story, "See How They Run," (Unit Three) and what purpose does the character "Toussaint" serve in the Shange choreopoem? (Unit Three) (a) Do some research and explore the life and achievements of Toussaint L'Ouverture (Pierre Dominique Toussaint-Breda) 1743-1803. (b) Then, or at the same time, discuss his important role as a symbol as well as a masculine version of romantic heroism for the narrator in the story.

28. Discuss the conflicting identities as developed in the works listed in Unit Four. Notice, in particular, (a) Angela De Hoyos' comparison with the brown spider. Why? (b) the slave mother's conflicting loyalties and how they are developed through the use of figurative language and imagery (c) Janet Rechtman's problems of adjustment as described by the young woman in "Chanukah, Camp Hill, Alabama." Consider if her sensitive, introspective concerns would have been different/the same in a community with more Jewish girls her own age.

29. In Unit Four, discuss the problems of Miss Sasagawara in the relocation camp as they are described by Ms. Yamamoto. (a) If she were not a dancer would her problems have been less intense? Why or why not? (b) How does the internal intensity of Miss Sasagawara compare with the lifestyle of the young girl who is telling the story? Her mental attitude? (c) Her father, the Reverend? (d) How would you have tried to cope with life in this camp? (e) Why is the story called "The Legend . . .?" Why not, just "The Story . . .?"

30. Compare the problems, pleasures and achievements of the narrator in Wiebe's "The Barriers Are Not Real" with those of Jason's narrator in "The Liberation of a First Generation Slovak-American Woman" as each has attempted to break out of the traditional role of the woman in a strong patriarchal family. (Unit Four).

31. Sharon Reneé Twombly writes that "the concept of the rings" is an important one in her work, "Ethnicity to Humanity" in Unit Four. Develop this concept and discuss its family, intellectual and emotional connotations.

32. Discuss the exploitation in human relationships as they are revealed in Unit Five. Consider the role of the woman as sex object, seductress, martyr and monster as evident in (a) LaVerne González' "Born to Suicide" (b) Marina Rivera's victim in "Chon" and (c) the black and the white woman

described in Gwendolyn Brooks' "Ballad of Pearl May Lee." (d) Which woman do you feel the most, the least sorry for, and why?

33. Read Harry Golden's *A Little Girl is Dead* and compare the rape-murder and lynching narrative that is based upon a true incident with the story described in Harper Lee's *To Kill a Mockingbird* and then compare both with Brooks' narrative poem, "Ballad of Pearl May Lee." (a) Consider the difference in the point of view, circumstances, the justice, poetic and otherwise, as revealed in the Brooks' poem. (b) Which work is the most moving of the three compared and why?

34. If you were telling an actress to read the Brooks' poem, "Ballad of Pearl May Lee," what kind of verbal tone would you tell her to use? Why? (b) What kind of body movements? Why? (Unit Five)

35. How does Eve Silver's controlled language underplay the terror in her tale, "Listen to My Story" in Unit Five?

36. Compare Eve Silver's experiences in the holocaust with those of the mother and the child in the Russian short story by Valentin Katayev, "Our Father Who Art in Heaven" written in 1946. (a) Notice the similarities in both tales of terror, for example, the attempts to escape fate by running constantly. (b) Which work is more powerful and why, in your opinion?

37. Compare the girlhood and family life of the young Polish woman in Eve Silver's "Listen to My Story" with those of the young German woman in Heidi Rockwood's "The Best of Two Worlds," (Unit Five and Unit Ten, respectively). How was the first unable to escape Nazi terrorism and the second able to do so?

38. Do a research paper discussing the holocaust experience by reading Eve Silver's "Listen to My Story" (Unit Five) as well as pertinent excerpts from the following books: (a) Elie Wiesel's *Night* (b) Lucy Dawidowicz's *The War Against the Jews* (c) Richard Rubenstein's *After Auschwitz* (d) Terrence Des Pres' *The Survivor* (e) F.E. Talmadge's *Disputation and Dialogue* and (g) Jozef Garlinski's *Fighting Auschwitz*.

39. Read Mary Antin's *The Promised Land* and Anzia Yezierska's *Hungry Hearts*, and then read, in this anthology, Rose Schneiderman's comments about the proper behavior of women from this ethnic culture as daughters, wives, career women within the family unit. ("The Childhood of an Immigrant Working Girl," Unit Six). (a) For example, were the sons favored when money was scarce and only one child could attend school? (b) Develop some other theories of your own after reading these works and then determine how many of these traditional roles still exist and why or why not? (c) Compare the lifestyles of these Eastern-European American immigrant women with Jade Snow Wong's comments in the "Introduction" and arrive at some conclusions about the traditional role of the Chinese-American woman compared with that of these others.

40. Compare and contrast the two women in Norma Rosen's story "What Must I Say to You?" (Unit Seven) as each gives insights into the lifestyles, values, and the thematic meaning of the story.

41. Discuss the symbolic significance of Valentina Sinkevich's "Kerosene Lamp" and Marie Prisland's "Old Wood Stove" from "Memories of Our Old Wood Stove" (Unit Eight), as each gives insights into the adjustment difficulties of the Eastern-European immigrant and/or the nostalgic memories of a lifestyle that is only a memory for them now.

42. Compare the magnificent courage and attempts to cope with the tragedies in her life as revealed by Leslie Silko's old Native American woman in "Lullaby" (Unit Two) and La Verne Gonzalez' old Puerto Rican woman in "Born to Suicide" (Unit Five). (a) In what specific ways does ethnicity give insight into the characters and lifestyles of both women and (b) in what specific ways are their problems universal and not related to ethnicity in any way?

43. Margaret Walker's "Now" was written in the early 1940's. What specific descriptive details focusing upon discrimination toward black women are (a) dated? (b) still relevant in contemporary America? (Introduction).

44. Discuss the stereotyped view of black women that the "vulgars" shouted in lines 17-23 in Margaret Walker's poem "Now" (Introduction) (a) Then, or at the same time, do some research and write an analytical paper detailing the image of the black women in the literature written by whites such as (a) William Faulkner's "That Evening Sun" and "Delta Autumn," (b) Carson McCullers' *The Member of the Wedding* and (c) Margaret Mitchell's *Gone with the Wind*, or others, as you wish.

(d) Then, read some of the works in this anthology written by black women and reach some conclusions about realistic/stereotyped character sketches. Decide which works (e) sketch one-dimensional types and which ones breathe life into the personalities. Be sure that you have taken into account the regional setting and the historical period when the work was written in order to reach accurate conclusions.

45. Joan Baez, in the beginning of this anthology, discusses her younger sister's alienation because the folk singer was darker skinned. Read about a similar situation in Piri Thomas' *Down These Mean Streets* and write a paper discussing the young protagonist's internal tensions and problems because he felt he was rejected by some members of his family. (a) Compare the family life and the world of the Puerto Rican barrio as described in "A Very Special Pet" from *El Bronx Remembered* (Unit Two) by Nicholasa Mohr with Piri Thomas' embittered experiences and (b) both with Joan Baez' interview. (c) Consider, for example, the difference in the point of view, the optimistic/pessimistic view of family relationships, the use of irony, figurative language, humor and whatever else you wish to discuss. (d) Finally, or at the same time, how has the narrator in the Thomas work been trapped by the brutal "code of machismo" and be sure that you have defined this term as you wish it to mean in your research project.

46. Irina Kirk's narrator in *Born with the Dead* (Unit One) says that ". . . every generation must create its own traditions . . ." while the Reverend in Ole Rolvaag's *Their Father's God* thunders that "a people that has lost its traditions is doomed!" Which point of view do you agree with and why? (a) Read some of the selections from *That Elusive Identity* (Unit Four) and other works such as Maxine Hong Kingston's "No Name Woman" (Unit One) and analyze how the narrators in the works chosen accepted or rejected their ethnic traditions and/or came to terms with their ethnicity. (b) Do certain ethnic groups have more problems? Why?

47. In several works, a young woman is humiliated because of her ethnic origins; in other words, she is made aware of her ethnicity as the story unfolds. She faces a "moment of truth" and the story is one of "initiation." Define "initiation" as a literary device and then discuss what important truths the narrator in each of the following stories learns as she leaves a state of innocence to one of self-awareness, and the significance: (a) Virginia Driving Hawk's "Special Places" (Unit One) (b) Kumi Kilburn's "No Dogs and Chinese Allowed" (Unit Four) (c) Ruby Reyes Flower's "Ruby's Discovery" (Unit Nine) and (d) Joan Baez' interview. (Introduction).

48. Read the poem "Incident" by Countee Cullen in the library and then compare the psychological wounds that the narrator experienced with some of the painful experiences by narrators in some of the works in this anthology because of prejudice and/or discrimination. Refer, for example, to the works listed in topic forty-six. (a) Why, in your opinion, do some people persist in "name calling"? (b) How, in each case, were the narrators able to come to terms with girlhood psychological wounds? (c) In what specific ways were they unable to do so? Elaborate.

49. Apply topic forty-seven to the following works: (a) Rose Mary (Shingobe) Bartow's school experiences in "Who Was Really the Savage?" (b) Eve Silver's "Listen to My Story," and (c) Teruko Ogata Daniel's "Such, Such Were the Joys . . . George Orwell" (Unit Nine, Unit Five and Unit Four, respectively).

50. Compare the experiences, point of view and attitude described in two works by Chinese ethnic women: (1) Edith Maud Eaton (Sui Sin Far) in "Mental Portfolio of a Eurasian" with (2) Diana Chang's "An Appearance of Being Chinese" and Two Poems: "Saying Yes" and "Otherness." Be sure that you take into account the fact that the first narrator lived and wrote during the end of the nineteenth century and the other is a contemporary artist in order for your conclusions to be as accurate as possible from an historical and from a literary point of view.

51. A critic has written that from "a psychological perspective, there are both common attributes, which . . . are common to . . . [the] Jewish heritage, and . . . cultural attributes, which are unique either to that geographical section of the country or to the city in which that person was raised." (Clinical Psychologist, Psychotherapist and Marriage Counselor Ira L. Tedoff, as quoted in *The Southern Israelite*, March 21, 1978, p. 17.) Dr. Tedoff also says that "the Southern Jew may . . . be a product of a culture where 'social grace' and 'good Southern manners' are given a higher priority than asserting one's feelings and ideas." Develop these theories, either agreeing or disagreeing, by

comparing the girlhood, family and community experiences and also the personalities of the two Jewish narrators in the works by Arlene G. Peck, "The Southern Jewish American Princess (In The Fabulous Fifties)" and Helen S. Garson, "Rich is Better" (Unit One).

52. Discuss the mother/daughter or grandmother/granddaughter relationship in the following works, analyzing personality traits, exploring the reasons for tensions, love, pride, rejection of ethnic traditions and the significance. Consider, too, the use of imagery, irony, figurative language, symbolism, sarcasm and the thematic meaning of each piece. (Some topics are more pertinent than others depending upon the work selected.) Then, or at the same time, do the works reveal unique ethnic or universal characteristics? Both? Elaborate. (a) Nila Northsun's "The Ways/The Way It Is," nine poems (Unit Two), (b) Doras Reed Benbow's "My Grandmother The Wasp" (Unit Two), (c) Alice Walker's "Everyday Use" (Unit Eight), (d) Phyllis J. Scherle's "A Trace of Gold" (Unit Eight), (e) Janice Mirikitani's "Sing With Your Body" (Unit Nine), and (f) Dorothy Burton Skardal's "The Norwegian-American Immigrant Girl and Morality" from *The Divided Heart* (Unit Ten).

53. Substitute the word "the father" for "the mother" and "the grandfather" for "the grandmother" in topic fifty-one, and use the following works" (a) Anne Webster's "My Father's War" (Unit Two), (b) Jeanne Wakatsuki Houston and James D. Houston's "Whatever He Did Had Flourish" from *Farewell to Manzanar* (Unit Two), (c) Camille Lessard's *Canuck*, "Vic's Revolt" (Unit Two), (d) Elizabeth Cullinan's "The Power of Prayer" (Unit Two), (e) Lisel Mueller's "The Cremona Violin" and "More Light" (Unit Two), (f) Lyn Lifshin's "Beryl" (Unit Two), (g) Hisaye Yamamoto's "The Legend of Miss Sasagawara" (Unit Four), (h) Eve Silver's "Listen to My Story" (Unit Five), (i) Ruby Ryes Flowers' "Ruby's Discovery" (Unit Nine), and (j) Jade Snow Wong's excerpt from "Puritans from the Orient" in the Introduction.

54. Find works that deal with family relationships and trace through them the following topics, as they are pertinent: (a) tensions/love between husband, wife and/or children, (b) the reasons for family cohesiveness or fragmentation, (c) attitudes toward assimilation, cultural pluralism, (d) ethnic pride/shame, and the significance.

55. Read the works by Native American authors and discuss the ways in which the Anglos have exploited them and their family relationships. Consider works by Leslie Silko (Unit Two), Liz Sohappy (Unit Nine) and the other Native American writers listed under Native American Authors in *Contents by Ethnic Groups*.

56. Apply topic fifty-four to an analysis of any other ethnic groups listed in the *Contents by Ethnic Groups Represented by Author's Name*, using the Asian-American, especially the Japanese-American works, for example.

57. In some of the works in this anthology, the narrator describes an easy adjustment to the American mainstream with no assimilation problems, while, in other works, cultural pluralism and visible ethnic differences result in discrimination, hostility, family tension and alienation. Develop this topic by using the works of (a) German-American Women (b) Asian-American Women and Native American Women as listed in the *Contents by Ethnic Groups Represented by Author's Name*. (Some works and some topics are more pertinent than others.)

58. In several of these works, lovers, husbands, and fathers are weak, sick, unemployed, selfish, unloving, drunkards, lechers, petty tyrants with few redeeming virtues. Many of these male symbols lack substance, are one-dimensional, frequently with suffering, strong, hard-working wives and daughters. Develop this statement, as it is pertinent, by using some of the following works by (a) Hispanic-Americans (b) Eastern-European Americans (c) Irish-Americans (d) Japanese-Americans and (e) Native Americans. (Refer to the authors you wish to use by looking under the listing in the *Contents by Ethnic Groups Represented by Author's Name*.) Consider differences if works had been written from a masculine viewpoint in each case too.

59. In several works, religion and ritual are important sources of strength for ethnic, immigrant families. In other works, religion and ritual result in internal tensions, alienation and/or discrimination. Develop this topic, using pertinent aspects, for each of the following works: (a) Janet Rechtman's "Chanukah, Camp Hill, Alabama" (Unit One), (b) Hisaye Yamamoto's "The Legend of Miss Sasagawara" (Unit Four), (c) Marya Zaturaska's "A Russian Easter 1920" (Introduction), (d) Emma Lazarus' "The Crowing of the Red Cock" (Unit Ten), (e) Laurraine Goreau's "Black

Baptism'' (excerpt) from Chapter Seven of *Just Mahalia, Baby* (Unit Seven), (f) Sister M. Florence Tusasz's ''Growing Up as a Polish American'' (Unit Seven).

60. The English, German and Scandinavian immigrants seem to have had less difficult adjustment problems as evidenced by the works written by Rockwood, Sutin and Jones. Do some research and find out why this was the case traditionally with Northern-European and English speaking peoples and less so with Eastern-Europeans, Mediterraneans and Asians. (a) Is this still the case? Find out, for example, how the recent ethnic groups, especially women from Southeast Asia and from Cuba, have adjusted to the American lifestyle. (2) Interview some recent arrivals, selecting women representing different ages, different homelands, different professional skills and arrive at some conclusions about the ease or difficulty of the adjustment as a result of this research.

61. Why do Eastern-Europeans seem to need to cling to possessions (cf. Valentina Sinkevich's ''Kerosene Lamp'' and Marie Prisland's ''Memories of Our Old Wood Stove'') (Unit Eight), while Native American women find spiritual nourishment in clinging to their tribal land? (cf. the Native American woman's point of view in the Introduction, and Joy Harjo's ''The Last Song'') (Unit Nine). Perhaps the Declaration of an American Indian Conference in 1961 will give insight into this point of view: ''Were we paid a thousand times the market value of our lost holdings, still the payment would not suffice. Money never mothered the Indian people, nor have any people become more closely attached to the land, religiously and traditionally.'' (a) Interview some members of your family and relatives and ask them if they have possessions from their immigrant ancestors that are important, of sentimental value to them. (b) Do you have any such possessions? Write a paper using the works in this book and the results of your research to analyze why possessions are important to people.

62. During the Ancient World, the Greeks and the Hebrews, in part, because of their religious doctrines, were proud of their advanced humanitarian civilizations during a time when their neighbors frequently practiced and participated in barbaric rituals resulting in the torture of prisoners, human sacrifices, sexual excesses and pagan orgies. As a result, both contemporary Greek-Americans and Jewish-Americans have been proud of their contributions to Western Civilization. Develop this statement, or disagree with it, using the following works: (a) Muriel Rukeyser's ''Letter to the Front'' (Unit Seven), (b) Maria B. Frangis' ''An Ancient Heritage in a New World'' (c) Evangeline Papageorge's ''My Father, My Mother and My Greek Heritage'' and John Keay Davidson's ''Emory's Evangeline'' and Loral Graham's ''A Greek Who Bore Warm Gifts'' (Unit One and Unit Six, respectively).

63. Several works in this anthology deal with the Japanese-American relocation camp experience. Using pertinent works listed under *Contents by Ethnic Groups Represented by Author's Name*, compare the experiences by these Japanese-American women. Consider, as pertinent, for example (a) the ability/inability to cope with camp life (b) the optimistic/pessimistic point of view (c) the long range repercussions of the events upon children, parents (d) and the internal feelings of guilt, self-loathing, Anglos rejections and/or exploitation and/or kindness that existed. You may wish to read the complete work, *Farewell to Manzanar*, by Jeanne Wakatsuki Houston and James D. Houston and Michi Weglyn's *Years of Infamy* for additional details about the relocation camp experience. *Executive Order 9066*, edited by Maisie and Richard Conrat and published in 1972 by the California Historical Society has some fine pictures describing the effect on the personal level of the internment of the 110,000 Japanese-Americans.

64. Do some research, and then discuss the classical, historical, biblical and/or ritual references in some of the following works, as each gives insight into character and/or theme: (a) Arlene G. Peck's ''The Southern Jewish American Princess (In The Fabulous Fifties)'' (Unit One), (b) Maxine Hong Kingston's ''No Name Woman'' from *The Woman Warrior* (Unit One), (c) Janet Rechtman's ''Chanukah, Camp Hill, Alabama '' (Unit Four), (d) Judith Plaskow's ''The Jewish Feminist: Conflicts in Identies'' (Unit Four), (e) Liz Sohappy's ''The Parade'' (Unit Eight), (f) Angela De Hoyos' ''HERMANO'' (an excerpt) (Unit Eleven), (g) Emma Lazarus' ''The Crowing of the Red

Cock'' (Unit Ten), (h) Juliana Geran Pilon's ''Return to Romania'' from *Notes from the Other Side of Night* (Unit Ten), (i) Norma Rosen's ''What Must I Say to You?'' (Unit Seven), (j) Aviva Barzel's ''Pass Over the Blood'' (Unit Nine), (k) Adrienne Rich's ''The Burning of Paper Instead of Children'' (Unit Eleven), (l) Rowena Wildin's ''Children'' (Unit Eleven), (m) Nikki Giovanni's ''Adulthood'' (n) Lisel Mueller's ''More Light'' (Words attributed to Goethe on his deathbed) (Unit Two) (o) Lisel Mueller's ''The Cremona Violin'' (After E.T.A. Hoffmann's story) (Unit Two), (p) Ntozake Shange, ''Toussaint'' (Unit Three), (q) Buffy Sainte-Marie's ''Refuse to Be a Victim'' (Unit Eleven), (r) Lyn Lifshin's ''Seder'' (Unit Seven), (s) Sister M. Florence Tumasz' ''Growing Up as a Polish American'' (Unit Seven).

65. Which work, from those that you read in this anthology, left you with some unanswered questions? If you could speak with the author of the work, what would you like to ask her and why?

66. Which work read in this anthology was most meaningful to you in terms of your own personal experiences, one that evoked an intellectual and an emotional response? Try to explain this response in depth.

BIOGRAPHICAL SKETCHES OF ARTISTS AND WRITERS

The Artists

Martha E. Clayton, from Atlanta studied architecture at Georgia Tech where she now works with graphics and design in the Solar Energy and Material Technology Division of the Engineering Experiment Station. She has been painting for ten years and is of British and French ancestry. She entered the Dogwood Festival Art Show in Atlanta and the Student Center at Georgia Tech purchased this painting.

Maria de Noronha (Gallman), from Portugal, has aristocratic roots that include Ponce deLeon and Fernando de Noronha, who discovered an island named after him. Her father, "a complete authoritarian," put her mother, gentle and artistic, "on a pedestal" and growing up was difficult. She sketched the cosmopolitan world she saw and wanted a more independent life than women had, so she studied at Hunter College, receiving a degree in Fine Arts and then embarked upon a rewarding career. She has taught drawing and art in New Jersey and was Artist-in-Residence at Oglethorpe University; she was awarded the M. Grumbacher Award as Painter of the Year in 1962. She has exhibited at the National Academy of Design, the National Art Club Gallery, the State Department and the Metropolitan Museum of Art where she had her own show in October, 1977. She has worked in the White House, studied in Paris, speaks five languages and now makes her home in Atlanta.

Harriett Warshaw, from Atlanta, studied and worked with art all her life, combining a fulfilling life as wife and mother with artistic enrichment. She studied at the Atlanta College of Art in The Atlanta Memorial Art Center. Having explored all mediums, she now has become a watercolorist. Her juried work has been exhibited at the Callanwolde Fine Arts Center and the Atlanta Artists Club Gallery of which she is a member. Warshaw paintings have been added to private collections in Atlanta, in New Jersey, in Colorado, in Miami and in California.

The Writers

Joan Baez, born in 1941, the daughter of "a gypsy queen and a visionary scientist," traveled extensively as a girl moving from New York, to Bagdad and to California. Music provided an early haven, and she taught herself to play on a mail order guitar. She remained apart from her schoolmates due to the color of her skin. "It's hard to be a Princess in the States when your skin is brown." Her father was Mexican, her mother was "born in Scotland . . . a mystic . . . a blue blood and God moves about her more freely than He does most people." The daughter helped establish the Institute for the Study of Nonviolence in 1965, embarked upon an active musical career, opposed segregation on college campuses and achieved recognition as an accomplished folk artist, winning many awards. When asked if she considers herself a politician or a musician first, she replies, "A human being first."

Toni Cade Bambara, from Long Island, New York, received a B.A. from Queens College in 1959, studied at the University of Florence and received an M.A. from City College in 1964. She has been a teacher, writer, critic whose works have appeared in magazines and scholarly critiques. She is the editor of *The Black Woman* and the author of a challenging collection of short stories, *Gorilla, My Love*, one of which is in this anthology. She has a clever command of the language and captures the nuances of dialogue in a unique way. She is now living in Atlanta and working on a novel.

Aviva S. Barzel, from Jerusalem, is a Professor of Hebrew Literature at the Jewish Theological Seminary in New York, having studied at Hebrew and Columbia Universities. She has taught at Lehman College, published, in Hebrew, articles and poems. She is a literary critic with works in *Yediot Aharonot*, the Israeli Daily, Literary Supplement.

Doras Reed Benbow, from a distinguished New England family, moved to Georgia in 1950 where she is an artist, musician, writer, poet. The first of her three poetry books, "Sometimes In The Soft Of Night," won the Author of the Year Poetry Award from the Dixie Council of Authors and Journalists in 1973, at which time she also received an honorary Doctor of Letters degree in London where her poems appeared in *Poetry of the Americas*. She has conducted workshops at Breneau College, Mercer University and the Georgia Alliance for Arts Education. Her books include *Lantern In The Moonlight* and *Beyond The Farthest Star*. She wrote Celestine Sibley at The Atlanta *Constitution* that life "has been a continuing education for me. . . . I have admired the masters, but knowing that I will never be one doesn't stop me from experiencing the joys of trying all the arts."

Gwendolyn Brooks, grew up in Chicago and was awarded the Pulitzer Prize in 1950 for *Annie Allen*, after having received Guggenheim Fellowships in 1946 and 1947. In 1968, she was chosen as the successor to the late Carl Sandburg as Poet Laureate of Illinois. She writes that her father "had loved education and the arts" but because the family was poor, he could not become a doctor, so he was forced to work as a janitor. A critic has said that her verse "mirrors a world not merely personal or racial, but universal." She finds inspiration in the world she knows but adds her own philosophic wisdom. Her works include *A Street in Bronzeville, The World of Gwendolyn Brooks*, and an autobiography, *Report from Part One*. She edits a yearly magazine, *The Black Position* and loves to read her poetry to students on college campuses where she is received with affection.

Diana Chang, born in New York, was taken before she was a year old by her Chinese father and Eurasian mother to live, in the 1930's, in Nanking, Peking and Shanghai. After the Second World War, the family returned to America where Diana graduated from Barnard College. A John Hay Whitney Foundation Fellowship enabled her to complete her first novel, *The Frontiers of Love*. Her other novels include *A Woman of Thirty, A Passion for Life* and *The Only Game in Town*. Many of her poems have been anthologized and she is a talented painter with several shows to her credit. She was awarded the *Mademoiselle Magazine* Woman-of-the-Year Award and her latest book, *A Perfect Love*, is scheduled for release in 1978.

Armand B. Chartier, from Massachusetts, received his Ph.D. from The University of Massachusetts and is a French Professor at the University of Rhode Island at Kingston, having been Chairman of the Modern Language Department at North Adams College. He was appointed by Governor Frank Licht to the American and Canadian French Cultural Exchange Commission in 1972 and by Governor J. Joseph Garrahy to the Rhode Island Heritage Commission in 1977. He is an editor of *Modern Language Studies* and an executive officer of *The Society for The Study of the Multi-Ethnic Literature of The United States*. He has published many scholarly articles and his translation of Camille Lessard's *Canuck* is the first English excerpt of this French novel.

Elizabeth Cullinan, grew up and still lives in New York. She received her B.A. at Mary Mount College and published *House of Gold* in 1969, obtaining a literary fellowship from Houghton Mifflin to work on this volume. A year later she received a New Writer's Award from The Great Lakes College Association. Her other publications include *The Time of Adam* and *Yellow Roses* with sixteen of these short stories originally published in *The New Yorker*. Frequently, she writes about Irish Catholic family life and the concerns of women, in particular, with sensitive perception and powerful command of the language.

Borghild Dahl, writer, teacher, lecturer and woman of indominable courage in spite of increasing blindness, was born in Minneapolis, of Norwegian-American parents. She was a Professor of Literature and Journalism at Augusta College and the first woman granted a scholarship to study in Norway from the American-Scandinavian Foundation. In 1950 she was awarded the St. Olaf medal by King Haaken for promoting good relations between Norway and America. She never let her affliction handicap her, and she has written thirteen books for young people. Other publications include *Karen, Homecoming* and *Minnetonka Summer.* Her stories depict women of notable courage, sometimes a composite of her own mother who came to America in the 1870's. One hundred years later when the daughter approached her 80th birthday, she wrote: "I am an optimist if there ever was one. I believe the world is getting better." She was voted the most representative Norwegian-American Writer in 1975, when The Sesquicentennial of Norwegian-American Settlements in America was celebrated.

Teruko Ogata Daniel grew up in Washington where she has taught high school English both in Washington and in Oregon. She is now an instructor at Olympic College in Bremerton, Washington where she lives with her Turkish-Norwegian husband and adopted Filipino-American child. She writes, "A famous Japanese poet said: 'Write me down/as someone who loved/persimmons and poetry.' This captures the essence of my lifetime as a Japanese-American woman. Throughout, the bittersweet beauty of life complements, balances, and harmonizes all experiences whether they be in the past, present or future." She is a poet with publications in many magazines.

Angela de Hoyos, a Mexican-American painter and poet, attended San Antonio College and Fine Arts Institute. She has received art and literary awards including Second Prize for Poetry, CSSI International Competition, Italy. A collection of her poems has been published by Cuadernos Del Caballo Verde, University of Veracruz, Xalapa, Mexico with other works published both in America and abroad. Her book entitled *Chicano Poems for the Barrio* was published in 1975, and *Arise Chicano! and Other Poems* in 1978. (Spanish translation by Mireya Robles.)

Ruby Reyes Flowers was born in Houston, Texas, the daughter of an Alabama mother and Filipino father. She has worked as an X-ray technologist and her husband is a radiologist. She has two children, now lives in Monroeville, Alabama, does free-lance writing, with this contribution her first published work in an anthology.

Maria B. Frangis, of Greek immigrant parents, graduated from Randolph-Macon Woman's College in Virginia, followed by creative writing work at Iowa State University. She has worked in radio and television in Columbia, South Carolina, and is currently writing children's books. She has published in *Datebook, Teen,* and *Young World,* lives in Atlanta with her family and is a leader in community and church activities, currently editing the Greek Church Publication. She contributed the picture of her Greek Church to this anthology.

Dorothy Friedman, born of Eastern-European parents in New York, began writing poetry at ten and became school poet. Too poor to go to college, she did not embark upon a professional writing career until she became a widow, although she did obtain an art scholarship to study in the Brooklyn Museum. Her art has been exhibited at home and abroad and now she has an active free-lance career, publishing in literary reviews, anthologies and newspapers. She now lives in California and is writing her autobiography which will be illustrated by her own sketches. She is a social worker in Los Angeles.

Helen S. Garson, married and the mother of three children, is of German ancestry and has had a distinguished professional career. She studied at George Washington University, The University of Georgia and got her Ph.D. from the University of Maryland with Post Doctoral Studies at Oxford University. Formerly Associate Dean at George Mason University, she is now a Coordinator of Graduate English Studies there. Her numerous publications include "Variations of the Gothic and Grotesque: Sexual Motifs in Southern Literature," and "Southern Girls: Memories of Loneliness and Loss." She has been active in the Popular Culture Association with her scholarly works in all its publications.

Nikki Giovanni, who was born in Knoxville, Tennessee in 1943, says, "I write what I see, and I take responsibility for it." She is a popular poet who reads her poetry on television, on college campuses and has a best-selling record album. She continues to ask "Who am I?" and "What am I?" with family love stressed as important in producing a strong black society. She studied at Fisk University and is an English Professor at Rutgers University. Her poetry books include *Black Feeling, Black Talk, Black Judgment,* and *My House.* She has also written poems for children and biographies of Langston Hughes and Nina Simone.

LaVerne González, of Irish ancestry, married a Puerto Rican, and "found the fierce pride of Self and love of freedom duplicated and revitalized in my 'Spanish heritage' through marriage." She entered college as a freshman with an understanding husband and five children, getting her Ph.D. in six years from Purdue University where she is now an English Professor and Director of Developmental Composition. She also teaches Caribbean and Chicano literature and her publications include *Your Line Into Infinity*, poetry, reviews and a short story "Loteria. She is editor of *Multi-ethnicity in America*, active in the National Council of Teachers and received the Best Teacher of English Department Award in 1975-76 and the Innovations in Teaching Award in 1977.

Laurraine Goreau, grew up in New Orleans where she became managing editor of a newspaper at twenty-two. She had produced and performed for television, is a recorded composer, lyricist, playwright and an accomplished actress. Her editorials, articles and publications have given her numerous awards, and she became the friend and chosen biographer of Mahalia Jackson with whom she traveled extensively. She is now popular on campuses as a talented lecturer, combining wit and humor with anecdotes about her career.

Rose Basile Green, a descendant of Roman Italians, was born in New York, received her Ph.D. from the University of Pennsylvania, taught English at Temple University, helped establish Cabrini College where she organized the Department of English and became Chairman until 1970. Her many poetry collections and books include *Primo Vino* (Sonnets), *Seventy-six for Philadelphia* (Sonnets), *Woman, The Second Coming* (Sonnets), *The Italian-American Novel: A Document of the Interaction of Two Cultures*. She received the Bicentennial Award for Literature given by the Daughters of the American Revolution and was cited in the Congressional Record in October 6, 1977 as one of the outstanding Italian-Americans of the twentieth century. Combining a rewarding professional career with marriage and motherhood, she now lectures and promotes ethnic studies courses in educational institutions.

Joy Harjo, of mixed ancestral ancestry, combines European roots with Creek Indian origins. She grew up in Oklahoma and she says that her writing "is a part of that history both past and current, but also grows past that, creating its own history."

Ann C. Hooper, grew up in Atlanta where her dentist father was a distinguished community leader and where her mother still lives. She studied at Talladega College, The Sorbonne, Indiana University and received her Ph.D. at Florida State University. She is a French Professor at Florida A & M, currently living with her husband and children in Tallahassee. She has written scholarly articles, received the Mason Modern Language and the Phi Sigma Iota French Honorary Award in 1953. She was coordinator of a Minority Intern Program and took students abroad to study during several summers.

Jeanne Wakatsuki Houston, was born in Inglewood, California and now lives in Santa Cruz with her talented husband and three children. She studied sociology and journalism at San Jose College and *Farewell to Manzanar* details her own family experiences in an internment camp during the Second World War. A film of the book was premiered in 1976 and the screenplay, which she and her husband Jim wrote together with John Korty, was nominated for an Emmy that year. It also won the Humanitas Prize and two Christopher Awards.

Sonya Jason, grew up as a child in a Pennsylvania mining town, with her mother "a little homesick for her native Slovenia." The daughter loved the beauty of her community until the ugliness of coal mine land-stripping took away much of her lovely environment. She writes that "ethnicity is a topic I feel deeply about. We must discover who we are and as much about our past as possible . . .; then we must get on with the job of becoming as much as we can be." She now makes her home in California with her husband and two sons, completing a novel about her Slovenian-American girlhood experiences.

Thelma Jones, of Norwegian-American immigrants, has used her parents' lives as inspiration for her works. Her father became an educator of national fame and her mother, the *Skinny Angel*, of her book, was descended from Mordecai Sofer, Ethan Allen's brother-in-law. The daughter grew up in Minnesota, the first professional librarian in Wayzata, the town that later named her as Citizen of the Year in 1966, and one of ten outstanding women in the state. Her book, *Skinny Angel*, was on display in a British Museum when the author was touring in England and her works also include *Once Upon a Lake* and *Piety Hill*. She is now completing her autobiography *Tonnie and Her Times*. (When she was a child, she could not pronounce her first name, calling herself "Tonnie" instead.)

Kumi Kilburn, born in Korea, then moving to Shanghi, makes her home with her doctor husband and children in Kirkland, Washington. She has been active in her school and community, serving in a leadership capacity on the school administrative board. She has also embarked upon a rewarding free-lance writing career with themes stressing pride in her ethnic heritage.

Maxine Hong Kingston, of Chinese-American parents, grew up in Stockton, California and she achieved fame with her best selling work, *The Woman Warrior*. She dedicated the book to her parents who cannot read English, and writes that her mother is "the creative one with the visions and the stories to tell. I'm the technician. She's the great inspiration. I never realized it until I finished the book." Ms. Kingston went to Berkeley where she met her husband and, in 1967, they moved to Hawaii where she teaches English and creative writing at Mid-Pacific Institute in Honolulu.

Irina Kirk, a Russian-born novelist, teacher and scholar of Russian literature, depicted the awesome dilemma of self-exile in her novel, *Born with the Dead*. Her works include interviews with dissidents, *Dostoevsky and Camus, Chekhov* (Twayne) and her book dedication to this editor was as follows: "May your voice [regarding oppression of the arts] be heard. For, as a Russian poet said, 'silence is the most insidious lie.' " She fled to Manchuria after the Russian Revolution, received her Ph.D. at Indiana University and now teaches at the University of Connecticut. She received the Eugene Bank Memorial Award, Best Short Story, 1960, and the Best Teacher Award in 1971.

Monica Krawczyk, grew up in Winona, Minnesota, of Polish-Americans. Her mother instilled in the girl a love of education, having purchased an encyclopedia set for the family with pin money as described in the story used in this anthology. Monica studied at the University of Minnesota and went into social work after teaching school. She had thirty short stories published and was a leader in disseminating information about her Polish heritage, organizing the Polanie Club of Minneapolis. During the First World War, she was decorated with the *Polonia Restituta* by the Polish government for her efforts in behalf of relief. She explained that her great pride in her culture was because her father took her to rehearsals of Polish plays as a child. She died in 1954 without ever having traveled abroad.

Lyn Lifshin, grew up in a small Vermont town and felt like an outsider as one of only two Jewish families. She started writing poems in the third grade and has published over thirty poetry books, including *Black Apples, Leaning South, Unstated Madonna* and an anthology of mother and daughter poems, *Tangled Vines*. She writes that "because my real life was more apart from 'Jewish Myths' than many other Jewish women's lives . . . what it's like being Jewish has been a much more prominant theme in poems. . . ." She has given poetry readings and was the recipient of fellowships at the Mac Dowell Colony and the Millay Colony. She has recorded *Offered by Owner*, a collection of her thirty-three poems.

Mary McCarthy, born in Seattle, is known for her polished writing style, occasionally biting satire and penetrating observations. She taught at Bard and Sarah Lawrence College and now lives in Paris. Her fictional works include *The Company She Keeps, The Groves of Academe, The Group* and *Birds of America*. Her nonfiction publication include *Memories of a Catholic Girlhood, Venice Observed* and *The Stones of Florence* as well as political publications about Vietnam and Hanoi.

Uma Majmudar, from West India, came to America in 1967 with her doctor husband and now makes her home in Atlanta. She was on the teaching faculty of Ahmendbad B.D. College in India, has worked as a dramatist and as a radio announcer. She is now a correspondent for *India Abroad*, a free-lance writer, studying journalism at Georgia State University.

Enid Mescon, of a first generation Irish-American mother and a Russian-American father, moved to Atlanta from Adel, Georgia where she attended the public schools, graduating from the University of Miami and doing graduate work in sociology at Columbia, The New School and New York University. She is married to a Georgia State University professor, has three children, is a community and religious school leader. Her previous publications are in the field of gerontology.

Janice Mirikitani, was born in Stockton, California, but "immediately after . . . was incarcerated in an American Concentration Camp." She graduated magna cum laude from The University of California/Los Angeles with advanced work at San Francisco State. She is a third-generation Japanese-American, proud of her heritage, and self-taught in painting, modern dance and photography. She writes: "I am/syllable/word/line where the poem begins/it smolders or lives; roots reaching back to where Japan swims" and she continues: "I am in opposition to all which attempts to negate me." Her works have appeared in *Mark in Time, Third World Women* and *Asian-American Heritage*, edited by David Hsin-Fu Wand. She is living and working in San Francisco as project director of a Japanese-American anthology. She states that works from the Third World are "like food: universal, essential, procreative, freeing, connective, satisfying."

Nicholasa Mohr, grew up in the inner city barrio of New York City in the South Bronx. Her first novel, *Nilda*, won acclaim and her second collection of stories about life in *El Bronx*, the Puerto Rican ghetto, during the 1950's, won a National Book Award nomination. She described in these stories, one of which is in this anthology, life in an ethnic community during the decade of the largest influx of migrants to New York. Her stories are written with warmth and with an understanding about people trapped by poverty and frustration and taking out their frustrations through violent outbursts. But she also writes of love, compassion and family concern. Ms. Mohr has artistic talent and she received a Merit Award from The Society of Illustrators for her *Nilda* book jacket.

Lisel Mueller writes that she was "born in Hamburg in 1924 and came to America in 1939. Technically this makes me a German-American, but I can't accept the term insofar as it implies a special ethos or community. I was the child of unorthodox, cosmopolitan parents. My father, a liberal intellectual, whose opposition to Nazism caused our emigration, fought against national insularity all his life. My 'sense of belonging' resides in shared values and attitudes that have nothing to do with ethnic lines. As a writer, my language has always been English. I am married to a native Midwesterner; we have two daughters. I have published four books of poetry and teach in the Goddard College MFA Writing Program." Her works include *The Private Life: Poems* and *Dependencies*.

Nila Northsun, a native Paiute Native American, taught tribal cultural tradition courses in a Missoula, Montana high school and now is making her home in Caprinteria, California. Her published works include poetry in *Sun Tracks, Pembroke, Yellow Brick Road, The Wormwood Review*, an anthology, *The First Skin Around Me*, and *Diet Pepsi & Nacho Cheese*.

Grace Paley, teaches at Sarah Lawrence College near New York City where she was born. She studied at Hunter College and New York University and has taught at Columbia and Syracuse. Her short stories have been published in *The American Monthly, New American Review* and have been collected in a volume entitled *The Little Disturbances of Man*. She writes of loneliness, about shrewd, colorful characters; her language is fanciful, imaginative and sometimes almost surrealistic. She probes the love/hate relationships between men and women and began to write poetry on a trip to Vietnam, emotionally involved with the American presence there.

Evangeline Papageorge, born in Turkey of Greek parents, came to America at the age of three and has lived in Georgia for fifty years. She has had a distinguished professional career; after graduating from Agnes Scott College and Emory University, she received her Ph.D. at the University of Michigan and was a Sterling Fellow at Yale University. She rose through the ranks at Emory University as Assistant in Biochemistry in 1929, then Acting Chairman, Assistant Dean at the School of Medicine, Associate Dean and finally Professor Emeritus of Biochemistry in September, 1975. She was a Phi Beta Kappa, a charter member of Sigma Xi at Emory and an honorary member of Alpha Omega Alpha. She has led cultural trips to Athens and has been devoted leader of the Greek Orthodox Parish in Atlanta.

Arlene G. Peck, grew up in Atlanta where she now resides with her husband and three children. She completed her education at Columbia College where she studied Business Administration. She has a role of active leadership in the Jewish community and founded the Woman's Division of Technion, becoming its first president. She was the first woman to become a vice-president of a synagogue, and has embarked upon a successful professional writing career, with articles appearing frequently in the *Southern Israelite, The Jewish Post and Opinion*. Ms. Peck led a discussion group at the Atlanta Federal Penitentiary, and she is writing a book about her experiences with this program.

Juliana Geran Pilon migrated to America from Romania in 1962, at the age of fifteen. Although she spoke no English, she received a scholarship to a summer course in creative writing within a few months, and three years later earned her B.A. at the University of Chicago. After a year at Princeton as a Woodrow Wilson Fellow, she received her Ph.D. in Philosophy from Chicago in 1974 as a Danforth Fellow. Among her many honors and publications, both philosophical and literary, the one she cherishes most is an article cited in the Congressional Record by way of argument for offering Solzhenitsyn American citizenship. She lives in Atlanta with her husband and is in the Department of Philosophy at Emory University.

Judith Plaskow, grew up in New England and attended Clark University and Yale where she received a Ph.D. in religious studies. Awarded a Danforth Graduate Fellowship, she studied in Edinburgh in 1966. The work used in this anthology was the text of an address to the National Jewish Women's Conference in New York in February, 1973. She is an authority on religion and women's studies, teaches at Wichita State University in Kansas where she lives with her husband and son. She is co-authoring a book entitled *The Woman Spirit: A Feminist Reader in Religion*.

Marie Prisland came to America as a young girl in 1906 and worked for six cents an hour while attending evening classes. Too poor to become an educator, she embarked upon a remarkable career as a teacher of Slovenian-American women, becoming, in 1926, the founder and then serving as president for over twenty years of the Slovenian Women's Union of America. In 1929, she created *Zarja (The Dawn)*, a magazine for which she still writes a monthly column. She has written articles and authored a book of her recollections, *From Slovenia to America*, published in 1968. She received the Order of St. Sava from the Yugoslav government in 1938 and was recognized by President Truman in 1946 for her leadership role. Still active in her eighties, she helps obtain scholarships for Slovenian-American students and is a senior associate of The Slovenian-American Institute.

Rose Mary Prosen, grew up in Cleveland, the second child of immigrant parents. She writes that "we lived in what today would certainly be called a ghetto; everybody was Slovenian, Roman Catholic and poor. We called it a community. The men and women of the neighborhood were mostly peasants from the foothills of the Swiss Alps where poverty had motivated them to emigrate to the New World. Men in love with the earth and its fruits gave their lives to . . . factories . . . without unions. . . . Though there was a railroad track . . . back of our house, my father defied dirt with beauty. There were two cherry trees in the front of our house and flowers on all four sides. There was wine in the basement and music in the kitchen." Ms. Prosen's works include her first prize winning reminiscence, "Looking Back" included in this anthology, scholarly articles in *College English*, and two publications, *Poems* and *O the Ravages*. She is currently an English Professor at Cuyahoga Community College in Cleveland, Ohio.

Heidi Rockwood, during the Second World War, grew up in Bavaria, in the Southwest corner of Germany. She studied at the University of Munich, then at Tubingin University, finally in England, before migrating to the United States in 1966. Awarded a scholarship, she studied at Florida Southern and received her Ph.D. at the University of Florida in 1973. She has written scholarly papers and is doing research at present on alchemy. She is married to a Georgia Tech English Professor and she teaches German and Linguistics in the Modern Language Department at the same school.

Janet Rechtman, born in Camp Hill, Alabama, was a member of the only Jewish family there. In 1960, her parents moved to Atlanta where she began her writing career. She has an M.A. in Victorian Studies from York University in Toronto and is enrolled in a Ph.D. program at Emory University. She is a founding member of the Atlanta Women's Poetry Workshop and her work has appeared in *Southern Poetry Review, Poem, Quest,* a feminist quarterly, *Other Harmonies* and *The Atlanta Gazette*.

Adrienne Rich, whose father was Jewish and mother, Protestant, said in a poem, "Readings of History" in 1960: "Split at the root, neither Gentile nor Jew/Yankee nor Rebel, born/In the face of two ancient cults,/I'm a good reader of history." She grew up in Baltimore, graduated from Radcliffe and had her first poetry book, *A Change of World,* published in the Yale Younger Poets Series in 1951. She spent a year in Holland learning Dutch and translating poetry before returning to New York to teach poetry workshops at Columbia and to participate with the SEEK program at City College. She also worked with a tenants' movement and attempted to improve the conditions of women prisoners. Her works include *The Diamond Cutters, Snapshots of a Daughter-in Law, The Will to Change.* A new poetry collection, *Poems 1974-77,* is scheduled for publication in 1978.

Marina Rivera, born in a small Arizona mining town, moved to Phoenix where she now lives. She grew up in both the Chicano and the Anglo culture and some of her poems deal with this theme. She graduated summa cum laude from Northern Arizona University and is currently teaching in an advanced high school community program. Since she received a scholarship from a Phoenix-group dedicated to college aid for Chicano youth, she has pledged her own poetry profits for this purpose. Her first collection *Mestiza* was published in 1977 and she has been anthologized in works such as La Verne Harrell Clark's *The Face of Poetry*.

Norma Rosen, born in New York, received her B.A. from Mount Holyoke and her M.S. from Columbia University. She published her first novel, *Joy to Levine!* in 1962 and her highly praised novella and eight poems, *Green*, in 1967, both under her maiden name, Norma Stahl. "The Open Window," was adopted for television by the Canadian Broadcasting System and her story, "What Must I Say to You?" appeared first in The *New Yorker*. She has taught writing at Harvard, The University of Pennsylvania and Lehman College. The recipient of a Radcliffe Institute Fellowship and a New York State CAPS Grant for fiction writing, she is at present working on a novel.

Muriel Rukeyser, is a poet, prose writer, teacher. She grew up in New York, attended Vassar College and Columbia University; since 1956 she has taught at Sarah Lawrence. Her first poetry book, *Theory of Flight*, reveals knowledge of statistical work after a ground course at Roosevelt Aviation School. Her works include *Beast in View, Orpheus, Waterlily Fire*, a novel, *The Orgy*, and a biography of Willard Gibbs. She has been awarded numerous prizes and critics have praised her inventiveness and force. Kenneth Rexroth once said, "I consider Muriel Rukeyser by far the best poet of her exact generation"—(the generation that first came to literary expression in the 1930's).

Phyllis J. Scherle, from Southern Illinois, is of German-American ancestry. She graduated cum laude from Southern Illinois University and is a member of Phi Kappa Phi and Kappa Delta Pi. She received the Betty Rhodes Memorial Scholarship and the Thelma Louise Kellog Scholarship in English. She has taught at Southeast Missouri State, Wabash Valley College and is currently an English Professor at Purdue University/Indianapolis. She was past president of the Indiana College English Association and is Editor of *The Associator*.

Esta Seaton, a first generation Polish-American poet and the daughter of a shoemaker father who "had an odd talent for finding small towns in which to settle," was raised in Tuckahow, New York, with a degree from New York University and a Ph.D. from the University of Minnesota in American Studies. She is an English Professor at Georgia Tech with more than ninety poetry publications including appearances in the *Atlantic Monthly, Poem, College English* and the *Georgia Review*. She and her husband both "share a passionate love for New York City, that greatest of all melting pots."

Ida Cohen Selavan, has been teaching Hebrew and Jewish Studies for twenty-five years and Yiddish for five. She is a member of the Jewish Feminist Organization, a contributor to *Lilith* and has read scholarly papers at the Modern Language Association Conventions. She translated the Aviva Barzel poems into English and is busy with other important translation projects and some important research of her own about Jewish activist women.

Ntozake Shange, from Trenton, New Jersey, attended Barnard and received an M.A. at the University of Southern California. She has been a women's studies and Afro-American studies instructor and is currently a full-time writer. She began a series of seven poems to explore the realities of seven different women which eventually evolved into *For Colored Girls Who Have Considered Suicide When the Rainbow is Enuf*, a choreopoem, a selection of which is included in this anthology. The work was named a Literary Guild Alternate for August, 1977, the Main Selection of the Fireside Theatre of the Literary Guild and was nominated for a Tony Award. Ms. Shange says that her work described a young black girl's growing up, ''her triumphs, and errors, our struggle to become all that is forbidden by our environment, all that is forfeited by our gender, all that we have forgotten.''

Leslie Marmon Silko, a Laguna Pueblo Native American, grew up in Albuquerque, New Mexico, was educated in Bureau of Indian Affairs schools, graduated magna cum laude from the University of New Mexico and was elected to Phi Beta Kappa. She is a creative writing teacher at this same school and describes herself as ''Laguna Pueblo, Mexican and white.'' Her short story, ''Lullaby,'' in this anthology, was in *The Best American Short Stories 1975* and she was also featured in *Two Hundred Years of Great American Short Stories*. Her novel, *Ceremony*, was well received and she is proud of her cultural heritage which she sometimes uses in her poems and publications. As a child ''I listened to my great grandmother . . . tell stories which ranged from tales about Coyote's misadventures to accounts of Apache and Navajo raids upon the Pueblo.'' This editor has contributed the Leslie Silko entry to the *Encyclopedia of American Women Writers*, which Lina Mainiero is editing and Frederick Ungar is publishing.

Eve Silver, born in Southwestern Poland, in that territory ''that was always considered Polish as opposed to other sections that have belonged to Russia, Austria or Germany,'' was admitted to Warsaw University but never studied there because the Second World War disrupted her life. She migrated to America after losing some members of her family in the holocaust, attended Emory University and received a B.A. from Georgia State in Atlanta where she now lives. She freelances for Atlanta newspapers, including the *Journal-Constitution* and the *Southern Israelite*. She is now engaged in a research project about her heritage, having received a grant to study in Illinois.

Valentina Sinkevich, a Russian-American poet, who authored two books, *Ogni* (Lights) in Russian and *The Coming of Day,* in Russian with English translations, emigrated to America from Germany in 1951 where she had been in a labor camp. She is a staff writer of the New York Russian language newspaper, *Novoye Russkoye Slovo*, contributing to its literature and art section, co-editor of the Russian Poetry and Art Almanac, *Perekrestki* (Crossroads), gives poetry readings where she now lives in Philadelphia, working as a librarian.

Virginia Driving Hawk Sneve, raised on the Rosebud Reservation in South Dakota, and an enrolled member of the Rosebud Sioux tribe, attended Bureau of Indian Affairs Day schools, graduated from St. Mary's School for Indian Girls in Springfield, South Dakota and received her B.A. and M.A. from South Dakota State University in Brookings. She is married to a teacher-administrater at the Flandreau Indian School, has authored five children's books and four adult books on South Dakota history. Ms. Sneve also works as a producer-writer for the South Dakota Public Television—Radio Network.

Liz Sohappy, a Palouse Native American, makes her home in Topperish, Washington. She attended the Institute for Indian Arts and continued her art career in Portland combining interests in art with anthropology. Her poetry has appeared in *The Whispering Wind* and she reveals in her works pride in her cultural heritage.

Avril Sutin, born in Liverpool, England, went to a technical college where she learned ''some shaky secretarial and bookkeeping skills.'' She became assistant to a buyer in a large merchandizing firm until 1956 when she left for America to join her American fiance. She has lived in Connecticut and now makes her home in Atlanta with her husband and two sons. She has embarked upon an active free-lance career and is studying creative writing at Georgia State University in Atlanta.

May Swenson, whose parents were Swedish-American immigrants, grew up in Logan, Utah, graduating from Utah State University. She has lived and worked in New York and received a Guggenheim Fellowship and grants from the National Institute of Arts and from the Ford Foundation. She has edited New Directions and her poetry has appeared in *Saturday Review, Harper's* and *The New Yorker*. Her works include *To Mix With Time, Poems to Solve, Half Sun, Half Sleep* and*Iconographs*. She says that she has been inspired to write many of her poems "directly on the scene . . . in much the same way as a painter sketches from life." Her works reveal a sensitivity to the awakening of self-awareness and concern for the human condition.

Ferris Takahashi, (also known as M.H. Constable and Mary Takahashi) was born in Boston, moved to Chicago, and now lives in Colorado with her doctor husband. Her poems and short stories have appeared in *Common Ground* and*Pacific Citizen*. Some of her works have described the difficulties of adjustment to the United States of Japanese-Americans, due to real or imagined Anglos hostility and/or their own internal sensitivities and insecurity.

Sister M. Florence Tusasz, born in Philadelphia of Polish-American parents, entered the Roman Catholic Congregation of the Sisters of the Holy Family of Nazareth in 1927. She obtained two degrees from the Catholic University and her Ph.D. from Fordham. Her doctoral dissertation on "Eighteenth Century English Literature and the Polish Enlightenment (1764-1822)" was published by the Kosciusko Foundation. After becoming the first Academic Dean of Holy Family College in 1954, she now serves as Public Relations Director and Professor of English, with an active professional career as lecturer and scholar. Her prose and poetry have been published in Polish and English and she has a leadership role in the American Association of Teachers of Slavic and East European Languages, the Polish American Historical Association and the Polish Heritage Society.

Sharon Reneé Twombly, whose father was born in America and whose mother came from Germany, graduated from Georgia Tech in 1977 with highest honors, receiving the American Association of University Outstanding Woman Senior Award. Her degree was in experimental psychology and a World Student Fund Scholarship enabled her to study in Zurich during 1977-78. Her mother's ethnic roots "beckoned to me" and she studied European classicism while abroad. She plans to obtain an advanced degree in animal behavior psychology and was a student of this anthology editor at Georgia Tech.

Evangeline Vigil, labels herself a "pure Chicana" with pride in her San Antonio heritage. She received her B.A. from the University of Houston and won first prize in a national poetry contest sponsored by the Coordinating Council of Literary Magazines in the Spring of 1977 for her poem "Ay Que Ritmo." She is presently poet-in-residence at Harlandale, San Antonio, actively involved with the problems of inner city ethnic children. She has adapted her poems to song and is an accomplished guitarist. She is proud of her large family, especially of her grandmother who "helped me develop a philosophy of life" that was linked with ethnicity. "Pure Chicana" represents for this young woman "the newest race of people, created by the union of the European and the native Indian of the Americas" with "the use of the Spanish language, recreated as an evolving language within an evolving culture."

Mary Elizabeth Vroman was born in 1925 and died in 1967. Before her untimely death, she was the first black woman accepted as a member of the Screen Writers Guild when her short story "See How They Run" (included in this anthology) was made into a movie, *Bright Road*, in 1953. Her other works include *Esther, Harlem Summer,* and *Shaped to Its Purpose*.

Alice Walker, born of sharecropping parents in Eatonton, Georgia, attended Spelman College, graduated from Sarah Lawrence and has taught writing courses at Jackson State and Tougaloo in Mississippi where she was writer-in-residence, and where she now sponsors the Alice Walker Literary Award. Her first volume of poetry, *Once*, was published in 1968 and her other works include *Revolutionary Petunias* and *Other Poems*. She has written two novels, *The Third Life of Grange Copeland*, and *Meritian*, a Langston Hughes biography and her collection of short stories is entitled *In Love and Trouble*, one work included in this anthology. She writes that her themes concern "the loss of compassion, trust, and the ability to expand in love . . . and about (and for) those few embattled souls who remain painfully committed to beauty and to love. . . ."

Margaret Walker, grew up in Birmingham where her father was a minister and she achieved prominence with her first poetry book, *For My People*, which won the Yale Younger Poets Award in 1942. She studied in Mississippi and in Louisiana, earning her Ph.D. from the University of Iowa. She has worked as a reporter, as a social worker and she is now an English Professor and Director of The Institute for The Study of The History, Life and Cultures of Black People at Jackson State University in Mississippi. Her works include a novel, *Jubilee,* about the Civil War, translated into French, Spanish, German and Swedish, and four works in progress: *Mother Broyer*, a novel; *Goose Island*, a collection of short stories; *A New Introdction to the Humanities*, a textbook; and *An Anthology of Afro-American Literature.*

Anne Webster, came from a family consisting of "two camps—my fair mother and sister who inhabited house and kitchen, and my lean, dark father with whom I gardened, took long walks, and sat by the river holding our bamboo poles. My looks mirrored his down to the shape of our fingernails. Even his weakness for drink and love of running played out the stereotype of his heritage. His trace of Cherokee blood was marked by straight black hair and walnut skin much like mine—so opposite the Scotch-Irish milkiness of my mother and sister." Ms. Webster lives in East Point, Georgia where she combines a profession as nurse with one as poet. Her poems have appeared in *13th Moon, The Sunstone Review, Phantasm*, the *New York Quarterly* and *Southern Poetry Review.*

Katie Funk Wiebe, grew up in Saskatchewan, Canada, of Mennonite parents who left "the terrors of war, revolution and famine behind them in the Ukraine in Russia." Early in her life, she began "a love-hate relationship with the Mennonites, loving their faithful devotion to God's truth, but frustrated with their unreadiness to open their lives to creativity and beauty." Early widowhood forced Ms. Wiebe to return to school, receiving a B.A. from Tabor College and an M.A. from Wichita State University. She is now an English Professor at Tabor in Hillsboro, Kansas and her published works include *Alone: A Widow's Search for Joy* and *Day of Disaster*. She contributes to scholarly and Mennonite publications and admits that if "it had not been for some of the limitations placed upon me by my cultural background, I might never have pushed so hard to cross the barriers to becoming a writer."

Rowena Wildin, of Japanese ancestry, from Algona, Iowa, is a student majoring in Japanese. She plans someday to embark upon a career involving translation work.

Jade Snow Wong, grew up in San Francisco, the untraditionally independent daughter of first generation Chinese-American parents. *Fifth Chinese Daughter*, published in 1950, detailed her attempts to seek a ceramics career in spite of her father's opposition. In 1951, she received the Non-Fiction Award of the Commonwealth Club, and her works include *Puritans from the Orient* and *No Chinese Stranger.*

Hisaye Yamamoto, born of first generation Japanese-American parents in Redondo Beach, California, has been writing since she was fourteen. Evacuated with her family to a relocation camp in Arizona during 1942, she worked for the camp newspaper. Ironically, during this internment, her brother, who had enlisted with the United States 442nd Regiment, was killed in action in Italy. After the war, she worked as a columnist for the *Los Angeles Tribune* and was the recipient of a John Hay Whitney Opportunity Fellowship in 1950. She has contributed articles to the *Catholic Worker, Partisan Review, Kenyon Review, Harper's Bazaar* and numerous anthologies.

Marya Zaturenska, born in Kiev, in 1902, migrated to the United States at the age of seven where she worked in a factory. She attended Valparaiso University and the University of Wisconsin. After marrying poet and critic Horace Gregory, she edited several anthologies with him. Her second volume of poetry, *Cold Morning Sky*, won the Pulitzer Prize in 1938 and a selection is included in this anthology. Other works of hers are *Golden Mirror* and *Terraces of Light.*

Details about the following writers are described with their work: (1) Shirley Chisholm (2) Rose Mary (Shingobe) Barstow (3) Edith Maud Eaton (Sui Sin Far) (4) Eva Jessye (5) Emma Lazarus (6) Buffy Sainte-Marie (7) Rose Schneiderman and (8) Sojourner Truth.

SUGGESTED READINGS

(Also see contributor's publications)

Maya Angelou, *Gather Together in My Name*, New York: Bantam Books/Random House, 1974.

Mary Antin, *The Promised Land*, Boston: Houghton Mifflin Company, 1912, 1940.

Hannah Arendt, *Rahel Varnhagen*, translated by Richard and Clara Winston, New York: Harcourt, Brace, Jovanovich, 1974.

Dora Askowith, *Three Outstanding Women*, New York: Bloch, 1941.

Lois C. Banner, *Women in Modern America*, New York: Harcourt, Brace, Jovanovich, 1974.

Mildred Barker, *Women: Feminist Stories by Nine New Authors*, New York: Eakins Press, 1972.

Pauline Bart, "Depression in Middle-Aged Women," In Vivian Gornick and Barbara Moran, eds., *Woman in Sexist Society*, New York, Basic Books, 1971.

Charlotte Baum, Paula Hyman and Sonya Michel, *The Jewish Woman in America*, New York: New American Library, 1975.

Frances Beale, "Double Jeopardy: To Be Black and Female," in *The Black Woman*, ed., Toni Cade Bambara, New York: New American Library, 1974.

Beatrice Bisno, *Tomorrow's Bread*, New York: Liveright, 1938.

La Verne Harrell Clark, ed., *The Face of Poetry, 101 Poets in Two Significant Decades—The Sixties and the Seventies,* Gallimaufry Press, P.O. Box 32364, Washington, D.C. 20007.

La Verne Harrel Clark, ed., *Re-visiting the Plains Indian Country of Mari Sandoz*, Gallimaufry Press, P.O. Box 32364, Washington, D.C. 20007.

La Verne Harrell Clark, ed., *They Sang for Horses, the Impact of the Horse on Navajo and Apache Folklore*, Gallimaufry Press, P.O. Box 32364, Washington, D.C. 20007.

Paulette Cooper, ed., *Growing Up Puerto Rican*, New York: New American Library, 1972.

Angie Debo, *The Rise and Fall of the Choctaw Republic*, Norman, The University of Oklahoma Press, 1934.

Pat Cruchfield Exum, *Keeping the Faith: Writings by Contemporary Black American Women*, Greenwich: Fawcett Publications, Inc., 1974.

Erna Ferguson, *Dancing Gods*, Albuquerque: The University of New Mexico Press, 1931.

Elsa Honig Fine, *The Afro-American Artist*, New York: Holt, Rinehart & Winston, 1973.

Alice C. Fletcher, *The Hako, a Pawnee Ceremony*, Bureau of American Ethnology, 2nd Report, Washington, 1903.

J.E. Franklin, Black Girl, *From Genesis to Revelations*, Washington, D.C.: Howard University Press, 1977.

Betty Frieden, *The Feminine Mystique*, New York: W.W. Norton, 1963.

Verta Mae Grosvenor, *Thursday and Every Other Sunday Off, a Domestic Rap*, New York: Doubleday, 1972.

Ossie Guffy as told to Caryl Ledner, *Ossie the Autobiography of a Black Woman*, New York: Bantam Books, 1971.

Rosa Guy, *The Friends*, New York: Bantam Books, 1973.

Lorraine Hansberry, *Raisin in the Sun*, New York: New American Library, Signet Books, 1959.

Lorraine Hansberry, *A Sign in Sidney Brustein's Window*, New York: Random House, 1965.

Lorraine Hansberry, *To Be Young, Gifted and Black*, New York: Signet Books, 1970.

June Jordan and Terri Bush, *The Voice of the Children*, New York: Washington Square Press, 1974.

Jane B. Katz, *I Am the Fire of Time*, New York: E.P. Dutton, Inc., 1977.

Josephine Zadovsky Knopp, *The Trial of Judaism in Contemporary Jewish Writing*, Urbana: University of Illinois Press, 1974.

Elizabeth Koltun, *"The Jewish Woman; an Anthology,"* *Response* Magazine, No. 18, Summer 1973.

Elizabeth Koltun, *The Jewish Woman, New Perspectives*, New York: Schocken Books, 1976.

Judith R. Kramer and Seymour Leventman, *Children of the Gilded Ghetto*, New Haven: Yale University Press, 1961.

Nella Larsen, *Passing*, New York: Macmillan, 1971.

Nella Larsen, *Quicksand*, New York: Macmillan, 1971.

Anita Lebeson, *Recall to Life; the Jewish Woman in America*, New York: Yoseloff, 1970.

Gerda Lerner, *The Female Experience, an American Documentary*, Indianapolis: Bobbs-Merrill Educational Publishing, 1977.

Gerda Lerner, *"Making a Living,"* in *Black Women in White America: A Documentary History*, New York: Vintage Books, 1973.

Alexandra Levin, *The Szolds of Lombard Street: A Baltimore Family 1859-1909*, Philadelphia: Jewish Publication Society, 1960.

Nancy O. Lurie and Stuart Levine, ed., *The American Indian Today*, Baltimore: Penguin Books, 1965.

Alice Marriott and Carol K. Rachlin, *American Indian Mythology*, New York: New American Library, 1968.

Paule Marshall, *Brown Girl, Brownstones*, New York: Random House, 1959.

Paule Marshall, *The Chosen Place, the Timeless People*, New York: Harcourt, Brace & World, 1969.

Paule Marshall, *"The Negro Woman in American Literature"* (speech at the Harlem Writers' Guild Conference, New York City, Spring 1965), *Freedomways*, 6, Winter 1966, pp. 20-25.

Paule Marshall, *"Reena,"* In *American Negro Short Stories,* ed., John Henrick Clarke, New York: Hill & Wang, 1966.

Paule Marshall, *Soul Clap Hands and Sing*, New York: Antheneum, 1961.

Louise Meriwether, *Daddy Was a Number Runner*, New Jersey: Prentice-Hall, 1970.

Caroline Mirthes, *Can't You Hear Me Talking to You?* New York: Bantam Books, 1971.

Anne Moody, *Coming of Age in Mississippi*, New York: Dell Publications, 1970.

Toni Morrison, *The Bluest Eye*, New York: Holt, Rinehart & Winston, 1970.

Toni Morrison, *Sula*, New York: Alfred A. Knopf, 1974.

Toni Morrison, *"What the Black Woman Thinks About Women's Lib,"* *Time Magazine*, August 22, 1971.

Cecyle S. Neidle, *America's Immigrant Women*, Boston: Twayne Publishers, 1975.

Katharine D. Newman, *The American Equation, Literature in a Multi-ethnic Culture*, Boston: Allyn and Bacon, Inc., 1971.

Katharine D. Newman, *Ethnic American Short Stories*, New York: Washington Square Press, 1975.

Gloria Oden, *Resurrections*, Olivant Press, P.O. Box 1409, Homestead, Florida, 33030.

Martha Ostenso, *The Dark Dawn*, New York: Dodd, Mead & Company, 1926.

Martha Ostenso, *Love Passes This Way*, New York: Dodd, Mead & Company, 1942.

Martha Ostenso, *The Mad Carows*, New York: Dodd, Mead & Company, 1927.

Martha Ostenso, *A Man Had Tall Sons*, New York: Dodd, Mead & Company, 1958.

Martha Ostenso, *The Mandrake Root*, New York: Dodd, Mead & Company, 1938.

Martha Ostenso, *Milk Route*, New York: Dodd, Mead and Company, 1948.

Martha Ostenso, *O River, Remember!* New York: Dodd, Mead and Company, 1943.

Martha Ostenso, *Prologue to Love*, New York: Dodd, Mead and Company, 1932.

Martha Ostenso, *The Stone Field*, New York: Dodd, Mead and Company, 1937.

Martha Ostenso, *The Sunset Tree*, New York: Dodd, Mead and Company, 1949.

Martha Ostenso, *There's Always Another Year*, New York: Dodd, Mead and Company, 1933.

Martha Ostenso, *The Water's Under the Earth*, New York: Dodd, Mead and Company, 1930.

Martha Ostenso, *The White Reef*, New York: Dodd, Mead and Company, 1934.

Martha Ostenso, *Wild Geese*, New York: Dodd, Mead and Company, 1925.

Martha Ostenso, *The Young May Moon*, New York: Dodd, Mead and Company, 1929.

Elena Padilla, *Up from Puerto Rico*, New York: Columbia University Press, 1958.

Esther Panitz, "In Defense of the Jewish Immigrant (1891-1924)," *American Jewish Historical Quarterly* LV, 1 September 1965, pp. 57-97.

Esther Panitz, "The Polarity of American Jewish Attitudes towards Immigration (1870-1891)." *American Jewish Historical Quarterly* LIII, 2 December 1963, pp. 99-130.

Ann Petry, *The Street*, Boston: Houghton, Mifflin Co., 1943.

Rabbi Sally Priesand, *Judaism and the New Woman*, New York: Behrman House, Inc., 1975.

Agnes Roisdal, *Defend My Mother*, New York: Vantage Press, 1951.

Lillian Ross, *Vertical and Horizontal*, New York: Simon and Schuster, 1963.

Ruth Rubin, *Voices of a People*, 2nd edition, New York: McGraw-Hill, 1973.

Sonia Sanchez, ed., *We Be Word Sorcerers*, New York: Bantam Books, 1973.

Mari Sandoz, *The Battle of Little Bighorn*, New York: Modern Literary Editions Publ Co., 1966.

Gwen Gibson Schwartz and Barbara Wyden, *The Jewish Wife*, New York: Wyden, Inc., 1969.

Patricia Cayo Sexton, *Spanish Harlem*, New York: Harper and Row, 1965.

Margarethe E. Shank, *The Coffee Train*, New York: Doubleday, 1953.

Barbara Miller Solomon, *Ancestors and Immigrants: A Changing New England Tradition*, Cambridge: Harvard University Press, 1956.

Monica Itoi Sone, *Nisei Daughter*, Boston: Little Brown and Co., 1953.

Lois Mark Stalvey, *The Education of a WASP*, New York: William Morrow and Co., 1970.

Hope Sykes, *Second Hoeing*, New York: Putnam, 1935.

Donna M. Terrell and John Upton Terrell, *Indian Women of the Western Morning, Their Life in Early America*, New York: The Dial Press, 1974.

Linda Ty-Casper, *The Peninsulars*, Manila: Bookmark, 1964.

Linda Ty-Casper, *The Secret Runner and Other Stories*, Manila: Florentino, 1974.

Linda Ty-Casper, *The Transparent Sun and Other Stories*, Manila: Peso Books, 1963.

Enriqieta Longauez y Vasquez, "The Women of La Raza," *El Grito del Norte*, Vol. 2, No. 9, July 6, 1969. El Grito, Box 466, Fairview Station, Espanola, New Mexico 87532.

Michele Wallace, "A Black Feminist's Search for Sisterhood," New York: *The Village Voice*, July 28, 1975, pp. 6-7.

Mary Helen Washington, *Black-eyed Susans, Classic Stories by and About Women*, New York: Anchor Press/Doubleday, 1975.

Michi Weglyn, *Years of Infamy, The Untold Story of America's Concentration Camps*, New York: William Morrow and Co., 1976.

Violet Weingarten, *Mrs. Beneker*, New York: Simon and Schuster, 1968.

Rita Wellman, *The Gentile Wife*, New York: Moffat/Yard (Dodd, Mead and Co.), 1919.

Phyllis Wheatley, *Poems on Various Subjects, Religious and Moral, 1773*, Chapel Hill: University of North Carolina Press, 1966.

Kenny J. Williams, *In the City of Men: Another Story of Chicago*, Baltimore: Townsend Press, 1974.

Kenny J. Williams, *They also Spoke*, Baltimore: Townsend Press, 1970.

Jeanne Wilson, *Mulatto*, New York: M. Evans and Company, Inc., 1967.

Emma Wolf, *Other Things Being Equal*, Chicago: A.C. McClurg, 1892.

Martha Wolsenstein, "Two Types of Jewish Mothers," In Margaret Mead and Martha Wolfenstein, eds., *Childhood in Contemporary Cultures*, Chicago: University of Chicago Press, 1955.

Grace Steele Woodward, *The Cherokees*, Norman: The University of Oklahoma Press, 1963.

Anzia Yezierska, *Hungry Hearts*, Boston: Houghton Mifflin Co., 1920.

Jean F. Yellin, *Intricate Knot: The Negro in American Literature, 1776-1863*, New York: New York University Press, 1971.

Rose Zeitlin, *Henrietta Szold: Record of a Life*, New York: Dial Press, 1952.